THE ESSENCE OF INTERSTATE LEADERSHIP

Debating Moral Realism

Edited by
Yan Xuetong and Fang Yuanyuan

First published in Great Britain in 2024 by

Bristol University Press
University of Bristol
1-9 Old Park Hill
Bristol
BS2 8BB
UK
t: +44 (0)117 374 6645
e: bup-info@bristol.ac.uk

Details of international sales and distribution partners are available at bristoluniversitypress.co.uk

© Bristol University Press 2024

British Library Cataloguing in Publication Data
A catalogue record for this book is available from the British Library

ISBN 978-1-5292-3261-5 hardcover
ISBN 978-1-5292-3262-2 paperback
ISBN 978-1-5292-3263-9 ePub
ISBN 978-1-5292-3264-6 ePdf

The right of Yan Xuetong and Fang Yuanyuan to be identified as editors of this work has been asserted by them in accordance with the Copyright, Designs and Patents Act 1988.

All rights reserved: no part of this publication may be reproduced, stored in a retrieval system, or transmitted in any form or by any means, electronic, mechanical, photocopying, recording, or otherwise without the prior permission of Bristol University Press.

Every reasonable effort has been made to obtain permission to reproduce copyrighted material. If, however, anyone knows of an oversight, please contact the publisher.

The statements and opinions contained within this publication are solely those of the editors and contributors and not of the University of Bristol or Bristol University Press. The University of Bristol and Bristol University Press disclaim responsibility for any injury to persons or property resulting from any material published in this publication.

Bristol University Press works to counter discrimination on grounds of gender, race, disability, age and sexuality.

Cover design: blu inc
Front cover image: stocksy/3554847/Giada Canu

Bristol Studies in East Asian International Relations

Series Editors: **Yongjin Zhang**, University of Bristol, UK,
Shogo Suzuki, University of Manchester, UK and
Peter Kristensen, University of Copenhagen, Denmark

This series publishes cutting-edge research on the international politics of East Asia, the ongoing transformation of the region, as well as the impact of such transformation on the wider global order. It welcomes theoretically informed and theoretically innovative works that can help develop and establish new Asian schools of thought in International Relations theory.

Also available

A Hierarchical Vision of Order
Understanding Chinese Foreign Policy in Asia
By **Antoine Roth**

Middle Powers in Asia Pacific Multilateralism
A Differential Framework
By **Sarah Teo**

China's Rise and Rethinking International Relations Theory
Edited by **Chengxin Pan** and **Emilian Kavalski**

China Risen?
Studying Chinese Global Power
By **Shaun Breslin**

The Responsibility to Provide in Southeast Asia
Towards an Ethical Explanation
By **See Seng Tan**

Find out more at

bristoluniversitypress.co.uk/
bristol-studies-in-east-asian-international-relations

Forthcoming

Disciplined Democracies
Human Insecurity in Japan-Myanmar Relations
By **Lindsay Black**

International advisory board

Amitav Acharya, American University, Washington D.C., US
Mark Beeson, University of Western Australia, Australia
Barry Buzan, London School of Economics and Political Science, UK
Zhimin Chen, Fudan University, Shanghai, China
Ja Ian Chong, National University of Singapore, Singapore
Paul Evans, University of British Columbia, Canada
Rosemary Foot, University of Oxford, UK
Evelyn Goh, Australian National University, Australia
Linus Hagström, Swedish Defense University, Sweden
Miwa Hirono, Ritsumeikan University, Japan
Yuichi Hosoya, Keio University, Japan
Weixing Hu, University of Macau, China
Xiaoming Huang, Victoria University of Wellington, New Zealand
Christopher R. Hughes, London School of Economics and Political Science, UK
Yang Jiang, Danish Institute for International Studies, Denmark
Hun Joon Kim, Korea University, South Korea
Jing Men, College of Europe, Belgium
Nele Noesselt, University of Duisburg-Essen, Germany
John Ravenhill, University of Waterloo, Canada
Masayuki Tadokoro, Keio University, Japan
Yu-Shan Wu, National University of Taiwan, Taiwan

Find out more at

bristoluniversitypress.co.uk/
bristol-studies-in-east-asian-international-relations

Contents

List of Abbreviations		vi
Notes on Contributors		viii
Preface		ix
1	Interstate Leadership, Moral Realism, and their Critics *Yan Xuetong and Fang Yuanyuan*	1
2	IR Moral Realism as a Universal Theory *Yan Xuetong*	16
3	Moral Realism as an Alternative Approach to the Agent–Structure Problem *Fang Yuanyuan*	31
4	Prospects, Promise, and Limitations of Moral Realism *Qingxin K. Wang*	52
5	Ideal Morality and Realist Interest of Moral Realism *Kai He*	74
6	The Conception of Morality in Moral Realism *Feng Zhang*	93
7	Moral Realism and Hegemonic Transition *Athanasios Platias and Vasilis Trigkas*	113
8	Innovation of Moral Realism and Dialogue with It *Mario Telò*	143
9	Moral Realism and Sino–American Relations *Deborah Welch Larson*	162
10	Moral Realism on Interstate Leadership in Response to Critics *Yan Xuetong*	179
Appendix 1:	Written Discussion between Rajesh Rajagopalan and Yan Xuetong	204
Appendix 2:	'Chinese School' as an Inappropriate Title	216
Selected Bibliography		221
Index		245

List of Abbreviations

AIIB	Asian Infrastructure Investment Bank
AOSIS	Alliance of Small Island States
ASEAN	Association of Southeast Asian Nations
BCE	Before Common Era
BRI	Belt and Road Initiative
COMECON	Council for Mutual Economic Assistance
COP 21	21st United Nations Climate Change Conference
COVID-19	Coronavirus Disease 2019
CPC	Communist Party of China
CPTPP	Comprehensive and Progressive Agreement for Trans-Pacific Partnership
CS	Chinese School
EC	European Community
EU	European Union
FDR	Franklin D. Roosevelt
FPA	Foreign Policy Analysis
GATT	General Agreement on Tariff and Trade
GDP	Gross Domestic Product
GIR	Global International Relations
IMF	International Monetary Fund
IR	International Relations
IRT	International Relations Theory
LGBTQIA+	Lesbian, Gay, Bisexual, Transgender, Queer/Questioning, Intersex and Asexual +
NATO	North Atlantic Treaty Organization
P5	Permanent Five
PLA	People's Liberation Army
PRC	People's Republic of China
QUAD	Quadrilateral Security Dialogue
RCEP	Regional Comprehensive Economic Partnership
UK	United Kingdom
UN	United Nations
UNDP	United Nations Development Programme

LIST OF ABBREVIATIONS

UNESCO	United Nations Educational, Scientific and Cultural Organization
UNICEF	United Nations International Children's Emergency Fund
US	United States
USSR	Union of Soviet Socialist Republics
WB	World Bank
WHO	World Health Organization
WWII	World War II
TPP	Trans-Pacific Partnership
TTIP	Transatlantic Trade and Investment Partnership

Notes on Contributors

Kai He is Professor of International Relations and Director of the Centre for Governance and Public Policy at Griffith University: k.he@griffith.edu.au.

Deborah Welch Larson is Research Professor of Political Science at the University of California, Los Angeles: dlarson@polisci.ucla.edu.

Athanasios Platias is Professor of Strategy in the Department of International and European Studies at the University of Piraeus: platias@unipi.gr.

Mario Telò was Professor of International Relations at LUISS University and the Free University of Brussels.

Vasilis Trigkas is Postdoctoral Teaching Fellow at the Schwarzman College at Tsinghua University: vasilis.trigkas@sc.tsinghua.edu.cn.

Qingxin K. Wang is Professor of the School of Public Policy and Management at Tsinghua University: wangqingxin@tsinghua.edu.cn.

Yan Xuetong is Professor and Director of the Institute of International Studies at Tsinghua University: yanxt@mail.tsinghua.edu.cn.

Fang Yuanyuan is Instructor of the School of International Relations at Beijing Language and Culture University: fyyhbwh@163.com.

Feng Zhang is Professor of International Relations and Executive Dean of the Institute of Public Policy at the South China University of Technology: zhangfeng@ipp.org.cn.

Preface

The purpose of writing this book is to strengthen the study of the international relations (IR) theory of moral realism through discussions between myself and eight IR scholars who are also interested in moral realism. Since the publication of *Leadership and the Rise of Great Powers* in 2019, more than 40 reviews have appeared. I found it necessary to sponsor discussions on IR moral realism and put some of them into a collection. On the one hand, it is important to clarify certain misunderstandings about IR moral realism; on the other, it is helpful for further development of this theory.

Producing a book of this kind meant there were some difficult decisions to make, giving the writers' multiplex perspectives and portraying aspects such as morality, ideology, leadership types, leadership formation, political institutions, power structure, level analysis, international norms, international order, China–US rivalry, and so on. It became clear that there are too many outstanding essays about moral realism to be included in one volume. For the sake of following a specific theoretical theme, fresh chapters would be necessary. To provide readers with an understanding of the significance of moral realism, I invited the eight IR scholars to contribute new chapters to this project. With a solid grounding in IR theories and remarkable views on Chinese political culture, these scholars have been successful with their writings on IR theory and Chinese foreign policy.

Chapters in this collection set the stage for the understanding of and debating on IR moral realism. In addition, those debates will give IR students new insight into aspects of ontology, epistemology, and methodology in IR theory construction. For other readers, this collection may provide insightful opinions about the differences between interstate leadership and domestic leadership, the relations between leadership and political institutions, the different views on leadership morality's influence on the historical trends of international politics, and the impacts of major powers' leadership on the present world order.

In addition, the outbreak of the war in Ukraine in 2022 adds a practical dimension to the theoretical significance of this book. Since the war began, many IR scholars have paid increasing attention to the role of world leaders along with the war-impacted international order. Because moral realism attributes the international changes to the leadership of major powers, many writers, in their discussions in the book, show particular concern about the related national or international leadership embodied by war.

In the process of editing this collection, I have noticed that the unique nature of interstate leadership has not received enough academic attention. The indistinction between domestic and international leadership has also engendered considerable misunderstanding of IR moral realism. For the sake of improving our knowledge of interstate leadership, I have embedded my responses to various critiques into research of the nature, morality, measurement, and impact of this leadership. Although the response chapter cannot cover all the critiques in the previous chapters because of the concern of embroidering the core theme, it answers the major questions or meets main challenges from each writer's contribution.

In addition, my response also delves into the relationship between international leadership and international institutions. Moral realism believes that political leadership has the power to establish, maintain, revise, and destroy political institutions. This argument can find many facets of evidence from the current trend of counter-globalization. Since Brexit in 2016, the existing international institutions have failed to prevent policy makers of major powers from adopting deglobalization policies. Without a progressive global leadership, major powers prefer a decoupling policy for their own economic security; thus, counter-globalization gains momentum.

I do not agree with the popular view that moral realism is a branch of the 'Chinese School' of IR theory. Since the national culturalism's viewpoint of IR theory hinders a healthy development of IR theoretical studies, I have included Chapter 2 that mainly and specifically addresses the point that IR moral realism is universal rather than national. Beside this, I have also attached a short essay as Appendix 2, discussing the inappropriate title 'Chinese School'. Appendix 1 is the pen discussion between Professor Rajesh Rajagopalan and myself, which focuses on the epistemology of moral realism and also illustrates its universality.

I want to express my deep appreciation to the contributors to the volume. The unique academic perspectives of their chapters underpin the value of this book. Although Professor Mario Telò is no longer with us, his legacy lives on in the pages of this book. I am especially grateful to Dr Fang for editing the whole book and keeping in close contact with every author. Without her assistance, this collection would hardly have been able to see the light of day as originally planned. I am pleased to acknowledge the support from the Chinese Fund for Humanities and Social Science. Finally, I am indebted to Bristol University Press for appreciating the scholarly potential in this collection.

Yan Xuetong
Tsinghua University, September 2022

1

Interstate Leadership, Moral Realism, and their Critics

Yan Xuetong and Fang Yuanyuan

The intensive major power rivalry, the increasing uncertainty of international relations, the decline of democracy, the prevailing deglobalization, the devastating impacts of pandemics, and many other emerging global issues are becoming daunting. In the wake of these escalating challenges, there is a need for robust international leadership, which unfortunately is absent. Regarding the global spread of pandemics, Tedros Adhanom Ghebreyesus, Director-General of the World Health Organization (WHO), notes that the major threat we are facing now is not from the COVID-19 pandemic, but from the lack of global leadership.[1] The reality could be even worse than mere lack of a global leadership because the prevalence of populist leadership in major powers is driving the world towards a more conflicting, rather than cooperative, order.

The absence of a positive global leadership has its root in both power structure and individual causes. Structurally, there is a leadership dilemma accompanying the power transition process, with both the declining hegemon and the rising state. With a declining relative comprehensive capability, it is difficult for a hegemon to continue to bear the burden of providing necessary common goods for maintenance of the global order. However, reneging on such commitments will deteriorate its leadership and leave the opportunity for the rising power to replace it. For the rising state, the leadership dilemma exists as well, because if it lobbies for leadership in international affairs, it will provoke hostility and containment from the hegemon and its client states. Meanwhile, the rising power is unable to provide the same amount of public goods to the world as the hegemon because of its material power being less than the latter. Due to the leadership dilemma, a vacuum of interstate leadership is likely to occur during the power transition between major states.

Another factor often overlooked is the strategic preferences of leaders of major powers, which was vividly demonstrated in the case of the United States (US) during the administration of Donald Trump. When taking over the reins from the Barack Obama administration, it possessed the same power resources as its predecessor. Nevertheless, the US witnessed a dramatic decline in its global influence as well as leadership in the first year of Trump's administration. Actually, Trump's administration was neither the first nor the last populist leadership. This type of leadership had already existed in other major states before it obtained power in the US. It failed to attract the timely attention of the IR academic because the global influence of these states is much less than the US.

Since Trump's administration wielded the US global leadership, a growing number of scholars have been recognizing the need and the urgency for researching interstate leadership as an independent study. Among all IR studies on interstate leadership in recent years, moral realism is one of the major theoretical achievements. Using scientific methods and drawing on ancient Chinese thoughts, moral realism combines with observations of contemporary international relations, and provides a systemic and theoretical analysis of interstate leadership. It has not only advanced the development of interstate leadership studies, but is also paradigmatically innovative in a broader sense. Ontologically, moral realism presents a dualist theory, seeing structure and agent as coexisting variables affecting the status as well as behaviour of a leading state. Methodologically, it provides a dynamic rather than static, and relative rather than absolute, perspective on interstate leadership.

This book takes moral realism as a focal point to explore several key issues regarding interstate leadership. This chapter starts with a reconstruction of the diffusive debate on interstate leadership, then proceeds with an elaboration of moral realism's construction of the subject. After that, it concludes with a brief overview of the contributions in this volume.

Power, social contract, or influence

Leadership and the Rise of Great Powers was published in 2019 and Joseph Nye published *Do Morals Matter? Presidents and Foreign Policy from FDR to Trump*[2] in 2020. Both of these books focus on interstate leadership and morality. Such convergence of realist and liberalist scholars vividly reflects the importance of the issues of interstate leadership in this changing world. While issues of leadership have powerfully reclaimed significance in preserving stability and prosperity in international relations, the essence of interstate leadership and its function has remained understudied. The existing studies of leadership in international affairs present two routes, one practical, closely associated with specific countries and their foreign policies, and the other theoretical. The practical route has been more prominent as its importance is largely taken for granted with its practical value. Nevertheless, the importance of theoretical analysis is often overlooked in dominant IR theories, mainly because more IR students prefer environmental factors to cognitive factors for explaining differences and changes in international relations. To those who 'place great stress on the incentive and constrains posed by the environment be it domestic or international',[3] leadership does not truly matter. The popularity of *Guns, Germs, and Steel: The Fates of Human Societies*[4] by Jared M. Diamond illustrates well this social preference.

The reason for the sluggish theoretical development of interstate leadership does not only rest in the inadequate attention; what also impedes its development is the lack of consensus on the underlying assumptions about definition, categorization, and measurement of interstate leadership, as well as at which level of analysis it should be studied. It is true that some other prevail concepts of IR theory, such as power and interests, also lack common definitions, but theoretical studies of interstate leadership suffer more because leadership is a subjective art rather than an objective environment. As reflected in Chapter 3, while Yan and Nye both converged with their interests in moral leadership, there is a clear difference in their conceptualization of leadership.

There is no consensus among scholars on basic assumptions about the definition and categorizations of interstate leadership. Even scholars who conceptualize interstate leadership as power hold different views about it. Hegemonic stability theorists, such as Charles Kindleberger, view interstate leadership as a form of power, and that the legitimacy of power can be derived from the military and economic capabilities of the leading state, and can directly affect the behaviour of other states in international politics.[5] Being a behaviourist, Oran Yang holds a leader-centred perspective, emphasizing the importance of legitimacy in interstate negotiation, and dividing the power in international negotiation into structural leadership, entrepreneurial leadership, and intellectual leadership.[6] Nye defines leadership as 'the power to orient and mobilize others for a purpose'.[7] When discussing the future of US international leadership, John Ikenberry argues that although the US may not play a direct leadership role in the future as it did in the past, the political institutions and structures of relations that were built under American support after World War II will still provide channels and routines of cooperation.[8]

Those who consider interstate leadership as a social contract view legitimacy as both a source and a constraint on the power of a leading state. Hedley Bull argues that a great power needs to follow two principles for exercising its governing function: one, it must function in an interstate community of shared interests and values; and two, it must be recognized by other states.[9] In contrast to the loose nature of the interstate compact in Bull's theory, David Lake regards the interstate relationship as relatively structured and stable. With the tacit consent, the security of the following states is enhanced, and they cede a portion of their policy sovereignty to the leading state in return. While the leading state benefits from the privilege of making rules, the cost may also be substantial, as they must provide sufficient value to their followers.[10]

In addition to power and social contract, certain IR scholars regard interstate leadership as influence. Chen Zhimin and Zhou Guorong, based on the various definitions and categorizations, define interstate leadership as the behaviour and process by which actors in the international system lead and drive the members of the system to achieve specific goals through the use of critical influence. They study interstate leadership in a comprehensive manner in terms of the number of interstate leaders, and the purpose, means, manner, field, performance, and legitimacy and recognition of interstate leadership.[11] Yu Yixuan differentiates interstate leadership from hegemony. She argues that interstate leadership relies on cooperation and negotiation rather than coercive forces, and it exists in specific areas and issues rather than holistic control or dominance.[12] Chang Jian and Yin Haozhe propose a triangular model of 'leader–follower–leader competitor' and divide the replacement cycle of interstate leadership into four different stages: leadership weakening, making up for leadership deficiency by force, fiercely competing for leadership positions, and new leaders standing out.[13]

In addition to divergences on definition, interstate leadership is divided into different types according to different criteria. Oran Yang divides interstate leadership into structural leadership, entrepreneurial leadership, and intellectual leadership.[14] Like Yang, Ikenberry also divides interstate leadership into three types: structural leadership, institutional leadership, and situational leadership.[15] Nye divides interstate leadership into only two types: leaders who prefer hard power are categorized as those with transactional leadership, while leaders who prefer soft power have transformational leadership.[16]

Political psychologists criticize studies of leadership in IR as always narrowly focusing on 'power balances, correlations of forces, and other structural features of the international system'.[17] Focusing on leaders, decision-making groups, and bureaucratic processes, it intends to open the black box of the decision-making process and explore how leadership, in the form of individual and collective groups, influences a country's domestic and foreign policy.[18] For instance, James David Barber argues that 'the crucial differences in the whole thrust and direction of national politics can be anticipated by an understanding of a potential President's character, his world view, and his style'.[19] Margaret G. Hermann studies the impact of six personal characteristics (nationalism, belief in one's own ability to control events, need for power, need for affiliation, conceptual complexity, distrust of others) of 45 heads of government on the foreign policy behaviour of their nations and shows how these six personal characteristics of national heads interact to form two orientations, namely, independent orientation and participatory orientation, on foreign affairs.[20]

Political psychology contributes significantly to the studies of leadership in international relations as it brings back micro-level analysis to international politics, and challenges rational theorists' perception of leaders and makes the study of international relations more humane. James Barber argues that the mission of political psychology should 'reach for life, liberty, and the pursuit of happiness for the human race, recognizing that reason has to be fostered in the context of political reality'.[21] However, political psychology also has its shortcomings. For instance, it is difficult to fully explain the causes of international conflicts and wars merely by psychological approaches. Additionally, most of the present-day psychoanalytic theories are limited to European and American cultural contexts, while developing countries and oriental culture are rarely addressed.[22] The other defect is that their analyses are based on modern history, giving limited attention to historical cases. It is difficult to apply their theories to explain policy making in ancient history.

Few studies have specified that interstate leadership in international relations is fundamentally different from its variation in the form of organizational leadership, such as corporate leadership and governmental leadership. Leadership, of any type, can be analysed from three core aspects – actor, relation, and situation.[23] Interstate leadership is different from organizational leadership in at least three aspects. First, the main actors of interstate leadership, both leaders and followers, are autonomous entities with independent power. They can be state leaders as individuals, or governments as groups, or states as unitary actors. Second, it is not possible to establish absolute mandatory hierarchical relations between leading powers and followers in an anarchical system because of each state's independent material power. Therefore, interstate leadership presents a non-hierarchical and non-subordinate leading–following relationship. Third, the solidarity of interstate leadership is based on shared interests between leaders and followers. Unlike corporations or governments, the most important factor in establishing and sustaining leadership is the institutional setting that gives leaders the legitimacy to lead; interstate leadership, being non-organizational leadership, is formed and maintained by states' material power and authority of leaders.

IR moral realism: from thoughts to theory

Being prudent with the distinction between interstate and domestic leadership, moral realism connects the three levels of analysis to construct a new explanatory mechanism of how individuals as political leaders of great powers change the power structure at the systemic level. It will be helpful to understand moral realism by reviewing its epistemology and methodology of studying interstate leadership. Moral realism, a theory of political determinism, postulates that political leadership functions as an operational variable that supercharges resource elements, namely, military, economy, and culture; thus, it plays a determinative role in the growth or decline of a state's comprehensive capability. Such political determinism originates from the study of ancient Chinese thought of interstate relations, especially Pre-Qin thoughts, which could date back to 2,700 years ago.

The Pre-Qin period refers to Chinese history before the first Emperor of Qin united China in 221 BCE. Histories usually divide the last five centuries of Pre-Qin history into the Spring and Autumn period (ca. 770–476 BCE) and the Warring States period (ca. 475–221 BCE), where states strove to protect their own security and 'sought to develop and resolve the relationship among themselves … thus they accumulated a rich and prolific experience in politics'.[24] The complex political configuration and dynamics during that period provided the space for scholars to look at the interstate system, interstate relations, and interstate political philosophy. By studying the thoughts of the Pre-Qin philosophers on interstate politics, we found that Chinese Pre-Qin thinkers attributed the dominant power transfer between states to rulers of monarchs. Confucius focuses on the moral cultivation of rulers; Mencius focuses on whether rulers practise benevolent governance; Xunzi pays attention to the political principles adopted by rulers; Mozi emphasizes whether rulers appoint people on merit; Guanzi focuses on the rationality of rulers' strategy; Laozi treasures the moral accumulation of rulers, mainly virtual pacifists; and Hanfeizi focuses on whether rulers govern a state with law.[25] Although Pre-Qin thinkers focused on different political elements, they were all political determinists agreeing that the leadership directly influences the policies of a state, thus changing the power structure between states.

These Pre-Qin interstate political philosophies are further elaborated and discussed in the book *Ancient Chinese Thought, Modern Chinese Power* published in 2011. Where those studies cultivated new IR thoughts, the theoretical arguments in the book were then labelled as moral realism by the IR community.[26] This book received attention from both academic professors and policy analysts. Different from dominant IR theories originating from European philosophers and political thinkers, such as Socrates, Plato, and Aristotle in ancient times, and Thomas Hobbes, John Locke, Jean-Jacques Rousseau, Max Weber, Karl Marx, and others in modern times, moral realism, based on ancient Chinese political thought, enriches the current mainstream IR theory. Practically, the photo of then US Vice President

Joe Biden holding the book at the Chengdu airport in 2011 confirms its empirical value to politicians beyond China.

However, two criticisms have driven me to further develop these thoughts into theory. First, it is necessary to explain the instrumental role of morality in international relations because some critics argue that moral realism is not true realism where morality involves theoretical analysis.[27] IR moral realism developed from existing IR theories and is not related to the school of 'moral realism' in philosophy. In the philosophical debate, moral realism (or moral objectivism) refers to the meta-ethical view that there exist objective moral facts and moral values, which are independent from human perception, beliefs, preferences, or characteristics. Whereas in the discipline of international relations, moral realism views morality as dependent on human perception, beliefs, preferences, and historical context. IR moral realism uses an instrumental definition of morality: behaviour that falls within the norms accepted by the majority is perceived as 'moral'. Thus, what is 'moral' is not objectively unchanging, but is subjectively decided based on the international norms of the time and externally judged by other countries within the same interstate system.

IR moral realism proposes that a leadership that is 'moral', aka one which follows the international norms of its time, will become strong and durable, while a leadership that is 'amoral', aka one which goes against the international norms, will decline. This idea is derived from the ancient Chinese thought *dedao duozhu, shidao guazhu* (得道多助, 失道寡助, a just cause enjoys abundant support while an unjust cause finds meagre support). IR moral realism attributes international changes to the type of changes in political leadership of major powers.

Second, some scholars suspect moral realism is constructed especially for China, and is unable to be applied to cases beyond China.[28] Such criticisms encouraged me to develop existing thoughts into a rigorous theory that is universally applicable to states that would like to obtain interstate leadership in an interstate system. After seven years of work, my book, *Leadership and the Rise of Great Powers*, was published in 2019, where I developed my thoughts into a theory of political leadership explaining the rise and fall of great powers in world politics. In the book, I have devoted my attention to using the dual-variable method to construct a rigorous theoretical model that can adequately explain the past and the present, aiming to make significant universal applications.

IR moral realism regards the leadership of major powers as the key variable that determines international configuration, norms, and order. Methodologically, political leadership serves as an independent variable in moral realism and its values are leadership types characterized according their governmental morality. When the leadership of a major power changes in type, that state's comprehensive capability as well as its international status will also change in response, which leads to a change in the international configuration. Therefore, moral realism proposes that political leadership alone is enough to explain 'the decline of the dominant state, the success of a given rising state, and the failure of other rising states during the same historical period'.[29] When the type of international configuration changes, a new interstate leadership will emerge. If the new leadership is a different type from the previous one, it will shape a new order with the norms that it prefers. That is why the types of interstate leadership define the features of international norms and order.

While it is preferable to categorize domestic and interstate leadership by using the same criteria, the different nature of domestic and interstate social systems makes it impossible. Domestic leadership is based on legitimacy of a hierarchical system while interstate leadership is established on the power relatively stronger than others in an anarchic system. As such, I categorized state leadership into inactive, conservative, proactive, or aggressive types,[30] and interstate leadership into humane authority, hegemony, anemocracy, and tyranny.[31]

Moral realism's analysis of leadership is dynamic rather than static. According to moral realism, proactive state leadership and humane interstate leadership are the most ideal leadership types that can possibly lead to a country's peaceful rise. Proactive leadership of a rising state opts for strategies that 'enlarge international support for its cause'[32] and 'strives to improve its state's international status by carrying out political reform'.[33] If the rising state has proactive state leadership that can effectively use its existing military, economic, and cultural strength in the right direction to enhance its comprehensive national power, it is possible for the country to narrow its power gap with the dominant state. If the rising state establishes a humane interstate leadership with universal moral standards (valuing strategic credibility and being consistent between domestic and foreign policies), it can gain more interstate support. Where it is so, the rising state will receive higher interstate authority, which ultimately means it has a great chance to surpass the dominant state who provides an interstate leadership with lower-level morality. However, the ideal type of leadership does not ineludibly and unequivocally lead to the success of a rising state, as power transition is a dynamic process that depends on the leadership types and strategic decisions by both sides. I also note that the type of leadership is subject to change due to regime change or self-transformation of leadership.[34]

Moral realism attributes China's rise to the government's greater capability of reform than that of the US during the four decades after the Cultural Revolution ended in 1976. Moral realism treats reform as a kind of governmental morality for people's interests. According to the theoretical logic of moral realism, the power gap between China and the

US will continue to be reduced if the Chinese government can maintain greater reform capability than that of the US. The present situation shows that China's rise and America's relative decline are jointly transforming the unipolar world dominated by the US to a bipolar one of Sino–US rivalry. Thus, the main challenge facing the policy makers of both countries in the future is how to peacefully manage their competition for global leadership. The bipolar configuration implies that neither the Chinese nor the American leadership is able to provide dominant values for the world. There is a slight chance for liberalist values to resume global influence in the coming decade, while different regions may have different dominant values.[35]

Criticisms of IR moral realism

IR moral realism presents a theoretical attempt at systemically discussing the nature, typology, and function of interstate leadership. Along with the recolonization of moral realism, it has received criticism from various perspectives. As noted previously, moral realism has normative and practical values; thus, the criticisms are also twofold. One is on the theoretical conceptualization and approaches; the other regards the implications of this theory, including the policy implications and predictions of the future international order. Some scholars, such as Feng Zhang, Kai He, Mario Telò, and Vasilis Trigkas, have closely and critically followed my researches on Chinese thoughts from the early stage.[36] This volume invites these scholars to present their takes and criticisms on moral realism, for two purposes. First, for the sake of providing IR students with a coherent understanding of moral realism and related debates, it is necessary to collect the debates on moral realism in their newest development, reflecting mainly on the book *Leadership and the Rise of Great Powers*, along with my other relevant works. Second, in order to further develop moral realism, it requires the gathering of criticisms from different perspectives. Having different theoretical backgrounds, the scholars invited to contribute to this volume provide various valuable views about moral realism.

In Chapter 2, I review the construction process of moral realism driven solely by academic inquiry, rather than political concerns, and explain why it is misleading to put moral realism under the umbrella of 'Chinese School of IR'. Moral realism is not a theory about Chinese exceptionalism, but a universal theory attempting to explain interstate changes at the system level as a common question shared by IR researchers across the world. It is also not a Sinocentric theory as it draws from both Chinese ancient philosophy and foreign literatures. Moral realism does not argue that China is going to provide a world leadership that is superior to that of others, but suggests a recipe that can be used for all leading states, including both rising powers and hegemons. Given that moral realism, like other universal or scientific theories, faces the test of time, in this chapter, I test the validity of three moral realism models with the ongoing war in Ukraine.

Fang Yuanyuan, in Chapter 3, notes the convergence of Yan's and Nye's researches on moral leadership, but emphasizes their differences in level of analysis and conceptualization of morality. Focusing on moral realism, Fang notes that, with its implicit emphasis on the impact of structure determining national interests and treating systemic change as a dependent variable, the theory provides an alternative approach to the agent–structure problem in international relations as a dualist theory exploring the mutual interaction of agent and structure. Fang further elucidates the significant ontological and epistemological differences between moral realists and constructivists in their analysis of agent and structure. She, however, indicates that the conceptualization of leadership is ambiguous and there is limited explanation by moral realism of the causal framework of the two categories of leadership, state and international, demonstrating that it could be achieved differently.

In Chapter 4, Qingxin K. Wang, adopting a comparative perspective, reviews moral realism in relation to neorealism and constructivism. Wang agrees with the constructivist view that national interest is socially constructed, that is, the decision of national leaders will be affected by various complicated factors, and the quality of political leadership is not the only aspect that determines the rise and fall of a country. Furthermore, he argues that Yan's empirical evidence of the impact of political leadership on international change is flawed. He believes that history has shown that the US is still likely to regain its strength after austerity, and therefore we cannot yet judge the impact of the Trump administration's foreign policy. Wang thinks that Yan may have overestimated China's strength while underestimating the ability of the US, and made a controversial judgment on the future direction of Sino–US relations and changes in the international system. He also thinks that the concept of hegemony in moral realism theory has negative connotations and may have a misunderstanding of American hegemony.

Kai He, in Chapter 5, regards moral realism as a revelatory challenge to the development of the three paradigms of international relations known as realism, liberalism, and constructivism, as well as a brave prediction of policy practice at the realistic level. He questions the unclear conceptualization of morality and political leadership, the internal interaction logic of political leadership, the undefined conceptualization and mechanism of moral norms, and the ignorance of institutions in moral realism. He finds the two key concepts of moral realism, 'morality' and 'political leadership', to be quite blurred when they refer to different analyses at the levels of individuals, governments, and states. Further, he points out that there is probably interactive logic between state leadership and international leadership, which could be deeply and respectively analysed as 16 outcomes. Then, he also puts forward some questions about norms, especially 'moral norms'. Last but not least, he has noticed the significance of moral realism in multilateral institutions and international orders, which is ignored by Yan.

In Chapter 6, Feng Zhang, from a constructivist perspective, critically analyses Yan's moral concept in combination with the four moral approaches that have dominated the history of Chinese and Western thought: deontology, consequentialism, virtue ethics, and role ethics. Zhang argues that although Yan's moral concept is inspired by Chinese traditional thought, it gradually breaks away from Confucianism and tends towards Western realistic tradition, which is narrow and instrumental, and ignores the relationship of integrity and morality. Zhang also note the parallels in Yan's and Nye's theories of moral foreign policy and compares and contrasts their conceptions of morality. Regarding morality as a tool to realize interests and power, Yan ignores the true meaning of moral value and is contrary to the moral values of Xunzi. The concept '*yi*' (virtue) put forward by Xunzi reflects the combination of virtue ethics and principle-based deontology. This criticism is also noted in Wang's section. Lastly, he criticizes Yan for ignoring the relationship of honesty and morality in the moral outlook of Xunzi. Zhang thinks that the '*xin*' (credibility) of Xunzi emphasizes the virtues or habits of promoting credibility and trust in constructive relations; however, the concept of strategic reliability put forward by Yan turns the relational '*xin*' into international leadership in the practice of moral principles.

In Chapter 7, Athanasios Platias and Vasilis Trigkas, unlike Fang, treat moral realism as a dualist theory, and perceive it as an agent-based ontology and the polar opposite of Waltz's system-based ontology. Arguing from a neoclassical realist theoretical framework, they point out that moral realism underestimates the structural dimension of leader choice as an empirical condition, and suggest that political leadership should be treated as a mediating variable rather than an independent one. The two authors conduct a comparative analysis of Chinese classical corpuses and Greek classics, and find that similarities of Sino-Hellenic classical writings with these two interstate systems are prevailing. For instance, the case of Themistocles which Thucydides presents in great detail and finesse, demonstrates quite paradigmatically Yan's thesis that leadership can reshape interstate configuration, order, norms, system centre, or even the interstate system as a whole. They also find that strategic credibility has also been noted by Thucydides when describing the way that Themistocles cultivated the Athenian alliance system and advanced Athen's strategic credibility. The similar perception of leadership and strategic credibility shared among Ancient Greek and Chinese philosophers further attests the universal value of moral realism.

Mario Telò, in Chapter 8, provides a critique of the conceptualization of some crucial concepts in moral realism, such as bipolarity, liberalism, and hegemony. Telò contests that Yan's prediction of the Sino–US bipolar structure is problematic and suggests that Yan underestimates the capability of the US, India, Japan, Brazil, Russia, and the EU, as well as the role of complex interdependence and institutional resilience. From a European perspective, he criticizes Yan for not realizing the severe divisions within the West, which he considers to be a crisis of liberalism. In addition, he also criticizes Yan's definition of liberalism as narrow historicization of political theory. Similar to Wang, he believes that Yan's attachment of negative connotation to the concept of hegemony is contrary to its meaning in Western political science and refers to new institutionalism, new realism, and Italian Marxism. Based on that, he also questions Yan's conceptualization and categorization of hegemonic leadership.

In Chapter 9, Deborah Welch Larson, from an empirical perspective, contrasts moral realism with power transition and other realist theories to shed light on the current Sino–American relations. Larson believes the competition between China and the US is different from that during the US–Soviet Cold War, and is more about status and technology rather than military and territory. In particular, President Biden has pledged to restore US moral leadership by re-emphasizing liberal values and norms, raising the possibility of a competition with China to shape global norms. Given the power held by the two states, historical lessons suggest dialogue is the best approach in avoiding protracted conflicts. Hence, he proposes that the two superpowers should pursue international leadership by focusing on peace and stability.

In Chapter 10, I respond to the criticisms discussed by the eight scholars mentioned previously by discussing unique nature, relative morality, quality measurement, functional conditions, and further studies of interstate leadership. The response aims at clarifying my ambiguous or confusing arguments in my writings instead of defending them. Responding to He, Platias, Trigkas, and Fang's criticisms of the level of analysis of moral realism, I clarify that moral realism treats interstate leadership at an individual level, and it is composed of a group of individual policy makers. While acknowledging the structural impact on determining a state's interests, 'moral realism treats power structure as a constant rather than a variable' in a given situation. Regarding the question about the connotation of hegemony raised by Telò, Wang, Platias, and Trigkas, this chapter addresses the connotation variation in history. Responding to Larson and Wang's scepticism on assessing interstate leadership and related questions on how to improve or evaluate the decline of leadership in international affairs, I note that measurement of interstate leadership should take into account not only the number of followers but also their relative capabilities and their credibility. Regarding Telò and He's emphasis on the autonomous role of international institutions and their influence on states, I explore the relation between international leadership and international institutions, noting that the former is the precondition for the latter's formation and function.

As it has been revealed by several authors in the book that there are many puzzles about interstate leadership that have not been solved, I suggest two interrelated paths of interstate leadership studies, one theoretical and one empirical. Besides studying its functions as an independent variable, I agree to treat interstate leadership 'as a dependent variable, studying its formation, continuation, decline, and vanishment'. Empirically, I accept Telò and Fang's concerns of categorizing American leadership by individual administration without taking into account the similarities between their policies, and He's suggestion of taking the ideology element into consideration when studying the ongoing interstate leadership competition.

Summary

Different from most realist theorists offering an environmental explanation for the rise and fall of great powers, moral realism treats national leadership as the key factor in winning the competition between major powers. It regards exercising humane leadership to win international support as the most important aspect of obtaining interstate leadership, which is even more crucial than exercising material strength to win the military competition. Humane authority requires the leading power to practise humane norms both domestically and internationally, which, as Daniel Bell notes, is not the same as soft or cultural power because it is a type of political leadership that underpins national power and international stability.[37] While a rosy theoretical vision is unfolded, critics in this book generally question whether it will be realized empirically.

Although contributors in this volume commonly agree on the significance of morality in interstate leadership, they differ in terms of what constitutes morality, how to assess it, and to what extent it matters in relation to environmental constraints. However, acknowledging virtue as an important element of morality, I still believe that it will be more practical to approach morality in interstate leadership more as a duty than a virtue, because the non-compliance to interstate leadership is the main character of an anarchic system. In this volume, the debate on the nature of morality reveals the fundamental epistemological differences between realism and other IR theories, such as liberalism and constructivism. The fact that the progress of digital technology is accompanied by a worldwide decline of democracy at present reminds us that scientific studies of interstate leadership have more chance of being consistent with harsh realities than normative perception.

The purpose of this volume is not to reach a consensus on the understanding of interstate leadership, or to search for a solution for the leadership competition between China and the US, but to intrigue reflections among readers on related subjects. Under the condition that institutional determinism is still the most influential mentality, it would be a great achievement if this volume could bring about more research on interstate leadership. From an empirical perspective, I wish this volume to trigger off more studies on the leadership offered by the Chinese or American governments when their joint leadership is unrealistic at present. Divergences, as well as convergences, have their value in contributing to the advancement of social inquiry. None of the theoretical and empirical issues discussed in this volume can be resolved in the near future, but they can be presented to attract more scholars' attention and inquiry.

Notes

1. WHO Director-General opening remarks at the Member State Briefing on the COVID-19 pandemic evaluation – 9 July 2020.
2. Joseph S. Nye, *Do Morals Matter? Presidents and Foreign Policy from FDR to Trump*, New York: Oxford University Press, 2020.
3. Robert Jervis, 'Do Leaders Matter and How Would We Know?', *Security Studies* 22, no. 2 (2013): 153.
4. Jared M. Diamond, *Guns, Germs, and Steel: The Fates of Human Societies*, New York: W.W. Norton & Company, 1997.
5. Charles P. Kindleberger, 'Dominance and Leadership in the International Economy: Exploitation, Public Goods, and Free Rides', *International Studies Quarterly* 25, no. 2 (1981): 242–54; Robert Gilpin and Jean M. Gilpin, *The Political Economy of International Relations*, Princeton: Princeton University Press, 1987.
6. Oran Yang, 'Political Leadership and Regime Formation: On the Development of Institutions in International Society', *International Organization* 45, no. 3, (1991): 285, quoted in Chen Zhimin and Zhou Guorong, 'Guoji lingdao yu Zhongguo xiejinxing lingdao juese de goujian' ('International Leadership and China as One Facilitative Leader'), *Shijie jingji yu zhengzhi* (World Economics and Politics) 3 (2017): 18.
7. Joseph S. Nye Jr, *The Powers to Lead*, New York: Oxford University Press, 2008, p 19.
8. G. John Ikenberry, 'The Future of International Leadership', *Political Science Quarterly* 111, no. 3 (1996): 385.
9. Hedley Bull, *The Anarchical Society: A Study of Order in World Politics*, London: Macmillan, 1977.
10. David A. Lake, 'Regional Hierarchy: Authority and Local International Order', *Review of International Studies* 35 (2009): 20–1, 35–339.
11. Chen Zhimin and Zhou Guorong, 'Guoji lingdao yu Zhongguo xiejinxing lingdao juese de goujian': 21.
12. Yu Yixuan, 'Chaoyue baquan: Guojiguanxi zhong lingdao de xingzhi ji qi guannian jichu' ('Beyond Hegemony: The Nature of Leadership in International Relations and Its Conceptual Basis'), *Fudan International Studies Review* 27 (2020): 42.
13. Chang Jian and Yin Haozhe, 'Guoji lingdao diwei xin gengti zhouqi yanjiu' ('A Study of the New Replacement Cycle of International Leadership'), *Fudan International Studies Review* 27 (2020): 21–2.
14. Oran Yang, 'Political Leadership and Regime Formation: On the Development of Institutions in International Society'.
15. G. John Ikenberry, 'The Future of International Leadership': 388–96.
16. Joseph Nye, *The Powers to Lead*, p 21.
17. Ole R. Holsti, 'The Political Psychology of International Politics: More than a Luxury', *Political Psychology* 10, no. 3 (1989): 497.

18 Yin Jiwu, 'Xinli yu Guoji guanxi fenxi: Geti xinli fenxi de lilun yu shijian' ('Psychology and International Relations: The Theory and Practice of Individual Psychoanalysis'), *Ouzhou yanjiu* (Chinese Journal of European Studies) 1 (2004): 69.
19 Ruth P. Morgan, 'Reviewed Work(s): The Presidential Character: Predicting Performance in the White House by James David Barber', *The Journal of Politics* 37, no. 1 (1975): 305.
20 Margaret G. Hermann, 'Explaining Foreign Policy Behaviour Using the Personal Characteristics of Political Leaders', *International Studies Quarterly* 24, no. 1 (1980): 7–46.
21 James David Barber, 'The Promise of Political Psychology', *Political Psychology* 11, no. 1 (1990): 183.
22 Yin Jiwu, 'Xinli yu Guoji guanxi fenxi: Geti xinli fenxi de lilun yu shijian': 78–9.
23 Peter G. Northouse, *Leadership: Theory and Practice*, 7th Edition, California: SAGE Publications, Inc, 2015.
24 Yang Qianru, 'An Examination of the Research Theory of Pre-Qin Interstate Political Philosophy', in Daniel A. Bell and Sun Zhe (eds), *Ancient Chinese Thought, Modern Chinese Power*, Princeton: Princeton University Press, 2011, p 148.
25 Yan Xuetong, *Shijie quanli de zhuanyi: Zhengzhi lingdao yu zhanlue jingzheng* (The Shift of World Power: Political Leadership and Strategic Competition), Beijing: Beijingdaxue chubanshe, 2015, pp 180–2.
26 Feng Zhang was the first one to use the term in the article Feng Zhang, 'The Tsinghua Approach and the Inception of Chinese Theories of International Relations', *The Chinese Journal of International Politics* 5, no. 1 (Spring 2012): 73–102.
27 'Yan Xuetong Duihua Mearsheimer: Zhongguo Nengfou Heping Jueqi?' (A Dialogue between Yan Xuetong and Mearsheimer: Can China Rise Peacefully?), *iFeng Academia*, 29 September 2013, http://news.ifeng.com/exclusive/lecture/special/yanxuetong/#pageTop.
28 Svetlana Krivokhizh and Elena Soboleva, 'The Past Serving the Present: Yan Xuetong's Theory of Moral Realism and the Future of the Global Order', *World Economy and International Relations* 61, no 11 (2017): 76, www.imemo.ru/en/publications/periodical/meimo/archive/2017/11-t-61/china-domestic-and-foreign-policies/the-past-serving-the-present-yan-xuetongs-theory-of-moral-realism-and-the-future-of-the-global-order.
29 Yan Xuetong, *Leadership and the Rise of Great Powers*, Princeton: Princeton University Press, 2020, p xiv.
30 Yan Xuetong, *Leadership and the Rise of Great Powers*, p 29.
31 Ibid., p 40.
32 Ibid., p 35.
33 Ibid., p 193.
34 Ibid., pp 37–40.
35 Ibid., pp 197–206.
36 See Kai He, 'A Realist's Ideal Pursuit', *The Chinese Journal of International Politics* 5, No. 2 (Summer 2012): 183–97; Feng Zhang, 'The Tsinghua Approach and the Inception of Chinese Theories of International Relations'; Mario Telò, 'Building a Common Language in Pluralist International Relations Theories', *The Chinese Journal of International Politics* 13, no. 3 (Autumn 2020): 455–83.
37 Daniel A. Bell and Sun Zhe, *Ancient Chinese Thought, Modern Chinese Power*, 'Introduction', pp 1–18.

2

IR Moral Realism as a Universal Theory

Yan Xuetong

A decade or so has passed since Nele Noesselt published 'Is There a "Chinese School" of IR?' in 2012.[1] Now, many international relations (IR) scholars regard IR moral realism as one of the major theories affiliated with the 'Chinese School' and view it as a theory that shares the same defects of that school. This is a common misunderstanding about IR moral realism. Thus, this chapter will address these criticisms and illustrate that they are not applicable to moral realism.

Disagreement on the issue of 'Chinese school'

In 2004, Chinese IR scholars held a conference on 'Constructing Chinese Theories, Establishing Chinese School'.[2] Faced with the new upsurge of constructing Chinese IR theories, I took the opposite stance to that of most Chinese IR scholars. It may be because my thinking was so different on this issue, that *Shijie Jinji Yu Zhengahi* (World Economics and Politics) invited me in 2006 to write an essay to give my opinion.[3] In the opening paragraph I argue that 'IR theories themselves do not have national identities, thus it is impossible to construct Chinese IR theories'.[4] From then on, Qin Yaqing, the leading advocate for the 'Chinese School', and I have continuously debated on this issue.

At the moment, Qin's position has been widely accepted by both Chinese and international adherents, while mine has received little support. The term 'Chinese School' or 'Chinese IR theories (IRT)' have increasingly appeared in papers, dissertations, and books.[5] Nevertheless, this popularity does not make it reasonable to categorize moral realism as a theory of 'Chinese School'. Although moral realism, relational theory, and the *tianxia* system are often regarded as '[t]he "big three" of Chinese IR thinking', these three theories are different in terms of ontology, epistemology, and methodology.[6] As Yongjin Zhang noted, '[T]here is significant epistemological and methodological diversity within the Chinese School, even though the notion of a singular "Chinese School" seems to suggest otherwise'.[7] Furthermore, scholars such as Peter J. Katzenstein have pointed out that '[s]ome prominent scholars like Qin are committed to building a Chinese School. Others like Yan regard this as an unnecessary, even harmful exercise. These moves have been widely debated in and across other national schools of IR'.[8]

I have clearly expressed my disagreement with the idea of constructing a 'Chinese School' in the article 'Why Is There No Chinese School of International Relations Theory?', which I have attached as an appendix to *Ancient Chinese Thought, Modern Chinese Power* published in 2011. Nevertheless, others persist on viewing me as an advocate for the 'Chinese School'. For instance, although Yevgeny N. Grachikov acknowledged, 'The only opponent to the creation of the "Chinese School" was Yan Xuetong, who emphasized that IR theories should be universal',[9] he also said, 'Despite the difference in their approaches, Yan Xuetong and Qin Yaqing are regarded as major scholars contributing content for the "Chinese School"'.[10] Salvatore Babones wrote, 'Yan Xuetong is well known as the arch-empiricist of Chinese IR theory, interpreting social science as a universal, positivist science of hypothesis testing and prediction. But he is equally well known for eschewing the development of specifically Chinese concepts, preferring instead to see the Chinese discipline develop by importing well-established Western theories and methods'.[11] In 2021, Yih-Jye Hwang said that 'the main advocates of the CS [Chinese School] such as Yan, Zhao, and Qin have indeed juxtaposed China and the West, believing that there can be a "distinctive" Chinese world order'.[12]

Qin argues that Chinese IR scholars 'all explore explicitly the traditional philosophies and thoughts embedded in the Chinese culture for their intellectual inspiration and theoretical construction. It is exactly because of this feature that they all bear their cultural birth marks'.[13] Similarly, Yongjin Zhang argues, 'Rather than one homogenous school of thought, it is a conversation about how to theorize a distinct perspective on world politics that draws on Chinese cultural resources and is informed by a historically contingent situation of China's rise to a global power status'.[14] Nevertheless, history shows that shared culture does not sanction either Chinese or foreign scholars' building of IR theories affiliated with a certain academic school.

Differing from the views of cultural identification, I agree with Beate Jahn's argument that 'there is no unitary Chinese or Western theory but rather internal theoretical diversity and differential power'.[15] I have several reasons for opposing the concept of 'Chinese School' but they are criticized by Babones who says, 'It must be said that Yan's reasoning seems quite facile: He argued that schools of thought shouldn't be named by their creators, that they are rarely named after countries (the "English School" notwithstanding), and that China is too diverse to be associated with a single school'.[16]

Academic rather than political motives

The popular criticism of the 'Chinese School' or the 'Chinese IRT' is that their motives are political rather than academic. However, there is no evidence that IR moral realism is a politically driven theory.

The suggested political motives for constructing a 'Chinese School' or the 'Chinese IRT' are: serving Chinese national interests, improving China's soft power, and decolonizing Western IR knowledge. Noesselt stated that 'the search for a "Chinese" paradigm of international relations theory is part of China's quest for national identity and global status', and 'to safeguard China's national interests and to legitimize the one-party system'.[17] Similarly, Matteo Dian said, 'The Chinese School in particular tends to "speak for power", producing concepts and analyses that can be considered functional to legitimate the political narrative promoted by the Chinese government'.[18] Beate Jahn argued that 'these Chinese IRT include an intellectual goal, namely the provision of a "better" understanding of international relations and a political goal, consisting in challenging the hegemony of Western international theories and by extension the hierarchical international order these theories prop up'.[19] Protesting the idea of a national school of IR,[20] Barry Buzan stated that its aim 'could also be read as complementary to the broader political aim of the Chinese government to improve China's ability to resist and contest Western hegemony, both academically and politically'.[21]

It is true that there are many Chinese scholars who are eager to establish Chinese IRT in order to propagate the government's strategy and protect national interests.[22] After the concept of 'soft power' was introduced into China, both Chinese scholars and officials regarded the construction of Chinese IRT as a way to improve national soft power.[23] According to an interview by *Zhongguo Xinwen Zhoukan* (China News Week), these ideas are mainly popular among leftists of different fields.[24] In 2022, their ideas were buttressed by an official document jointly issued by the Propaganda Department of the Chinese Communist Party and the Chinese Education Ministry. The document requires China's universities to construct an education system that meets the state's needs to improve national soft power and a discourse system that leads international communication to use Chinese concepts.[25]

In contrast, the formation of moral realism did not have such concerns. In 2004, Xu Jin and I began to incorporate Pre-Qin Chinese philosophies into modern IR theoretical studies. Initially, we had no intention of establishing a new theoretical model as we were merely hoping to enrich modern IR theories from a new perspective. In 2008, our work produced a collection of Pre-Qin political thoughts on interstate relations. In the editor's notes, I stressed, 'We will be able to enrich existing IR theories, if we draw inspiration from the political thoughts of Ancient Chinese thinkers'.[26]

Subsequently, my Tsinghua colleagues and I interpreted the Pre-Qin philosophies through a modern IR framework. Our work produced another collection in 2009. In the preface of that book, I restated our academic motivation: 'The purpose of this book is to provide a repository of Chinese traditional thoughts for scholars so that they may draw upon Pre-Qin thoughts about interstate politics to enrich existing IR theories'.[27] Three articles from this collection were translated into English, providing the main context for *Ancient Chinese Thought, Modern Chinese Power* in 2011. This book received wide attention from foreign IR scholars, followed by a new wave of discussion about the 'Chinese IRT'. In 2012, Feng Zhang dubbed the theoretical thoughts in the book as 'moral realism'.[28]

In response to the many criticisms about IR moral realism, I began to conscientiously construct a systematic theory. Katzenstein said, 'Neither the Copenhagen nor the Chinese School is spurred by problem solving theorizing. ... It [Chinese School] is not interested in the unique problem created by the simultaneity of preindustrial, industrial, and post-industrial processes'.[29] Actually, I started to think about the core theoretical question of moral realism from the publication of *Ancient Chinese Thought, Modern Chinese Power*. Yongjin Zhang rightfully pointed out that 'the central theoretical puzzle that moral realism must crack is why a rising state is able to displace a dominating hegemon even when it is inferior to the latter in terms of economic power, technological invention, education system, military strength, and political system'.[30] Perplexed by this puzzle, I focused my attention on addressing the question of international power transition between great powers, especially the emergence of China–US bipolarity. My initial efforts produced the book *Shijie Quanli de Zhuanyi: Zhengzhi Lingdao Yu Zhanlue Jingzheng* (World Power Transition: Political Leadership and Strategic Competition) in 2015.[31] In the preface of that book, I stressed, 'This book provides a comprehensive explanation about moral realism and urges China to adopt the humane authority strategy to aid its rise. This does not mean that the Chinese government will or must adopt this strategy, only that there is a historical basis for it'.[32] Following the previous book, I published *Leadership and the Rise of Great Powers* in 2019. In this book, I argued,

> As Chinese political institutions have fewer constraints on national leadership than is the case in the United States, there could be two different trends of the present bipolarization. If the Chinese government carries out more political reforms over the next decade than its American counterpart, the bipolarization will speed up.

Otherwise, it will stop if the Chinese government commits more strategic mistakes and retrogression than the United States.[33]

Universalism not Chinese exceptionalism

Many foreign scholars belittled the theoretical achievements of the 'Chinese School' or 'Chinese IRT'. As Yongjin Zhang noticed, 'It grants recognition of its existence, but not as a theory on a par with other (American) theories. … Compared with American IR, which presents itself as pluralistic, these schools of thought would look hopelessly parochial and provincially monotonous'.[34] A major criticism of 'Chinese School' or 'Chinese IRT' is that they are forms of 'Chinese exceptionalism'. Hun Joon Kim said that 'the Chinese School's references to historical documents and classics are either inaccurate or overly romanticized. It is a kind of anachronism, which also infers an imperious form of Chinese exceptionalism – a form of wishful thinking that China will be different from any other great power in its behaviour or disposition'.[35]

The accusation of Chinese exceptionalism has also been applied to moral realism, not because of the content of moral realist theory but because of its erroneous association with the 'Chinese School'. For example, Dian claimed, 'This fusion of exceptionalism, prescription, and description appears clearly from Yan's words', by quoting some of my recommendations to China's foreign policy as:[36]

> Learning from the distinction between humane authority and hegemony in Pre-Qin times, the strategy for China's rise in its foreign policy should be distinct from that of the United States in three areas. First, China should promote an international order that takes as its principle a balance between responsibilities and rights. Second, China should reflect on the principle of reverse double standards, namely, that more developed countries should observe international norms more strictly than less developed ones. Third, China should promote the open principle of the traditional idea of all under heaven as one, that is, China should be open to the whole world and all the countries in the world should be open to China.[37]

Dian is erroneously equating my recommendation for China's deviation from the US's strategy as support for Chinese exceptionalism. Suggesting that China should take a different path to international supremacy does not in and of itself imply China as an exception to the rule. My recommendation for the Chinese government to adopt a different set of foreign policies from that of the US stems from the assumption that the circumstances of the two countries' foreign relations share some similarities. The recommendations derived from studying ancient Chinese philosophies are not specialized for China but are applicable for all leading states, including the US. China is merely the example used because it is, at the time of writing, the rising state, while the US is the hegemon. Moral realism has never suggested that the Chinese civilization is superior to other civilizations, nor does it imply that the Chinese civilization can be an exception to the rules governing how states rise or fall. The theory advocates for leading by example as a strategy for any interstate leadership of humane authority, no matter whether it is Chinese or foreign.

Moral realism does not assert that China is going to provide a world leadership that is more moral than America's. While moral realism recommends that the Chinese government should adopt foreign policies according to the principle of humane authority, it does not influence China's foreign policy. Take, for instance, the strategy of forming alliances: moral realism has asserted for years that China is unable 'to provide a global leadership in the next decade as long as it adheres to the non-alignment principle and does not provide security protections for any country, including its neighbors'.[38] And yet, the Chinese government has firmly adhered to the non-alliance principle.[39] In contrast, Joseph Biden's administration has adopted certain foreign principles that are similar to those advocated by moral realism, such as leading by example. In the presidential inauguration address in 2021, Biden said, 'We will lead not merely by the example of our power but by the power of our example'.[40]

With regard to the strategy for rivalry between great powers, moral realism stresses the importance of competition for talent in both ancient Chinese history and modern times.[41] Moral realism theory posits that adopting the principles of a humane authority is a strategy for obtaining interstate leadership, which is as applicable to China as to other major powers. Guilherme Vilaça stated 'that the focus on recruitment and the morality of leaders or elite officials parallels a recent turn in international relations and international law literatures towards virtue ethics and how international organizations' reputation and success largely depend on the exercise of leadership and virtues by their highest officials'.[42] He also added, 'In this respect, albeit Yan's proposal is mostly directed at Chinese institutions, it can easily be translated into the international sphere not to mention the indirect contribution that better Chinese officials and leadership produce'.[43]

Cultural hybrid rather than Sinocentrism

Another criticism of the 'Chinese School' or 'Chinese IRT' is that they are Sinocentric. Babones said, 'A more likely explanation, though, is that Chinese IR scholars prefer to draw lessons from a time when China was at the center, if not of the world, then at least of its own neighborhood.

The Chinese School is nothing if not Sino-centric'.[44] Hwang stated, 'The enterprise of the CS [Chinese school] does indeed essentialise and fixate the existence of a "Chinese culture" and has the potential to be another hegemonic construction based on Sinocentric ideology'.[45] Lu Peng noted how Sinocentrism hindered the progress of a 'Chinese School', saying, 'The slow progress is attributed to the prevalence of the Sino-centrism in Chinese IR which assumes the superiority of Chinese international experience in knowledge making and evaluation. … Under its influence, the Chinese School Movement is constantly applauded by Chinese IR scholars despite the difficulty in yielding scientific output'.[46]

Sinocentrism is the practice of theory construction based on Chinese history and literature, relating to China's interstate status as a dominating power. While moral realism does draw on ancient Chinese philosophies for inspiration, it is not an example of Sinocentric theory crafting. First, moral realism is based on both Chinese and foreign literature, especially modern IR works by American and European scholars. For instance, when we consulted ancient Chinese texts, Xu Jin and I compared the similarities and differences between ancient Chinese and European political thinkers. We identified that pre-Qin Chinese thinkers and modern IR scholars shared some similar views on interstate affairs, such as '[m]odern IR theories assume an international system that is anarchical, and therefore states fall into many conflicts and wars for the sake of their own interests. This idea is consistent with Xunzi's view that "a social group without hierarchical distinctions leads to rivalry"'.[47] In my book *Leadership and the Rise of Great Powers*, which systematized the assumptions, logics, corollaries, and leadership categories of moral realism, there are more foreign literature sources than Chinese in the bibliography.

Second, moral realism draws on both Pre-Qin Chinese history and modern IR records. In *Leadership and the Rise of Great Powers*, the four types of interstate leaderships are purposely illustrated using both Chinese and foreign cases. The book cites examples of humane authority with the leadership of the early Western Zhou Dynasty and Franklin Roosevelt's administration, hegemonic leadership with the rule of Duke Huan of State Qi and the governments of the US and the USSR during the Cold War, anemocratic leadership with King You of the late Western Zhou Dynasty and Donald Trump's administration, and tyrannical leadership with the first Chinese empire, the Qin Dynasty established by Ying Zheng, and German Nazi government headed by Adolf Hitler.[48] By using both Chinese and Western examples, I hoped to show the categorization is not Sinocentric but universally applicable.

Third, the purpose of moral realism is not to explain China's rise; instead, it is meant to provide a mechanism for the rise and fall of all great powers in history. The modern rise of China is only one of many cases. Moral realism attempts to address the current shortcoming of modern IR theories, which is the inability to explain how a rising power overtakes a hegemon. Moral realism models political leadership as an independent variable and attributes both the rise and fall of great powers to it.[49] The theory attributes the rise of China to the national leadership headed by Deng Xiaoping who initiated the reform and opening-up strategy in 1978 instead of Mao Zedong from 1957 to 1976.[50] The two different types of leadership resulted respectively in social progress and disaster in China. Similarly, in the US after the Cold War, the two types of political leadership headed by Bill Clinton and Trump brought about the respective improvement and decline of America's global leadership. The former increased the US's international strategic credibility while the latter undermined it.[51] The Chinese and American cases are two examples of how moral realism can be applied to explain the rise and fall of great powers beyond the Chinese experience.

Being tested by the coming international order

All IR hypotheses face the test of time; those that survive the test are often deemed as universal or scientific theories. The ongoing war in Ukraine brings about changes in the international order that serves as a new test for moral realism. This section will examine the validity of three assertions of moral realism's model: state leadership determines the direction of change in national strength; different types of state leadership adopt different strategies for pursuing the same interests; different types of international leadership advocate for different international orders.[52]

The interaction between state leadership and national strength

Moral realism argues that responsible decision makers can provide a stronger leadership than irresponsible ones.[53] A responsible government will display the characteristic of leading by example, namely spearheading whatever it calls on its followers to implement in difficult situations. The effect of governmental responsibility is illustrated by the contrast between the Ukrainian government headed by Volodymyr Zelenskyy and the Afghan government headed by Mohammad Ghani. The former organized a strong resistance to Russia's invasion while the latter abandoned its regime.

According to the standard dogma of strength, military power determines who succeeds during a military conflict. Therefore, in February 2022, based on the large gap in military power between Russia and Ukraine, almost everyone predicted that the Ukrainian government would collapse after a week of Russia's attack. The belief in this outcome is evident in the Biden administration officials' discussions. They made plans with the Ukrainian government to relocate Zelenskyy from the capital Kyiv to Lviv, a town near the Polish border, in response to Russia's invasion.[54] Russian President Vladimir Putin's decision to initiate a regime change in Ukraine through a special military action demonstrates that he similarly underestimated the effect of Zelenskyy's leadership. Contrary to the predictions, Zelenskyy refused to flee and broadcasted that he and his family members would stay and defend his country alongside his fellow citizens.[55] In the following two weeks, Ukrainian troops successfully resisted Russia's attack against Kyiv, and the success was followed by substantial military aid from NATO members.

Moral realism explains the discrepancy between Ukraine's relatively weaker military power and initial military success as a result of Zelenskyy's demonstration of governmental responsibility. This success cannot be attributed to foreign military aid because NATO members did not provide substantial aid to Ukraine in the first two weeks. Similarly, the successful resistance cannot be attributed to the resilience of democratic institutions because the same political institutions headed by acting president Oleksandr Turchynov failed to prevent Russia's annexation of the Crimean peninsula from Ukraine in March 2014. Since the only factor that changed was the Ukrainian leadership, the only logical conclusion is that the type of leadership brought about a corresponding outcome in the first two weeks.

This stands in sharp contrast with Ghani's governmental responsibility when the US withdrew from Afghanistan. Ghani fled Kabul in August 2021 and the Taliban took over as Afghanistan's government on the same day.[56] Ghani's governmental troops possessed much more advanced military equipment than the Taliban when the US troops withdrew from Afghanistan. In addition to NATO's aid, Ghani's government was also supported by UN P5 while Zelenskyy's government is not yet. Despite the military and public relations advantage, Ghani's government still could not withstand the assault from the much more poorly equipped Taliban troops, once again demonstrating that military power is not an accurate enough predictor of success.

Different leadership types adopt different strategies when pursuing similar interests

In 2012, I classified Putin as an example of an aggressive leader according to moral realism after he resumed presidency[57] and argued that this type of leadership is prone to military expansion.[58] According to moral realist thought, it was Putin's strategic preference that triggered the war in Ukraine. In contrast, there are different results of the Cuban crisis in 1962 and the Ukrainian crisis in 2022. In 2022, Russia desperately wants to prevent Ukraine from joining NATO, because if Ukraine became a NATO member, the consequent deployment of an American weapons system in Ukraine would pose a serious strategic threat to Russia. In 1962, John Kennedy's administration also desperately wanted to prevent Cuba from deploying the Soviet Union's short-range missiles because it would pose a serious strategic threat to the US. While the Cuban missile crisis resolved peacefully, the war in Ukraine broke out in 2022.

Not every IR theory can offer a satisfactory explanation for why two similar international incidences with similar strategic interests would result in two different outcomes. For instance, offensive realism believes that all the policy makers of great powers have the same preference, aka they all prefer pre-emptive action in anticipation of a danger from the adversaries to preserve their national security. John Mearsheimer said that 'one should never underestimate how ruthless great powers can be when they believe they are in dire straits'.[59] Although offensive realism successfully predicted Putin's war in Ukraine, it cannot explain why Kennedy's administration did not act in the same way as Putin's government during the Cuban missile crisis. In contrast, moral realism believes that different types of leadership have the corresponding strategic preferences in protecting national security within the self-interests international system.[60] Putin prefers a military solution while Kennedy prefers diplomatic settlement. Ergo, the Cuban missile crisis resolved peacefully while the Ukrainian crisis did not.

The interaction between political leadership and international order

In 2019, moral realism modelled two important changes to the international order in the 2020s. The first was an increase in international strategic uncertainty, because '[t]he recent popularity of one-man decision making in major states will devalue the strategic credibility and increase the uncertainty of international politics in the coming decade'.[61] The war in Ukraine and its related disturbances to the current world order support this prediction. International strategic uncertainty is reflected not only in the war itself but also in the sudden global shortage of energy, food and fertilizer, ocean shipping, and rail transportation.[62] Fallout from the war raised global fears of economic interdependence, which manifested in the trend of decoupling policies to restructure international supply chains. Even the EU, a former steadfast advocate of globalization, has decided to strengthen internal supply chains over international ones. At the European Council meeting held in March 2022, EU leaders called for reduced strategic dependencies in key sectors such as critical raw materials, semi-conductors, health, digital technology, and food.[63]

The second change was the renewed value of sovereignty, because '[w]hen leading powers lack strategic credibility, most states may value their own national sovereignty as much as they did during the Cold War'.[64] When the US established unipolar domination at the end of the Cold War, Western countries collectively pushed for human rights norms to prevail over sovereignty. NATO and the US initiated wars with the excuse of protecting human rights in non-democracies, such as the Kosovo War (1999), the

Iraq War (2003), the Libya War (2011), and the war in Syria (2011). In 2022, Russia waged war in Ukraine with the same allegation of protecting human rights. Putin claimed that the aim of Russia's military actions was to protect Ukrainian Russians subjected to what he called eight years of bullying and genocide by Ukraine's government.[65] Instead of engaging on the issue of human rights protection, NATO members switched tracks and condemned Russia's violation of Ukrainian sovereignty. In addition to vocal condemnation, they provided economic and military aid to the Ukrainian government to resist Russia's invasion.[66] According to the European Council, 'EU leaders demanded on several occasions that Russia immediately cease its military actions, unconditionally withdraw all forces and military equipment from Ukraine and fully respect Ukraine's territorial integrity, sovereignty and independence'.[67] When the Western countries consider sovereignty superior to human rights, they hold the same stance as non-Western states. The renewed priority of sovereignty will inevitably shape a new international order.

Summary

Methodological education at the University of California, Berkeley taught me that scientific IR theories require universal explanatory power when analysing the same kind of IR phenomena, no matter when and where they happened. With respect to the debate about 'Chinese IRT' between Chinese IR scholars, P.M. Kristensen and R.T. Nielsen said that

> Yan Xuetong is known as a staunch opponent emphasizing a universal approach to IR. For example, at a 2003 conference on building Chinese IRT the debate stood between Yan Xuetong strongly advocating the scientific method, Shi Yinhong in favor of a humanistic, historical approach, and Qin Yaqing who adopted the middle ground by proposing a 'third culture' in the intersection of scientific and humanistic approaches.[68]

However, because moral realism is viewed as a part of the 'Chinese School' or the 'Chinese IRT', it garnered the same generic criticisms despite its scientific approach. I feel compelled to defend moral realism from these criticisms, such as political motivation, exceptionalism, and Sinocentrism. Furthermore, my defence that moral realism should not be categorized as part of the 'Chinese School' or the 'Chinese IRT' should not be seen as an endorsement of or defence against those criticisms towards other theories, including those self-claimed Chinese IRTs, constructed by Chinese scholars.

Although moral realism is not as influential as the existing major IR theories, it is still a universal theory. It is true that offensive realism is much more popular than moral realism and has never been viewed as a national IR theory or doubted as a universal IR theory. However, moral realism offers a stronger explanatory power than offensive realism when similar security crises lead to different outcomes, such as the Cuban crisis in 1962 and the Ukrainian crisis in 2022. As such, I believe moral realism provides an alternative realist paradigm for development of modern IR theories.

Notes

1. Nele Noesselt, 'Is There a "Chinese School" of IR?', *GIGA Research Programme* 188 (March 2021), pp 1–28, https://www.jstor.org/stable/resrep07521#metadata_info_tab_contents.
2. Guo Shuyong (ed), *Gouji Ganxi: Huhuan Zhongguo Lilun* (International Relations: Calling for Chinese Theory), Tianjin: Tianjin People's Press, 2005, p 357.
3. In opposition to the idea that human rights are universal, the Chinese governmental institutions of social science have disapproved of the term 'universal' since the end of the Cold War. Because of publishing my essay, World Economics and Politics was deprived of the annual award for Excellent Journal of 2006 by the authority of the Chinese Academy of Social Science.
4. Yan Xuetong, 'Guoji Guanxi Lilun Shi Pushixing de' (International Relations Theories Are Universal), *Shijie Jingji yu Zhengzhi* (World Economics and Politics) 2 (2006): 1.
5. Yongjin Zhang and Teng-Chi Chang (eds), *Constructing a Chinese School of International Relations: Ongoing Debates and Sociological Realities*, New York: Routledge, 2016; The China Association of International Relations and the Shanghai Association of International Relations, *Guoji Guanxi Lilun de Zhongguo Tansuo* (Chinese Studies of IR Theories), Shanghai: Shanghai People's Press, 2018.
6. Salvatore Babones, 'Taking China Seriously: Relationality, Tianxia, and the "Chinese School" of International Relations', *Oxford Research Encyclopedias*, 26 September 2017, p 6, https://doi.org/10.1093/acrefore/9780190228637.013.602.
7. Yongjin Zhang, 'The Chinese School, Global Production of Knowledge, and Contentious Politics in the Disciplinary IR', *All Azimuth* 9, no. 2 (2020): 294.
8. Peter J. Katzenstein, 'The Second Coming? Reflections on a Global Theory of International Relations', *The Chinese Journal of International Politics* 11, no. 4 (2018): 382–3.
9. Yevgeny N. Grachikov, 'Chinese School of International Relations: How Theory Creates Diplomatic Strategy and Vice Versa', *Russia in Global Affairs* 17, no. 2 (April–June 2019): 160.
10. Ibid.
11. Salvatore Babones, 'Taking China Seriously: Relationality, Tianxia, and the "Chinese School" of International Relations', p 4.
12. Yih-Jye Hwang, 'Reappraising the Chinese School of International Relations: A Postcolonial Perspective', *Review of International Studies* 47, no. 3 (2021): 16, doi:10.1017/S0260210521000152.
13. Yaqing Qin (ed), 'A Multiverse of Knowledge Cultures and IR Theories', in *Globalizing IR Theory Critical Engagement*, London: Routledge, 2020, p 150.
14. Yongjin Zhang, 'The Chinese School, Global Production of Knowledge, and Contentious Politics in the Disciplinary IR': 289.
15. Beate Jahn, 'Chinese International Theory – A Politics of Knowledge Approach', presented at the webinar on 'Chinese School' in August 2021, p 6.
16. Salvatore Babones, 'Taking China Seriously: Relationality, Tianxia, and the "Chinese School" of International Relations', p 3.

17 Nele Noesselt, 'Revisiting the Debate on Constructing a Theory of International Relations with Chinese Characteristics', *The China Quarterly* 222 (2015): 430.
18 Matteo Dian, 'The Rise of China between Global IR and Area Studies: An Agenda for Cooperation', *Italian Political Science Review*, 52 (2022): 253, https://www.cambridge.org/core/services/aop-cambridge-core/content/view/B6A319ECD1FE8CD46F33E1FD34B91DA2/S0048840221000319a.pdf/rise_of_china_between_global_ir_and_area_studies_an_agenda_for_cooperation.pdf.
19 Beate Jahn, 'Chinese International Theory – A Politics of Knowledge Approach', a speech presented at the webinar on 'Chinese School' held on 27 April 2021, p 1.
20 Barry Buzan, 'How and How Not to Develop IR Theories: Lessons from Core and Periphery', in Yaqing Qin (ed), *Globalizing IR Theory Critical Engagement*, p 60.
21 Barry Buzan, 'The "Chinese School": An Outsider Perspective', presented at the webinar on 'Chinese School' held on 27 April 2021, p 2.
22 Guo Shuyong (ed), *Gouji Ganxi: Huhuan Zhongguo Lilun*, p 357.
23 Guo Shuyong, 'Zhongguo Gouji Guanxi Lilun Jianshe Zhong de Zhongguo Yishi Chengzhang Ji Zhongguo Xuepai Qiantu' (The Growing Concourse of China and the Prospect of Chinese School in Constructing Chinese IR Theories), *Gouji Guancha* (International Review) 1 (2017): 20.
24 Cai Rupeng, 'Chuixiang Zhongguo Xuepai de Zong Haojiao' (The General Trumpet of the Chinese School), *Zhongguo Xinwen Zhoukan* (China News Week) 46 (2017): 16, www.inewsweek.cn/2/2017-12-08/3720.shtml.
25 'Zhonggong Xuanchuanbu, Jiaoyubu Lianhe Yinfa "Mianxiang 2035 Gaoxiao Zhexue Shehuikexue Gaozhiliang Fazhan Xingdong Jihua"' (The Propaganda Department of the CPC Central Committee and the Ministry of Education Jointly Issued 'Action Plan for High Quality Development of Philosophy and Social Sciences in Colleges and Universities in 2035'), *Guangming Ribao*, 28 May 2022, p 2, https://epaper.gmw.cn/gmrb/html/2022-05/28/nw.D110000gmrb_20220528_2-02.htm.
26 Yan Xuetong and Xu Jin (eds), *Zhongguo Xianqin Goujiajian Zhengzhi Sixiang Xuandu* (Pre-Qin Chinese Thoughts on Foreign Relations), Shanghai: Fudan University Press, 2008, p 1.
27 Yan Xuetong and Xu Jin (eds), *Wangba Tianxia Sixiang Ji Qidi* (Thoughts on World Leadership and Implications), Beijing: World Affairs Press, 2009, p 1.
28 Feng Zhang, 'The Tsinghua Approach and the Inception of Chinese Theories of International Relations', *The Chinese Journal of International Politics* 5, no. 1, (2012): 95–6.
29 Peter J. Katzenstein, 'The Second Coming? Reflections on a Global Theory of International Relations': 377–8.
30 Yongjin Zhang, 'The Chinese School, Global Production of Knowledge, and Contentious Politics in the Disciplinary IR': 290.
31 Yan Xuetong, *Shijie Quanli de Zhuanyi: Zhengzhi Lingdao Yu Zhanlue Jingzheng* (World Power Transition: Political Leadership and Strategic Competition), Beijing: Peking University Press, 2015.
32 Ibid., p 3.
33 Yan Xuetong, *Leadership and the Rise of Great Powers*, Princeton: Princeton University Press, 2019, pp 82–3.
34 Yongjin Zhang, 'The Chinese School, Global Production of Knowledge, and Contentious Politics in the Disciplinary IR': 294.
35 Hun Joon Kim, 'Will IR Theory with Chinese Characteristics be a Powerful Alternative?', *The Chinese Journal of International Politics* 9, no. 1 (2016): 59–79.
36 Matteo Dian, 'The Rise of China between Global IR and Area Studies: An Agenda for Cooperation': 8.
37 Yan Xuetong, *Ancient Chinese Thought, Modern Chinese Power*, Princeton: Princeton University Press, 2011, p 219.

38 Yan Xuetong, *Leadership and the Rise of Great Powers*, p 199.
39 'Guofangbu Tan Meimeng Tixi: Jianjue Fandui Lengzhan Siwei He Linghe Boyi Linian' (Defense Ministry Talking about American Alliance System: Firmly Opposing Cold War Mentality and the Idea of Zero-Sum Game), *Chinanews.com*, 29 October 2020, https://baijiahao.baidu.com/s?id=1681885955997681047&wfr=spider&for=p.
40 President Joseph R. Biden, Jr, inaugural address at the White House, 20 January 2021, www.whitehouse.gov/briefing-room/speeches-remarks/2021/01/20/inaugural-address-by-president-joseph-r-biden-jr/.
41 Yan Xuetong, *Ancient Chinese Thought, Modern Chinese Power*, p 67.
42 Guilherme Vasconcelos Vilaça, 'Strengthening the Cultural and Normative Foundations of the Belt and Road Initiative: The Colombo Plan, Yan Xuetong and Chinese Ancient Thought', in Wenhua Shan, Kimmo Nuotio and Kangle Zhang (eds), *Normative Readings of the Belt and Road Initiative Road to New Paradigms*, Cham, Switzerland: Springer International Publishing AG, 2018, pp 30–1.
43 Ibid., p 37.
44 Salvatore Babones, 'Taking China Seriously: Relationality, Tianxia, and the "Chinese School" of International Relations', p 7.
45 Yih-Jye Hwang, 'Reappraising the Chinese School of International Relations: A Postcolonial Perspective': 19
46 Lu Peng, 'Chinese IR Sino-Centrism Tradition and Its Influence on the Chinese School Movement', *Pacific Review* 25 (2018): 150, https://www.tandfonline.com/doi/full/10.1080/09512748.2018.1461681.
47 Yan Xuetong and Xu Jin (eds), *Zhongguo Xianqin Goujiajian Zhengzhi Sixiang Xuandu*, p 1.
48 Yan Xuetong, *Leadership and the Rise of Great Powers*, pp 43–7.
49 Ibid., p 191.
50 Ibid., p 133.
51 Ibid., pp 41–2.
52 Ibid., pp 56, 62–3.
53 Ibid., pp 24, 29–30.
54 Carol E. Lee, Courtney Kube and Kristen Welker, 'US Officials Discussed Ukrainian President Leaving Capital if Russia Attacks', *NBC NEWS*, 22 February 2022, www.nbcnews.com/politics/white-house/us-officials-discussed-ukrainian-president-leaving-capital-russian-att-rcna17094.
55 'President Zelensky Refuses to Leave Ukraine, Asks for Ammunition Instead of "a Ride"', *MARCA*, 26 February 2022, www.marca.com/en/lifestyle/world-news/2022/02/26/6219c92aca4741db0e8b461b.html.
56 Ken Bredemeier, 'Ghani Says He Fled Afghanistan to Avoid Kabul Bloodshed', *VOA*, 8 September 2021, www.voanews.com/a/south-central-asia_ghani-says-he-fled-afghanistan-avoid-kabul-bloodshed/6219383.html.
57 Yan Xuetong, *Leadership and the Rise of Great Powers*, p 38.
58 Ibid. p.36.
59 'John Mearsheimer on Why the West Is Principally Responsible for the Ukrainian Crisis', *The Economist*, 19 March 2022, www.economist.com/by-invitation/2022/03/11/john-mearsheimer-on-why-the-west-is-principally-responsible-for-the-ukrainian-crisis.
60 Yan Xuetong, *Leadership and the Rise of Great Powers*, pp 193–4.
61 Ibid., p 204.
62 'Brief No 1: Global Impact of War in Ukraine on Food, Energy and Finance Systems', United Nations, 13 April 2022, https://unctad.org/system/files/official-document/un-gcrg-ukraine-brief-no-1_en.pdf; Tan Weizhen, 'How the Russia–Ukraine War Is Worsening Shipping Snarls and Pushing up Freight Rates', *CNBC*, 11 March 2022, www.cnbc.com/2022/03/11/russia-ukraine-war-impact-on-shipping-ports-air-freight.html.

63 'European Council, 24–25 March 2022', *European Council*, www.consilium.europa.eu/en/meetings/european-council/2022/03/24-25/.
64 Yan Xuetong, *Leadership and the Rise of Great Powers*, p 204.
65 Paul Kirby, 'Why Has Russia Invaded Ukraine and What Does Putin Want?', *BBC News*, 9 May 2022, www.bbc.co.uk/news/world-europe-56720589.
66 Katharina Buchholz, 'Where Military Aid to Ukraine Comes From', *Statista*, 2 June 2022, www.statista.com/chart/27278/military-aid-to-ukraine-by-country/.
67 'EU Response to Russia's Invasion of Ukraine', *European Council*, 3 June 2022, www.consilium.europa.eu/en/policies/eu-response-ukraine-invasion/.
68 P.M. Kristensen and R.T. Nielsen, 'Constructing a Chinese International Relations Theory: A Sociological Approach to Intellectual Innovation', *International Political Sociology* 7, no. 1 (2013): 5–6, https://doi.org/10.1111/ips.12007.

3

Moral Realism as an Alternative Approach to the Agent–Structure Problem

Fang Yuanyuan

The agent–structure problem has been the root cause of deeply entrenched disputes of international relations (IR), stretching from the late medieval differentiation between the individual and the state to contemporary metatheoretical controversies within epistemology and political ontology. Despite their many differences, however, the 'agent–structure', 'parts–whole', and 'micro–macro' problems all reflect the same metatheoretical imperative of the need to explain the ontological and explanatory relationship between social actors or agents (in this case, states) and societal structures (in this case, the international system). The agent–structure problem has 'at present evolved into what is often claimed to constitute the central problem in social and political theory'.[1]

Knafo argues that the agent–structure debate shows how hard it is to integrate a structural conception of power with a concept of social change associated with an agency. He maintains that, by overemphasizing the dynamics of social reproduction, the notion of structural power has made it hard to account for social change.[2] Moral realism, by treating political leadership as the independent variable explaining the rise and fall of great powers, and potentially the changes of international norms and systems, provides an answer to such social change and an alternative perspective to the existing agency and structural analyses, linking individual, state, and system levels of analyses.[3] Instead of simply granting agents the determinative role in relation to structure, moral realism provides a dualist theory, valuing the importance of leaders in decision making and the importance of a nations' relative capability and status in the international system.

This chapter follows a three-tier structure. First, it provides an in-depth analysis of how moral realism deals with the problem of agent–structure. Second, it revisits the agent–structure debate and compares moral realism's take on the debate with other prominent analyses. Third, it critically analyses the problems and the challenges lying ahead of moral realism and provides related suggestions for the further development of this valuable theory.

Bringing agent back to realist discourse

Engaging classical realism and Chinese philosophy, moral realism brings agent-level analysis back to realist discourse by explaining the rise and decline of great powers through political leadership as the key independent variable. Neorealists believe that national interests determine a nation's policy, which is believed to be defined by the international structure. The state has often been understood as a unitary and rational actor. Therefore, it does not matter who the leader is.[4] Structural determinism, as such, refers to the underlying distribution of material capabilities that gives states the ability to direct the overall shape of world political order. Even though structural theories of leadership vary, they have one thing in common: leadership is rooted in the distribution of power (defined in terms of material capacities) and the structure of the international system. It is not really people or policy that makes a difference, but the structure itself. Briefly, moral realism differs from neorealism by arguing that the leader matters.

Reviewing the discourses of classical realism, one could find that there were explicit interests in agent-level units, exploring human nature as the explanation for the permanent struggle for survival and power that characterizes interstate relations. Two founding classical realist concerns of international politics, what explains states' behaviour and the problem of international order, drove classical realists' exploration of the natural individual.[5] Neal identifies individualism and instrumentalism as two of the realists' core tenets, which he traces directly to Hobbes.[6] Hobbes sees the nature of man lying at the core of the classical realists' quests to find the prime mover of states, as the desire for power, the sole moving force driving the world.[7] Niebuhr puts simply that war has its origin in 'dark, unconscious sources in the human psyche'.[8] Morgenthau notes 'the ubiquity of evil in human action' arising from man's ineradicable lust for power and transforming 'churches into political organizations ... revolutions into dictatorships ... love for the country into imperialism',[9] not only attributing frictions and wars among states to human nature, but also domestic ills. Aside from such pessimistic attribution of political problems to the nature of men, the optimistic ideal accepts the possibility of cooperation and the elimination of war as a product of rational reasoning and morality.[10]

In the Pre-Qin philosophical thoughts, the method employed by Confucius and Mencius is at the level of the individual person, specifically, the ruler. Confucius believes that the stability level of the world order is wholly determined by the moral cultivation of the political leader. Mencius inherited Confucius's analysis and ascribes the presence of absence of world order and the survival of states to whether the ruler has implemented benevolent governance, not simply to the ruler's own moral cultivation. He holds that the reason the first kings of the three dynasties of Xia, Shang, and Zhou rose to leadership of their states whereas the last three kings of the same dynasties lost their positions was that the former governed benevolently and the latter did not.[11] Xunzi's analysis is also largely at the individual level. In analysing the nature of international society, Xunzi regards 'the nature of the ruler of the leading state and his ministers as an independent variable – that is, whether international society is that of a sage king or a hegemon is determined by the nature of the ruler of the leading state and his ministers'.[12]

Deeply influenced by Chinese ancient thoughts on rulers, Yan focuses on the agent level, promoting leadership determinism as an addition to the existing explanation of the rise and fall of great powers.[13] Moral realism is not merely a reinterpretation and theoretical development of classical realism or ancient Chinese thoughts, but a novel theory that attempts to explain the new situation and changes in international relations today. Unlike classical realism, which attempts to explore the nature of state and international order, moral realism aims at explaining the changes of the international order. The empirical background of the development of moral realism is the rise of China and the relative decline of the US after the 2008 financial crisis. The international order dominated by the US since the Cold War is changing, and how to explain the causes of such changes and predict the trend of this change is what drove Yan's theoretical inquiry. Existing works of literature on the rise and fall of great powers attributing the transition of power to external variables, such as structural shift, and internal variables, such as overstretch of foreign policy,[14] failed to explain the dynamics of the current struggle for leadership between China and the US. Firstly, how could China bridge its power gap with the US without fundamentally changing its political system? Secondly, how could the US international leadership drop drastically while its material capability remained the strongest? Attempting to develop a parsimonious theory using one independent variable to explain both the rise and fall of great powers, Yan locks in the analysis of international political leadership as the key determinant.

Yan's theorization of moral realism consists of two parallel logics of reasoning centred on his division of capability and authority (see Figure 3.1). First, political leadership, more specifically, the types of political leadership, is an operational variable determining a state's strategic preferences and comprehensive capability. The reform capability of the leadership determines

Figure 3.1: Political leadership type and a state's international status

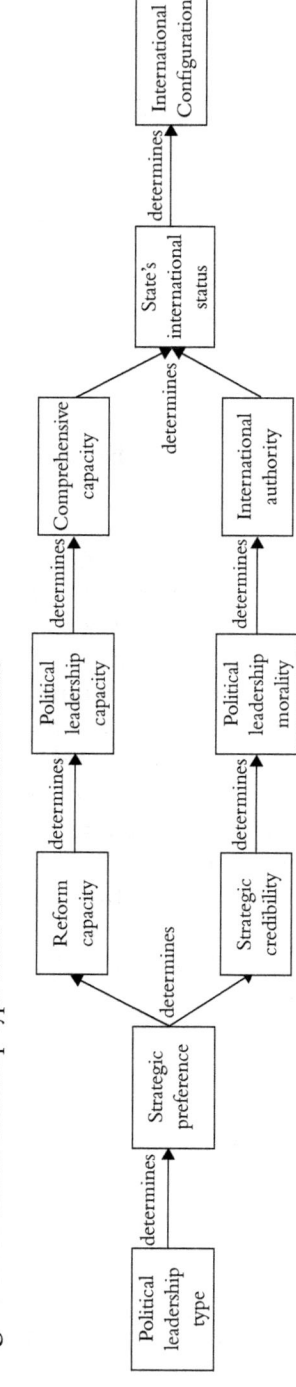

Source: Fan Yuanyuan, illustrating theorization by Yan Xuetong

the state's comprehensive capability. Second, the notion of morality analysed in moral realism refers to public governmental morality at the political leadership level. Strategic credibility is the lowest level of international morality and a prerequisite to a leading power's establishment of international authority. Yan notes that morality gives a country the authority to lead, thus enhancing the power of that country.[15]

Giving agent, leadership, the primary role in determining the changes of structure enables moral realism to not only explain the rise but also the decline of global leadership. Ontologically, leadership at the agency level is treated here as an autonomous and functional member of the polity, instead of coexisting with or being constrained by the structure. Moral realism follows the tradition of classical realism, seeing agents, specifically leaders and leading states, as rational actors featuring a decision-making process aiming at maximizing their benefits. If one still harbours doubt about Yan's conception of agents as rational, his perception of morality in moral realism makes it evident.

Interestingly, Joseph Nye and Yan, coming from different theoretical backgrounds, converge at leadership level of analysis, even more specifically at the moral aspect of leadership. Nye published the book *Do Morals Matter?* in 2020, in which Nye works through each presidency from FDR to Trump to examine the role of ethics in US foreign policy during the American era after 1945. In this book, he emphasizes the importance of morals and develops a scoreboard consisting of intentions (stated goals, as well as presidents' stated values and personal motives), means (assessed from both quality and efficiency), and consequences (which should be morally good for Americans and others) to make moral judgments. He challenges realists because they devalue the role of morality and oversimplify national interest,[16] which Yan, emphasizing moral leadership, would firmly oppose. However, Nye and Yan diverge on their perception of morality as Nye treats morality as an autonomous concept, while Yan treats it more as a heteronomous concept.

Some critics question the compatibility of morality in realist discussion and argue that by emphasizing morality, Yan has become a liberalist or constructivist.[17] Two points justify Yan's notion of morality in accordance with realist tradition: first, moral realism elucidates morality solely as 'governmental morality',[18] whereby leaders' actions will be judged according to the accepted codes of conduct pertaining to national interests and national capability. 'Therefore, it is a public, rather than a private morality, as well as a universal rather than a national morality.'[19] Leaders' policies rather than their personality or the beliefs of any individual are judged in moral realism, which differentiates it from constructivism and liberalism. Second, moral realism adopts an instrumental-based approach of morality, rather than a value-based approach. Instead of arguing about the moral aspect of the leaders defining national interests or the priority of national interests as Brostrom suggests,[20] Yan notes that morality is instrumental as it 'influence[s] policy makers' concerns about how national interests should be achieved rather than what national interests ought to be'.[21] By treating morality in such an instrumental way, Yan makes rationality and morality compatible in the sense that being moral is a way of maximizing one's utility.

While both Nye and Yan narrowed down leadership as a focused level of analysis and described it as an essential independent variable, their perception of leadership in terms of level of analysis also varies. Nye identifies that a leader is someone who helps a group create and achieve shared goals, and leadership should be a mutual 'process' that works under the interdependence of a leader and followers.[22] Leadership thus is identified as a social relationship with its components being based on leaders and followers, where they interact freely. However, Yan's perception of leadership is more complex, not only limited to the individual level, but also referring to leadership at the state level.

Furthermore, leadership is studied in moral realism to understand the current power transition, which is a structural problem. According to moral realism, the state leadership types of rising states and dominant states play a joint role in changing international configurations. Yan even argues that leadership changes in dominant states are more likely to change the international configurations as it is easier to undermine a state's comprehensive capability than to improve it. With the changes in power configuration, a new type of international leadership will emerge, which might lead to changes in international norms depending on the continuity or changes of the type of international leadership between the previous and current leadership. If the new international leadership brought about changes in international norms, the combination of changes in power configuration and the international norms leads to system transformations, which Yan thinks is unlikely to happen even if China replaced the US to claim the new international leadership, as the Chinese government has no intention of changing the Yalta system.[23] The transition of power, potentially the transformation of international order, is then a bottom-up process, initiated by rational agents, which provides an alternative answer to the agent–structure debate.

Revisiting the agent–structure debate

The agent–structure problem consists of three interrelated problems: two are ontological and the other is epistemological. The first, and more fundamental, issue concerns the nature of both agents and structures – in other words, what kind of entities are they? The first is about the choice of the form of explanation corresponding respectively to agents and structures. This choice depends largely on the kinds of properties of agents and the structures that have been deemed causally significant. Thus, approaches to social inquiry that conceive of human beings as reflective, goal-directed subjects, such as rational choice theory, generate agent explanations that are, broadly speaking, 'interpretive' – that is, cast in terms of the goals, beliefs, and self-understandings of agents. On the other hand, approaches that conceive of human beings as nothing more than complex organisms processing stimuli – such as behaviourism – generate agent explanations that are more mechanistically causal in form. Built on Porpora's analysis of 'structure', Colin Wight neatly laid out five different conceptualizations of 'structure' and the problem of contradictory uses of the term.[24] The second, and more essential, problem is about how they are interrelated. There has been a fundamental agreement that 'agent and structure are in some way mutually implicating, of their interrelationship';[25] however, there is no consensus in international relations on how they are interrelated. The third is an epistemological question regarding how to approach the agent–structure problem. There are two basic ways: either by 'making one unit of analysis ontologically primitive or by giving them equal and therefore irreducible ontological status'.[26] Depending on which entity is made primitive, these approaches generate three possible answers to the ontological question: structuralism, individualism, and structuration.

Structural analysis of international relations can be divided into three groups based on their ontological perception of the complex nature of structure and the relation of structure in relation to agent. First, constructivists generally adopt the concept of structure as rules and resources.[27] David Dessler and Nicholas Onuf unambiguously, and systematically, make the case for an account of structure as rules and resources.[28] Dessler argues the scientific realists' solution to the agent–structure problem starts from a single premise, namely, that all social activity presupposes social forms. Hence, 'state action is possible and conceivable only if there exist the instruments through which that action can be carried out'.[29] Structural refers 'to the social forms that pre-exist action'.[30] The conceptualization of structure as rules and resources is also embedded within the English School but equally, it has also been deployed by Keohane and can be said to be consistent with neoliberal approaches in general.[31] It is also apparent in Gramscian and neo-Gramscian perspectives, although these are best understood as the subset dealing with intersubjective understandings.[32]

Second, structural realism and post-structuralism are apt to adopt a relational view of structure.[33] Waltz argues that the definition of structure requires that we concentrate on how the units stand in relation to one another. How units stand in relation to one another, the way they are arranged or positioned, is not a property of the units. The arrangement of units is a property of the system.³⁴ According to Doty, agents and structures are seen to be effects of practices. Or, as she puts it, 'The subject, agent, is determined not determinative';³⁵ practices are autonomous and determinative; what stops, halts, the charge of determinism is that that which determines, namely practises, what are themselves radially indeterminate.³⁶ Koran (2007) observes that structure is the most important factor in determining outcomes since the structure is given methodological or explanatory priority while agents or units have a very limited explanatory or methodological role.

Third, neo-Marxists and structural Marxists, led by Immanuel Wallerstein, conceptualize structure in structuralist terms rather than in terms of relations between, and properties of, primitive individuals.³⁷ Wallerstein follows Althusser's insistence on 'absolute ontological priority of the whole over the parts', and proposes that the only meaningful unit of analysis in comparative or international political economy is the whole world system. In contrast to the neorealist definition of system structure as the distribution of capabilities across pre-existing states, world-system theorists define the structure of the world system in terms of the underlying organizing principles of the world economy, and in particular of the international division of labour, which constitutes or generates state and class agents.³⁸

While holding different conceptualizations of the nature of structure, structural analysis commonly grants priority to the system level of analysis and values the importance of structure to the inquiry of social reality over that of agent. Moreover, their ontological conceptualization led to the methodological preference of systemic approaches to international relations over agent level of analysis. For instance, Waltz argues that '(t)he formula for the acceleration of a freely falling body does not explain how the body falls. For the explanation one looks ... to the whole Newtonian system. ... Once the system is ... grasped, the phenomena are explained'.³⁹ Even though Waltz outlined three levels of analysis – individual, state, system – as an anti-reductionist, he intentionally limits his attention to a structural theory of international systems, eschewing the task of linking it to a theory of foreign policy, which is regarded by Waltz as reductionism as foreign policy analysis treats the system as a dependent variable but focuses on analysing independent variables.⁴⁰ The parsimonious theory of neorealism is compromised by criticism of its deficiencies in explaining system change, variables and interactions between different unit levels, and interests and preferences.⁴¹ Moral realism overcomes these deficiencies by providing a reductionist theory, giving priority to agent, and linking foreign policy making with structural changes. According to Yan, foreign policy making indeed is an essential process in determining the rise, sustainment, and decline of a state's material capability, during which leadership plays the decisive role. Agreeing with Waltz in that there is an unbalanced development of nations' material capability, according to Yan, the answer to this question rests in the leader's capability of reform, rather than structural reasons.[42]

Like Yan, Wendt notes the limitation of the basic assumptions and international logic of structural analysis, which he attributes to structural analysts' ontological and epistemological commitments regarding the agent–structure problem. Wendt was the first scholar to explicitly introduce the debate of agent and structure to IR, starting with a critique of two key theories in international relations: the structural realism theory and the world-system theory.[43] Wendt opens up 'a promising avenue for the theorization of agency'[44] to IR, which encouraged a wave of bringing the micro level to, or, in other words, bringing back to, the social inquiry of IR.[45] In addition to Wendt's influence, Bhaskar and Ian state: 'human agents have different properties to those of structures and we should care to distinguish between them',[46] also contributing to the exploration of the nature of agents in IR. The agency answer to the ontological question reduces the epistemological issue to a choice between either treating actors wholly as objective maximizers of utility, most commonly formalized in rational choice theory, or viewing them as subjective, interpretative agents pursuing individual goals, an approach deeply rooted in phenomenology, hermeneutics, and Wittgenstein's later philosophy, as well as contemporary constructive theories of international relations.[47]

A rational agent is a key site for the convergence of classical realism, liberalism, and rational choice theory in political science. There is a rationalist-individualist ontology embedded in these theoretical schools, in which individuals can be understood apart from society, 'the fundamental characteristics of men are not products of their social existence'[48], and their self-action is the basis of social agency and the foundation of society.[49] Thus, individual human beings are understood as 'conceptually prior to political society but also to all social interactions'.[50] Along this line, the rational individual is theorized as a self-interested maximizer of utility.[51] There is an underlying analogy of rational individual and the state as rational actors embedded in classical realists', even neorealists', understanding of world politics, which is also reflected in Yan's mixture of leadership at individual and state level.

The most significant challenge to a rational understanding of agency in IR is the alternative constructive understanding of individual proposed by constructivists and post-structuralists.[52] Since then, the agency level of analysis has been largely dominated by constructivists and decision-making analysts that explore not only how agents act and impact the structure, but, more importantly, deconstruct what the agents are.[53] Constructivists' understanding of agency is deeply rooted in human consciousness, which perceives agents as socially constructed and subjective rather than rational beings. The three distinct traditions that enable agents to arise are post-structuralism, actor-network theory, and performance studies. These bodies show how social practices produce subjects. Despite their differences, they view the agency as situational, relational, and reflexive.[54] Consequently, the current agency analysis introduced a broad variety of levels and corresponding agents, including states, regions, human beings, bureaucracies, and the global system,[55] broad enough that almost every actor in the international system can be justified as an agent.

In either case, the individual is viewed as the primary source of social structure, and hence all conceptions of the link between agents and social structure are ultimately reduced to explanations in terms of individual action. In Karl Popper's classic formulation, 'all social phenomena, and especially the functioning of all social institutions, should always be understood as resulting from the decisions, actions, attitudes, etc. of human individuals ... we should never be satisfied by an explanation in terms of so-called collectives'.[56]

Wendt, by introducing structuration theory, attempts to find a reciprocal or middle road between agent and structure. However, in search of such a middle road, scholars following Wendt limited their analyses to the constitution of identities and interests, while bracketing other aspects of agency.[57] Proposals to endogenize corporate identity and study 'processes involving the appearance and disappearance of political actors as well as boundary transformations'[58] went mainly unheard. As Fearon and Wendt note, 'like rationalists, modern constructivists have been largely content to take as "exogenously given" that they were dealing with some kind of actor, be it at state, transnational social movement, international organization or whatever. The middle road thus turned out to be a "one-way street" in constitutive theory'.[59] Critics argue that constructivism provides very little to the issue of substantive knowledge as well as hypotheses about the behaviour of states and their systems. It was not until the mid-1990s that some theorists in international relations began some alternative works to assist in developing constructivism as a substantive theory of international behaviour.[60]

Upon scrutiny, what is intertwined in moral realism is a dualist approach to the agent-structure problem, similar to Wendt's structuration theory, seeing the relation between agent and structure as reciprocal. The emphasis on the role of agents, as analysed in the previous section, is evident in moral realism, and what is often overlooked is its interpretation of the role of structure in the power transition process. The structure is obviously the dependent variable in the theoretical framework of moral realism, as it attempts to explain the changes of international configuration and possibly of international system. However, moral realism does not simply treat structure as the outcome of the actions of agents. According to Yan, moral realism provides 'a dualist theory that stresses the importance of both political leadership and a state's capability in decision making'.[61] State capability in moral realism is more of a structural, rather than an agent-centred, concept, as it is not solely determined by a state's absolute comprehensive capability, but depends on its relative capability and status in the international system. Yan further explains that 'on the one hand, the anarchical nature of the international system requires all policy makers to define their strategic interests prudently, according to their state capability; on the other hand, it gives policy makers room to develop the distinct strategic approaches through which to pursue national interests'.[62] Following this logic, a state's position in the system determines the context of which leadership is exercised, which then makes moral realism a structural theory as well as an agency theory.

Despite the similarity of treating agents and structures as mutually determined, there are ontological and epistemological differences between moral realists' and constructivists' analyses of agent and structure. First, not only interpreting agent and structure as mutually determined, Wendt sees them as coexisting;[63] however, Yan perceives agent and structure as independent variables influencing different aspects of a state's foreign policy-making process. Second, constructivism perceives structure as socially constructed, while moral realism sees it as an objectively anarchical system, the characteristic of which is not subject to change. Third, while constructivism conceives individuals as subjective, moral realism follows the tradition of realism conceiving leadership objectively as a unitary rational being. Yan believes that a state's national interests are objectively determined by national comprehensive capability, while constructivists commonly see national interests as socially constructed.[64] Fourth, current agency analysis inquires into how agency is constructed, contested, and transformed, treating individuals as equally important to the social structure, but moral realism considers individuals' different levels of importance and treats leadership only as an influential agent to the structure.

Challenges lying ahead of moral realism

While contributing to the current power transition theories by bringing the agent level back and reflecting on the interaction between agent and structure, the problem of moral realism also lies in its conceptualization of agent. It is unclear which level of leadership moral realism treats as the primitive unit of actor: the president as an individual, the government as a group, or the state as a collective unit. The current manuscript seems to discuss all in one, but they are indeed different actors as the president could not simply equate to the government or to the state.

As Bhaskar notes, 'the structures that constitute the international system have their emergent powers; states as structures within that system have their own emergent powers; and human agents have a set of different emergent powers … for the ways in which each entity is structured endow it with properties not possessed by entities with differing structures'.[65] The ambiguity in the conceptualization comes from three aspects: the definition of leadership, the explanation of leadership actors, and the treatment of the scope of leadership. What is apparent is that moral realism treats political leadership as the independent variable, explaining the changes of the relative statuses of states. However, the concept of leadership compromises a huge variety of definitions, which can refer to the actor who is leading a group of people or an organization, or the position or state of being in control of a group of people, or the capability of leading. Yan prudently clarified a couple of key concepts at the beginning of the book *Leadership and the Rise of Great Powers*, including power, capability, and authority; unfortunately, leadership, as the key factor of moral realism, is not included.

At first glance, it seems that Yan perceives leadership more as the policy maker; as he notes, moral realism treats national leadership as 'a key factor in shaping a country's foreign policies, political principles, official ideologies, and political institutions, while different types of leaderships have corresponding attitudes toward reform and strategic preferences'. Therefore, 'the different leadership types of the dominant state and of rising states could reshape the international configuration, order, norms, world center, or even the international system as a whole'.[66] In the Chinese version of *Leadership and the Rise of Great Powers*, Yan prudently translated political leadership into 领导力, which refers to leadership capability.

Besides this ambiguous conceptualization of leadership, what needs more clarification is, if moral realism labels political leadership more from the perspective of actors, then what kinds of actors is it discussing? This brings us to the issue initially mentioned in this section: how does moral realism define an agent? In Chapter 2 of *Leadership and the Rise of Great Powers*, Yan clearly claims that he regards decision making as a collective action rather than the result of a single leader's individual decision; in other words, political leadership refers to a group of decision makers as a collective actor, rather than the top leader of that decision-making group. Additionally, Yan's attempt to distinguish the study of leadership in moral realism from the study of leaders in political psychology is evident. Yan notes that 'political leadership is categorized according to its concrete policies rather than the supreme leader's personality or the beliefs of any individual'.[67] However, when he starts to categorize types of state leadership, he gives most of the examples as individual leaders, such as Emperor Taizong of the Tang Dynasty, Mao Zedong, Donald Trump, and so on, rather than as collective actors.

As noted, moral realism is based on the review of ancient Chinese thoughts on domestic and interstate relations. It is worth mentioning that Confucius and Xunzi's thoughts that moral realism referred to leadership is largely focused on individual actors, instead of collective actors. As cited from Confucius at the beginning of the book 为政以德,譬如北辰,居其所而众星共之 (He who exercises governance through virtue will be like the North Star keeping its position surrounded by other stars), which talks about how the leader at the top could attract followers,[68] 'Governing is regulating. If you regulate yourself properly, no one dares not to regulate oneself'. Mencius went a step further and stated, 'no one is not benevolent if the emperor is, no one is not righteous if the emperor is, no one is not just if the emperor is. If the emperor is moral, the state will be settled'.[69] Emperor, as Son of Heaven, is the moral model that represents the highest moral standard and is responsible for leading by example to all his followers, including government ministers and civilians.

Upon scrutiny, Yan's unconscious equation of leaders' behaviours and influences with those of the collective decision-making group is influenced by Chinese ancient culture, which perceives governance as a hierarchical relationship, in which a leader at the top of the hierarchy can determine the policy and action of the collective group, disregarding disagreement within this group. It is true that strong leaders can determine and lead group thinking, just like the examples given in the book, such as Emperor Taizong of the Tang Dynasty and Mao Zedong, but this might not be the same with weak leaders. In the book, Yan also referred to group thinking, attempting to rationalize the simple equation of leader and the collective decision-making group; however, the leader is not necessarily always the one that is the most provocative and leading the group thinking – other players might also influence the decision making, even though they are maybe not bureaucratically categorized as a part of a state's decision group, such as interest groups. Therefore, to further develop moral realism, it will be helpful to move down further towards the micro level of analysis, to explore what the core actor of state and international leadership is, instead of putting them in a melting pot.

As noted previously, Yan's theorization of moral realism consists of two parallel logics of reasoning centred on his division of state leadership and international leadership, in other words, domestic and international leadership. Yan categorized state leadership and international leadership into different typologies. State leadership is categorized into four types: inactive, conservative, proactive, and aggressive leadership; while international leadership is classified as humane authority, hegemony, anemocracy, and tyranny.[70] However, Yan did not explore the causal relations or even the interaction between these two levels of leadership, and the typologies of state leadership and of international leadership do not correspond with each other. He noted that 'the leadership of a leading state that is able to improve its national capability does not necessarily provide a benevolent international leadership or create a stable order of the international system. It is also true to say that a government that undermines its international status is not necessarily a tyrannical international leadership,'[71] which implies that state leadership and international leadership can only be analysed independently.

That Yan categorized these two levels of leadership into different types can be justified as they are executed in different contexts, one under a hierarchical power structure, and the other in an anarchical system. However, treating these two levels of leadership in a parallel way significantly reduces the empirical value of moral realism as it would be hard to categorize a state's leadership comprehensively and predict its preferences and outcomes in a parsimonious way, for example, Donald Trump, who is recognized as having significantly reduced US international strategic credibility but has implemented the domestic policies he promised and, to a certain extent, has stabilized the US employment rate. How should we evaluate this when there is such a contradiction?

One of the major breakthroughs of moral realism in the existing literature on power transition and rising states is that using political leadership as an explanatory variable can parsimoniously and effectually explain both the rise and fall of a state. But how about the sustainability of a state's relative comprehensive capability through different types of leadership? At the micro level, how could moral realism explain the continuity of a state's foreign policy with different types of political leaders? While George W. Bush and Barack Obama are different types of leadership, Shea asserts that 'the Obama administration has pursued the "Global War on Terror" with as much, if not more vigor than George W. Bush',[72] which reflects that Obama's foreign policies are more of a continuity than a change in comparison with that of Bush.[73] As Noah Smith notes, FDR and Reagan, as two transformational presidents, actually implemented changes that began under their predecessors of the opposite party with different leadership types. Just as Reagan expanded on Jimmy Carter's accomplishment, Roosevelt got a running start from Herbert Hoover.[74] Additionally, despite the vast differences between Trump's and Biden's administrations, there are some issues on which their policies are more of continuity, such as their China policy.

Since Biden took office, it has been increasingly evident that America's China policy under Biden is just as assertive as it was under Trump. At the contentious meeting in Alaska, Secretary of State Antony Blinken and National Security Adviser Jake Sullivan followed the Trump administration's direct attack on Chinese suppressive domestic governance and aggressive international behaviours. 'Biden's economic policy, though it does not involve the president yelling at companies to put, it does not change that much from that of Trump'.[75] Until now, Biden has followed Trump's footmark regarding the strategic framework of Indo-Pacific, constantly framing its bilateral relations with South Korea and Japan and its multilateral relations with the QUAD within the Indo-Pacific strategic framework.[76] That is to say, changes of political leadership types do not necessarily bring about changes in strategic preferences, at least not on all issues. What, then, are the conditions under which a change of president type would lead to a change of strategic preference, and ultimately to the rise and fall of a state? It might be helpful if the future studies of moral realism further elaborate on the boundary of the impact of structure and that of leadership. What is decided by the structure or agent might be an issue-based question, relating to the degree of relevance of each issue to the core national interests of a state.

Additionally, facing a similar problem of structural and geopolitics determinism, Yan's perception of regional states as constrained by dominant states and small states as not able to exercise any kind of leadership might be too pessimistic.[77] Specifically, facing climate change and a chain of environmental problems, middle power and small states have contributed significantly in initiating, sustaining, and implementing international cooperation and driving the introduction of specific rules and regulations. If one is interested in looking at the record of UN climate proposals, one will find that the aggregate numbers of proposals proposed by small and middle powers are actually greater than that of the two major countries, China as the rising state and the US as the dominant state. Small states, like the Alliance of Small Island States (AOSIS), have enhanced their collective bargaining power to promote agenda that is beneficial to them, giving full play to the advantages of small countries in institutional design and knowledge shaping, and attempting to realize small states' leadership in climate negotiations.[78] How does moral realism explain middle and small states' leadership in specific issues of international politics? Middle and small states are largely analysed as followers in Yan's current theoretical framework, whose leadership is overlooked.

Summary

In this review chapter, moral realism is critically analysed in the context of the agent–structure debate in IR. It is noteworthy that the purpose of reviewing the theory from the agent–structure perspective is to decipher the ontological and epistemological background of this theory and reconnoitre hidden logical flaws in a more focused way, but by no means should the discussion and development of moral realism be constrained in the agent–structure debate. The world is going backwards, as many scholars have already noted. To get back on track, moral leadership is an important antidote. With Vladimir Putin tightening authoritarianism in Russia, Recep Tayyip Erdoğan, Rodrigo Duterte, and Viktor Orbán's undermining of democratic norms in Turkey, the Philippines, and Hungary, and the list goes on, it certainly appears that Huntington's post-Cold War 'third wave' of democratization is witnessing a strongman-inspired reversal, which makes the study of the agent, such as moral realism, urgent and important.

Amitav Acharya once commented on Yan's moral realism that the focus on the leadership variable promoted is a very timely contribution, given the widespread global attention to and dismay over Donald Trump's leadership of the US, the West, and the world.[79] Yan notes that, with the end of American hegemony, China will cautiously avoid war, consequently a bipolar US–Chinese order will be shaped by fluid issue-specific alliances rather than rigid opposing blocs, which means mos states will adopt a two-track approach siding with the United States on some issues and China on others.[80] Nye notes that the key to realizing this assumption is that both sides have skilled leadership to manage the current US–China conflict.[81] Leadership matters, especially in a turbulent era.

If Trump's destruction of US international leadership during his administration had not yet highlighted the importance of leadership, Biden's rapid restoration of US leadership in just a few months in office has made it undeniable. Since Donald Trump took the Oval Office in 2017, the US's retrenchment has been evident with its withdrawal from several international commitments, such as withdrawing the military from Syria, the Iran Nuclear Deal, and the Paris Agreement. This changing policy, featured in the 'America first' principle, seems to have only diluted US leadership further, rather than prevent the US from declining as an international leader, as it has not only degraded its relations with allies but, more importantly, has dented US authority and credibility in the world. As an adversary of Trump, President Biden laid out different foreign policy visions for America to restore respected leadership at home and on the world stage. Biden has recommitted alliances and re-entered the agreements mentioned earlier and is keen on restoring the US's global leadership. He has termed Trump's move on immigration as morally bankrupt and racist. He has put in place a comprehensive immigration reform. He has emphasized the need of addressing the root cause of immigration in the countries of origin.[82]

Despite the absence of fundamental changes in the relative comprehensive capability of the US as well as his political system, with the change of president, the US's international leadership turned around in a short period of time. Biden promised to 'lead by example', repair the damage wrought by the former administration, and rally the world to meet the common challenges, such as climate change, terrorism, nuclear proliferation, cyberwarfare, that all nations are facing, which presents a vivid example of what Yan categorized as humane leadership. Although not explicitly stated, the Biden administration's actions suggest that they believe that moral realism offers a viable course for accelerating the US international leadership. Given this, the further development of moral realism is not only of theoretical importance but also of practical significance.

Notes

1. Walter Carlsnas, 'The Agency–Structure Problem in Foreign Policy Analysis', *International Studies Quarterly* 36, no. 3 (1992): 245–70.

2. Samuel Knafo, 'Critical approaches and the legacy of the agent/structure debate in international relations', *Cambridge Review of International Affairs* 23, no. 3 (2010): 493–516.
3. Moral realism was firstly proposed as a systematic defence of the idea that there are objective moral standards. The term was then borrowed by Feng Zhang who further developed the concept by combining Western realist theory with Chinese ancient thoughts on morality; Pavlos Kontos, *Aristotle's Moral Realism Reconsidered: Phenomenological Ethics*, New York: Routledge, 2011; Feng Zhang, 'The Tsinghua Approach and the Inception of Chinese Theories of International Relations', *The Chinese Journal of International Politics*, 5, no. 1 (2012): 95–6. Moral realism in this article only refers to the theory developed by Yan Xuetong in a series of articles and books: Yan Xuetong (ed), *Ancient Chinese Thought, Modern Chinese Power*, Princeton: Princeton University Press, 2011; Yan Xuetong, 'Gaige Nengli Yingxiang Guojia Shili' (Reform Capability Determines National Comprehensive Capability', in *Daoyi Xianshi Zhuyi Yu Zhongguo de Jueqi Zhanlue* (Moral Realism and China's Rising Strategy), Beijing: China Social Science Press, 2018, pp 267–70.
4. Kenneth W. Waltz, *Man, the State and War*, New York: Columbia University Press, 1893.
5. Charlotte Epstein, 'Theorizing Agency in Hobbes's Wake: The Rational Actor, the Self, or the Speaking Subject?', *International Organization* 67 (2013): 287–316.
6. Patrick Neal, 'Hobbes and Rational Choice Theory', *Western Political Quarterly* 41, no. 4 (1988): 635–52.
7. Hans J. Morgenthau, *Politics Among Nations: The Struggle for Power and Peace*, 3rd edition, New York: Knopf, 1960.
8. Niebuhr Reinhold, *Beyond Tragedy*, New York: Charles Scribner's Sons, 1938, p 158.
9. Hans J. Morgenthau, *Scientific Man vs. Power Politics*, Chicago: University of Chicago Press, 1946, pp 194–55, cited in Kenneth W. Waltz, *Man, the State and War*, p 24.
10. Saint Augustine, *The City of God*, Marcus Dods (trans), 2 volumes, New York: Hafner Publishing Co, 1948.
11. Yan Xuetong (ed), *Wangba Tianxia Sixiang Ji Qidi* (Thoughts of World Leadership and Implications), Beijing: Shijie zhishi chubanshe, 2009, pp 130–52.
12. Yan Xuetong (ed), *Ancient Chinese Thought, Modern Chinese Power*, p 28.
13. Paul Kennedy, *The Rise and Fall of the Great Powers*, New York: Random House, 1987); Charles A. Kupchan, 'Empire, Military Power, and Economic Decline', *International Security*, 13, no. 4 (1989): 36–53; Jessica T. Mathews, 'Power Shift', *Foreign Affairs*, 76, no. 1 (1997): 50–66; Vassilis K. Fouskas and Bülent Gökay, 'The Power Shift to the Global East', in *The Fall of the US Empire: Global Fault-Lines and the Shifting Imperial Order*, London: Pluto Press, 2012, pp 111–32; David A. Lake, 'Legitimating Power: The Domestic Politics of US International Hierarchy', *International Security* 38, no. 2 (2013): 74–111.
14. Ibid.
15. Yan Xuetong, *Leadership and the Rise of Great Powers*, Princeton: Princeton University Press, 2019, pp 1–51.
16. Joseph S. Nye, *Do Morals Matter? Presidents and Foreign Policy from FDR to Trump*, New York: Oxford University Press, 2020.
17. Amitav Acharya, 'From Heaven to Earth: "Cultural Idealism" and "Moral Realism" as Chinese Contributions to Global International Relations', *The Chinese Journal of International Politics* 12, no. 4 (2019): 467–94.
18. To clarify the notion of morality, Yan notes that there are three levels of morality: personal, governmental, and international. As moral realism is a theory that specifically addresses international relations, 'morality refers solely to governmental morality. See Yan Xuetong, *Leadership and the Rise of Great Powers*, p 8.
19. Yan Xuetong, *Leadership and the Rise of Great Powers*, p 24.
20. Jannika Brostrom, 'Morality and the National Interest: Towards a "Moral Realist" Research Agenda', *Cambridge Review of International Affairs* 29, no. 4 (2015): 1624–39.

21. Yan Xuetong, *Leadership and the Rise of Great Powers*, p 6.
22. Joseph Nye, 'Transformational Leadership and US Grand Strategy', *Foreign Affairs* 85, no. 4 (2006): 68
23. Yan Xuetong, *Leadership and the Rise of Great Powers*, pp 165–71.
24. Porpora notes the four most uses of the term structure: (1) Patterns of aggregate behaviour that are stable over time; (2) Law-like regularities that govern the behaviour of social facts; (3) Collective rules and resources that structure behaviour; (4) Systems of human relationships among social positions. Wight adds one more use of the term as relations of difference that constitute and define the properties of elements. See Douglas Porpora, 'Four Concepts of Social Structure', *Journal for the Theory of Social Behaviour* 19, no. 2 (1989): 195–212; Colin Wight, *Agents, Structures and International Relations: Politics as Ontology*, Cambridge: Cambridge University Press, 2006.
25. Alexander Wendt, 'The Agent–Structure Problem in International Relations Theory', *International Organization* 41, no. 3 (1987): 335–370.
26. Ibid.
27. See Alexander Wendt, 'Anarchy is what States Make of it: The Social Construction of Power Politics', *International Organization* 46, no. 2 (1992): 391–425; Alexander Wendt, *Social Theory of International Politics*, Cambridge, UK; New York: Cambridge University Press, 1999.
28. See David Dessler, 'What's at Stake in the Agent–Structure Debate?', *International Organization* 43, no. 3 (1989): 441–73; Nicholas G. Onuf, 'World of our Making: Rules and Rule', in *Social Theory and International Relations*, Columbia, SC: University of South Carolina Press, 1989; Vendulka Kubalkova, *Foreign Policy in a Constructed World*, New York: Routledge, 2001.
29. David Dessler, 'What's at Stake in the Agent–Structure Debate?': 453.
30. Ibid., 452.
31. Robert Keohane and Joseph Nye, *Power and Interdependence: World Politics in Transition*, Boston; Toronto: Little, Brown, 1977; Robert Keohane, *International Institutions and State Power: Essays in International Relations Theory*, New York: Routledge, 1989; Quddus Z. Snyder, 'Taking the System Seriously: Another Liberal Theory of International Politics', *International Studies Review* 15, no. 4 (2013): 539–61.
32. Jonathan Pass, 'Gramsci Meets Emergentist Materialism: Towards a Neo Neo-Gramscian Perspective on World Order', *Review of International Studies* 44, no. 4 (2018): 595–618.
33. Kenneth Waltz, *Theory of International Politics*, New York: McGraw-Hill, 1979.
34. Ibid., p 80.
35. Roxanne L. Doty, 'Aporia: A Critical Exploration of the Agent–Structure Problematique in International Relations Theory', *European Journal of International Relations* 3, no. 3 (1997): 365–92.
36. Roxanne L. Doty, 'Aporia: A Critical Exploration of the Agent–Structure Problematique in International Relations Theory': 377.
37. Louis Althusser and Etienne Balibar, *Reading Capital*, London: New Left Books, 1970, pp 180–1; Steven Smith, *Reading Althusser*, Ithaca: Cornell University Press, 1984, pp 192–200.
38. Alexander Wendt, 'The Agent–Structure Problem in International Relations Theory': 346.
39. Kenneth Waltz, *Theory of International Politics*, p 9.
40. Ole R. Holsti, 'Theories of International Relations and Foreign Policy: Realism and Its Challengers', in *Controversies in International Relations Theory*, London: Red Globe Press, 1995.
41. Robert Keohane (ed), *Neorealism and Its Critics*, New York: Columbia University Press, 1986; Steven M. Walt, *The Origin of Alliances*, Ithaca: Cornell University Press, 1987; Joseph Grieco, *Cooperation among Nations*, Ithaca: Cornell University Press, 1990.

42 Yan Xuetong, *Leadership and the Rise of Great Powers*, pp 20–85.
43 Alexander Wendt, 'The Agent–Structure Problem in International Relations Theory'.
44 Structuration theory asserts that agents and structures are mutually constitutive, and reifies both agents and structures as entities of distinct ontological qualities. For more discussions, see Alexander Wendt, 'The Agent–Structure Problem in International Relations Theory'.
45 Barry Buzan, 'The Level of Analysis Problem in International Relations Reconsidered', in Ken Booth and Steve Smith (eds), *International Relations Theory Today*, Cambridge: Polity, 1995; Bryan Mabee, 'Levels and Agents, States and People: Micro-Historical Sociological Analysis and International Relations', *International Politics* 44 (2007): 431–49; Jennifer L. Selin, 'What Makes an Agency Independent?', *American Journal of Political Science* 59, no. 4 (2015): 971–87; Colin Wight, *Agents, Structures and International Relations: Politics as Ontology*; Jan-H. Passoth and Nicholas J. Rowland, 'Who Is Acting in International Relations?', in Daniel Jacobi and Annette Freyberg-Inan, *Human Beings in International Relations*, Cambridge: Cambridge University Press, 2015, pp 266–85.
46 Roy Bhaskar, *The Possibility of Naturalism: A Philosophical Critique of the Contemporary Human Sciences*, 2nd edition, Brighton: Harvester, 1979, p 62.
47 James Fearon and Alexander Wendt, 'Rationalism v. Constructivism: A Skeptical View', in Walter Carlsnaes, Thomas Risse, and Beth Simmons, *Handbook of International Relations*, London: Sage, 2001.
48 David Gauthier, 'The Social Contract as Ideology', *Philosophy and Public Affairs* 6, no. 2 (1977): 139.
49 Jean Hampton, *Hobbes and the Social Contract Tradition*, Cambridge: Cambridge University Press, 1986.
50 Ibid., p 6.
51 Thomas Hobbes, *Leviathan*, edited by Michael Oakeshott, Oxford: Basil Blackwell, 1946[1651].
52 Charlotte Epstein, 'Theorizing Agency in Hobbes's Wake: The Rational Actor, the Self, or the Speaking Subject?'
53 For constructivist analyses, see Alexander Wendt, 'The Agent–Structure Problem in International Relations Theory'; Alexander Wendt, *Social Theory of International Politics*; Cynthia Weber, 'Performative States', *Millennium: Journal of International Studies* 27, no. 1 (1998): 77–95; for decision-making analyses, see Graham Allison, *Essence of Decision: Explaining the Cuban Missile Crisis*, Boston: Little, Brown, 1971; Walter Carlsnaes, 'The Agent–Structure Problem in Foreign Policy Analysis', *International Studies Quarterly* 36, no. 3 (1992): 245–70.
54 Christian Bueger and Felix Bethke, 'Actor-Networking the "Failed State": An Enquiry into the Life of Concepts', *Journal of International Relations and Development* 17, no. 1 (2014): 30–60; Bernd Bucher, 'Moving beyond the Substantialist Foundations of the Agent–Structures Dichotomy: Figuration Thinking in International Relations', *Journal of International Relations and Development* 20, no. 2 (2017): 408–33; J-H. Passoth and Nicholas J. Rowland, 'Who Is Acting in International Relations?'
55 Benjamin Braun, Sebastian Schindler, and Tobias Wille, 'Rethinking Agency in International Relations Performativity, Performances and Actor-Networks', *Journal of International Relations and Development* 22 (2019): 787–807.
56 Karl Popper, *The Open Society and Its Enemies: Vol 2*, London: Routledge & Kegan Paul, 1966, p 98.
57 Mary F. Katzenstein, *The Culture of National Security: Norms and Identity in World Politics*, New York: Columbia University Press, 1996.
58 Lars-Erik Cederman and Christopher Daase, 'Endogenizing Corporate Identities: The Next Step in Constructivist IR Theory', *European Journal of International Relations* 9, no. 1 (2003): 6.

59. Benjamin Herborth, 'Die via media als konstitutionstheoretische Einbahnstraße: Zur Entwicklung des Akteur-Struktur-Problems bei Alexander Wendt' (The via Media as a One-Way Street in Constitutional Theory: On the Development of the Agent–Structure Problem in Alexander Wendt's work), *Zeitschrift für Internationale Beziehungen* 11, no. 1 (2004): 61–87.
60. Erik Ringmar, 'How the World Stage Makes Its Subjects: An Embodied Critique of Constructivist IR Theory', *Journal of International Relations and Development* 19, no. 1 (2016): 101–25.
61. Yan Xuetong, *The Rise and Fall of Great Powers*, Princeton: Princeton University Press, 2020, p 61.
62. Ibid.
63. Alexander Wendt, 'The Agent–Structure Problem in International Relations Theory': p 350.
64. Yan Xuetong, *The Rise and Fall of Great Powers*; Alexander Wendt, 'The Agent–Structure Problem in International Relations Theory'.
65. Roy Bhaskar, *The Possibility of Naturalism: A Philosophical Critique of the Contemporary Human Sciences*, p 62.
66. Yan Xuetong, *The Rise and Fall of Great Powers*, p xiv.
67. Ibid., p 27.
68. Ibid., p 1.
69. Mencuis, 4; *Li Lou*, A20 [(cf. Legge, *The Chinese Classics*, 2, pp 293–94).]
70. Yan Xuetong, *The Rise and Fall of Great Powers*, pp 25–52.
71. Ibid., p 52.
72. Timothy J. Lynch and Robert S. Singh, *After Bush: The Case for Continuity in American Foreign Policy*, Cambridge: Cambridge University Press, 2008.
73. There are several researches that share this argument, for example, Mike Aaronson, 'Interventionism in US Foreign Policy from Bush to Obama', in Michelle Bentley and Jack Holland (eds), *Obama's Foreign Policy: Ending the War on Terror*, Abingdon: Routledge, 2014; Aiden Warren and Adam Bartley, *US Foreign Policy and China: The Bush, Obama, Trump Administrations*, Edinburgh: Edinburgh University Press, 2021.
74. Noah Smith, 'Trump Blazed a Trail That Clears the Way for Biden', *Bloomberg Opinion*, 20 April 2021.
75. Ibid.
76. On 20 January 2021, the State Department released *The United States of America and the Republic of Korea on Working Together to Promote Cooperation between the Indo-Pacific Strategy and the New Southern Policy*, which notes that 'the Republic of Korea (ROK) and the United States of America continue to work together to create a safe, prosperous, and dynamic Indo-Pacific region through cooperation between the Republic of Korea's New Southern Policy and the United States' Indo-Pacific Strategy based on the principles of openness, inclusiveness, transparency, respect for international norms, and ASEAN centrality', www.state.gov/the-united-states-of-america-and-the-republic-of-korea-on-working-together-to-promote-cooperation-between-the-indo-pacific-strategy-and-the-new-southern-policy/; on 12 March 2021, Biden said at the Virtual Quad Leaders Summit that 'We've got a big agenda ahead of us. ... The Quad is going to be a vital arena for cooperation in the Indo-Pacific', www.whitehouse.gov/briefing-room/speeches-remarks/2021/03/12/remarks-by-president-biden-prime-minister-modi-of-india-prime-minister-morrison-of-australia-and-prime-minister-suga-of-japan-in-virtual-meeting-of-the-quad/; on 16 March 2021, Secretary of State Antony J. Blinken and Japan's Minister for Foreign Affairs Toshimitsu Motegi reaffirmed the vital importance of the US–Japan Alliance as the cornerstone of peace, security, and prosperity in the Indo-Pacific region.
77. Yan Xuetong, *Leadership and the Rise of Great Powers*, pp 59–61.

78 Louise van Schaik, Stefano Sarris, and Tobias von Lossow, *Fighting an Existential Threat: Small Island States Bringing Climate Change to the UN Security Council*, The Netherlands: Clingendael Institute, 2018.
79 Amitav Acharya, 'From Heaven to Earth: "Cultural Idealism" and "Moral Realism" as Chinese Contributions to Global International Relations'.
80 Yan Xuetong, *Leadership and the Rise of Great Powers*, pp 198–206.
81 Joseph S. Nye, 'Perspectives for a China Strategy', *PRISM* 8, no. 4 (2020): 120–31.
82 Aaron Ettinger, 'Rumors of Restoration: Joe Biden's Foreign Policy and what It Means for Canada', *Canadian Foreign Policy Journal* (2021): 1–18.

4

Prospects, Promise, and Limitations of Moral Realism

Qingxin K. Wang

Drawing on Confucian morality, Professor Yan Xuetong has developed an ambitious theory of moral realism that aims to improve on neorealism by incorporating morality into the neorealist theory of international politics. Yan has been heavily influenced by ancient Confucian thinkers as he stresses the importance of states' responsible political leadership in bringing about international change and international humane authority that promotes universal moral norms. Nonetheless, his theory is more than just a synthesis of the neorealist theory with Confucian morality. Yan's emphasis on the effects of morality on international politics also resonates with the constructivist concern about moral norms to a certain extent.[1]

This chapter examines the basic assumptions and arguments of Yan's moral realism, analyses its prospects and promises by comparing moral realism with two mainstream Western international relations (IR) theories, neorealism and constructivism, and also critically evaluates the limitations of moral realism. The first part of the chapter provides an overview of mainstream IR theories and the potential contributions of moral realism. The second part places moral realism in the context of cross-cultural academic dialogue between moral realism and mainstream Western IR theories, with a detailed comparison between moral realism on the one hand and neorealism and constructivism on the other. The third part critically evaluates moral realism and identifies its limitations.

Mainstream Western IR theories and the promise of moral realism

The field of mainstream IR has been dominated by three major international relations: neorealism, neoliberalism, and constructivism. Kenneth Waltz formulated his influential neorealist theory based on three important assumptions about international politics. First, international politics is anarchic, meaning the absence of world government. Second, states are unitary actors in international politics, and domestic politics is not important in international politics. Third, states are rational and utility maximizers, which means states tend to act to maximize their national interests defined as power. Power is measured mainly in terms of economic and military resources. Thus, Waltz postulated that given the anarchic nature of international politics, states' behaviours are mainly determined by anarchy and the distribution of states' capabilities (or material power) in the international system. The upshot is that states tend to adopt a balancing strategy to cope with security dilemmas in the world of anarchy.

Robert Gilpin has developed the theory of hegemonic stability to account for international changes based on Waltz's neorealism. Gilpin stresses that the differential rates of economic growth leads to the rise and decline of states' power and capability in the international system, eventually bringing about international change and possibly war. The theory has helped many IR scholars to forecast the future direction of international politics and, in particular, predict the potentially adverse impact of China's rise on world politics. Gilpin has focused on material resources as the sole measurement of state power to account for international change while paying little attention to the role of international ideas and norms in effecting international change. As Gilpin has emphasized, rules and norms are created by leading states to pursue their national interests in the maintenance of international order, and have no staying power independent of the material power that has created them. When the material power of leading states declines, rules and norms will decline as well because the leading states no longer have material power to enforce these rules and norms.[2]

Neorealism has been criticized for putting too much emphasis on the distribution of material power in international systems as the sole determinant of states' interests and behaviour, while neglecting many important factors such as domestic politics, institutions, ideology, culture, norms and identities. Neoliberals share the neorealist assumptions that international politics is anarchic and states are rational and utility maximizers. Nonetheless, neoliberals emphasize the constraining effects of international institutions and argue that institutions can reduce transaction costs through issue linkage and hence enhance cooperation among states. They also believe that states tend to prefer absolute gains, rather than relative gains.[3]

Constructivism has presented a more formidable challenge to neorealism. It has rejected neorealism's assumption that states are rational and utility maximizers. Constructivism argues that state interests are socially constructed. Subjective factors like ideas, beliefs, norms, and identities are important factors that may shape states' decisions and actions. States form their interests and identities on the basis of intersubjective meanings that they assign to material objects in the process of interaction and practices. Material objects have no independent meanings aside from the intersubjective meanings that states attach to them. In other words, ideas, norms, and identities are constitutive of states' power and interests. Moreover, constructivism has also rejected the neorealist argument that anarchy necessarily leads to self-help and competitive power politics. Rather, it believes that self-help is one kind of intersubjective structure resulting from interaction and practices among states, rather than a reified structure. In other words, self-help is not a necessarily logical outcome of anarchy. While anarchy can lead to self-help and power politics, it can also can lead to cooperation if states share common values, norms, and identity. In short, power politics is also socially constructed and 'anarchy is what states made of it'.[4]

Yan's moral realism presents an alternative to neorealism and constructivism. Yan's main argument is that states' political leadership is an important driving force for changes in the international system. As he argues, the states that possess responsible political leadership will likely initiate necessary reforms that may promote faster economic growth and attract international support in the international struggle for power, and eventually enhance their comprehensive capability and even bring about major changes in international systems.

Yan's national comprehensive capability is much more than material power resources, as neorealists have defined. As he suggests, comprehensive capability is a function of states' economic resources, military resources, cultural resources, and political capability combined. Political capability is crucial because it functions as an operational element as opposed to a resource element, and exerts a multiplicative effect on the sum of the three resource elements. Political capability is determined by the efficiency of state political leadership, which is mainly measured by the adoption of good reform policies, and the efficient and faithful execution of these reform policies. A state's political leadership may improve, maintain, or undermine the state's political capability and hence its comprehensive capability depending on how political leadership is effectively and responsibly executed.[5] Thus, rather than accepting neorealists' definition of power as constituted only by resources, Yan follows a neo-Confucian tradition that emphasizes the importance of human agency in enhancing states' comprehensive capability and in ultimately bringing about major international change.

The most innovative and perhaps most controversial issue in Yan's theory is his argument that responsible (or moral) political leadership is essential in promoting positive domestic changes and enlisting international support, ultimately bringing about international change. For Yan, morality means 'governmental morality, whereby leaders' action will be judged according to the accepted codes of conduct pertaining to national interests and national capability'.[6] As he defines, 'political leadership refers to a leading body that has the capability to enlist the support of other individuals, teams, organizations in the accomplishment of a common task'.[7] As Yan emphasizes, 'a political leadership plays the essential role in improving, maintaining, or undermining state capability and hence the changes in international configuration'.[8]

Yan suggests that a good political leadership can be measured by the efficiency with which the political 'leadership is able to win both domestic and foreign support, which improves a state's capability and international power'. Drawing on Chinese ancient philosopher Guanzi, Yan further suggests that the different efficiency with which states exercise political leadership contributes to differential growths of international capability among states in two aspects: 'First, the differing efficiencies of state leadership cause the resource elements to increase at different rates. Second, these differing efficiencies cause the same amounts of resource elements to enact different capabilities'.[9] As Yan suggests, the collapse of the former Soviet empire in 1991 was a direct result of the lack of efficiency of the Soviet state leadership, which eventually led to the change of international configuration from bipolarity to unipolarity.[10]

In other words, Yan suggests that a state's possession of power resources does not automatically translate into capability and influence. Rather, power resources need to be converted into actual capability and influence by the effective exercise of political leadership. A morally responsible political leadership will mean the effective and efficient conversion of power resources into capability and influence; morally irresponsible political leadership would mean inefficient conversion of power resources into capability, or undermine a state's comprehensive capability.

As Yan postulates, a rising state that possesses efficient political leadership may accumulate sufficient comprehensive capability to surpass or even openly challenge the power of the dominant state and the international order it has helped to establish. If the rising state succeeds in defeating the dominant state and becomes the new dominant state, it may bring about major international change by creating a new type of international leadership and accompanying international norms.[11]

Overall, Yan has provided a distinctly Chinese perspective of international relations theory. His concern about the moral exercise of state leadership in accounting for international change is a welcome correction of neorealism's single-minded focus on the change in the distribution of material capability as the primary source of international change. Yan's arguments are very original and provocative. The book is well written with intellectual vigour and clarity. Specifically, his study has made three potential contributions to the study of international relations.

First, Yan's stress on the importance of state political leadership for the change of international power distribution shows a lot of promise for future research on the subject. As he suggests, state political leadership, or the responsible and efficient exercise of political leadership, is construed as the extent to which political leaders can build domestic political consensus as well as international support for his policy reforms. This argument has gone beyond the conventional argument of domestic politics which says states' foreign policy can be significantly constrained by domestic politics. In the past, a lot of Western studies have showed that states are not unitary as political leaders invariably face different kinds of political opposition and bureaucratic resistance when making foreign policy decisions. Their studies lent support to Yan's argument for state political leadership.

Aaron Friedberg has provided an important study that focuses on the irrational nature of foreign policy making in Great Britain when adapting to the relative decline of British hegemony prior to World War I. As Friedberg argues, due to factional infighting and bureaucratic squabbles, British leaders were not able to adopt an effective foreign policy to arrest the trend of their relative decline. Friedberg suggests that if British leaders had increased national defence spending and instituted national conscription, there was a good chance that Britain could have avoided the fate of its decline as a world hegemon in the early part of the 20th century.[12] Fareed Zakaria's study on the foreign policy of the US in the late 19th century has provided another example of domestic political constraints on foreign policy making of the would-be hegemon. As his study has showed, the growth of US national wealth had not been necessarily translated into the nation's assertive foreign policy and international influence. Surprisingly, the US, as one of wealthiest nations in the world prior to 1889, had not adopted an assertive foreign policy to promote international influence commensurate to its economic might. He argues that the division of political power within the US state between the federal government and state governments were the main reason for the US to adopt a conservative foreign policy to maintain its international status quo. The reason the US had adopted a very assertive foreign policy after 1889 and become the world's leading power was mainly because US policy makers had gained their political power by making foreign policy with the centralization of state power or the assertion of the power of the federal government over state governments. Thus, domestic politics explains the international ascendancy of the US after 1889, rather than the responsible execution of US political leaders at the time.[13]

What Yan is saying is that domestic politics can be subsumed into the variable of political leadership. Those leaders who do not exercise good leadership will encounter strong resistance from political opposition; those who can exercise good leadership may overcome the resistance of political opposition by commanding an overwhelming amount of political leadership for particular reform policy or foreign policy. Aside from the Soviet example, Yan mentions three other cases to substantiate his arguments.

The first case is the Roosevelt administration whose policies enjoyed a lot of domestic and international support and thus significantly strengthened the American global leadership in the early post-war period. As Yan also suggests, the political leadership in the post-Mao period is another example of efficient exercise of political leadership. China's political leadership under Deng Xiaoping has adopted good reforms at home to set the country on the right path for economic growth and a proactive foreign policy to enlarge foreign support, has executed these policies responsibly, and has led China ultimately to rapid international ascendance vis-à-vis the US. Susan Shirk's study of the political logic of Deng's reform will certainly support Yan's argument.[14] As Yan suggests, President Trump's weak political leadership has undermined American global leadership. This is because Trump has adopted divisive social policies that have discriminated women and minorities, such as opposition to abortion and same-sex marriage, which may have greatly undermined the Democrats' support and contributed to the loss of the Republican majority in the House of Representatives. Internationally, President Trump adopted an isolationist foreign policy towards Europe by pushing NATO allies to fulfil their promises for military budget and in a way resulting in frictions and divisions among NATO allies.

I may add that the Biden administration's policy may lend support to Yan's argument, even though Yan's book does not discuss the Biden administration. Domestically, President Biden has, since his inauguration, tried to unify American society across different religions and ethnicities, reversing the Trump administration's divisive social policy. The personnel appointment of his administration has reflected his intention to mend the fences across the racial and political divide, with unprecedented amounts of minority cabinet-level officials, in a way placating the black minorities, and women who were alienated by the Trump administration's racist overtone and opposition to abortion. Internationally, President Biden has taken advantage of the Russian–Ukrainian war to strengthen the unity of NATO by adopting concerted stringent sanctions on Russia for the invasion of Ukraine. He also injected new life into NATO by admitting Finland and Sweden into NATO and by beefing up American military presence in Eastern Europe, especially in Poland at a time when NATO faces the danger of losing its purpose. The Biden administration has also managed to put forth an Indo-Pacific strategy that has galvanized the American alliance in the region. Thus, President Biden's effective exercise of political leadership domestically and internationally may have strengthened American global leadership.

Second, Yan's study has an important practical value. The publication of the book is timely because it coincides with the growing tensions between China and the US that have resulted from China's rapid economic and political ascendancy. It is incumbent on political leaders and foreign policy analysts of China and the US to find ways to avoid the likely catastrophic clash of civilizations as the two countries step up their economic and geopolitical competitions. Yan's study will contribute to the current debates about the future direction of Sino–US relations in the foreign policy community of both China and the US. As Yan stresses, a civilizational dialogue between the Chinese civilization and the Western civilization is necessary to avoid potentially catastrophic conflicts as neither Western liberalism nor Confucian political ideology alone is strong enough to dominate the entire world. As he suggests, the two ideologies may actually complement each other and the prospect of peace between the US and China can be strengthened if these two different ideologies can be reconciled and a new and unifying political ideology can be developed by integrating the Western liberal values of equality, democracy, and freedom with Confucian cultural norms of benevolence, righteousness, and rites of propriety.

Third, Yan's moral realism will definitely deepen the epistemic dialogue between Chinese IR scholars and mainstream Western IR scholars. The contemporary mainstream IR field has been criticized for being ethnocentric as it has been dominated by the theories that are developed based on Western traditions and historical experiences. As the conduct of contemporary Chinese foreign policy has been deeply rooted in ancient Chinese traditions, cultural bias may have blinded many mainstream IR scholars and analysts and prevented them from correctly grasping the logic of contemporary Chinese foreign policy. Thus, Amitav Acharya has proposed the idea of developing the global international relations theories (GIR) based on a diverse variety of different cultures and traditions.[15] Yan's study may help us to promote a deepening dialogue between Chinese IR scholars and mainstream Western IR scholars, clarify misunderstanding and misperception of China and Chinese foreign policy that may occur in the foreign policy-making community of many Western countries, and enable Chinese and Western IR scholars to work together towards building global IR theories.[16]

Comparing moral realism with neorealism and constructivism

This section places moral realism in direct academic dialogue with two mainstream Western IR theories, neorealism and constructivism. Through a detailed comparison of moral realism with neorealism and constructivism, it clarifies the similarities and differences between moral realism and the two other Western IR theories.

To some extent, Yan's moral realism has been built on neorealism. It shares with the neorealists the two basic assumptions about international politics.

First, states are rational and utility maximizers. Second, international politics is anarchic, namely, there is an absence of world government. Drawing on these two assumptions, Yan postulates that the distribution of international material power, or what he calls the international power configuration, is an important factor in determining states' interests and behaviour. In other words, he accepts Waltz's argument that states may engage in self-help and power politics to enhance their security.

Like Gilpin, Yan believes that international change is mainly initiated by the rising states overtaking the dominant state in terms of comprehensive capability. As the international redistribution of comprehensive capability takes place, the conflicts between rising states and the dominant state are inevitable and may cause major disturbances in international order and even war.[17] International norms and order are deliberately created by the dominant state to serve its own strategic interests. Changes in the international configuration may lead to changes in the international normative order.

Nonetheless, moral realism differs from neorealism in two important aspects. First, moral realism provides a much broader definition of states' capability than neorealism. While neorealism single-mindedly focuses on the distribution of states' material capability as the sole determinant of their interests and behaviours, moral realism insists that states' capability is a function of their material capability, cultural capability, and political leadership combined.

Secondly, moral realism does not completely accept the neorealist argument that the differential rates of economic growth are the main driving force for the rising state to overtake the dominant state in terms of international capability, eventually causing international instability. As moral realism believes, the differentiation in states' political leadership is the main driving force for international change. The state that exercises political leadership effectively and responsibly can amass a lot of domestic and international support and accumulate a lot of comprehensive capability; the state that does not exercise political leadership effectively cannot convert material resources into international influence. Thus, a rising state with effective exercise of political leadership may overtake the hegemonic state in capability, eventually leading to changes in the international system.

Moral realism's stress on the importance of political leadership suggests that it shares some similar concerns with constructivism. This can be seen in two aspects. First, moral realism shares the constructivist emphasis on the importance of ideational factors, especially morality, to a certain extent. Constructivism stresses that moral norms and ideals can motivate human action and help political leaders establish international cooperation and peace. Yan's concern about the efficient and responsible exercise of political leadership suggests that he is being influenced by the neo-Confucian stress on the importance of human agency in exercising political leadership. As the renowned neo-Confucian scholar Wang Yangming of the Ming [D]ynasty suggested, men can transform the material environment and overcome adverse material conditions if they are highly motivated by moral passion. In other words, with moral passion, men can be motivated to accomplish seemingly impossible tasks and effectively carry out political responsibility. But moral realism sees morality as instrumental to leading states' interests, rather than serving as the intersubjective basis for states to form interests – this point will be elaborated later.

Second, while Yan is sympathetic to Waltz's argument that international anarchy may lead to self-help and power politics, he does not believe that anarchy necessarily leads to this. This position resembles that of constructivism to a certain extent. As Yan suggests, international anarchy determines states' interests and goals, but political leadership determines their approach and strategy to achieve their interests and goals. Thus, states with efficient political leadership can adopt a range of different and flexible strategies such as non-alignment strategy, trade war, or violent war to enhance security.[18]

While moral realism shares with the constructivists the concern about the importance of moral power of leading states, it also differs from constructivism in four important ways.

First, Yan's moral realism differs from constructivism in its conceptualization of states' interests and power. Constructivism questions neorealism's understanding of states' interests as based on material power. Constructivists believe that intersubjectively shared ideas such as beliefs, norms, and identity can shape states' interests independent of material basis and can guide their behaviours. This is because ideas, norms, and identity provide meanings to material power structures and serve as an important basis for states to define their interests independent of material power. A norm is defined as collective expectation about states' proper behaviours that implies a certain logic of appropriateness.[19] State identity is a state's 'relatively stable, role-specific understandings and expectations about self'.[20] For example, as Thomas Risse-Kappen argues, the diffusion of democratic norms among members of the North Atlantic Treaty Organization (NATO) has meant that members treat one another as equal partners and their cooperation is achieved through persuasion and compromise, rather than through coercion or threats based on power asymmetry.[21] Likewise, identity matters in terms of perception of threat. A stranger holding a gun will pose much more threat to us than a friend holding a gun. In other words, the identity of the gun holder can determine whether a gun is a threat to us or not. Likewise, Iranian nuclear weapons will pose a much larger threat to American security than British nuclear weapons would pose to American security because Americans consider the British the most friendly ally and consider Iranians as a bitter enemy.

Nonetheless, unlike constructivism, moral realism treats material resources as the primary basis of states' power, and treats morality as a secondary basis of power derived from material resources, rather than independent power resources. As Yan writes, 'objective national interests are defined by state capability, and that their existence is not determined by people's perceptions'.[22] States' moral power manifested in state political leadership can enhance their overall power in bringing about international change, but states' moral power cannot substitute their material power. In other words, to borrow Max Weber's terms, moral realism stresses instrumental reason of morality, rather than value reason of morality. In Yan's own words, the 'characterization of national interests is what distinguishes my view on national interests from Alexander Wendt's. I believe that national interests are objective, while Wendt suggests that national interest is subjectively constructed by social perceptions'.[23]

Likewise, Yan also believes that international order is maintained mainly on the basis of leading states' material capabilities, with their moral political leadership as a supplementary basis. As Yan writes, 'national capability is the precondition for effective moral actions. ... Without superior capability, no leading state would be able to maintain international order through moral actions alone'.[24]

Second, moral realism also differs from constructivism in its conception of the relations between state agency and international structure. For constructivism, state agency and international social structure are mutually constitutive. As Wendt argues, states can produce, reproduce, or alter international social structure such as norms and identities by their discursive practices, and international norms and identities can then come back to shape and constitute states' interests and action. In other words, international social structures are not reified objects that cannot be changed by states; rather, international social structures exist only through the reciprocal interaction and practices between states.[25]

Constructivists recognize the important role state agency plays in creating and promoting international norms strategically. As Martha Finnemore and Kathryn Sikkink suggest, international norms originate with norm entrepreneurs, be they states or individuals, and states comply with norms because of states' voluntary socialization with norms in the absence of dominant states' coercion or material rewards.[26] Moreover, they also see the interconnection and interaction between states' strategic preferences and norms change, rather than a one-sided relationship between preference and norms, what they call 'strategic social construction'.[27] They stress that international norms created by certain states or individuals can become internalized by other states or become intersubjectively shared and come back to shape states' interests and actions.

The constructivist conception of mutual constitution between state agency and international social structure poses a major challenge to Waltzian neorealism's argument that international material structure imposes deterministic constraints on states and that there are universal laws of international politics.[28]

Unlike constructivism, moral realism does not see the relations between state agency and international social structure as mutually constitutive. Moral realism, like constructivism, stresses the importance of state agency in promoting international change. For moral realism, state agency consists of two dimensions. The first dimension is the exercise of material power, and the second is the efficient exercise of state political leadership. Moral realism only focuses on the effects of international power structure on states' interests and action, and pays no attention to the effects of international social structures on states' interests and actions.

This is because moral realism, unlike constructivism, stresses that international norms are primarily created by leading states due to leading states' preponderant capability and their ability to enforce international norms and order. When lesser states accept or comply with leading states' international norms, their compliance is mainly a result of the strategic calculation of interests rather than their internationalization of the norms. When leading states' power is in decline, lesser states are less willing to accept or comply with the norms.

Third, moral realism differs from constructivism in how international order is created and maintained. As constructivists believe, ideational factors are the driving force for international change and changes in the international material structure alone cannot be the driving force for international change without states assigning intersubjective meanings to it. As Finnemore and Sikkink suggest, 'In an ideational international structure, idea shifts and norm shifts are the main vehicles for system transformation. Norm shifts are to the ideational theorist what changes in the balance of power are to the realist'.[29]

Likewise, Wendt also suggests that intersubjectively shared norms and identities as practised by states are the main driving force for international systemic change. He proposes the concept of the culture of anarchy and argues that anarchy is a product of a historical contingent idea born out of international practices of states. By engaging in new practices, states can overcome mutual distrust and arrive at different cultures of anarchy with different degrees of cooperation. He postulates that there is a unidirectional historical progression of states' intersubjectively shared identities from the lower form of the culture of anarchy with intense conflicts to the higher form of the culture of anarchy with close cooperation. That is to say, the Hobbesian culture existed among states before the Treaty of Westphalia whereby states identified each other as mortal enemies and engaged each other in a constant struggle for power and survival while denying each other's rights to existence. The Lockean culture emerged after the Westphalian Treaty of 1648 when states identified each other as sovereign actors and restrained competitors while recognizing states' sovereign rights to existence. The Kantian culture emerged after the end of the Cold War with democratic states identifying each other as friendly partners and engaging in close cooperation with each other with no prospect of military conflicts among them.[30] Wendt further argues that this historical progression will not regress. As he writes,

> With each 'higher' international culture states acquire rights — to sovereignty in the Lockean case, freedom from violence and security assistance in the Kantian case — that they will be loathe to give up, whatever new institutions they may create in the future. This process may not survive exogenous shock, like invasion (the barbarian invasion of Rome), or a revolution in the domestic constitution of member states (the American and French revolutions). But with respect to its endogenous dynamic, the argument suggests that the history of international politics will be unidirectional.[31]

Moral realism does not agree with constructivism that ideational change is the primary source of international change. As Yan suggests, ideas and norms are primarily a result of the deliberate promotion of the leading states to serve their national self-interests through the exercise of their material power, rather than originating through norm entrepreneurs or states' intersubjective practices. In other words, international changes are driven primarily by leading states' material capability, with norms serving as a secondary role. As Yan writes, 'leading states selectively promote the norms in favor of their interests rather than being persuaded into accepting all good norms including those unfavorable to their interests'.[32]

Leading states create international norms and order to provide public goods such as security and economic prosperity because such norms and order benefit the leading states the most. When the cost of maintaining international norms and order outweighs their benefits, leading states will dismantle or revise these norms and order.[33] The recent US proposal to create the Trans-Pacific Partnership (TPP) and the Transatlantic Trade and Investment Partnership (TTIP) to replace the mal-functioning World Trade Organization (WTO) are cases in point. China's creation of the Asian Infrastructure Investment Bank (AIIB) is another case in point.

As Yan stresses, leading states' strategic credibility is an important consideration in their creation and maintenance of international order. Leading states lead by example through complying with international norms they themselves create so that the lesser states will follow the lead by complying with the international norms.[34] Thus, Yan is more in agreement with neoliberalist John Ikenberry and Charles Kupchan's quasi-realist view that leading states play an important role in promoting norms to the lesser states through their exercise of dominant power, that is, through a combination of normative persuasion, material inducement, or coercion.[35]

Yan disagrees with Alexander Wendt's single-minded focus on state identity and norms in accounting for international change without taking into consideration states' material interests and power. He also disagrees with Wendt that international norm types will evolve unidirectionally from the Hobbesian culture of power struggle among bitter enemies, through the Lockean culture of restrained competitors, to the Kantian culture of close cooperation among democratic states. Yan thinks the direction of norm changes is uncertain and unpredictable, depending on the strategic preference of the leading states.[36]

Moreover, as Yan suggests, the creation of a particular type of international norms and order is closely associated with the nature of international leadership. Drawing on his study of Xunzi's three international leaderships in his earlier book on Chinese thought and Chinese power, Yan suggests that there are four types of international leadership: humane authority, hegemony, tyranny, and anemocracy. These four different types of international leadership give rise to four types of international norm respectively: moral norms, double-standard norms, realpolitik norms, and coward-bullying norms.

Moral norms are nurtured and promoted universally to all states by an international humane authority which practises moral norms universally at home and abroad. Humane authority treats morality as the foundation of foreign and domestic policy. It also creates and promotes international moral norms for other states to follow. Its foreign policy conforms to international moral norms it itself creates. Yan suggests two examples of international humane authority, one that of the founding Zhou rulers in ancient China, the other the American international leadership under the Roosevelt administration. The Zhou rulers through superior moral power assembled a multi-state coalition to defeat the oppressive Shang ruler and created an international humane authority based on moral norms of Zhou rites (周礼). The Roosevelt administration in the US also established an international humane authority after the end of World War II through its preponderant material power and moral norms of liberalism.

Hegemonic leadership is founded on double-standard norms. On the one hand, the hegemonic state promotes moral norms among its allies. On the other hand, it practices realpolitik norms and coward-bullying norms towards its rivals and enemies. While tyrannical leadership always adopts foreign policy in accordance with the principle of realpolitik, anemocratic leadership maintains its international order, often through bullying weaker states.[37] Realpolitik norms and coward-bully norms are derived inherently from the nature of international anarchy as states are inherently self-regarding and are engaged in constant struggle for power among one another.[38]

Yan applies his theory to predict China's future role in international politics. As he suggests, China may not be a new hegemonic leader, because while it may catch up with the US in terms of its economic capability, it lacks a universal ideology to lay a normative basis for future Chinese hegemony that may attract many lesser states. Since neither the US nor China are powerful enough to create a new international authority alone, Yan suggests that the new norm in the world will likely be a combination of American ideology founded on liberalism and the Chinese ideology founded on Confucianism.

Fourth, moral realism and constructivism also differ in their assessment of the prospects of international peace. Constructivism is more sanguine about the prospect of future international peace. Some constructivists like Wendt have been inspired by Kant's ideal of perpetual peace and his loathing of war as an instrument to resolve international conflicts. Constructivists believe that norms and identity can constitute states' interests and action, and that the formation of collective identity may reduce the chance of international conflicts and enhance the likelihood of international peace. As Wendt postulates, a collective action problem that results from egoistic interests can be overcome if states form a collective identity which may generate collective interests among states. Wendt identifies two systemic processes of international interaction between states – deepening interdependence among states and the transnational convergence of domestic values such as democracy or human rights – that may help general collective identity and foster collective interests among states. Furthermore, strategic cooperation among states initially motivated by egoistic interests may encourage states to redefine who they are in relation to their partners as states repeat acts of cooperation. Gradually, the systemic process of international interaction and repeated acts of cooperation among states may lead to the emergence of a collective new identity and eventually the creation of international states such as NATO and the European Union. Furthermore, as discussed previously, Wendt also argues that the establishment of the culture of Kantian democratic states is also a recipe for international peace.[39]

While constructivists aspire to the moral ideal of perpetual peace, moral realism has no such aspiration. Like neorealism, Yan is pessimistic about the prospects of international peace. He seems to believe that international conflicts and even war may be inevitable as states compete for hegemony and international leadership. Influenced by classical realists like Morgenthau and neorealists like Gilpin, Yan seems to suggest that international violent conflicts are a fact of life in world politics. International conflicts are particularly acute between the rising state and the dominant state as the two states approach power parity and struggle to create competing international orders that will reflect their respective national interests, which tend to be a zero-sum game. In Yan's own words, 'structural contradiction between the rising state and the dominant state is inevitable because both pursue domination within a closed system'.[40] In fact, he seems to think that

China and the US currently are locked in such a zero-sum competition for international hegemony.

Unlike constructivists who emphasize the transformation of states' identities as a solution to world peace, moral realism's hope for international peace lies in the creation of international humane authority to ultimately pacify international conflicts. Moral realism's normative order seems to be inspired by Confucian morality. It seems to aspire to the creation of humane international authority in order to replace an immoral world whereby international hegemony, tyranny, or anemocracy rule and international violent conflicts abound. The international humane authority may pacify the world by promoting universal moral norms that can be socialized by other states, which will replace the norm of double standard created by hegemonic leadership, the norm of realpolitik created by tyrannical leadership, and the norm of coward-bullying by anemocratic leadership. But such an aspiration is bound to be difficult.

Moreover, moral realism seems to suggest that the responsible state leadership's use of force against irresponsible state leaderships can be morally justified and may be indispensable for the creation of international humane authority and its maintenance. This is because the leading states bear a special moral responsibility to maintain the stability of the international system. As Yan writes in regard to the responsibility of leading states to protect allies and international order,

> That the head of an alliance that has become involved in war is immoral or irresponsible is a misconception. Holding the opposite view in this regard, I would argue that indiscriminate refusal to use military force is a policy of national suicide, as well as an immoral principle, and antithetical to the behavior of a humane authority leadership. In the anarchical international system, small states seldom have enough military capability to protect their security and must rely on a powerful state for protection. A leading state's adoption of a policy of absolute nonuse of military force amounts to a denial of its duty to protect international order and justice.[41]

Yan's argument here echoes the Confucian theory of use of force and has little resemblance with constructivism. As we know from ancient Chinese history, the establishment of the international humane authority by the founding Zhou rulers was accomplished by a violent war known as the War of Muye (牧野之战). Moreover, the maintenance of international humane authority may also require coercive force. While Confucius touted the rule of virtue, he still believed that coercive force may be necessary for rulers to discipline some people's recalcitrant behaviours. Thus, Confucius openly endorsed the military force used by the famous minister Guan

Zhong to expel the barbarians' invasion of the Zhou empire and called him a benevolent man.[42]

While Yan's conception of morality of state political leadership stresses the ability of political leaders to formulate good policy reforms responsibly and win the support of the majority of people at home and the support of the majority of countries in the world, his conception of morality also stresses the special moral duty that political leaders owe to their people, that is, the arduous duty of providing national security to the people. In other words, Yan's interpretation of morality has some affinity to the morality as conceived by classical realists such as Hans Morgenthau. Like Yan, Morgenthau also thought political leaders should be judged by a different moral standard than one that is applied to the ordinary people. Political leaders are in charge of an arduous duty of protecting the lives of ordinary people and their nation, they should be judged by whether or not they succeed in discharging this arduous duty, rather than by the moral principles commonly applied to ordinary people. For Morgenthau, the moral exercise of political leadership is defined in terms of the pursuit of national interests and national capability. Those leaders who act in contrast to national interest will not be considered as a morally good or responsible leader.

The limitations of moral realism

Like any other good studies, Yan's work is not free of weaknesses despite its intellectual vigour and ingenuous innovation. Several weaknesses are identified here.

First, and perhaps the most difficult and controversial question, is Yan's argument that the efficient exercise of state political leadership may result in the adoption of good reforms at home and proactive foreign policy to attract international support, which may enhance leading states' international capability and ultimately cause major international change.[43] As Yan has suggested, a responsible political leadership can be defined by pursuing good reforms and efficient and faithful execution of these reforms.[44] But his definition of political leadership begs the further question of what constitutes good reforms as opposed to bad reforms. As Yan seems to stress, the most morally responsible leaders are those who can adopt the most rational domestic and foreign policies to promote national interests after carefully weighing up costs and benefits of alternative foreign policies, and then exert their moral responsibility to the upmost with passion in order to efficiently and faithfully execute political leadership. In this regard, Yan links the exercise of political leadership with different kinds of foreign policies with the introduction of four categories of foreign policy: inactive, conservative, proactive, and aggressive. Inactive leadership believes the best strategy is to maintain status quo and take no action at all domestically and internationally.

Conservative leadership views economic development as the foundation of comprehensive capability and as the best strategy to maintain status quo, while refraining from being assertive internationally. A proactive leadership is one in which political leaders responsibly execute their political leadership with good reform policy domestically and with a proactive foreign policy of enlarging international support. Aggressive leadership believes in social Darwinism and tends to adopt aggressive foreign policy bent on military expansion. For Yan, the adoption of a proactive foreign policy by the rising states' political leadership is a recipe for their successful challenging the dominant state and effecting international change.[45]

Thus, Yan's conception of responsible and efficient political leadership seems to combine the Waltzian assumption that states are unitary and rational actors, and always weigh up carefully the cost and benefits of pursuing good reforms and rational foreign policy, with the neo-Confucian emphasis on the power of human will and moral passion to overcome adverse material conditions.

Nonetheless, the reasons for the rise and fall of leading states are very complicated and may be multiple. The moral quality of political leadership certainly may be an important factor, but it cannot be the only factor determining the rise and fall of nations. The causes for the rise and fall of states may include many factors such as culture, geography, demography, economy, market size, or technology. For example, while realist Robert Gilpin believes the uneven economic growth among states leads to change in the international system, he thinks the ultimate cause for the rise and fall of states is technological innovation. Historian Kenneth Pomeranz thinks demographic change is an important factor that has caused the great economic divergence between the West and the East after the 18th century.[46] Some causes for the changes may be a result of human agency or human will. For example, German sociologist Max Weber believed the ascendancy of modern capitalism in the West was a result of the rise of Protestantism, which provided the ethical basis for the rationalization of all economic activities.[47] Economist Douglass North thinks the man-made rules of protecting private property and their institutionalization are the causes that led to the rise of the Western world.[48]

Even if we grant the importance of human agency, there are also limits to human rationality. Contrary to the Waltzian understanding of rationality, men's rationality is bounded, as suggested by economist Herbert Simon. National leaders invariably face a lot of uncertainty when they are making policy decisions. No national leaders are prescient about the correct direction of domestic reforms and foreign policy that may bring their nations to the correct path of international ascendancy. No national leaders can exert their moral responsibility with utter passion without taking into consideration informational uncertainty; many national leaders are just muddling through with their bounded rationality in policy making.⁴⁹ Paul Kennedy has provided a classical study of the rise and fall of the great powers that contradicts the logic of rationality and the power of human will. As he suggests, national leaders have often fallen into the trap of imperial overstretch. As nations mobilized resources to expand international influence, national leaders tended to face a difficult dilemma and became the victims of their own success: to further expand their nations' international power would mean to drain their national resources and undermine their nations' international power, but to curtail their international expansion would also undermine their nations' international power.⁵⁰

Secondly, one related issue is the correct assessment of comprehensive national capability. With Yan stressing the importance of state political leadership, one wonders whether or not he may have overestimated the power of China and underestimated the capability of the US. Yan's conception of political leadership in terms of formulating good reform policies and efficiently promoting national interests overseas is very much related to how we estimate the extent of the rise of China and the relative decline of the US, and its implications for the future of Sino–US relations. Yan has suggested that it is quite likely that China will continue to rise economically and politically and that future international systems may evolve into bipolarity. But some critics disagreed. As Amitav Acharya suggests, Yan has dismissed the significant role that the middle powers like India, Japan, and Brazil may play in world politics. Acharya argues that the world may move towards multipolarity in the future.⁵¹ Others suggest that Yan is too optimistic about the inevitable rise of China and underestimates the power and resilience of the US. These critics have suggested that future world politics may not be bipolar because the power disparity between the US and China is still very wide-ranging as the size of the US economy is much larger than that of China and its technological capability is still far more advanced than that of China, let alone the overwhelming number of nuclear warheads that the US possesses.⁵²

Last but not least is the issue of the conception of hegemony, which is related to the evaluation of American hegemony in the post-war period. Yan's conception of hegemony is based on the great ancient Confucian scholar Xunzi's conception of it (霸权), which had a clearly negative connotation of hegemony. Xunzi's hegemon did not pay any attention to moral norms, but only stressed the importance of its strategic credibility. Yet the mainstream Western understanding of hegemony has been heavily influenced by Charles Kindleberger's conception of it which emphasizes the importance of a benevolent hegemon in providing international public good.⁵³ The different conceptions of hegemony have led to very different understandings of the nature of American hegemony. Yan's conception of hegemony leads to his negative portrait of American hegemony as relying on promoting the norm of double standard to maintain international order. This is in sharp contrast to the understanding of the mainstream Western IR literature that the US has played a benevolent hegemonic leadership role in the Western world during the Cold War and beyond by providing international public goods such as international security and economic prosperity through the construction of post-war international order that was founded on international institutions such as the United Nations (UN), the General Agreement on Tariff and Trade (GATT) and the WTO, and the World Bank. Moreover, notwithstanding creating certain double-standard norms, the US may have played an important role in promoting some universally acceptable moral norms in the post-war international order such as that of collective security in the UN, protecting human rights evident in the UN Charter and the UN Declaration on Human Rights, trade reciprocity and the principle of Most-Favoured Nations in the GATT/WTO, and the principle of mutual assistance in the World Bank.[54] Obviously, these two different conceptions of hegemony have stemmed from two very different cultures. Perhaps there may need to be deeper scholarly dialogue and reconciliation between these two different conceptions of hegemony in order to avoid misunderstanding.

In short, Yan has provided a Chinese perspective of IR theory that has posed some very important questions regarding the sources of international capability and international systemic change, and in particular the relevance of moralism in the study of contemporary IR. While he has not answered all the questions he has raised, his study may likely challenge mainstream Western IR theories as to how we approach and investigate the sources of international capability and in particular the moral quality of state political leadership in bringing about international change. It has also pointed us in a new direction as to how to reconcile ancient Chinese interstate relations theories with contemporary Western IR theory informed by realism and constructivism.

Summary

This chapter examined the basic assumptions and arguments of Yan Xuetong's moral realism, analysed its prospects and promises by comparing it with two mainstream Western IR theories, neorealism and constructivism, and also critically evaluated the limitations of moral realism. The first part of the chapter provided an overview of mainstream IR theories and the potential contributions of moral realism. In particular, Yan's study on moral realism has three potential contributions. First, it holds the promise of integrating the study of the impact of domestic politics on foreign policy with moral realism. Second, Yan's moral realism will definitely deepen the epistemic dialogue between Chinese IR scholars and mainstream Western IR scholars.

Third, his study has important practical value in that it will likely deepen the civilizational dialogue between China and the US in a time of growing tension between the two countries.

The second part of the chapter placed moral realism in the context of cross-cultural academic dialogue between moral realism and mainstream Western IR theories with a detailed comparison between moral realism on the one hand and neorealism and constructivism on the other. The third part critically evaluated moral realism and identified its limitations.

Notes

1. Yan Xuetong, *Leadership and the Rise of Great Powers*, Princeton: Princeton University Press, 2018, pp 1–206.
2. Robert Gilpin, *War and Change in International Politics*, New York: Cambridge University Press, 1981, pp 28–31.
3. Robert Keohane, *After Hegemony: Cooperation and Discord in World Politics*, Princeton: Princeton University Press, 1984.
4. Alexander Wendt, 'Anarchy Is What States Make of It: The Social Construction of Power Politics', *International Organization* 46, no. 2 (1992): 394–403; Ronald L. Jepperson, Alexander Wendt, and Peter J. Katzenstein, 'Norms, Identity, and Culture in National Security', in Mary F. Katzenstein (ed), *The Culture of National Security*, New York: Columbia University Press, 1996, pp 33–75.
5. Yan Xuetong, *Leadership and the Rise of Great Powers*, pp 13, 56.
6. Ibid., p 8.
7. Ibid., p 29.
8. Ibid., p 56.
9. Ibid., p 56.
10. Ibid., p 57.
11. Ibid., p 78.
12. Aaron L. Friedberg, *The Weary Titan: Britain and the Experience of Relative Decline, 1895–1905*, Princeton: Princeton University Press, 1988.
13. Fareed Zakaria, *From Wealth to Power: The Unusual Origins of America's World Role*, Princeton: Princeton University Press, 1998.
14. Susan Shirk, 'Playing to the Provinces: Deng Xiaoping's Political Strategy of Economic Reforms', *Studies in Comparative Communism* 23, no. 15 (1990): 2227–258.
15. Amitav Acharya, 'Global International Relations (IR) and Regional Worlds: A New Agenda for International Studies', *International Studies Quarterly* 58, no. 4 (2014): 647–59. Alastair Iain Johnston seems to disagree that mainstream Western IR theories are culturally biased and is more sceptical about the extent to which East Asian history-based IR studies can contribute to resolving theoretical controversies, lead to theoretical breakthrough, or drive the field forward. See Alastair Iain Johnston, 'What (if Anything) Does East Asia Tell Us about International Relations Theory', *Annual Review of Political Science* 15 (2012): 53–78.
16. Mario Telò, 'Moral Realism: Innovation and Dialogue in International Relations Theory', unpublished paper.
17. Yan Xuetong, *Leadership and the Rise of Great Powers*, pp 67–77.
18. Ibid.
19. Ronald L. Jepperson, Alexander Wendt, and Peter J. Katzenstein, 'Norms, Identity, and Culture in National Security', in Mary F. Katzenstein (ed), *The Culture of National Security*, pp 33–75.

20. Alexander Wendt, 'Anarchy is What States Make of It': 397.
21. Thomas Risse-Kappen, *Cooperation among Democracies: European Influence on US Foreign Policy*, Princeton: Princeton University Press, 1995.
22. Yan Xuetong, *Leadership and the Rise of Great Powers*, p 68.
23. Ibid., p 68.
24. Ibid., p 74.
25. Alexander Wendt, 'The Agent–Structure Problem in International Relations Theory', *International Organization* 41, no. 3 (1987): 335–70.
26. Yan Xuetong, *Leadership and the Rise of Great Powers*, pp 105–106; Martha Finnemore and Kathryn Sikkink, 'International Norm Dynamics and Political Change', *International Organization* 52, no. 4 (1998): 901–2.
27. Martha Finnemore and Kathryn Sikkink, 'International Norm Dynamics and Political Change': 888, 894.
28. Jeffrey T. Checkel, 'The Constructivist Turn in International Relations Theory', *World Politics* 50, no. 2 (1998): 325–7; Dale C. Copeland, 'The Constructivist Challenge to Structural Realism: A Review Essay', *International Security* 25, no. 2 (2000): 189–91.
29. Martha Finnemore and Kathryn Sikkink, 'International Norm Dynamics and Political Change': 888, 894.
30. Alexander Wendt, *Social Theory of International Politics*, New York: Cambridge University Press, 1999, pp 266, 297, 323.
31. Ibid., p 3127.
32. Yan Xuetong, *Leadership and the Rise of Great Powers*, p 105.
33. Ibid., p 69.
34. Ibid., pp 70–7.
35. Ibid., pp 106–7; G. John Ikenberry and Charles A. Kupchan, 'Socialization and Hegemonic Power', *International Organization* 44, no. 3 (1990): 290.
36. Yan Xuetong, *Leadership and the Rise of Great Powers*, pp 120–1.
37. Ibid., pp 43–5.
38. Ibid., p 109.
39. Alexander Wendt, 'Collective Identity Formation and the International State', *American Political Science Review* 88, no. 2 (1994): 388–92.
40. Yan Xuetong, *Leadership and the Rise of Great Powers*, p 72.
41. Ibid., p 66.
42. D.C. Lau, *Analects*, New York: Penguin Classics, 1979, Book XIV, Verse 16, p 126.
43. Yan Xuetong, *Leadership and the Rise of Great Powers*, pp 13, 56.
44. Ibid., p 56.
45. Ibid., pp 29–36.
46. Kenneth Pomeranz, *The Great Divergence: China, Europe and the Making of the Modern World Economy*, Princeton: Princeton University Press, 2000.
47. Max Weber, *The Protestant Ethic and the Spirit of Capitalism*, New York: Oxford University Press, 1905.
48. Douglass C. North and Robert P. Thomas, *The Rise of the Western World: A New Economic History*, New York: Cambridge University Press, 1973.
49. Rajesh Rajagopalan criticizes Yan's definition of political leadership as tautological because Yan defines it in terms of foreign policies of leading states and then uses foreign policies to explain foreign policies of leading states. But Rajagopalan seems to misunderstand Yan's argument that the quality of political leadership is the cause for the rise and fall of leading states. See Rajagopalan, 'Book Reviews', *India Quarterly* 75, no. 3 (2019): 407.
50. Paul Kennedy, *The Rise and Fall of the Great Powers: Economic Change and Military Conflict from 1500 to 2000*, London: Vintage, 1989.

51. Amitav Acharya, 'Global International Relations (IR) and Regional Worlds: A New Agenda for International Studies': 648.
52. Mario Telò, 'Moral Realism: Innovation and Dialogue in International Relations Theory'.
53. Charles Kindleberger, *The World in Depression, 1929–1939*, New Haven: Yale University Press, 1973.
54. Mario Telò, 'Moral Realism: Innovation and Dialogue in International Relations Theory'.

5

Ideal Morality and Realist Interest of Moral Realism

Kai He

Yan Xuetong's *Leadership and the Rise of Great Powers* is a path-breaking project, which integrates ancient Chinese philosophy, historical and contemporary cases, and modern international relations (IR) theory.[1] Yan proposes 'moral realism' – a new realist theory – to explain the rise of great powers as well as the transformation of international order. He argues that 'political leadership serves as the core independent variable' in explaining why only a 'few rising states have been able to replace the dominant state'.[2] In addition, he suggests that political leadership can also account for the changing international power configurations, norms, orders, and systems.

His argument is parsimonious and elegant, fitting the golden standard of the political science discipline because his 'moral realism' theory has only one key variable – political leadership – which explains the power dynamics, the transformation of international order, as well as the rise and fall of international norms. It is really ambitious and provocative because political scientists normally draw a clear explanatory boundary around their theories in order to avoid academic criticisms. For example, Kenneth Waltz, the founding father of neorealism, famously stated that neorealism is a theory of IR, not a theory of foreign policy because it cannot explain 'why state X made a certain move last Tuesday'.[3] On the contrary, Yan claims that the explanatory power of 'moral realism' can cross three different levels of analysis: individual, state, and system.

Moreover, moral realism has already bridged materialism and ideationalism in that morality and norms – two ideational variables in constructivism – are well integrated with material power in Yan's definition of 'political leadership'. It is obvious that Yan's 'moral realism' has posed some tough challenges to the major canons of contemporary IR theory. Although scholars might not necessarily agree with Yan's arguments, they will be inspired by many insights from the book, which will in turn encourage them to seek new light through both theoretical innovation and empirical investigation in IR.

In this review chapter, I first highlight some major contributions of Yan's book to both IR theory building and the study of China's rise. Namely, it takes leadership in IR seriously, breaks the boundary between materialism and ideationalism, and crafts bold but nuanced predictions on the US–China competition in the future. In the second section, I discuss three areas that Yan's moral realism might need to further clarify: the conceptualizations of morality and political leadership, the interactions and mechanisms between state leadership and international leadership, and the holistic view of norms and leadership. These three issue areas can be seen as an opportunity for other scholars to further explore in order to advance moral realism as a new IR theory in the future.

In the third section, challenging traditional power-based transition and Yan's morality/norm-oriented order transition, I propose an institution-based order transition in which I argue that multilateral institutions play an important and constitutive role in shaping the international order transition. It will be beneficial for moral realist scholars to take multilateral institutions into consideration for future research. In conclusion, I argue that although Yan's moral realism might have some weaknesses in theory and practice, it reflects a genuine ideal pursuit of a leading realist for a better and more peaceful world. The more influential the moral realism theory is, the more peaceful the world will be.

Three contributions as theory, practice, and prediction

As one of the most influential IR scholars in China, Yan's books and arguments have fascinated Western IR scholars. For example, the idea of 'moral realism' proposed by this book has been seen as a major theoretical backbone of Chinese foreign policy transformation under Xi Jinping.[4] Other commentators argue that Yan's book reflects how Chinese scholars view IR, which might influence China's foreign policymakers in the long run.[5] Besides the significant policy relevance, Yan's book has made three theoretical and empirical contributions to the study of China's foreign policy in particular and international relations in general.

Taking leadership seriously

Yan's moral realism highlights the role of leadership in shaping the rise and fall of great powers in the international system. It argues that 'when the rising state's leadership is more capable and efficient than that of the dominant state and that of other contemporary major states, international influence is redistributed in a way that allows the rising state to eclipse the dominant state'.[6] The importance of leadership is not new for scholars in the field of foreign policy analysis, which focuses on the role of agency in the decision-making process. However, Yan's moral realism is not confined to the study of foreign policy. Instead, he argues that political leadership can not only explain a state's power trajectory, but also shed light on the transformation of international order. According to Yan, 'when a rising state's political leadership surpasses that of the dominant state, the power disparity between the two states reverses, rendering the rising state the new dominant state'.[7] In other words, Yan's moral realism is not only a foreign policy analysis (FPA) theory, but also an IR theory, which can explain the interactions and dynamics among great powers in the international system.

It is worth noting that classical realists, like E.H. Carr and Hans Morgenthau, also highlight the role of leadership in driving states' policy behaviours. For example, Morgenthau strongly opposed the Munich accords because the Nazis were different and dangerous.[8] Classical realists seem to emphasize history, ideology, and domestic politics in analysing the nature of political leadership. In contrast, Yan's moral realism highlights the political capability of leadership, not only the nature of leadership.

Why is political leadership so important? Yan traces the root of political leadership to a state's capabilities. He argues that a state's comprehensive capability includes both material resources and non-material elements. While the material resources consist of military, economic, and cultural capabilities, the non-material force refers to a state's political capability, the core of which is a state's political leadership. He further suggests, 'Political capability exerts a multiplicative effect on the sum of the other three elements. Should political capability decrease to zero, then the effect of the other three is reduced to nothing'.[9] As the core component of political capability, leadership plays an operational and dynamic role in shaping a state's decision-making process.

Yan proposes two typologies to further define political leadership. Domestically, a country's 'state leadership' can be categorized as inactive, conservative, proactive, and aggressive. Inspired by the Chinese Pre-Qin philosophies, especially that of Xunzi, Yan typologizes a state's 'international leadership' as humane authority, hegemony, anemocracy, and tyranny. More importantly, he argues that different types of political leadership will lead to different strategic behaviours. For example, inactive leadership is more likely to choose to avoid conflicts, while a conservative leadership might prefer imposing economic impacts. Proactive leadership is more likely to enlarge international support, but aggressive leadership is inclined to choose military expansion.[10]

Similarly, the four types of international leadership will lead to different foreign policy behaviours. For example, a humane authority will follow international norms and moral standards as well as behave in a strategically trustworthy way. A hegemony will maintain strategic credibility towards its allies but adopt 'the law of the jungle as the principle for dealing with non-allies'.[11] Anemocratic leadership is irresponsible and adopts foreign policies based on its perceived interests with others. And last, a tyrannical leadership always adopts foreign policies that are 'consistent with the principle of realpolitik, thus neither ally nor rival is willing to trust it'.[12]

It is worth noting that Yan makes it clear that all these categorizations of state leadership and international leadership are ideal types. In real life, most states or international leaderships are hybrids in nature. For example, in the ongoing Russian–Ukrainian war, President Putin and President Zelenskyy have shown different styles and capabilities in political leadership. However, it is quite difficult to place these two leaders in one category of leadership. More research is needed to unpack the political leaderships of both leaders because it will help us to understand the origins, processes, outcomes, and implications of this ongoing war. Yan suggests that 'in the era of globalization, the principle of humane authority maintains certain advantages with respect to becoming the doctrine of international leadership'.[13] Domestically, proactive state leadership is preferable because it encourages appropriate reforms domestically and alliances internationally. Recalling the key question of why rising powers can rise up in the international system, Yan's answer lies in two types of political leadership: proactive state leadership and humane authority international leadership.

Breaking the boundary between materialism and ideationalism

Yan's moral realism is an exemplary work integrating materialism and ideationalism in the study of IR. In IR, realism is seen as a school of thought rooted in materialism because it emphasizes the role of material interests in shaping state behaviour and international politics in general. Both liberalism and constructivism, on the other hand, highlight the role of ideas in world politics, although they differ in how ideas influence or change the world. Yan's moral realism creatively integrates both material interests and ideational morality into one research framework in explaining state behaviour as well as the change of international system.

Moral realism is a realist and materialist theory in essence because it argues that states pursue national interests in terms of power and capability in the anarchic international system. However, it also suggests that the best way for a state to pursue its materialist interests is to follow the moral codes and norms in the international system. Unlike most realists, Yan believes that there are certain moral codes and international norms in the ideational system which states should follow. The motive for states to follow these moral codes is not rooted in altruism, but instrumental in nature. In other words, it is in a state's best interest to follow these moral codes because this kind of 'humane authority' leadership can help states to gather strategic credibility as well as international support.

It should be noted that Yan is not the first scholar who has integrated materialism and ideationalism in the study of IR. For example, some scholars in the study of strategic culture also highlight the importance of both culture and power in shaping a state's strategic behaviour.[14] In addition, many neoclassical realist scholars also suggest that a state's foreign policy behaviour is influenced by both system-level power configurations and various domestic transmission belts. The domestic transmission belts include some ideational variables, such as threat perceptions, leaders' images, and strategic cultures.[15]

However, Yan's theoretical innovation lies in his treatment of morality, especially the instrumental view of morality and norm building in general. He argues that 'the role of morality is to influence policy makers' concerns about how national interests should be achieved rather than what national interests ought to be'.[16] In other words, Yan is still holding a realist view in defining a state's national interests. However, he suggests that political leaders should pay attention to moral codes in pursuing these materialist interests because 'morality is a contributing factor to its leadership's strategic preferences'.[17] Here, Yan's treatment of universal morality is different from classical realists, like George Kennan and Morgenthau, who argue that traditional or universal morality cannot be used to explain and inform state behaviours.[18] The reason is simply that the so-called morality in the eyes of classical realists often serves some particular interests of states. Differing from classical realists, Yan's moral realism highlights the utility of morality in constructing political leadership. To a certain extent, his moral realism is more 'realist' than classical realism because it is more instrumental in dealing with morality.

It is clear that Yan's moral realism will be at odds with many realists as well as liberals and constructivists. For hardcore realists, the so-called morality or moral code is just a reflection of national interests as well as the result of power struggle. Liberals and constructivists might share a similar view on the importance of morality; however, they will not be comfortable with Yan's instrumental view of morality. Instead, they believe that morality or moral codes in the international system can play an independent role in shaping a state's national interests as well as its strategic preferences. In other words, morality or moral codes are independent variables in the eyes of ideationalists, such as liberals and constructivists, but they only serve as an intervening or dependent variable in Yan's moral realism. To a certain extent, Yan's moral realism has posed a serious theoretical challenge to all three major IR paradigms: realism, liberalism, and constructivism. It is expected that moral realism will contribute a new wave of theoretical debates among IR scholars over the role of morality in world politics.

Crafting bold but nuanced predictions

Last but not least, Yan's moral realism is exceptionally policy-relevant with high predictive value. It is an open secret that political scientists are not good at forecasting.[19] It is why some scholars explicitly state that their theories aim to explain what has happened in world politics, not to predict what will happen in the future.[20] It is understandable because too many unpredictable variables might influence a state's foreign policy decisions as well as the dynamics of international politics. It is a safe bet to confine a new theory to the domain of explanation instead of going for prediction.

It is clear that Yan is a risk taker and a true scientific believer in the study of international relations when he states that 'all scientific theories have the function of prediction'.[21] In the conclusion chapter, he is not just satisfied with the explanatory power of his moral realism in explaining what has happened. Instead, he makes some bold but nuanced predictions on what will happen in the future international order transition against the background of US–China competition. Prediction is risky business because it is easier to be judged as right or wrong. As mentioned before, too many unmeasurable and unpredictable variables might change the course of world politics. However, Yan confidently believes that his theory of moral realism can pass this 'prediction' test.

Yan has forecasted three major changes in international politics in the next decade (2019–2028). First, the world will experience 'bipolarization without a global leadership'.[22] China's rise will change the US-dominant unipolar world to a bipolar one, in which the US and China will be the two poles in the system. Other states will have to choose between the US and China based on their respective interests. Neither the United States nor China will be able to provide global leadership. Second, we will witness an unstable international order but not the Cold War.[23] Yan argues that nuclear weapons will effectively prevent direct war between the US and China. However, this nuclear deterrence will not guarantee peace among regional powers. The ongoing war between Russia and Ukraine seems to vindicate Yan's prediction of the instability of international order in the next decade or two.

Last, Yan suggests that there will be no new mainstream value in the international system in the next ten years. Although liberalism according to Yan is in decline, 'there is no ideology able to replace liberalism through establishing a set of new mainstream values to guide international community in the coming decade'.[24] Therefore, Yan predicts that we will witness a competition of various ideologies for regional dominance or influence although he believes that the leadership of humane authority advocated by his moral realism will offer a better solution for a more peaceful world in the future.

The book was published in 2019 and the time frame of Yan's prediction should be 2018–2028. At the time of this writing in 2021, we can preliminarily assess the predictive value of Yan's moral realism. First, the world is indeed moving in a bipolar direction in which the US and China are the two superpowers while others are not in the same league. The COVID-19 pandemic has further accelerated the power transition due to the different handlings of the pandemic between the US and China. Although the US might retain its military advantage for some time, China will eventually catch up if it can sustain its economic growth and technological advancement. Moreover, the pandemic has also revealed the lack of global leadership in the international system because neither the US nor China could take up the global leadership to fight against the pandemic. Although the Biden administration intends to resume the US leadership in the world, the reputational and credibility damages caused by Trump will not easily be repaired. China has indeed tried to pursue international leadership. However, as moral realism suggests, the different domestic value system is the major hurdle for China to be accepted by other countries in the world. Therefore, the world, as Yan wisely predicted, is moving towards bipolarization without leadership.

As for the prediction of the possibility of a new Cold War, we might need more time to provide a full evaluation. The US is indeed augmenting its new 'Cold War' efforts against China. Since Pompeo's China speech at the Nixon Library, the US has waged its own new 'Cold War' on China by targeting the Chinese communist ideology. Although the Biden administration appears to tone down the ideological narrative against China, it proposed a 'grand alliance' with other democracies to counter China.[25] It is clear that the US intends to form an anti-China ideological alliance similar to the one against communism and the Soviet Union during the Cold War. However, the US will not be able to wage a Cold War by itself. If no other states, especially its European and Asian allies, follow suit, an anti-China 'grand alliance' will not emerge and the new Cold War will be an illusion for the US. Therefore, the key issue here is how China responds to the US ideological challenges as well as alliance pressures. If China closes up its ideological openness by embracing anti-US value systems, the new Cold War will become inevitable because US allies will have no choice but to join the US camp. However, if China successfully evades the US ideological trap and continues to promote political tolerance and economic openness, other countries, including American allies and partners, will hesitate to join the anti-China 'grant alliance'. The economic attraction of the Chinese market might be irresistible for those states recovering from the pandemic.

Yan's third prediction is about the lack of a mainstream value in the international system in the next ten years. One interesting point from moral realism is that liberalism will decline but no other value can replace it. In the past three years, we have witnessed indeed a crisis of liberalism. However, it might be too early to suggest that liberalism is in decline. The 2008 global financial crisis, Brexit, the rise of populism in the world, the COVID-19 pandemic, as well as the ongoing Ukraine war have all posed serious challenges to liberalism as a mainstream value and to democracy as a political system built on liberalism. However, it is not the first time for liberalism and democracy to face setbacks and difficulties. Even during the Cold War, the civil rights movement in the 1960s and the oil crisis in the 1970s posed similar challenges to the stability of democracy and the value system of liberalism. However, no value system is static in nature. It is possible for liberalism to evolve and for democracy to rebuild after the current crises. Therefore, it might be too early to predict the decline/demise of liberalism as a mainstream value. However, moral realism's argument on the ideology-rooted and value-based competition is valid because we have witnessed some value clashes between the US and China as well as among other states in the world. Nevertheless, whether the current ideological competition will lead to one dominant value system in the future is not clear. Ten years might be too short to assess ideational trends in the world in history. Moreover, a true diversity will mean that different values and ideologies can coexist in the international system although ideological competitions among states are inevitable.

As readers, we should applaud Yan's scientific bravery in making these bold but nuanced predictions for the next ten years. A decade is not a long period of time in IR. However, the next decade will be the most dynamic era of international order transition between the US and China in world politics. Will China's rise really lead to bipolarity in the international system? Will liberalism really decline? Most importantly, are we going to experience a new Cold War in the future? It seems that Yan is holding a cautiously optimistic view on the future order transition. Readers can definitely revisit Yan's book after ten years to see how his moral realism performs in predicting world politics. No matter the outcome of the test, we should appreciate Yan's scientific courage in making predictions, which are eschewed by most IR scholars.

Moral realism in scrutiny

Despite the theoretical and empirical contributions, there are three analytical issues in moral realism that Yan and other researchers need to further clarify in order to improve the academic rigour and policy relevance of this new theory in the field of IR. These three issues are the conceptualization of morality and political leadership, the interactive logic between state leadership and international leadership, as well as the relationship between norms and leadership.

Conceptualizing morality and political leadership

Two key concepts of moral realism are morality and political leadership. However, both need to be further scrutinized. First, moral realists need to clarify where the morality lies. Yan points out that there are three levels of morality: personal, governmental, and international. In addition, he argues that 'since moral realism is a theory that specifically addresses international relations, discussions in this book of "morality" refer solely to governmental morality, whereby leaders' actions will be judged according to the accepted codes of conduct pertaining to national interests and national capability'.[26] It is clear that the morality of moral realism lies at the governmental level with respect to a state's self-defined national interests.

However, Yan later claims that 'governmental morality addresses such concepts as the responsibility to protect national interests, the duty to practice international norms, and strategic credibility with regard to allies. The government's responsibility to the country it represents and the people it governs is the core of governmental morality. ... Governmental morality thus refers to those universal moral codes'.[27] Here, Yan seems to be contradicting his previous definition of governmental morality. It is understandable that governmental morality refers to the responsibility to protect national interests, but it is not clear why governmental morality also means the duty to practise international norms, and strategic credibility with regard to allies. It seems to ask too much of this one concept. In other words, this governmental morality seems to conflate both state and international levels of morality.

Second, moral realists need to further explain the relationship among three types of morality, which has been at the centre of philosophical and theoretical debate for centuries.[28] For example, in *The Prince*, Machiavelli tried to draw a distinction between the ethics of state behaviour (the behaviour of 'princes') and the ethics of individual behaviour. As Arnold Wolfers pointed out, 'down through the centuries Machiavelli and Machiavellianism have stood for a doctrine that places princes and sovereign states under the rule not of ordinary morality but of the "reason of state," considered an amoral principle peculiar to the realm of politics'.[29] Even Georg Hegel, a non-realist philosopher, held that the state has moral standards different from and superior to those of individuals.[30] Hans Morgenthau, a founding father of contemporary realism, clearly pointed out that '[R]ealism maintains that universal moral principles cannot be applied to the actions of states in their abstract, universal formulation, but that they must be filtered through the concrete circumstances of time and place'.[31]

Yan's moral realism seems to assume that there are some universal moral codes in the international system, which can potentially guide states' policy behaviours. It is true that the utopian and cosmopolitan understandings of morality are different from what realists think. While realists define morality or ethics as a function of politics, the utopians and cosmopolitans believe that 'universal moral standards provide a basis for evaluating state behaviour'.[32] However, this utopian and cosmopolitan view of morality still fails to specify how universal morality can be defined or measured in real politics. States are self-regarding and autonomous under anarchy in the international system. They are only responsible for the security and interests of their own citizens. Therefore, a moral action for one state or for the citizens in one state may or may not be a moral one for another state or the citizens of that state. As Carr clearly stated, 'these supposedly absolute and universal principles were no principles at all, but the unconscious reflexions of national policy based on a particular interpretation of national interest at a particular time'.[33]

It is a mistake to believe that realists do not care about morality or ethics in world politics. Instead, realists such as Carr and Morgenthau distinguish individual morality from the morality of states and refuse to define politics in terms of universal morality. Realists believe that there is a fundamental dilemma of international morality. As Carr suggested,

> On the one hand, we find the almost universal recognition of an international morality involving a sense of obligation to an international community or to humanity as a whole. On the other hand, we find an almost equally universal reluctance to admit that, in this international community, the good of the part (i.e., our own country) can be less important than the good of the whole.[34]

In other words, just because it is difficult to achieve a harmony of interests among states, international morality is hard to apply to states. Realists are not guilty of 'moral neutrality' as Richard Ashley criticizes.[35] Instead, realists understand that the morality of states is different from individual morality as well as universal morality. It is defined by power and interests of individual states. If there is any responsibility associated with governmental morality, it should refer to a state's own citizens instead of the international norms or universal morality.

Another key concept that needs to be further defined is political leadership. As mentioned before, political leadership is the key variable of moral realism in explaining the rise and fall of great powers. It is innovative for Yan to typologize political leadership in both domestic and international domains. However, two unaddressed problems might need further research. First, the unit of analysis of political leadership needs to be further clarified. On the one hand, Yan clearly states that 'decision making [is regarded] as a collective action rather than the result of a single leader's individual decision; therefore, political leadership in this book refers to the leading group of policy makers rather than a single supreme leader'.[36] On the other hand, he later suggests 'since the leading body's policies are usually in alignment with those of the supreme leader, the supreme leader can be used as a proxy when conducting qualitative analyses'.[37] It is not clear whether political leadership in moral realism refers to an individual leader or to a collective leadership group.

It is important to clarify the unit of analysis of political leadership. Because if political leadership means individual leaders, then a 'sage king' seems to be a necessary condition for a rising power to succeed according to moral realism. However, if political leadership does not refer to individual leaders, then we need to ask what other factors might contribute to a good political leadership. Here, we can conduct more research on political institutions, political culture, and even social factors that may constitute a strong 'political leadership'. Yan claims that his moral realism theory is rooted in political determinism in philosophy. However, if the unit of analysis of political leadership is not further clarified, it is easy to misperceive moral realism as an individual deterministic view, which advocates for the emergence of a 'sage king' in world politics.

This ambiguity over unit of analysis is related to the second conceptual concern: the under-specified source of political leadership. In order to typologize different domestic leadership, Yan introduces two interacting factors: (1) a leading body's attitude towards its state's international status quo, and (2) a leading body's responsibility towards the possible result of its policies.[38] Similarly, Yan uses two variables to typologize a state's international leadership: (1) strategic credibility, and (2) a consistent principle of actions.

While these different typologies are intriguing, two unanswered questions remain. On the one hand, people might question the theoretical and empirical underpinnings of these two typologies. For example, why should we use a state's attitude towards 'international status quo' to define the state leadership? Should a state's domestic leadership refer more to how a state treats its own people domestically? For international leadership, it is not clear how strategic credibility is linked to universal morality. On the other hand, people might also be curious about what factors can contribute to these different types of leadership, domestically and internationally. In other words, even though we know 'proactive leadership' and 'humane authority' are preferred leadership types, how a state could embrace such political leaderships is not clear.

Related to the previous unit of analysis question, if Yan's moral realism indeed applies to collective leadership instead of individual leadership, then an interesting and more important question for future researchers in the school of moral realism is to specify what kind of political environment or institution is more conducive to nurturing such a 'proactive' leadership domestically with a 'humane authority' in the international domain. Although as Yan suggests these leadership types are ideal in nature, some empirical research on the tendency towards these ideal types will provide invaluable information for the improvement of state governance as well as the peaceful change of international relations among great powers.

Interactive logic between state leadership and international leadership

As mentioned before, Yan's moral realism presents an elegant political science model, relying on one key variable – political leadership – to explain a state's foreign policy preferences as well as the rise and fall of great powers. Yan further specifies two types of political leadership: state leadership and international leadership, which are categorized into four ideal types. However, his moral realism model did not link these two types of political leadership together. Instead, he argues that 'these four categories each of state leadership and of international leadership, however, do not correspond with each other. The leadership of a leading state that is able to improve its national capability does not necessarily provide a benevolent international leadership or create a stable order of the international system'.[39]

It is clear that Yan's moral realism only proposes an ideal situation to explain the rise and fall of great powers in the system, in which a rising power should feature 'proactive' political leadership domestically with 'humane authority' internationally. It is understandable because Yan intends to propose the necessary conditions for a rising power to successfully challenge a dominant power. However, theoretically, one unanswered question is the other interactive outcomes between these two types of political leadership. For example, if a country has a proactive state leadership but tyrannical international leadership, how will this state behave in foreign policy? In a similar vein, if a country embodies a conservative state leadership but a humane-authority international leadership, will it have a chance to rise up and challenge the existing hegemon in the international system?

If state leadership and international leadership each have four variations, the combination of these two variables will lead to 16 outcomes. The interplay between proactive state leadership and humane-authority international leadership is only one of the 16 outcomes although it might be the best or ideal situation in which a rising power can successfully displace the hegemon. Yan's book has paved a path for future researchers to follow in that they can theoretically explore and empirically test other variable combinations as well as their related policy outcomes.

More importantly, Yan's moral realism seems to argue that the international order transition can only take place if the rising power and the declining hegemony have different types of political leaderships, especially the international leaderships because international leadership embraces competing norms. One interesting question, however, is the situation in which two states, like China and the US, have similar international leaderships but different state leaderships. The different state leaderships lead to different growth rates, through which a rising power can eventually challenge and surpass the declining hegemon. However, because these two states hold similar international leaderships, the power dynamics between these two states do not change the prevailing norms in the system. If this is the case, can we say that there is no order transition in the system? In a concrete example, if China indeed replaces US hegemony in the future, but China does not change the liberal norms in the system, can we say that the China-led liberal order is the same as the US-led one?

Leadership and norms

Norms are another key concept in Yan's moral realism because they are the linkage connecting morality and leadership. It is argued that different types of international leaderships advocate different international norms. In particular, humane authority promotes 'moral norms', while a hegemony sticks to 'double-standard' norms. For an anemocracy, the preferred norms are 'coward-bully' ones. A tyranny will promote 'realpolitik' norms.[40] Moreover, Yan adopts a realist view to rank the efficiency of these different norms for sustaining a state's international leadership as well as power in general. According to Yan, 'moral norms are more helpful than other norms in maintaining a leading state's international leadership for a longer period. Double-standard norms are less effective than moral norms in maintaining a state's international leadership, but more efficient than coward-bully and realpolitik norms'.[41]

Like morality, Yan also takes an instrumental view on norms, through which norms are treated as a rationalist tool for states to pursue their material interests. In other words, international norms, such as human rights, could not successfully emerge and diffuse without the endorsement from the dominant power.[42] For realists, norms are like institutions, that is, they are only epiphenomenal to the material interests and the distribution of power in the system. However, Yan does not just submit himself to this realist version of norms. For him, the imposition of norms by a great power is a necessary but not sufficient condition for the internalization of norms. Instead, he argues that the 'interaction between leading states and other states is the medium through which the leadership type alters international norms'.[43] Moreover, Yan suggests three mechanisms for leading states to change international norms: (1) example imitation; (2) support reinforcement; (3) punishment maintenance.[44]

Although Yan's moral realist version of norm replacement or norm diffusion is insightful, there are two analytical problems. First, other scholars might challenge his holistic view of norms. According to Yan, there are four dominant norms in the ideational system: moral, double standard, coward bully, and realpolitik. To be fair, Yan is not the only scholar holding this kind of holistic view of the ideational system. For example, drawing on the philosophical views of Thomas Hobbes, John Locke, and Immanuel Kant, Alexander Wendt suggests that there are three cultures of anarchy characterized respectively by 'enmity', 'rivalry', and 'friendship'.[45] However, this holistic view of norms or cultures sometimes scarifies the nuances of norms and cultures in shaping and constituting a state's interests and behaviours. For example, what are the moral norms according to moral realism? How could we differentiate some moral norms from others? In particular, are human rights moral norms or double-standard norms? Is non-proliferation a moral norm or a double-standard norm? It is clear that there are many unanswered but important questions on norms in moral realism, which encourage other scholars to continue this type of research in the future.

Another problem lies in the mechanism of norm change. The 'example-imitation' mechanism is indeed interesting, but it is not clear why the dominant power is voluntarily constrained by the norm it has created as well as how long it will keep this 'example-imitation' mechanism. Yan seems to suggest that moral norms are the most efficient way for states to maintain their international leadership. If so, then we should see all states, not only humane authority leadership, advocate moral norms. However, the reality is that humane authority is rare in history. Moreover, it might be rational for a state to adopt the 'example-imitation' mechanism at the beginning of its hegemony. Furthermore, the rise and fall of great powers also lead to changes of national interests. Therefore, what will the dominant power do when its interests are seriously undermined or threatened by the norms it has created? If a state cannot protect its own interests, its material power will be undermined. Sooner or later, the humane authority will lose its dominant position in the system. Consequently, the norms it used to advocate will also be replaced by other norms set by the new dominant powers. Therefore, logically, it is not rational for a dominant power to prefer norms over its own interests. It seems that moral realists need to further clarify the relationship between norms and interests.

The last question related to norms is the outcome of the great power competition. Yan suggests that 'When the rising state and the dominant state believe in different ideologies, the rivalry between them will include competition to make their own particular ideologies the mainstream global value. Ideological confrontation is often fiercer than rivalry purely for material interests'.[46] Here, it is not clear whether ideology is part of norms. If it is, then the US–China competition based on different norms should inevitably lead to ideological confrontation no matter whether China wants it or not. Then we will witness a new Cold War with ideological antagonism between the US and China. This conclusion seems to be at odds with Yan's prediction of 'bipolarization without a Cold War' in world politics for the next decade. Therefore, how to consolidate norms change and ideological competition seems to be a new task for moral realists in the future.

Institutions as a missing link of moral realism?

Although Yan's moral realism highlights the role of norms and morality in shaping the dynamics of great power politics, it does not pay enough attention to international institutions. For example, Yan suggests, 'as long as the United States and China handle conflicts mainly through bilateral diplomacy rather than multilateral approaches, global multilateral institutions will play a lesser role in international affairs'.[47] It is understandable because the Trump administration preferred a bilateral approach, that is, trade war or bilateral sanction, to multilateralism in dealing with China. However, it is problematic to argue that bilateralism will be the dominant model of interaction between great powers especially against the background of deepening globalization in the world. It seems to be an unfortunate omission for moral realism to downplay the role of multilateral institutions in world politics.

International institutions are an important component of the international order. According to the English School,[48] there are two types of international institutions: normative foundations (primary institutions) and intergovernmental organizations or accords (secondary institutions).[49] Here, the primary institutions refer to the normative norms in world politics, such as sovereignty and territorial sovereignty, non-intervention, and the equality of peoples. In Yan's moral realism, morality and international norms could be seen as the primary institutions. However, besides primary institutions, secondary institutions or multilateral institutions in a general sense, especially intergovernmental organizations, are also a constitutive part of the international order, which should not be ignored for two reasons.

On the one hand, primary institutions, such as sovereignty and territoriality norms, are embodied through secondary institutions such as the UN. As ideational constructs, primary institutions are difficult to be challenged directly without involving secondary institutions. Compared with secondary institutions, primary institutions are more resilient and deeply entrenched, and they cannot be as easily altered or overturned. On the other hand, these secondary institutions are the actual points of contact and interaction among states. If a state intends to change or challenge a particular norm, it will usually have to address a relevant secondary institution (even if by evasion or withdrawal). In other words, secondary institutions serve as a material cover of norms (primary institutions) in the international order.[50]

More importantly, multilateral institutions are the most dynamic, constitutive part of international order. Multilateral institutions are responsible for the provision of global public goods such as the open trading system under the World Trade Organization (WTO) as well as the financial stability ensured by the International Monetary Fund (IMF) and the World Bank in the post-war era. In addition, states interact with one another through rules and institutions on a daily basis. Multilateral institutions can be modified and changed according to shifting state interests as well as power struggles among states within institutions.[51]

The relationship between institutions and power distribution, the two main components of international order, is complex. The changes in multilateral institutions will gradually constitute an incremental transition in international order. Some liberal scholars such as G. John Ikenberry argue that the US decline will not lead to the demise of the basic logic of the liberal international order 'as a system of open and rule-based order'.[52] However, the rules, institutions, and even the logic of the liberal international order are not static in nature. Instead, they will change, not only because of the decline of US hegemony but also due to the constant modifications of multilateral institutions embedded in the current liberal order. In other words, US decline is not a necessary or sufficient condition of international order transition, because the international order is inherently in flux no matter whether it is led by the US or not.

Therefore, it is true that the rise of China and the decline of US hegemony will lead to international order transition. However, we should not ignore the role of multilateral institutions in the process of international order transition. As Yan argues, nuclear deterrence has prevented a hegemonic war between the US and China. If it is the case, then the two great powers will hesitate to engage in a traditional military conflict. It is why we saw the 'trade war' and 'tech war' between two nations, but no 'hot war', under the Trump administration. This then leads to some critical empirical questions: what will these two giants compete for? Where do they 'fight' beyond the combat zone?

My answer is multilateral institutions. In other words, multilateral institutions will be a new battlefield for the US and China. For example, in order to advocate the Trans-Pacific Partnership (TPP), a trade bloc excluding China, President Obama publicly stated that the purpose of the TPP was to preclude China from writing 'the rules for the world's fastest-growing region' in international trade.[53] When President Biden came to power, he publicly stated that China would face 'extreme competition' from the US. But differing from Trump, Biden pledged to focus on 'international rules of the road'.[54] It is clear that rules embedded in multilateral institutions are the major target of US–China competition during the period of international order transition. Consequently, multilateral institutions will become a new battlefield between the US and China during the order transition.

Therefore, it is a real pity that Yan's moral realism ignores the role of multilateral institutions. Since morality and norms advocated by moral realism share the same theoretical root with multilateral institutions, it would be beneficial for moral realism to incorporate institutions in its future theoretical and empirical refinements. For example, moral realism suggests that proactive state leadership will seek to enlarge its international support. Then, the related question is how international support could be mobilized more efficiently. Apparently, multilateral institutions can facilitate states' pooling support from others. In addition, a humane authority would prefer to promote moral norms in the international system. Then, multilateral institutions could serve as a more efficient means for a humane authority to achieve this goal. In a word, multilateral institutions can bridge the gap between morality and power in moral realism.

Summary

Moral realism is one of the newest and most innovative variants of realist theories. Inspired by the Chinese Pre-Qin ancient philosophies as well as rigorous modern IR theorizations, Yan creatively integrates morality and power dynamics in one theoretical framework, which not only explains the rise and fall of great powers, but also sheds some light on the future trajectory of the international order. Because of its bold and provocative arguments, moral realism will be certainly scrutinized and criticized by scholars. This indeed reflects the real value of Yan's scholarship and contribution to the IR field. A truly valuable book is not for reaching agreement, but for stimulating discussions, igniting debates, and sparking inspiration. To a certain extent, Yan's moral realism has paved a new path for scholars to advance IR theory, especially realism, theoretically, as well as to study the dynamics of international order transition empirically.

More importantly, policy makers should also take Yan's moral realism seriously. No one can deny the role of leadership, especially individual leaders, in shaping, influencing, and even determining the trajectories of human history. The ongoing war between Russia and Ukraine has proved the importance of leadership in shaping world politics. The US–China strategic competition seems to be inevitable. However, how the leadership of each country engages in the competition will shape the outcome of the international order transition. If the leaders in the US or China or both can take Yan's suggestions to pursue 'humane authority' and promote moral norms, the power transition between the two nations will be definitely different from as well as more peaceful than the previous ones.

Notes

[1] Yan Xuetong, *Leadership and the Rise of Great Powers*, Princeton: Princeton University Press, 2019.
[2] Ibid., pp 190–1.
[3] Kenneth Waltz, *Theory of International Politics*, New York: McGraw-Hill, 1979, p 121.
[4] Huiyun Feng, Kai He, and Yan Xuetong (eds), *Chinese Scholars and Foreign Policy: Debating International Relations*, London: Routledge, 2019.

5. Michael Auslin, '"Leadership and the Rise of Great Powers" Review: No More "Sage Kings"', *The Wall Street Journal*, 11 August 2019; Shivshankar Menon, 'Book Review: Yan Xuetong, Leadership and the Rise of Great Powers', *China Report* 56, no. 1 (2020): 139–59.
6. Yan Xuetong, *Leadership and the Rise of Great Powers*, p 2.
7. Ibid.
8. Hans Morgenthau, 'International Affairs: The Resurrection of Neutrality in Europe', *American Political Science Review* 33, no. 3 (1939): 483–4.
9. Ibid.: 13.
10. Ibid.: 25–53.
11. Ibid.: 44.
12. Ibid.: 46.
13. Ibid.: 52.
14. Alastair Iain Johnston, *Cultural Realism: Strategic Culture and Grand Strategy in Chinese History*, Volume 178, Princeton: Princeton University Press, 1998; Huiyun Feng, *Chinese Strategic Culture and Foreign Policy Decision-Making: Confucianism, Leadership and War*, London: Routledge, 2007; Huiyun Feng and Kai He, 'A Dynamic Strategic Culture Model and China's Behaviour in the South China Sea', *Cambridge Review of International Affairs* 34, no. 4 (2021): 510–29.
15. Gideon Rose, 'Neoclassical Realism and Theories of Foreign Policy', *World Politics* 51, no. 1 (1998): 144–72; Norrin M. Ripsman, Jeffrey W. Taliaferro, and Steven E. Lobell, *Neoclassical Realist Theory of International Politics*, Oxford: Oxford University Press, 2016.
16. Yan Xuetong, *Leadership and the Rise of Great Powers*, p 6.
17. Ibid., 7.
18. George Kennan, *American Diplomacy 1900–1950*, New York: Mentor Books, 1951; Hans Morgenthau, *Politics Among Nations*, 5th edition, New York: Knopf, 1978.
19. Philip E. Tetlock, *Expert Political Judgment*, Princeton: Princeton University Press, 2009.
20. Kenneth N. Waltz, 'Evaluating Theories', *American Political Science Review* 91, no. 4 (1997): 913–17.
21. Yan Xuetong, *Leadership and the Rise of Great Powers*, p 197.
22. Ibid., p 198.
23. Ibid., p 200.
24. Ibid., p 203.
25. Bob Davis and Lingling Wei, 'Biden Plans to Build a Grand Alliance to Counter China', *The Wall Street Journal*, 6 January 2021, www.wsj.com/articles/biden-trump-xi-china-economic-trade-strategy-policy-11609945027.
26. Yan Xuetong, *Leadership and the Rise of Great Powers*, p 8.
27. Ibid., p 9.
28. Kai He, 'A Realist's Ideal Pursuit', *Chinese Journal of International Politics* 5, no. 2 (2012): 183–97.
29. Arnold Wolfers, *Discord and Collaboration: Essays on International Politics*, Baltimore: Johns Hopkins University Press, 1962, p 48.
30. James E. Dougherty and Robert L. Pfaltzgraff Jr, *Contending Theories of International Relations*, 5th edition, New York: Longman, 2001, p 70.
31. Hans Morgenthau, *Politics among Nations*, p 10.
32. Jame E. Dougherty and Robert L. Pfaltzgraff, *Contending Theories of International Relations*, p 508.
33. Edward Hallett Carr, *The Twenty Years' Crisis, 1919–1939*, New York: Harper & Row, 1964, p 87.
34. Ibid., pp 166–67.
35. For a criticism of the lack of morality in realism, see Richard K. Ashley, 'Poverty of Neorealism', *International Organization* 38, no. 2 (1984): 225–86. For a comprehensive

discussion of realism and morality, see Jack Donnelly, *Realism and International Relations*, Cambridge: Cambridge University Press, 2000, especially Chapter 6.
36 Yan Xuetong, *Leadership and the Rise of Great Powers*, p 27.
37 Ibid., p 28.
38 Ibid., p 29.
39 Ibid., p 52.
40 Ibid., p 195.
41 Ibid.
42 See G. John Ikenberry and Charles Kupchan, 'Socialization and Hegemonic Power', *International Organization* 44, no. 3 (1990): 283–315; Stephen Krasner, 'Sovereignty, Regimes, and Human Rights', in *Regime Theory and International Relations*, edited by Volker Rittberger, Oxford: Clarendon Press, 1993, pp 139–67.
43 Yan Xuetong, *Leadership and the Rise of Great Powers*, p 112.
44 Ibid., p 114.
45 Alexander Wendt, *Social Theory of International Politics*, Cambridge: Cambridge University Press, 1999.
46 Yan Xuetong, *Leadership and the Rise of Great Powers*, p 196.
47 Ibid., p 202.
48 Hedley Bull, *The Anarchical Society: A Study of Order in World Politics*, New York: Macmillan, 1977.
49 Barry Buzan, *From International to World Society? English School Theory and the Social Structure of Globalisation*, Cambridge: Cambridge University Press, 2004.
50 Kai He, Huiyun Feng, Steve Chan, and Weixing Hu, 'Rethinking Revisionism in World Politics', *The Chinese Journal of International Politics* 14, no. 2 (2021): 159–86.
51 Huiyun Feng and Kai He (eds), *China's Challenges and International Order Transition: Beyond 'Thucydides's Trap'*, Ann Arbor: University of Michigan Press, 2020.
52 It is worth noting that though Ikenberry recognizes the evolution of the liberal international order from 1.0 to 2.0 and 3.0, he argues that 'precisely because the crisis of liberal order is a crisis of success, leading and rising states in the system are not seeking to overturn the basic logic of liberal internationalism as a system of open and rule-based order'. See G. John Ikenberry, 'Liberal Internationalism 3.0: America and the Dilemmas of Liberal World Order', *Perspectives on Politics* 7, no. 1 (2009): 71–87, 84. See also G. John Ikenberry, 'Why the Liberal World Order Will Survive', in 'Rising Powers and the International Order', special issue, *Ethics & International Affairs* 32, no. 1 (2018): 17–29.
53 Barack Obama, 'Remarks of President Barack Obama – as Prepared for Delivery State of the Union Address', White House: President Barack Obama, Washington DC, 20 January 2015, obamawhitehouse.archives.gov/the-press-office/2015/01/20/remarks-president-barack-obama-prepared-delivery-state-union-address.
54 Amanda Macias, 'Biden Says There Will Be "Extreme Competition" with China, but Won't Take Trump Approach', *CNBC News*, 7 February 2021, www.cnbc.com/2021/02/07/biden-will-compete-with-china-but-wont-take-trump-approach.html.

6

The Conception of Morality in Moral Realism

Feng Zhang

Professor Yan Xuetong's moral realism is one of the most distinctive and influential Chinese theories of international relations (IR) to have emerged in recent years. The theory was first presented in *Ancient Chinese Thought, Modern Chinese Power*.[1] In a review article of that book, I suggested 'moral realism' to describe the theory.[2] It was further developed in *Leadership and the Rise of Great Powers*, which tries to explain international power transition from the perspective of leadership quality.[3]

Most IR scholars who come across moral realism for the first time will be more impressed by its enunciation of morality than by its account of realism. The moral element of the theory is derived from traditional Chinese thought, especially the insights of the ancient Confucian scholar Xunzi (298–238 BCE). These are largely unknown outside the circle of professional philosophers and political theorists, let alone IR scholars. Yan's exploration of ancient Chinese thought for IR theory building was a novelty even inside China, not to mention in the West. His realism, in contrast, is largely a restatement of Western realist thought, especially classical realism.

But what precisely is the contribution of Yan's conception of morality to IR theory? In this chapter, I will explore the conception of morality in moral realism by situating it within broad intellectual approaches to morality. Drawing on moral philosophy across China and the West, I identify four approaches to morality that have dominated Western and Chinese intellectual history: deontology, consequentialism, virtue ethics, and role ethics. I then examine Yan's conception of morality by a close reading of his writings. Drawing on Xunzi, Yan distinguishes two levels of morality: humane authority, which has a strong moral standing, and hegemony, which is moral to the extent that it possesses strategic reliability. But he seems unaware of the two senses in which Xunzi conceives of morality: morality as duties and morality as virtues. He also misses Xunzi's relational conception of the morality of trustworthiness.

In the third section, I offer a critique of Yan's conception of morality. This conception is explicitly instrumental in accordance with realist commitments. It is narrow in that it is restricted to governmental morality judged by the extent to which policies serve national interests and capabilities. Subjects of genuine moral significance, such as justice and care, are left out of the picture. This blinkered conception runs counter to the Confucian universalism which provided the original inspiration for the theory. Meanwhile, the theory's emphasis on the utility of strategic credibility as a foreign policy principle faces theoretical and policy difficulties. The virtue ethics and role ethics approaches to morality point to fascinating directions for the development of moral realism, but these remain unexplored. Moral realism reflects the logic of consequences understood as instrumental rationality, but this is a far narrower approach than consequentialism in moral philosophy, which may be another avenue for further theory building. My critique is not meant to obscure the contribution of moral realism, which is genuine, pioneering, and inspirational, especially for Chinese scholars like myself; it is to suggest the value of a broader conception of morality and pinpoint avenues for the further development of the theory.

Four approaches to morality

According to a standard definition, morality is 'an informal public system applying to all rational persons, governing behaviour that affects others, having the lessening of evil or harm as its main goal, and including what are commonly known as the moral rules, moral ideals, and moral virtues'.[4] But what are the sources of morality? To answer this question, Chinese and Western thinkers have developed four distinct approaches in moral philosophy, namely deontology (following rules), consequentialism (maximizing values), virtue ethics (pursuing excellence), and role ethics (performing roles). These by no means exhaust all available approaches to morality; I discuss them here only as a heuristic device for examining the conception of morality in moral realism.

Deontology

Deontology offers a principles-based and reason-grounded conception of morality. It sees morality as deriving from moral laws, rules, and principles; moral conduct is a matter of following moral rules. In Western intellectual history, Stoic, Jewish, and Christian thought all hold that 'there is a set of rules or precepts of conduct, constituting a divine law, which is binding upon all rational creatures as such, and which in principle can be ascertained by human reason'.[5] Jews and Christians referred to this universal or common code variously as 'morality', 'the moral law', 'the law of nature', and 'natural law'.

This Hebrew-Christian conception formed a very powerful moral tradition in Western history, but a full-blown philosophical theory of morality based on this tradition was only worked out by Kant during the Enlightenment era. Kant believes that common morality is not a matter of religious revelation or human feeling, but of autonomous reason. His overriding principle is respect for individual human beings, as expressed in his famous formula that 'so act that you use humanity, in your own person as well as in the person of any other, always at the same time as an end, never merely as a means'.[6]

There is nothing like Kantian deontology in Chinese Confucianism or the Chinese intellectual tradition more generally, but it is not wholly absent. To begin with, Confucianism does espouse certain fundamental principles. One of the most important is Confucius' golden rule 'do not impose on others what you yourself do not want'.[7] Mengzi says, 'exemplary persons preserve their hearts with humaneness and preserve their hearts with propriety. The humane love others, and those who have propriety revere others'.[8] This is the principle of humaneness understood as loving other people. It appears that Confucianism exhibits at least a weak form of principles-based morality.

Consequentialism

Consequentialism is the doctrine that the moral rightness of an act is determined solely by the goodness of the act's consequences. Utilitarianism, a prominent version of consequentialism, holds that an act is morally right if and only if it produces more happiness for people it affects than any other act available to the agent. In contrast to utilitarianism's promotion of happiness as the moral aim, other consequentialists pinpoint divergent aims such as achievement, autonomy, or fairness.[9]

Consequentialism in moral philosophy is considerably richer than the logic of consequences as commonly understood in IR theory. The IR version of the logic of consequences, which is essentially instrumental rationality, takes action to be 'driven by calculation of its consequences as measured against prior preferences'.[10] It describes an international system populated by autonomous, egoistic, self-interested maximizers in a perpetual state of competition. In contrast, the sort of consequences emphasized by moral consequentialism is goodness which does not rule out but is much broader than self-interest. Usually, it combines both self-interest and some other-regarding concerns. Such goodness may be understood subjectively in terms of its intrinsic value or preference satisfaction or objectively as consisting in some list of disparate objective goods such as achievement, friendship, or equality. Broadly speaking, consequentialism may be seen as a doctrine of value maximization, whether in regard to one's own value and well-being or to those of all agents affected by a given action. But it does not tell us what is good or valuable, and is therefore in need of an additional theory of value to buttress its specific positions.[11]

Consequentialism occupies a peripheral position in Chinese thought, although at times it has played significant roles. The first major theory of consequentialism in Chinese history comes from Mohism, which judges justice solely according to the consequences of action rather than the adherence of moral principles. Mohists hold that 'justice is but the attainment of benefit (li 利)'.[12] Wise rulers in ancient times, Mozi says, realized justice by 'benefiting Heaven, ghosts, and ordinary people'.[13] To Mohists, justice is a means to an end, the end being benefit, of which economic wealth and political order are held as the most important.[14] Justice, in this conception, is justified solely by the benefit that might be accrued from action. It is a consequentialist ethic par excellence. It is important to note, however, that this consequentialism is of a communitarian rather than individualistic sort.[15] Mozi always privileges the benefits of the community over those of the individual. The economic wealth and political order that he emphasizes are collective or public in nature. As he puts it, 'The business of the humane person must be to seek assiduously to promote *the world's* benefits and to eliminate *the world's* harms'.[16]

Legalism is a far narrower doctrine of consequentialism than Mohism. Han Fei, the greatest Legalist thinker, holds that people 'like benefit (li 利) and fear harm'.[17] Benefit is the only motive force of social development, and material interests are the real basis upon which human relationships are forged, including even the relationship between parents and children.[18] Han Fei exploits the crude instruments of punishment and reward – what he calls law (fa 法) – not to improve human nature but to orient it towards realizing the utilitarian ends of the wealth and power of the state. The Legalist obsession with material consequences of action might have been influenced by Mohism, but it is a cruel doctrine in comparison because it has nothing of Mohism's concern with universal and impartial care. If we classify Mohist consequentialism as a sort of rule consequentialism that adheres to moral rules in the quest for benefit, then Legalist consequentialism is but a stripe of amoral consequentialism.[19]

Virtue ethics

Virtue ethics traces the foundation of morality to the character of the person; moral action is action performed by someone with a virtuous character or that expresses a virtuous character. A virtuous character is one that embodies a commitment to some ethical value, such as justice or benevolence. Here, virtue is understood as 'the disposition to do the right thing for the right reason, in the appropriate way – honestly, courageously, and so on'.[20] There are two aspects of virtue: the affective and the intellectual. The affective aspect manifests itself when the agent does the right thing and has a variety of feelings and reactions to it. The intellectual aspect refers to the fact that virtue is in large measure acquired through a good moral education; one becomes virtuous by learning from others, both in making particular judgments about right and wrong, and in adopting some people as role models or teachers or following certain rules.[21]

Virtue ethics differs from deontology and consequentialism in fundamental ways. Locating morality in rules and principles about human rationality and autonomy, deontology pays little heed to actual agents in action. Assessing morality by the goodness of the consequences of action, consequentialism recognizes only a reduced notion of virtue as instrumental to the achievement of some independently defined good.[22] Virtue ethics bases morality in the good character of the agent. Its focus is on the virtuous individual and on those inner traits, dispositions, and motives that qualify her as being virtuous. Its attraction lies in the fact that it treats morality as a more deeply human matter than does deontology or consequentialism.[23]

Virtue ethics characterizes an important dimension of Confucian thought. Mengzi, for example, seems to advocate a theory akin to Aristotelian virtue ethics, in which conception of virtue is connected to a theory about human nature and a related view of human flourishing described in terms of an ideal agent. Thus, Mengzi presents a programme of moral self-cultivation that leads to a distinctive conception of human flourishing, which he describes in terms of the paradigmatic models of the 'exemplary person' (君子 *junzi*) and 'sage' (聖人 *sheng ren*). At the same time, Mengzi, by virtue of his emphasis on the role of emotions and empathy, also shares similarities with Western sentimentalists such as David Hume, who describe the virtues primarily in terms of certain broadly construed emotions.[24]

The virtue ethics interpretation of Confucianism helps to explain the extraordinary emphasis Confucians have placed on *ren* (仁 humaneness) and the associated qualities of *yi* (義 appropriateness) and *li* (禮 propriety). Joseph Chan argues that the Confucian ethics of humaneness is ultimately based on a common humanity rather than differentiated social roles and thus carries ethical implications beyond these roles. The Confucian view, as he puts it, 'is that human persons are first and foremost moral agents capable of realizing *ren*, which means, among other things, a certain ability or disposition to care for and sympathize with others'.[25] For Confucians, *ren* is the overriding virtue of human beings, and the moral duties emanating from *ren* need not all arise from roles, relationships, or institutions. As an emotion, *ren* generates an ethical concern for human suffering that is potentially unlimited in scope. And as a motive, it commands us to care for people in need, even if they are strangers living in faraway places without any relational claims on us.

Role ethics

Role ethics traces morality to the performance of social roles and the discharge of obligations. In Western history, role ethics was prominent in ancient Greece but has been eclipsed by individualistic approaches in modern times.[26] In China, role ethics was prominent in Confucianism from the beginning and is still influential in Chinese society today. Roger T. Ames and Henry Rosemont Jr are the major protagonists of Confucian role ethics. According to Ames, Confucian ethics is grounded in a distinctive, relational conception of role-bearing persons. There is, he says, 'no discrete, essential, innate, and reduplicated "nature" independent of a person's specific context; there are only unique yet analogically similar persons constituted by their always-specific roles and relationships'.[27] Similarly, Rosemont contrasts the Confucian conception of role-bearing persons with the modern Western notion of an abstract autonomous individual.[28] The most distinguishing feature of Confucian role ethics, as opposed to Western ethical theories, is a concept of a relationally constituted person who realizes a vision of the consummate life through a kind of moral artistry centred on the concept of *ren* (仁 humaneness).

Role ethics locates morality in how people live their roles in concrete relationships; it is a relational, not principles-based, morality. As Ames puts it, 'Confucian role ethics takes the substance of morality to be nothing more or less than positive growth in the constitutive relations of any particular situation'.[29] This aspect of moral thinking is captured by the concepts of *yi* 義 and *li* 禮. *Yi*, which is the closest Chinese equivalent to the Western concept of justice, is not about a person's compliance with some external principle or rule, least of all the divine command as in the Hebrew-Christian religious tradition. Rather, it is about conducting oneself appropriately in different kinds of relations within one's family and community. Related, *li* (ritual propriety) is not just the observation of formal rites, but is 'the quality of propriety achieved by personally and consistently doing what is most appropriate in the roles and relations that define one'.[30]

Morality in moral realism

As we have seen, Chinese and Western thinkers have offered at least four common ways of conceptualizing morality: following principles (deontology), maximizing values (consequentialism), pursuing excellence (virtue ethics), and performing roles (role ethics). How does the conception of morality in moral realism stand against this broad intellectual framework?

In his early work, Yan makes an important distinction between two levels of morality: humane authority, which has a strong moral standing, and hegemony, which possesses strategic reliability but is otherwise lacking in moral resources.[31] The distinction is based on a reading of Xunzi, which is worth further elaboration. In the passage that Yan quotes from Xunzi, the two key moral concepts are *yi* 義 and *wang* 王. *Wang*, in the ancient Chinese historical context in which Xunzi writes, means 'a true king' or 'a sage king', but the alternative translation of 'humane authority' preferred by Yan is fully justified in a contemporary IR context. *Yi* may be conveniently translated as justice, as is sometimes done in Yan's book. But it is such a rich and malleable concept that it can also be translated into duty, righteousness, rightness, or appropriateness. According to Eric L. Hutton, author of an excellent recent translation of the *Xunzi*, there are two meanings of *yi* in the text. On the one hand, it refers to a certain set of ethical standards that were created by the ancient sage kings to bring order to people, in which sense it can be translated as 'duties'. On the other hand, *yi* also refers to a virtue, namely the tendency to adhere to these standards and the order they contain, in which sense it can be translated as 'righteousness'.[32]

Yi is the central concept of morality upon which Yan builds his theory of moral realism, but its two meanings used by Xunzi seem to have escaped Yan's attention. Yan takes Xunzi to think that morality is the foundation of authority and leadership, but he falls short of spelling out the exact meaning and content of morality in Xunzi's thought. The passage quoted by Yan is not illuminating. It says:

> Hence it is said, 'If one takes the state and aligns it with *yi*, then in a single day one will become illustrious.' Such was the case with Tang and Wu. Tang used Bo, and King Wu used Hao – these were both territories of merely a hundred *li* in size. But the world became united under them, the feudal lords were their servants, and among those of penetrating intelligence, none failed to submit and to follow. There is no reason for this other than that they achieved perfection in yi. This is what I mean by saying, 'If *yi* is established as your foundation, then you will be a true king'.[33]

This is Xunzi's assertion about the efficacy of *yi*. His arguments about the causes of such efficacy lie in a preceding passage:

> Kongzi lacked even so much land as to plant an awl in, but he sincerely cultivated *yi* in his thoughts and intentions, attached *yi* to his person and conduct, and made it clear in his words. From the days he had perfected it, he has not been obscure in the world, and his name has been passed down to later generations. Now take also the most eminent feudal lord in the world. Let him sincerely cultivate *yi* in his thoughts and intentions, attach *yi* to his laws, standards, and measures, make it clear in his governmental affairs, and accordingly extend and reinforce it in the way he elevates some and lowers others, executes some and

lets others live, so that the end of one affair and the beginning of the next are as though united seamlessly in it. When it is like this, then the way his good reputation and fame will grow and spread through all the space between Heaven and Earth will be just like the light of sun and moon, or the sound of thunder, will it not?[34]

Here Xunzi applies the two meanings of *yi* to an analysis of the accomplishments of Kongzi and feudal lords. When he praises Kongzi and feudal lords for cultivating *yi* in their thought and conduct, he is speaking of *yi* as a personal virtue. When he commends them for attaching *yi* to laws and standards, he has in mind *yi* as ethical standards or moral duties. Going back to our earlier discussion of the four approaches to morality, one may argue that Xunzi's understanding of *yi* reflects the approaches of virtue ethics and principles-based deontology, and he may well have regarded them as complementary.

One level below the strong morality of humane authority, Yan contends, is the partial morality of hegemony (*ba* 霸) based on strategic reliability. 'Strategic reliability' is translated from the Chinese original of *zhanlüe chengxin* 戰略誠信, which in turn builds on Xunzi's concept of *xin* 信.[35] It is not clear if 'reliability' is the best translation of *chengxin*. *Cheng* refers to sincerity or integrity, while *xin* means trustworthiness. 'Credibility' or 'trustworthiness" might serve better. In any case, in the Confucian context, *xin* denotes 'trustworthiness'. The key passages carrying Xunzi's argument about hegemony's foundation in trustworthiness are as follows:

> There are some who, even though virtue is not yet completed in them and *yi* is not yet perfected in them, nevertheless order and control for all under Heaven advances under them. Their punishments and rewards and their promises to allow or not to allow things are trusted by all under Heaven. Their ministers and subordinates all clearly know that one can make pacts with them. When governmental orders have been put forth, then even though they see opportunities for gain or loss, they will not cheat their people. When covenants have been settled upon, then even though they see opportunities for gain or loss, they will not cheat their allies.
>
> When it is like this, then their soldiers will be energetic and their city walls solidly defended, and rival states will fear them. Their own state will be united and its fundamental standards clear, and their allied states will trust them. Then, even though they may reside in a remote and backward state, their power to inspire awe will shake the whole world. Such was the case with the five hegemons. They did not strive to become exalted and lofty. They did not pursue the extremes of culture and good order. They did not make people's hearts submit willingly.

They inclined to tactics and stratagems, paid attention to fatigue and rest for troops, were careful to store up provisions, and prepared the equipment necessary for war. Those above and those below had must trust as tight as the way one's upper and lower teeth come together, and no one under Heaven dared stand up to them. Thus, Duke Han of Qi, Duke Wen of Jin, King Zhuang of Chu, King Helü of Wu, and King Goujian of Yue were all from remote and backward states, but their power to inspire awe shook the whole world, and their strength threatened the central states. There is no other reason for this than that they mastered trustworthiness. This is what I mean by saying, 'If trustworthiness is established as your foundation, then you will be a hegemon'.[36]

It is clear that for Xunzi, trustworthiness manifests itself in the 'pacts' and 'covenants' that rulers make with domestic subordinates and foreign allies alike. It is a fascinating anticipation of the modern theory of alliance based on treaty obligations. Xunzi even draws a casual chain between trustworthiness of this kind and 'the power to inspire awe' (*wei* 威). Earlier, I noted that Xunzi's understanding of *yi* reflects both virtue ethics and principles-based deontology. In the case of *xin*, Xunzi seems to have in mind a principle of maintaining robust relationships.

It is, however, possible to give a relational interpretation of *xin*. According to Ames:

> *Xin* 信 denotes the situational rather than agency-centered combination of perceived 'credibility' and the concomitant 'trust' that such credibility inspires; it describes a situation in which its participants conduct themselves sincerely and honestly with mutual regard. The cultivation of these honest relationships entails integrity not only in the sense of the persistent particularity of persons, but also in the integrative sense of becoming one together in their concrete, social relationships.[37]

Xin is relational in that it connotes 'both the increased credibility of the benefactor and the increased confidence and trust of the beneficiary'.[38] *Xin* means 'making good on one's word', but mere words and good intentions are not enough; one must follow through and make good on what one proposes to do. *Xin* demands practical results. Although on a moral scale it ranks below *yi*, it is still a stringent requirement. Xunzi has the relational quality of *xin* in mind when he speaks of the 'mutual trust' between the ruler and his subjects and between the ruler and his foreign allies. He places an extraordinary premium on practical results when he lauds *xin*'s ability to create hegemony. The relational logic here is that with mutual trust, political and diplomatic relationships become more productive, enhancing the credibility of the benefactor and the trust of the beneficiary. Under the relational interpretation, *xin* is no longer an abstract principle, but a virtue or habit for promoting credibility and trust in constructive relationships. Yan has missed this relational aspect of the morality of *xin*.

In his later work *Leadership and the Rise of Great Powers*, Yan changes 'reliability' to 'credibility' and argues that it is the 'lowest level of international morality'.[39] He distinguishes four types of international leadership according to the level of their strategic credibility and the nature of their principles of action. The highest or the most admirable type – humane authority – is one which is trustworthy and which adopts foreign policies consistent with international norms. Yan says that a humane authority 'maintains high strategic credibility and pursues international order in the following three ways: (1) by setting itself as a good example to other states through actions in accordance with international norms; (2) by promoting beneficial international norms through rewarding the states that obey these norms; and (3) by punishing states that violate international norms'.[40] He equates this kind of international leadership with practising moral principles.[41]

Earlier, I identified two senses in which Xunzi deploys the concept of *yi* in his discussion of humane authority which has deeply influenced Yan: as a personal virtue and as moral principles. In *Ancient Chinese Thought, Modern Chinese Power*, Yan is vague on the content of morality, as noted. Now, in specifically relating humane authority to the practice of moral principles, especially international norms, Yan seems to be adopting a principles-based, deontological approach to morality.

Hegemony, the second type of international leadership, is one which is trustworthy but which follows a double standard, in the sense that it maintains strategic credibility with allies but adopts 'the law of the jungle' as the principle for dealing with non-allies.[42] The emphasis on trustworthiness is consistent with Yan's earlier work, but the new point about double standard is a curious digression. In distinguishing strategic credibility from the law of the jungle and applying the former to alliance relationships and the latter to non-alliance relationships, Yan has made *xin* into a particularistic moral principle. But one possible deontological reading of Xunzi is that he sets forth *xin* as a universal principle, the applicability of which is determined by situational particularities. Thus, to take the current example of Sino–American rivalry, some Chinese officials and commentators would still like the relationship to be based on *xin* as a matter of principle, but the adoption of a competitive strategy by the US since the Trump administration has made this impossible. The principle is universal; its application is not. Yan's use of *xin* starts by making practical determinations of two kinds of relationships (allies and non-allies) and then applying *xin* according to the nature of relationships. It has unduly limited the scope of credibility as a foreign policy principle.

Credibility in general means convincing or trustworthy communications about what one will do under future circumstances.[43] The distinction which Yan could have made is between two kinds of credibility – that of promises and that of threats. The credibility of promises enables actors to cooperate more than they would otherwise have done; the credibility of threats reduces the level of cooperation from what it would otherwise have been.[44] The former type of credibility is usually applied to allies, and the latter to non-allies. To allies, as Yan points out, the credibility lies in the commitment of security protection, which carries moral force. To non-allies, especially adversaries, an important kind of credibility is deterrence, namely, the ability to prevent an undesirable behaviour by convincing the party that may be contemplating it that the cost will exceed any possible gain. There is no morality in the credibility of deterrence. Mutual deterrence now dominates the Sino–American security relationship, and few observers would characterize the relationship after the Trump years as a moral relationship.[45]

We have seen that from *Ancient Chinese Thought, Modern Chinese Power* to *Leadership and the Rise of Great Powers*, Yan has clarified his approach to foreign policy morality by adopting a largely principles-based, deontological understanding of morality. There is another important evolution in his thinking about the nature of international morality. He now firmly approaches morality from an instrumental perspective, defining morality as 'governmental morality, whereby leaders' actions will be judged according to the accepted codes of conduct pertaining to national interests and national capability'.[46] Its scope is confined to three areas: the responsibility to protect national interests, the duty to practice international norms, and strategic credibility with regard to allies.[47]

Moral realism is thus 'the approach to understanding a major power's behavior when morality is a contributing factor to its leadership's strategic preferences'.[48] Yan asserts that national interests are determined objectively and defined by a state's material capability. The role of morality is to influence policy makers' concerns about how national interests should be achieved rather than what national interests ought to be. In other words, morality informs the means, not the ends, of foreign policy; ends consist perforce in the maximization of national interests.[49] Morality is useful because it can enhance the power of states by increasing the legitimacy of a state's leadership; it can also strengthen a state's capability indirectly by changing other actors' policies towards it.[50]

At this point, it will be interesting to compare Yan's conception of morality in foreign policy with that of Joseph Nye, a prominent American IR scholar and author of a recent book on moral reasoning in American foreign policy.[51] Nye's discussion follows the Western tradition in thinking about morality and foreign policy. He sees this tradition as a battle between realists who argue that foreign policy is largely amoral in an anarchic world and liberals who contend that even in such a world moral values have their roles to play. Nye's purpose is to clear away the conceptual confusion surrounding American thinking about morality in foreign policy. To that end, he proposes a three-dimensional framework of moral reasoning: moral judgment should include intentions, means, and consequences. He uses this framework to evaluate the morality of American foreign policy from Franklin D. Roosevelt to Donald Trump.

There are clear cultural differences in Yan's and Nye's conceptions of morality. Nye situates his argument in the Western traditions of realism and liberalism. Yan derives his theory from Confucianism in the first instance, even though Western-style realism is never far from his mind. The most distinguishing feature of moral realism is the concept of humane authority. Unsurprisingly, this concept finds no equivalent in Nye since it is a distinctive Chinese-Confucian concept. The animating questions for Yan and Nye are also different. Yan wants to harness morality for a more effective Chinese foreign policy; morality is useful to the extent that it can help China safeguard its national interests and build up its national power. Nye, in contrast, focuses on assessing whether American presidents have made the best moral choices in their foreign policy decisions.

Nevertheless, there are parallels in the two scholars' theories of moral foreign policy. The most notable is their common emphasis on the consequences of foreign policy. Yan does not make as clear-cut a distinction between intentions, means, and consequences as does Nye, but his discussions touch upon all three dimensions. Another similarity is their recognition of the thorny issue of credibility in foreign policy. These commonalities are perhaps an indirect support for Yan's long-standing contention about the universality of scientific theories.

A broader conception

Yan's instrumental view of morality owes much to classical realism, especially the works of Hans J. Morgenthau and Richard Ned Lebow.[52] The irony of this theoretical orientation is that although the original inspiration of moral realism comes from traditional Chinese thought, especially the Xunzi variant of Confucianism, the more developed version of the theory as presented in *Leadership and the Rise of Great Powers* has somewhat moved away from its Confucian provenance and edged closer to the Western realist tradition. Yan is hardly concerned about such a move; he might well have regarded it as a virtue since he believes in the universality of scientific theories. But we must wonder if a cost is incurred in this ingenious yoking of Confucian sensibilities with realist proclivities. In particular, we must ask whether Yan has remained true to Xunzi's conception of morality, from which he has derived so much inspiration.

Xunzi's conception of morality follows the Confucian tradition set down by Kongzi. This tradition believes in the Way (*dao* 道), that is, the proper way to live and to organize society as practised and taught by the ancient sages and sage kings. To live according to this Way required practising certain rituals (*li* 禮) and exercising certain virtues. The most important virtues are *ren* 仁, which includes caring for others, and *yi* 義, which involves doing what is right. The exemplary person and the sage cultivate these virtues and embody the Way. That is why the ancient sage kings were able to be great leaders who brought peace and prosperity to the whole world.[53] This outlook does not reflect an instrumental view of morality; the emphasis laid on the cultivation of virtues makes it very close to virtue ethics, as discussed earlier.

It is true that Xunzi is taken by the accomplishment of the hegemon in practical statecraft. The hegemon is moral to the extent that he manifests trustworthiness (*xin*), which enables him to build an effective government and a strong military. But it is a limited morality nonetheless. Although better than vicious tyrants, the hegemon ranks below the fully virtuous sage king. He is inferior because he is not committed to moral cultivation of himself or those he rules. In contrast, the sage king is someone who not only strives for utmost virtue in himself, but also aims to teach his people and reform their bad natures through ritual practices.[54]

Xunzi's ethics seems to be first of all a kind of virtue ethics in its emphasis on moral cultivation and secondly a principles-based deontology in its reference to moral duties. Although Xunzi's discussions about enriching and strengthening the state are the most distinctive in the Confucian canon, he does not approach these subjects from an instrumental or consequentialist perspective. Wealth and power are not for him the moral good; the good consists in virtues and duties. Wealth and power will naturally accrue, so Xunzi believes, if the ruler possesses the relevant virtues and fulfils necessary duties, as is the case with trustworthiness. Xunzi's ethics describes a Confucian way to live in domestic society and conduct foreign relations in which virtues and duties are primary; wealth and power are important effects which he also values, but only of secondary moral significance. Yan's instrumental conception of morality has therefore diverged from Xunzi's original vision.

It is also narrow. Yan limits morality to governmental morality, judged by the extent to which policies serve national interests and national capability in accordance with accepted moral codes.[55] This seems to leave out the entire agenda of global justice, with which, one would think, a rising power like China ought to be concerned.[56] It is true that the first moral duty of a state's leadership is to ensure national security and the well-being of its citizens. But beyond this, moral concerns may be expanded towards the well-being of other countries and other peoples, especially those stuck in the dire straits of extreme poverty, injustice, and insecurity.

In fact, a moral theory truthful to Confucianism would not overlook concerns for people beyond one's immediate family and community, for the most important and distinctive Confucian concept is *ren* (仁 humaneness). *Ren* stands for a basic and universalizable aspect of human feelings manifested as 'love' or care for others. Kongzi says '*ren* is to *ai* (愛 love or care for) others'.⁵⁷ As noted, Confucian caring for others is potentially unlimited in scope. *Ren* is not confined to those personally known but can reach all people within the Four Seas, as Kongzi suggested.⁵⁸ The Neo-Confucians in the Song-Ming period (960–1644) expanded its scope further to encompass nature and Heaven.⁵⁹

It is true that Confucian ethics favours a graded concern for others and emphasizes that we should care for our family and friends above strangers. But that does not mean that strangers should be left to their own devices. Confucian sensibilities centred on the universal *ren* give the doctrine a global or cosmopolitan flavour. Mengzi says that humane persons 'extend from what they love to what they do not yet love'.⁶⁰ This suggests 'extension' (*tui* 推) as the mechanism for practising *ren* as universal affection. Although it is Mengzi who gives the concept of 'extension' prominence, the idea is already manifest in Kongzi, who has developed what might be called the Confucian Golden Rule consisting in both a negative and a positive principle. The negative principle says: 'Do not impose upon others what you yourself do not want'.⁶¹ The positive principle says: 'Humane persons establish others in seeking to establish themselves and promote others in seeking to get there themselves'.⁶² And further, 'Being able to take what is near at hand as an analogy could perhaps be called the method of humaneness'.⁶³

Both the negative and positive principles are known as *shu* 恕 (putting oneself in the other's place).⁶⁴ Together, they teach that humane persons identify themselves with the whole myriad things of the world and harmonize their desires with the desires of the world. They extend their affection from near to far through a continuous gradation, eventually making it permeate the whole world. By caring for others while trying to realize themselves, and by trying to achieve public interests in this way, humane persons overcome their personal desires without eliminating them.⁶⁵ *Shu* is not altruism since it starts with oneself, but it acquires an other-regarding generosity as it requires taking into consideration the interests of others.⁶⁶ It dissolves the self–other dichotomy and integrates personal interests with public interests in the building of a common humanity.

Advances in Western virtue ethics and care ethics over the past several decades offer a complementary perspective to this conception of Confucian ethics with graded but nevertheless global concerns. Michael Slote, for example, suggests basing morality in a motive like caring or humaneness. He distinguishes three levels of caring: self-concern (concern about one's own well-being), intimate caring (our concern for near and dear), and humanitarian caring (our concern for people in general).⁶⁷ I would suggest that the Confucian concepts of *ren* and *shu* already encompass these three levels of caring.

Going back to our earlier discussion about the four approaches to morality, I have just suggested that moral realism can expand its conception of morality in the direction of virtue ethics. It can also move along the path of role ethics. In role ethics, the self is defined in terms of social roles in different kinds of social relationships. What does this entail practically? A.T. Nuyen observes:

> To each role is attached a set of obligations, and to be in a role is to be under a set of obligations. Which obligations go with which role is determined by more or less explicit social expectations. For the key social roles, it is encoded in the rites, li 禮. To be in a social relationship, then, is to stand under certain obligations. What one ought to do and how one ought to behave in a certain relationship are all set out in *li*, or in social expectations. Thus, *li* describes both the factual and ethical.⁶⁸

Moral realism already contains the sprouts of a role ethical theory of foreign policy. For example, Yan distinguishes four types of state leadership (inactive, conservative, proactive, and aggressive) and four types of international leadership (humane authority, hegemony, tyranny, and anemocracy). Presumably, each of these types entails different kinds of foreign policy obligations and behaviours. He emphasizes the importance of practising international norms for humane authority, and good or morally desirable norms may be seen as the modern manifestation of the Confucian concept of *li*.⁶⁹ These thoughts, however, are not developed in as much depth as a role ethics approach would have preferred.

To a large extent moral realism may be seen as a kind of deontology, especially in its emphasis on principles of action. Its differentiation between principles of humane authority and those of hegemony and its emphasis on developing strategic credibility as perhaps the overriding foreign policy principle reflect a deontological approach. But deontology can run aground if principles are taken out of context or stretched to extremes. Hegel criticizes Kant for reducing morality to an empty formalism by pure reasoning.⁷⁰ Intriguingly, moral realism runs the risk of exaggerating and misconstruing the significance of credibility as a foreign policy principle. It is instructive to see how.

Yan's argument about strategic credibility is built on Xunzi's insight into trustworthiness. There is a certain fixation with credibility in strategic relations and consequently the importance of alliance building. Alliances, Yan says, can improve the comprehensive capability of a rising state such as China, enabling it to compete with and perhaps even dislodge the dominant state from its privileged position. And building alliances and providing security protection for allies is the main means by which a leading state establishes international strategic credibility. Yan provides a glowing comment on NATO expansion after the Cold War, contending that it helped the US to contain Russia and constrain China. By contrast, he portrays China's non-alignment principle in disparaging terms, blaming it for undermining the country's international credibility.[71]

Yan has long been a forceful – and rare – advocate of alliance policy in China, so his approbation of alliances is not surprising.[72] But his understanding of the theory and policy of alliances faces two serious difficulties. First, alliances need not be the only or even the main approach whereby a state establishes strategic credibility. The most fundamental way, as Xunzi recognizes, is to make good on one's word; in foreign policy, this means putting into practice policy announcements and professed intentions. Alliance should be seen as a special case of the general principle of *xin* understood as making good on one's word; what is special is that in an alliance, 'one's word' takes the concrete form of treaty commitments.

Second, Yan's appraisal of NATO expansion is misleading. Rather than serving to contain Russia, the US decision to expand NATO into central and Eastern Europe, areas deemed by Russia to be its traditional spheres of influence, aroused Russian enmity and provoked Putin's multifaceted challenges to the West, the most violent being the wars in Georgia (2008) and Ukraine (2014). The initial optimism about US–Russia relations in the immediate aftermath of the Cold War has turned into bitter disappointment and despair three decades later. NATO expansion, even though it is not the sole cause of this downward spiral, must be responsible for a big part of it. Many US scholars rightly suggest that if there is one thing the US can do to improve relations with Russia, it is the termination of further NATO expansion into Ukraine and Georgia.[73] Strategic credibility built up through alliances is no panacea for foreign policy success. While it may enhance solidarity among alliance partners, it could aggravate relations with non-allies, with adverse consequences for the alliance itself and the overall relationship between the alliance and its target countries. The point is not to abjure alliance in principle, but to understand the conditions of its workings.

Finally, the logic of consequences, understood as instrumental rationality, clearly informs moral realism, which is after all an approach of pressing morality into the service of protecting national interests and building national capabilities. Morality is conceived as an instrumental means of realizing the desired – and self-interested – consequences of interests and power. A moral consequentialist approach, as discussed earlier, would supersede the instrumentality of moral realism. It would suggest that the first task for a consequentialist theory of foreign policy is to discover and justify the moral good of foreign policy. This good cannot consist in power and interests alone. While in a narrow sense these may be moral goods for the state that benefits from them, they entail no morality for other states and actors that are affected by that state's action.

There are many candidates for moral goods in international relations which are faithful to moral consequentialism, such as common security, peace, and justice. The Chinese government's so-called 'community with a shared future for mankind' may count as one too, although that notion, so vague as it stands now, will need a great deal of fleshing out.[74] Another promising alternative is the traditional Chinese value of sufficiency, in contrast to the modern Chinese quests for wealth and power, which bear a heavy Western imprint.[75] Taking sufficiency as the moral good in foreign policy would be more faithful to the Chinese tradition. The scope for moral realism in the direction of consequentialism is broad too.

Summary

Between 'morality' and 'realism', the former is clearly the more distinctive feature of moral realism. Not only has Yan reintroduced morality to realist theorizing, in a manner that is complementary to the classical realist tradition of Western IR, but he has brought a refreshing moral perspective from ancient Chinese thought. There is, however, an uneasy tension between Yan's long-time loyalty to Western realism and the new inspirations he draws from the Chinese Confucian tradition. His realist commitments lead him to adopt an instrumental conception of morality, but such instrumentalism rides roughshod over the Confucian tradition. In particular, it is at odds with Xunzi's conception of morality upon which Yan has built his theory.

I have tried to situate the conception of morality in moral realism within four broad approaches to morality developed by Chinese and Western philosophers over the centuries: deontology, consequentialism, virtue ethics, and role ethics. Moral realism bears some resemblance to principles-based deontology, but its fixation with strategic credibility as a foreign policy principle faces theoretical and policy difficulties. Moral realism follows the logic of consequences understood as instrumental rationality, but this is a narrower approach than consequentialism in moral philosophy. A moral consequentialist theory of foreign policy would take its first task to be the discovery and justification of the moral good of foreign policy, which cannot consist in power and interests alone. Virtue ethics and role ethics reflect different aspects of Confucianism, and a moral realism developed in accordance with these approaches would have been the most faithful to the Chinese tradition. But they remain unexplored.

Perhaps a theory of moral realism, owing to its realist commitments, cannot but conceive of morality in instrumental terms.[76] If so, Yan cannot really be faulted, even though his instrumental conception of morality can be further developed. I have tried to show, however, that a broader conception of morality opens up a new and fascinating space for developing moral theories of international relations, realist or not. And there may be other ways of integrating morality and realism than Yan's moral realism. But for the discovery of these new theoretical avenues, we are all indebted to it in the first place.

Notes

1. Yan Xuetong, Daniel A. Bell, and Sun Zhe (eds), Edmund Ryden (trans), *Ancient Chinese Thought, Modern Chinese Power*, Princeton: Princeton University Press, 2011.
2. Feng Zhang, 'The Tsinghua Approach and the Inception of Chinese Theories of International Relations', *Chinese Journal of International Politics* 5, no. 1 (2012): 73–102.
3. Yan Xuetong, *Leadership and the Rise of Great Powers*, Princeton: Princeton University Press, 2019.
4. Robert Audi (ed), *The Cambridge Dictionary of Philosophy*, 3rd edition, Cambridge: Cambridge University Press, 2015, p 686.
5. Alan Donagan, *The Theory of Morality*, Chicago: University of Chicago Press, 1977, p 6.
6. Immanuel Kant, trans Mary Gregor and Jens Timmermann, *Groundwork of the Metaphysics of Morals*, Cambridge: Cambridge University Press, 2012, p 41.
7. Roger T. Ames and Henry Rosemont Jr (trans), *The Analects of Confucius: A Philosophical Translation*, New York: Ballantine, 1998, p 189.
8. Bryan W. Van Norden (trans), *Mengzi: With Selections from Traditional Commentaries*, Indianapolis: Hackett, 2008, p 111.
9. Robert Audi (ed), *The Cambridge Dictionary of Philosophy*, pp 201–2.
10. James G. March and Johan P. Olsen, 'The Institutional Dynamics of International Political Orders', *International Organization* 52, no. 4 (1998): 943–69, at 950.
11. David O. Brink, 'Some Forms and Limits of Consequentialism', in David Copp, (ed), *The Oxford Handbook of Ethical Theory*, Oxford: Oxford University Press, 2007, pp 380–423.
12. Ian Johnston, *The Mozi: A Complete Translation*, Hong Kong: The Chinese University Press, 2010, p 381.
13. Ibid., p 183.
14. Huang Weihe, 'Mozi de yiliguan' (Mozi's View on Justice and Benefit), *Zhongguo Shehui Kexue* (Chinese Social Sciences) 3 (1985): 115–24, at 117.
15. Chris Fraser, 'Major Rival Schools: Mohism and Legalism', in William Edelglass and Jay L. Garfield (eds), *The Oxford Handbook of World Philosophy*, Oxford: Oxford University Press, 2011, pp 58–67, at p 62.
16. Ian Johnston, *The Mozi*, p 147 (emphasis added).
17. Chen Qiyou, *Han Fei Zi xin jiaozhu* (New Exegeses of the *Han Fei Zi*), Shanghai: Shanghai guji chubanshe, 2000, p 893.
18. Ibid., pp 683–4.
19. Huang Weihe, 'Mozi de yiliguan': 120.
20. Julia Annas, 'Virtue Ethics', in David Copp (ed), *The Oxford Handbook of Ethical Theory*, pp 515–36, at p 516.
21. Ibid., p 517.
22. Ibid., p 533.
23. Michael Slote, *Morals from Motives*, Oxford: Oxford University Press, 2001, Kindle version, location 2140.
24. Philip J. Ivanhoe, 'Virtue Ethics and the Chinese Confucian Tradition', in Daniel C. Russell (ed), *The Cambridge Companion to Virtue Ethics*, Cambridge: Cambridge University Press, 2013, pp 49–69.

25 Joseph Chan, *Confucian Perfectionism: A Political Philosophy for Modern Times*, Princeton: Princeton University Press, 2013, p 117.
26 Richard Ned Lebow, *The Tragic Vision of Politics: Ethics, Interests and Orders*, Cambridge: Cambridge University Press, 2003; Richard Ned Lebow, *A Cultural Theory of International Relations*, Cambridge: Cambridge University Press, 2008.
27 Roger T. Ames, *Confucian Role Ethics: A Vocabulary*, Honolulu: University of Hawai'i Press, 2011, p 73.
28 Henry Rosemont Jr, *Against Individualism: A Confucian Rethinking of the Foundations of Morality, Politics, Family, and Religion*, Lanham: Lexington, 2015.
29 Roger T. Ames, *Confucian Role Ethics*, p 258.
30 Ibid., p 112.
31 Yan Xuetong, *Ancient Chinese Thought, Modern Chinese Power*, p 91.
32 Eric L. Hutton (trans), *Xunzi: The Complete Text*, Princeton: Princeton University Press, 2014, p 346.
33 I have used Hutton's translation in Eric L. Hutton, *Xunzi*, p 100. The translation in Yan's book, *Ancient Chinese Thought, Modern Chinese Power*, pp 86–7, is confusing and misleading in that *yi* is translated as both justice and norm in the same passage.
34 Eric L. Hutton, *Xunzi*, pp 99–100.
35 See the Chinese original in Yan Xuetong and Xu Jin, *Wangba Tianxia sixiang ji qidi* (Thoughts of World Leadership and Implications), Beijing: shijie zhishi chubanshe, 2009, p 144.
36 Eric L. Hutton, *Xunzi*, pp 100–1.
37 Roger T. Ames, *Confucian Role Ethics*, p 127.
38 Ibid., p 206.
39 Yan Xuetong, *Leadership and the Rise of Great Powers*, p 19.
40 Ibid., p 43.
41 Ibid.
42 Ibid., p 44.
43 Jon Elster, *The Cement of Society: A Study of Social Order*, Cambridge: Cambridge University Press, 1989, p 272.
44 Ibid., p 273.
45 See Feng Zhang and Richard Ned Lebow, *Taming Sino–American Rivalry*, Oxford: Oxford University Press, 2020.
46 Yan Xuetong, *Leadership and the Rise of Great Powers*, p 8.
47 Ibid., p 9.
48 Ibid., p 7.
49 Ibid., pp 6–7.
50 Ibid., p 19.
51 Joseph S. Nye Jr, *Do Morals Matter? Presidents and Foreign Policy from FDR to Trump*, New York: Oxford University Press, 2020.
52 Hans J. Morgenthau, *Politics among Nations: The Struggle for Power and Peace*, New York: Alfred Knopf, 1948; Richard Ned Lebow, *The Tragic Vision of Politics*.
53 Eric L. Hutton, *Xunzi*, p xxiv.
54 Ibid., p xxviii.
55 Yan Xuetong, *Leadership and the Rise of Great Powers*, p 8.
56 For recent works on global justice, see, for example, Gillian Brock, *Global Justice: A Cosmopolitan Account*, Oxford: Oxford University Press, 2009; Mathias Risse, *On Global Justice*, Princeton: Princeton University Press, 2012.
57 Roger T. Ames and Henry Rosemont Jr, *The Analects of Confucius*, p 159.
58 Ibid., p 154.
59 Joseph Chan, *Confucian Perfectionism*, p 118.

60 Bryan W. Van Norden, *Mengzi*, p 185.
61 Roger T. Ames and Henry Rosemont Jr, *The Analects of Confucius*, p 153.
62 Ibid., p 110.
63 Ibid.
64 Ibid., p 195.
65 Huang Huaixin, *Lunyu huijiao jishi* (Corrections and Exegeses of the Analects of Confucius), Shanghai: Shanghai guji chubanshe, 2008, pp 552–3.
66 Roger T. Ames, *Confucian Role Ethics*, p 195.
67 Michael Slote, *Morals from Motives*, location 1524.
68 Nuyen, 'Moral Obligation and Moral Motivation in Confucian Role-Based Ethics', Dao (2009) 8: 1–11.
69 Yan Xuetong, *Leadership and the Rise of Great Powers*, Chapter 2.
70 Alan Donagan, *The Theory of Morality*, pp 9–12.
71 Ibid., p 41.
72 Feng Zhang, 'China's New Thinking on Alliances', *Survival* 54, no. 5 (2012): 129–48.
73 Jeffrey D. Sachs, *A New Foreign Policy: Beyond American Exceptionalism*, New York: Columbia University Press, 2018, Chapter 5.
74 Feng Zhang, 'The Xi Jinping Doctrine of China's International Relations', *Asia Policy* 14, no. 3 (2019): 7–23.
75 Qian Mu, *Zhongguo Wenhuashi Daolun* (An Introduction to the History of Chinese Culture), Beijing: Commercial Press, 1994.
76 For such an argument, see Jannika Brostrom, 'Morality and the National Interest: Towards a "Moral Realist" Research Agenda', *Cambridge Review of International Affairs* 29, no. 4 (2015): 1624–39.

7

Moral Realism and Hegemonic Transition

Athanasios Platias and Vasilis Trigkas

Croesus, the king of the Lydian Empire, was quite euphoric after he had received the Delphic Oracles' response about how to deal with the rising menace of the Persian Empire. If Croesus goes to war, Pythia said, then he will destroy a great empire. Yet, what the oracle did not clarify was the name of the empire that was to be destroyed. Ignoring the wise counsel of his advisors on the ambiguity of the Delphic prophesy and the inherent risk in war, wishful Croesus jumped into conclusions. He imagined that his own Lydian empire would be the victorious one in a war against the rising Persian Empire of Cyrus the Great. It did not turn out that way: Croesus was crushed, his own empire annexed. Herodotus, the first of the great Greek historians, attributed to the successful leadership of Cyrus and the failed leadership of Croesus the hegemonic shift from the Lydian to the Persian Empire in the Eastern Mediterranean. Herodotus further submitted that, he recorded the histories of both *small states* and *great states*, for 'many states that were once great have now become small; and those that were great in my time were small before'.[1] In a similar spirit, Guan Zhong (管仲), the prime minister to Duke Huan of Qi, declared that 'if a state is huge but the achievements of its government are insignificant, the state will become insignificant. If a state is small but the achievements of its government are significant, the state will become significant'.[2] Stories from early antiquity must always be read with a grain of salt, yet history abounds with statesmen making fateful strategic decisions.

The moderns, however, particularly those of the triumphant post-Cold War era, have opted to conform to a rather algorithmic view about national success. There is to them a perfect polity – a software of governance – which if it was to be downloaded and installed, national success would automatically ensue. Indeed, by 1991, scholars and politicians alike ascribed to a triumphal school of thought prophesizing the end of history built on the socioeconomic software that the great victor of the Cold War, the US, had provided.[3] The rest of the world would have to conform to the institutional ethos that America set if it was to develop economically or otherwise risk stagnation and entrapment into perennial poverty.[4] Even China, the world's most populous nation and an ancient civilization, could not avoid the destiny of Americanization as it liberalized its statist economy.[5]

Yet, China has defied much of the assumptions of modernization theory – which sees liberal democracy as an inescapable outcome of development and then as a normative prerequisite spurring innovation and taking a developing country into high-income territory.[6] Wealth and economic liberalization have not delivered electoral democracy as liberal intellectuals once prophesized. Some have attempted to explain this puzzle of China's unexpected success by undertaking elaborate studies of its allegedly distinctive domestic governance: democratic centralism with its experimentalization and mass mobilization. This constitutes another institutional argument. While it justifies why a one-size-fits-all polity is not panacea, it doesn't explain how these *sui generis* Chinese institutions came to be in the first place, let alone performed so diversely as senior leadership changed over time.[7] Yan Xuetong's latest opus is an effort to respond to that very question by bringing leadership and statesmanship back into the strategic equation. To him, political leadership that is able to *initiate and implement domestic reforms* may *improve a state's power* and eventually *reshape the very configuration of the international system*. Yan introduces a political theory of hegemonic transition, though, mostly based on the perspective of the rising power. The very political nature of that theory which has clashed with the materialist theoretical orthodoxy of the post-Cold War era has inspired an intense debate about the right metrics of national power, the causal process of hegemonic transition, and the ultimate potential of China to lead internationally without becoming a liberal democracy on America's image.

In this chapter, we first review Yan's theory of leadership as it applies to established international relations (IR) theories of hegemonic transition and current views about power differentials between China and the US.[8] Although Yan authoritatively argues that leadership can dominate systemic pressures, recent empirical evidence demonstrates that the way China and the US adapt to an era of great power competition is severely conditioned by the structural dimension. Still, leadership remains a pivotal variable, yet complexity among different *levels of analysis* (agent, state, system) is hard to systematically demarcate. Second, we further elaborate upon how a theory of hegemonic transition, built upon political leadership, could be refined within a neoclassical realist framework where structural imperatives condition and delimit strategic action. Third, we approach Yan's theory from a classical perspective. Although Yan mostly draws from the Chinese classical corpus of strategy to build his theory, his eloquence in modern IR allows him to transcend culture-specific contexts. Similarly, we draw from the rich classical tradition of Greece to highlight what we believe to be parallel concepts to Yan's core ideas on 'moral realism' and 'strategic credibility'. These parallels help us sketch out teachable behaviour (virtues) that may guide leaders and influence strategic outcomes. Developed independently into two heterogenous interstate systems (the Sinic and the Hellenic), these crucial virtues (again, strategic principles that leaders can follow) have an air of universality capable of both inspiring and educating strategic elites in pursuit of the enlightened national interest. We conclude by extrapolating the theory of moral realism to the future of Sino–US strategic competition.

Hegemonic transition and political reform

Two broad categories have emerged in the literature on the rise of China: the material determinists and the political determinists. The material determinists (structuralists) argue that it is only natural for technology to diffuse in the global interstate system as underdeveloped states copy and adopt the best methods and practices.[9] As the law of diminishing returns kicks in, poorer underdeveloped nations, and in the first place China, will grow faster than rich developed nations.[10] As Robert Gilpin put it,

> the economic techniques of the dominant state or empire are diffused to other states in the system or, more especially, to states on the periphery of the international system in question. That is to say, through a process of diffusion to other states, the dominant power loses the advantage on which its political, military, or economic success has been based. Thus, by example, and frequently in more direct fashion, the dominant power helps to create challenging powers.[11]

The modernization theorists then take over and argue that, eventually, as a society becomes richer, a middle class will not accept taxation without representation.[12] Economic growth will bring electoral democracy and electoral democracy will consequently spur a higher level of innovation due to the creativity of free individuals.[13] For modernization theorists[14] national success is apolitical as economic freedom drives political change.[15] 'Increase [in wealth] is thus natural and will occur wherever opportunity and security exist. Remove the obstacles, and growth will take care of itself.'[16] Convergence is concrete.[17]

The political determinists, on the other hand, have framed political ideas and leadership as the fundaments of China's unprecedented rise in wealth and power. Technology may indeed diffuse from leading states to laggards, yet the speed of technological evolution is such that only states with an advanced political domestic order – able to undertake appropriate reforms – will catch up and, most importantly, out-innovate established champions. In the words of a renowned theorist, 'Because of competition and changes in technology each entrant into the "industrialization race" faces a new game, with altered rules'.[18] Reform, adaptation, and political innovation to competently play that ever-changing game are therefore essential national qualities for economic success.[19] 'Convergence is conditional': power shifts are ultimately political phenomena anchored on domestic reform.[20] Yan Xuetong's treatise on *Leadership and the Rise of Great Powers* fits squarely in this category.

Yan has long stressed the prevalence of political variables over material variables in evaluating composite national strength.[21] In constructing his topical theory of 'moral realism', he explicitly uses political leadership (political capability) as the operational element supercharging the resource elements of national strength (military and economy). If political leadership endorses and implements appropriate reforms, then, over time, the very structure of the international system may change.[22] As Perry Anderson has observed, the core of Yan's theory is that 'the basic cause of shifts in international power lies in the thought of leaders rather than in material force'.[23] Anderson criticized this view, affiliating it with a dangerous Maoist dictatorial perspective. However, Yan's prioritization of leadership is not based on a rigid ideological world view imposed by an omnipotent monocracy but is, rather, pragmatically flexible; for he defines political leadership as the capacity of *political elites* to collectively reform towards the right direction. Reform, in Yan's words, is 'both a descriptive term and prescriptive one; it embraces a moral dimension and is antithetical to retrogression'.[24] This perhaps echoes the classic argument made by Arnold Toynbee, who saw the ability of 'creative minorities' – as he framed the political elites – to respond successfully to strategic challenges as being catalytic for a state's survival and progress.[25] Thus, as Yan puts it, 'the leadership capability of different states can never be the same, which explains the law of differential growth in states' national capability'.[26]

This is an important insight into the modern theory of hegemonic transition.[27] While Kenneth Waltz sees the balance of power as naturally (re)occurring,[28] A.F.K. Organski explains hegemonic transition by the diffusion of industrialization,[29] George Modelski sees deterministic periodical cycles of power (driven by core economic sectors and naval power),[30] and Robert Gilpin, like Paul Kennedy, explains hegemonic transition by the mistakes of the established hegemonic powers (imperial overstretch compounded by diminishing economic returns, increased social spending, and adverse demographic trends), Yan frames hegemonic transition as a *dyadic differential of leadership* between the rising state and the ruling state.[31]

It is changes in national power from within caused by *superior leadership* that ultimately drive changes in the relations between states.[32] Ultimately, this dyadic differential of leadership between established and rising hegemon is the cause of systemic effect (changing polarity of the international system).[33]

To be sure, Yan's argument that China has in recent decades outperformed the US in its direction of reform is not agonistic but rather agnostic when it comes to the merits of a liberal democratic polity.[34] Yan is non-ideological and thus remains sceptical of a one-size-fits-all institutional approach, echoing Philip Kuhn's view that 'nobody knows just what the appropriate polity format may be for governing a nation state with more than one billion inhabitants. Until very recently it had never been tried'.[35] Different national conditions may therefore demand different institutions which adept leadership must often establish *ex novo*.[36] Hence, Yan's declaration that the quality of leadership (understood as a capacity to undertake reform and address challenges) may not be affected by the type of polity serves as a genuine scientific hypothesis.[37]

Yan's theory on leadership and hegemonic transition clashes directly with the established view in the American academy which usually prioritizes the fundamental impact of the polity factor on leadership. Michael Beckley's recent work evaluating power dynamics between China and the US serves as the most comprehensive counter-argument to Yan's insights on hegemonic transition. Beckley argues that China will not surpass the US in the coming decades because America has solid material advantages and, most importantly, *accountable political institutions* which China clearly lacks. Where Yan is agnostic, Beckley seems categorical. In his interdisciplinary study, *Unrivaled: Why America Will Remain the Sole Superpower*, Beckley attempts to debunk established narratives on US decline and rightfully argues that America enjoys a much superior resource base compared with China, that is, healthier demographics, abundant natural resources, unmatched geographic conditions, a more advanced economic ecosystem, and a far superior military. Most importantly, Beckley argues confidently that the US's democratic capitalism because of its intrinsic qualities – open deliberation, the wisdom of the crowds, the rule of law, and the separation of powers – constitutes a superior polity compared with China's.[38] The American polity, according to Beckley, has *high governance capacity* (defined as per capita tax revenues) and a *high degree of accountability* which constrains the governing elites from arbitrary action.[39] Hence, Beckley sees in American democracy an automatic deterministic ability for self-correction able to cure domestic pathologies and ultimately reinvent the US's international authority.[40] Beckley also provides normative prescriptions: in the case of the detrimental influence of big wealth in politics, super-PACs must be outlawed. In the case of imperial overstretch and unnecessary wars, a war tax should be the fiscal norm rather than deficit spending – a 'war credit card' as he put it – so that the public clearly understands the monetary cost of war and thus is fully engaged in the decision-making process.

Yet, these therapeutic reforms were not achieved when the American society was less polarized, and the Supreme Court of the US less ideologically charged. The Citizens United case – crucial for the influence of big money in politics – was tried in 2011 when the court's memberships were less biased than recently after the Trump administration decisively tilted the balance to the right with three appointees.[41] Moreover, political violence in America has been on the rise and the 2021 storming of the US's capital offers ominous signs. Amid an unprecedented political predicament, the structural domestic reform required by Beckley seems difficult to accomplish.[42] As Yan puts it, addressing the inability of a dominant state to reform, 'the dominant state has weaker motivation than rising states to pursue reforms, because its advanced position engenders pride in its political and social institutions rather than an eager desire to reform them'.[43] To be sure, this argument looks similar to Robert Gilpin's views about established hegemons and has a clear structural explanation: the position of a state in the international system affects propensity of reform.

International politics and alliances

Domestic socioeconomic success based on solid reformist leadership is a springboard for material power, but how can reinvigorated national strength be utilized to support a country's international legitimacy and optimize the 'durability of a country's leading global position'?[44] Both Yan and Beckley agree that alliances matter in pursuing that goal.[45] Alliances for Yan are at the core of what he calls 'strategic credibility'.[46] Strategic credibility is built by winning the *good will* of other lesser states and it acts as an *operational element* on national power. A state which provides security to states that lack it and follows fair diplomatic rituals can expand its international authority and thus build legitimacy as it competes with the ruling state. Simply put, a state with higher strategic credibility can do 'more with less' on the international chessboard, thus economizing precious national resources. Consequently, an aspiring great power with high strategic credibility could shape an international environment supportive of its rise and sustained primacy.[47] But is China close to following Yan's advice and upgrading its strategic credibility by extending alliance commitments?

China's strategy of alliances

Yan's repeated calls for China to abandon its non-alliance doctrine have not been seconded by the Chinese leadership that rejected his calls for a fully fledged security treaty with Russia back in 2015.[48] Beckley accurately points out China's prolonged strategic solitude. He asserts that a key understanding in structural realism is that during unipolarity, secondary powers tend to create a balancing coalition to counter the menacing superpower. However, there has not been any balancing coalition against the US, and China is in fact encircled by US security partners and allies.[49] If the US continues to manage its alliances astutely and thus preserve its strategic credibility, Beckley posits, then no counterbalancing coalition could be formed in the coming years; the international balance of power would remain heavily tilted towards the US.[50] Furthermore, with India and Vietnam to its west and the south-west, Japan to its east and Indonesia to its south, and Australia lurking from the back, a balancing coalition out-matching China may soon be formed. American strategists have often debated an Asiatic version of NATO and formations such as the democratic quadrilateral could be steps towards its realization.[51]

Yan remains strategically optimistic that such a catastrophic scenario for China will not materialize. He sees a strategic opportunity for China, pointing out the US's domestic divisions and the mercurial foreign policy of former President Donald Trump which has created fear for inconsistent, long-term security guarantees by the US (Biden will not be president for life) and US political uncertainty remains a factor for the allied states.[52] US retrenchment on some fronts (institutions and development) and unnecessary zeal on other fronts (Eastern Europe) have created 'a global leadership vacuum for China to fill and undermine American strategic relations with allies'.[53] Political leadership was essential in building the transatlantic alliance and the hubs-and-spoke system in the Pacific Ocean. Trump's years have already undercut the US's strategic credibility, while the euphoria of a 'united West' in Europe may not survive the next political cycle.[54] As America's long-term strategic credibility declines, Asian states may prefer to *bandwagon with China* as Canada and Mexico did to America during the late 19th century when European powers were unable to offer any credible support as they were absorbed in their local hegemonic wars.[55]

Can China really have such an auspicious strategic opportunity in its periphery which Xi Jinping himself upgraded as a core region for Chinese strategic attention?[56] It seems that even if US strategic credibility was to incurably falter, certain big states near China – Japan, India, Australia, and Indonesia come to mind – seem unlikely to bandwagon. Because these states are sufficiently capable to develop significant deterrence capabilities (India has nuclear weapons, Japan can promptly acquire them, and Australia and Indonesia could eventually develop them too), China will find it hard to attract them into its own security orbit. Moreover, these countries could coordinate their own regional security policies and form a counterbalancing coalition against China.[57] Chinese behaviour could affect threat perceptions in those countries, but it would be hard to fully neutralize the impact of proximity.[58]

When it comes to small states or states sufficiently removed from China's near periphery (certain ASEAN, Central Asian, African, or Middle Eastern states) that may be indeed tempted to join alliances with China, then, solitary China would have to first abandon its non-alignment doctrine and perhaps resolve its maritime disputes with neighbours in the South China Sea. Here, Yan becomes analytically eclectic: he puts realism aside and draws from constructivism to argue that Chinese millennials – the next generation of governing elites – will have the moral and epistemological qualities required to provide humane authority and revise China's outdated non-alliance doctrine due to their solid training in both modern science and the Chinese classics.[59] But Chinese millennials are as well versed in humanities and science as they are in the nationalist curriculum of the 'patriotic education' campaign.[60] Which ideas will prevail in shaping their worldview? Strategic cosmopolitanism or the nationalization of opinion?[61] Recent trends in Chinese public opinion point towards the latter.[62]

Projecting the theory on the domestic front

Observing the current US administration's policies and their impact on the US's national strength, Yan makes another crucial point: China's rise is a relative concept. China, since the days of Deng Xiaoping, has indeed reformed in the correct direction, yet the US has digressed, and it is US digression *perhaps more* than China's progression that has led to an accelerated narrowing of the power gap between the two nations in recent years. From the war of choice in Iraq, to the long war in Afghanistan, to the ongoing meddlesomeness in the Middle East, to the 2008 Great Recession, to the inability of American political elites to provide affordable healthcare to the citizens of the richest nation in the world.

Yet, if America's gross inequalities and extreme partisanship have undermined the country's international standing, then recent signals coming from Beijing are worrisome for the direction of reform in China. The post-Mao era of tacit agreement among CPC elites that leadership is shared (democratic centralism) has been sidelined. Every dissent within the party has been silenced as Chinese president Xi Jinping has acquired complete power, surpassing even Deng Xiaoping.[63] The pendulum seems to be moving back to a 'great helmsman' governance model.[64] Will that return to a unitary model of leadership and a more intrusive ideological drive affect China's power?[65] It would not be far-fetched to support that China's spectacular recent accomplishments in innovation may be the culmination occurring after a period of strategic openness inspired by Deng Xiaoping's visionary and reformist leadership, an outburst of incremental innovation following the catastrophes of the great leap forward and the Cultural Revolution. As China is closing down, suspending academics and attacking 'Western values' as ideological opium, the backlog of ideas and initiatives could be depleted, innovation may eventually stumble, and convergence with the US may pause or at least decelerate substantially.[66] While it remains unclear if the Chinese polity by and of itself constitutes a natural drag to Chinese economic efficiency and international standing, what is clear is that it failed to prevent the rise of a new strongman while the American polity survived a president-incited insurrection by racial supremacists (a severe stress test that few political systems can pass only with a bloody nose).[67] Power transition from a Republican to a Democratic administration in the US was ultimately accomplished efficiently. The crucial challenge for China will be the post-Xi transition as the lack of a separation of powers can well precipitate a crisis of succession – an endemic phenomenon in non-republican polities.

Advances in the theory of international politics?

The aforementioned puzzle on the interplay between leadership and domestic political structures (separation of powers and institutions) and to a wider extent with systemic structural stimuli has inspired a major and perhaps endless theoretical debate in IR concerning the so-called 'level of analysis'.[68] From the three levels of analysis: system, state, and agent, Yan's theory prioritizes leadership and therefore abides to an *agent-based ontology*.[69] It then goes to great lengths to demonstrate how state behaviour (fully determined by leadership) reshuffles global power (structural change) and ultimately creates international norms and institutions. Clearly, for Yan *leadership dominates* other *domestic level variables* across the board and over time changes the international configuration of power (a system's polarity).[70]

The problem, however, with theories that purely focus on unit-level variables is that they attempt to explain systemic changes – the rise of a new power – which cannot be explained without resource to system-level factors. The extraordinary lucidity and parsimony of structural realism are that the position of a state in the international system affects its character more than its character affects the international system. As Kenneth Waltz put it, national ends change based on relative strength.[71] The explicit assumption in Yan that a state is rising because it is exercising 'moral realism' (progressive domestic reform and the pursuit of strategic credibility abroad) seems to be an 'algorithmic account' about grand strategy formation built on utilitarian morality by a state's idiosyncratic political leadership.[72] It does not take into full consideration the fundamental impact of structure on either incentivizing or hindering political reform in the first place. In fact, as John Mearsheimer argued, America's unrivalled primacy took the nation on 'a holiday from realism' and allowed idealist and liberal elites to hijack US foreign policy.[73] As Joseph Nye put it, 'America's "Unipolar Moment" of unbalanced power raised the risk of hubris'.[74] Hence, could the rise of China and the fear that it has inspired in America facilitate progressive socioeconomic reform in Washington?[75] Could China's recent techno-industrial success stimulate a new industrial policy in America that mobilizes the formidable US scientific community to pursue new moonshots?[76] On the external front, will the US foreign policy establishment be able to neutralize Trumpism and reinvigorate its alliance system to counterbalance China? Unlike anything else, the China threat now 'cuts across the political divide', uniting legislators as far apart ideologically as Ted Cruz is from Elizabeth Warren and Nancy Pelosi.[77] Consequently, the US Congress sensitized to structural pressure seems to act in a bipartisan manner on China-related legislation and supports presidential initiatives that target China. Competitive pressure may not determine but it does 'shape and shove' political behaviour.[78]

Indeed, as early Biden initiatives demonstrate, the US has begun to reform its domestic economy by increasing the role of the state (endless frontier act, chips act, infrastructure plan, supply chain resilience and reshoring) and using the 'China threat' as a political conciliator to end politics at the water's edge. China features prominently as a 'clear and present danger' in almost every major speech of President Biden who seeks to underscore why US domestic reform is essential for balancing China.[79] Biden as president today supports legislative projects that he opposed or was indifferent to as senator and vice president during America's unipolar era (industrial plans, financial reform, economic protectionism, disengagement from the Middle East, and so on).[80]

This surprising bipartisanship on China and the US's subsequent competitive mobilization begs the question of the fundamental impact of structural pressure (the third image) on grand strategy. Kenneth Waltz himself submitted that 'the vice to which great powers easily succumb in a multipolar world is inattention; in a bipolar world, overreaction; in a unipolar world, overextension'.[81] In that particular statement, Waltz seems to contradict his older argument that a theory of international politics should be categorically demarcated from a theory of foreign policy as he himself makes generalizations on foreign policy with *polarity* alone driving strategic behaviour: inattention, overreaction, overextension.[82] In fact, a relatively younger school of realism, that of 'neoclassical realism', has offered a potential solution to the exhaustive debate about the levels of analysis.[83] Neoclassical realists support that under a permissive structural environment (US unipolarity), domestic unit variables tend to dominate a state's strategic decisions.[84] Hence, when the US was unchallenged, it had a margin of safety to pursue wars of choice in the Middle East, support utopian ideological projects (democratization and state building abroad), and let powerful financiers highjack the domestic economic agenda and de-industrialize the nation.[85] On the other hand, a more restrictive international environment 'restricts' the impact of unit-level variables on grand strategy. The distinction between permissive and restrictive strategic environments, as neoclassical realists put it, 'relates to the imminence and the magnitude of threats and opportunities that states face'.[86] That does not mean that governing elites are unable to shape strategy but that the available set of strategic options narrows significantly when the structural pressure intensifies.

To be sure, neoclassical realism – as with its historical predecessor classical realism – constitutes a 'complex theory' and thus it is a much less parsimonious school of thought compared with a purely neorealist one.[87] Yet, as a scholar has put it,

> In order to achieve balance between the parsimony of a spare theory and greater descriptive accuracy, a first-cut theory can be layered successively with additional causes from different levels of analysis focusing on domestic regime types, bureaucracies, and statesmen. 'The larger the domain of a theory, the less accuracy we expect. ... The domain of theory is narrowed to achieve greater precision. Thus, the debate between advocates of parsimony and proponents of contextual subtle solves itself into a question of stages, rather than either-or choices. We should seek parsimony first, then add on complexity while monitoring the adverse effects this has on the predictive power of our theory: its ability to make significant inferences on the basis of limited information.'[88]

Thus, in neoclassical realism, the *system serves as a first cut* which affects the strength of domestic-level intermediary variables. This methodological inclusiveness is therefore fully justified to deal with the complexity of strategic action.[89]

Yan's theory clearly diverges from Waltz's structuralism, yet could it really be mapped into the neoclassical realist school? Yan states that leadership is clearly an independent variable.[90] If this is indeed the case, then the theory would fall completely outside the research paradigm of neoclassical realism and could even be framed as the polar opposite of Waltz's system-based ontology.[91] Instead of leadership as an independent variable, we believe that leadership as an intermediary variable (though allowing for a stronger effect of the first image on strategic choice across the board) would anchor the theory solidly in a neoclassical realist perspective and address complexity. This would consequently offer a more pluralistic future research agenda on moral realism and strategy, and avoid the perplexing debate built around Thomas Carlyle's great man theory.

In fact, if leadership is treated as an intermediate variable, then it would be theoretically fulfilling to frame the conditions under which leadership has a higher probability to drastically influence 'state power' by reforming domestic institutions and ultimately affect not only short-term crisis decision making but, most importantly, long-term grand strategic formation.[92] For instance, neoclassical realists argue that the impact of a leader tends to become more fundamental during an acute international crisis but as the time frame expands, it is harder to demarcate the impact of leadership from that of strategic culture, domestic institutions, society-elites relations, ideology, path dependence, and so on.[93] Overall, as neoclassical realists have put it, 'Given the causal primacy of systemic (material) variables, under what conditions are collective ideational variables at the unit level more likely to play an intervening role between systemic pressures, on the one hand, and the specific foreign and security strategies states pursue at a given time'.[94] What is crucial here is to investigate under what context the strategic elites can set the ultimate intentions of a state and consequently shape grand strategy effectively.[95] Lastly, it would be interesting to explore the impact of institutional arrangements on filtering leadership selection.[96]

To address these questions, a plethora of historical case studies investigated under a cautious counterfactual analysis would be methodologically promising.[97] Then and perhaps crucially for a general theory of leadership the *fundamental virtues* that are conducive to *strategic success* must be clearly recognized and framed. By virtues here we do not mean inherent character traits (nature) but rather teachable principles (nurture) about the conduct of leadership that may affect outcomes.[98] One may consider which teachable virtues are essential so that foreign policy elites avoid delusional mentalities and Napoleonian syndromes (propensity for grandeur) and other cognitive fallacies that may impair the formation and implementation of a successful grand strategy.[99] Interdisciplinarity with political psychology,[100] history, and philosophy will be essential for that research programme.[101] To be sure, such a research programme requires a much higher degree of complexity compared with structural realism and necessitates a methodological approach which can incorporate unit-level variables (leadership) in a *non-ad hoc* manner so that it can ultimately produce a generalizable, leadership-centric theory of hegemonic transition. Still, though, even in its current version, Yan's theory of moral realism constitutes an ambitious grand theory which can singularly assist future 'empirical research by generating important theoretical questions in the first place and then develop hypotheses that are worth testing'.[102] But the modern neoclassical realist path is not the sole path forward; classical realism could also be a promising research route. We explore this dimension in the next section.

Leadership, strategic credibility, and the classical dimension of grand strategy

It is a usual characteristic of political scientists (and perhaps of most social scientists) to stress the impeccable novelty of their theories and attempt to frame previous works as parochial. With the advent of neorealism, the tendency of neorealist scholars to frame classical realism as theoretically vacant and thus unable to increase our understanding of political phenomena has become omnipresent.[103] Neoclassical realism has attempted to respond to that perceived disadvantage and add theoretical rigour to classical realism, yet we believe that classical realism in and of itself can also be useful to further substantiate a leadership-centric theory of hegemonic transition. After all, as two learned authors have put it, 'It would be a grave loss to demean classical realists as markedly inferior because they did not have the foresight to practice political science in the present fashion. ... We ought to be wary of overdrawing the differences between the ancients and the moderns in a fit of temporal parochialism, estranging ourselves from kindred spirits and inspirational insights'.[104]

We believe that the kindred spirits of the Ancients studied in *ex antiquis et novissimis optima* offer another promising research path for Yan's theory.[105] Yan has himself paved this potential research path. He has declared, for instance, that 'Ancient Chinese thinkers shared the view that power shifts between states result from changes in the rulers of major states', and that 'this approach is not uniquely Chinese. In fact, we can find similar analysis in both ancient and modern Western political writings'. As he further argued in his comparative study of Xunzi and Kautilya's strategic thoughts, 'since Xunzi and Kautilya were unaware of each other's thoughts at the time, their similar thoughts reflect a cross-cultural understanding of inter-state politics. This kind of co-variance occurred in the Axial Age (about the eighth to the third century BCE) which implies an understanding of objective laws of human society'.[106]

Indeed, this type of comparative inter-civilizational study could be seen as a powerful natural experiment applied not only to the Sino-Hindu but also to the Sino-Hellenic interstate system. The evolution of ideas about strategy and statecraft in China occurred independently of the respective evolution of ideas about strategy and statecraft in Greece; after all, the two interstate systems were at the very least until the third century BCE completely insulated from one another. Simply put, hegemonic transitions in the Hellenic system and the Pre-Qin Chinese system took place independently. Thus, we pose the following question: is there any similarity in the concept of moral realism as it is developed by Yan Xuetong, who utilized the Chinese classical corpus as the intellectual understructure of his theory, with similar concepts found in the Greek classics? That is to ask, how consequential was *political leadership* anchored in *utilitarian morality* as an explanatory variable for the rise and success of states in the works of influential classical Greek authors?[107] If there is indeed, as we argue, a similar argument concerning strategy as a quintessential function of leadership that is to be found in the Greek classics, then it would follow that a universal canon of strategy that prioritizes political leadership could possibly exist.[108] In other words, a theory of rise and national success based on political leadership transcends geography and culture. From this conclusion follows the insight that 'there is an essential unity to all strategic experience in all periods of history because nothing vital to the nature and function of war and strategy changes'.[109] To be sure, changing conditions (for example, new technologies or new forms of organization such as the invention of the modern nation state) may lead to corresponding changes in tactics, which in turn may influence strategy. Yet, grand strategy (the very logic of interstate conflict), military strategy (the nature of war), operational art (generalship), and, most importantly, the *art of leadership*, which is the great multiplier, are timeless in character.[110]

Of all the authors of classical antiquity, Thucydides holds the prime position in political realism.[111] Thucydides was indeed the first classical author in Greece who stressed the impact of the structure of the international system as fundamental to the intensity of interstate competition. Thucydides, however, attributed the ultimate defeat of Athens to the degeneration of Athenian leadership which failed to understand the role of consequentialist morality in foreign relations and also defied systemic limitations by following an imprudent strategy that overextended Athenian power. Moreover, Thucydides illustrates his narrative on political leadership by a detailed presentation of the transformative leadership of Themistocles on the rise of Athens and the creation of the Athenian Empire in the first place. Themistoclean leadership was the prime cause of hegemonic transition in the Greek interstate system.

Themistocles, a proactive reformer, saved all of Greece from Persian conquest, and in the process of doing so, he turned Athens into a formidable naval empire that was capable of leading a coalition of other Greek city states. In a sense, the case of Themistocles, which Thucydides presents in great detail and finesse, demonstrates quite paradigmatically Yan's thesis that leadership can 'reshape the international configuration, order, norms, world center or even the international system as a whole'.[112] In our recent work, we have utilized an analytical methodology to investigate the impact of Themistoclean leadership on strategic outcomes. We have recognized six interrelated causal mechanisms linking agency to systemic outcome: a) diagnosis of national threats, b) the generation of domestic power resources, c) military organization and doctrinal reform, d) alliance formation and alliance management, e) the outcome of wars, and ultimately all these combined lead to f) redistribution of power in the international system.[113]

Most crucially, and in yet another similarity with Yan's Chinese inspired theory, it is *the effect of leadership on alliances formation and management* (mechanism d) that deserves further comparative investigation. In fact, Thucydides describes how Themistocles cultivated the Athenian alliance system, and advanced Athens's strategic credibility in the Hellenic world.[114]

At the time of the Delian League in the fifth century BCE, Athens provided security for its allies against the recurrent Persian menace. Themistocles himself[115] reasoned that as 'the Athenians would liberate the Greeks of Asia, they would then turn in goodwill to the Athenians because of this benefaction'.[116] As Thucydides put it, Athens's supremacy commenced with independent allies who acted on the resolutions of a common congress.[117] Moreover, Thucydides makes it clear that Athens's allies voluntarily handed over the command of the Delian League to the Athenians because of their hatred of the Spartan commander Pausanias, who acted despotically after the end of the Persian wars.[118]

Overall, the essential characteristic of the Delian league was that Athens enjoyed the *good will* (*eunoia*/εὔνοια) by its allies.[119] Athens engaged in no charity; it simply pursued the lowest level of necessary moral action and, by legitimizing its material superiority, it eventually managed to compound its overall power (this is exactly the concept of strategic credibility in Yan's theory of moral realism). Thucydides himself lucidly distinguishes this fact, arguing that the early alliance system of Athens was a hegemony (meaning a voluntary alliance based on Athenian leadership exercised through eunoia), so that the Athenian lust for power eventually turned the hegemony into an *arche* (that is, a tyranny imposed by the Athenians over other Greek city states).[120] Unsurprisingly, the Athenians lost the good will (eunoia) and were hated by the rest of Greece. Observing this Athenian predicament, the Spartans, when they declared war against Athens in 431 BCE, submitted that Sparta would fight to liberate the Greeks from Athenian oppression.[121] According to Thucydides, at that point, 'People's feelings were very much on the side of the Spartans especially as they proclaimed that their aim was the liberation of Hellas. States and individuals alike were enthusiastic to support them in every possible way, both in speech and action'.[122] As the Peloponnesian War intensified, the Athenians acted in various ways that further deteriorated their legitimacy among other Greek city states.[123] The Massacre in Melos exacerbated by imperial overstretch (Sicilian expedition), demagogy, and pleonexia led to the ultimate Athenian defeat.

The Athenian strategic overstretch in Sicily was neither an outcome of fortune nor other impersonal forces, but rather it was based on an *imprudent decision* driven by Athenian statesmen.[124] It is to these statesmen, and their imprudent chain of decisions, that Thucydides mainly attributed the causes of Athens's downfall. In contrast to his admiration for Themistocles (and Pericles), Thucydides was highly critical of the leadership of Alcibiades, seeing in his degenerative leadership the direct causes for the ultimate defeat of Athens.[125] Thucydides thus viewed agency and political leadership as key factors shaping decisions about war and peace, victory and defeat.[126] Consequently, he was a strong advocate of what he called strategic prudence (*sophrosyne*/σωφροσύνη).[127] We believe that his appeal to prudence – a nurtured virtue – is the single most important term about leadership that can be found in Thucydides's classic treatise.

In fact, this very virtue is present in the Chinese classical corpus too. As Xunzi noted, in a concept that truly parallels sophrosyne,

> Plan before any undertaking, and carry it out with circumspection; be as careful about the end as you are about the beginning, and end and beginning will be alike. This is the most auspicious policy. The success of all undertakings rests upon circumspection; their failure derives from negligence. Therefore, when circumspection prevails over carelessness, the result will be good fortune; when carelessness prevails over circumspection, the result will be annihilation. When planning prevails over personal desires, the result will be progress; when personal desires prevail over planning, the result will be disaster.[128]

Xunzi further advised leaders to 'be cautious in strategy and never neglectful; be cautious in your undertakings and never neglectful; be cautious in dealings with your officers and never neglectful; be cautious in using your men and never neglectful; be cautious in regard to the enemy and never neglectful. These are called the five things that must not be neglected'. These basic pillars of sophrosyne are not only present in Xunzi but there are also clearly articulated in Sun Tzu's art of war.[129] Sophrosyne as the amenity of fine leadership was at the core of China's Pre-Qin strategic thinkers. Yan's moral realism is built upon this rich theoretical understructure. It may well be said that Yan would have perhaps reached the same conclusion had he used the Greek classics too.

Lastly, the concept of strategic credibility, and alliance management, is further and perhaps more elaborately explored in the works of the Athenian rhetorician Isocrates, who was in fact an avid reader of Thucydides himself.[130] As the great Classicist Jacqueline de Romilly has identified, the term that Isocrates utilized to describe the importance of building good will among states and to becoming a hegemon (leader)] is 'eunoia'. This concept is brilliantly analysed within his treatise 'On the Peace', where Isocrates presents a complete theory of rise and fall that is built around the antithesis between eunoia (good will) and misos (hatred).[131] As Isocrates detailed, in order to ensure national success and increase our own power, we have to be willing

> to treat our allies just as we would our friends and not to grant them independence in words, while in fact giving them over to our generals to do with as they please, and not to exercise our leadership as masters but as helpers, since we have learned the lesson that while we are stronger than any single state we are weaker than all Hellas.[132]

As Yan Xuetong noted, Xunzi expressed an almost identical idea, arguing that 'When the hate of the people of other states against us is great, then they will want to fight us every day. ... This is why the formerly great will be weakened'.[133]

It is striking that Greek and Chinese authors that lived in completely separate interstate systems reached similar conclusions about the primacy of reformist leadership and strategic credibility in alliances. While this may not suffice to fully demonstrate that a universal code of strategy exists, it does allow us to extract strategic advice about prudent leadership amid intensifying Sino-American hegemonic transition. Most importantly, it further attests that the first principles of moral realism and its normative advice on prudence – *sophrosyne* and *eunoia* – are both intertemporal and intercultural. They are as Chinese as they are Greek.

Summary

From the ambitious Belt and Road Initiative (BRI), to peripheral diplomacy, to the new global security initiative, to leadership roles in UN specialized agencies (China heads four out of 15), to Xi Jinping's very declaration in the 19th party congress that China may serve as a model for developing nations to achieve modernization while retain their cherished sovereignty, it has become abundantly clear that the 'hide and bide' strategy has been replaced by a much more proactive strategy.[134] Yet hegemonic leadership cannot be sustained on smart slogans and euphemisms about China acting altruistically; it requires a formidable domestic power base.[135] Hence, Yan in his theory of moral realism puts a premium on reformist domestic leadership which strives to achieve domestic excellence as the sine qua non for China's continued power rise. Progressive reform and opening up thus remain essential for China if the nation is to sustain its civilizational recovery and advance its national strength as it intensively competes with the US.

Internationally, Yan hopes that China will surpass America and establish precedence, not dominance. But he believes that this can only be achieved if Chinese political leadership continues to reform towards openness and, most importantly, China takes more international responsibility by abandoning its anachronistic non-alliance doctrine. The key concept for international leadership is *strategic credibility* advanced by prudent/sophron statesmanship. Yan refers to the Soviet Union and its mismanagement of its alliances to highlight the significance of strategic credibility. The US's alliance strategy during the Cold War was far superior to the Soviet Union's and thus by the time the Soviets unleashed their tank battalions to suppress the Prague spring in 1968, their strategic credibility had suffered an irreversible self-inflicted blow.[136] Their leadership over Eastern Europe – won in their valorous fight against Nazism – had been delegitimized precipitating the unravelling of the Warsaw Pact.[137]

Hence, at a time when China and the US marshal their strengths and acutely securitize their bilateral relationship, Yan's theory of leadership with its agent-based ontology is both germane and topical. As bilateral competition may soon become a cut-throat rivalry, we can only hope that the strategic communities in the US and China will realize the benefits of prudence, which calls for a 'disciplined use of very great power'. Political expediency may sometimes be necessary but an aspiring hegemon which is apathetic to the utilitarian moral dimension of its conduct delegitimizes its international authority, undercuts its strategic credibility, and ultimately plants the seeds of its own hubristic downfall unifying the world against him.

Morality in realism may thus not be categorical but instrumental and to an extent commensurable. As the Athenian ambassadors at the conference of the Peloponnesian confederate put it in 434 BCE, 'praise is due to all who, while so far subject to human nature as to rule over others, yet are juster than they have to be considering their power'.[138] The Athenians in their speech attempted to reconcile structure with agency: 'Power tends to corrupt', but absolute power need not corrupt absolutely as leaders have leeway to exercise it.[139] In other words, there can be no perfectly moral superpower but some superpowers can opt to exercise prudent restraint and 'disciplined use of very great power'. As a modern student of strategy has put it, America triumphed over the Soviet Union for there was a 'persistence, throughout that conflict, of something worse than American hegemony. For as long as the Soviet Union was the alternative, there was always something worse, in the eyes of most of the rest of the world, than the prospect of American domination. That minimized the "friction" – to use Clausewitz's term – that hegemony might otherwise have generated'.[140] Thus, the question naturally arises: can China create a new persistence of 'something worse than Chinese hegemony?' *Political leadership* anchored in *prudence* that is able to *build domestic excellence* and *nurture international eunoia* will be consequential if China is to lead in the 21st century.

Notes

1. Herodotus, *Histories* 1.5.
2. Quoted in Yan Xuetong, *Leadership and the Rise of Great Powers*, Princeton: Princeton University Press, 2019, p 56.
3. Charles Krauthammer, 'The Unipolar Moment', *Foreign Affairs* 70, no. 1, (1990): 23–33; Francis Fukuyama, *The End of History and the Last Man*, London: Penguin, 1992.
4. As liberal patriarch John Ikenberry put it, the teleology of American unipolar primacy was seen as systemic, for the robustness of the unipolar order was safeguarded by a 'deep congruence between the American model and the functional demands of modernization [which boosted] the power of the United States and made its relations with the rest of the world more harmonious'; John Ikenberry (ed), *America Unrivalled: The Future of the Balance of Power*, Ithaca: Cornell University Press, 2002, pp 296, 310.
5. For a prophetic and dissenting position, Samuel Huntington, 'The West Unique not Universal', *Foreign Affairs* 75, no. 6, (1998): 28–46.

6 On the theory of modernization, see the classic works of Seymour Martin Lipset, 'Some Social Requisites of Democracy: Economic Development and Political Legitimacy', *American Political Science Review* 53, no. 1 (1959): 69–105; Seymour Martin Lipset, *Political Man and the Social Bases of Politics*, New York: Doubleday & Company, 1960. For other optimistic predictions about China's inescapable democratization, see Dali L. Yang, 'China's Long March to Freedom', *Journal of Democracy* 18, no. 3 (2007): 58–64; Minxin Pei, 'Transition in China? More Likely than You Think', *Journal of Democracy* 27, no. 4 (2016): 5–20. For a comprehensive critique of the theory of modernization as it applies to China, see James Mann, *The China Fantasy: Why Capitalism Will not Bring Democracy to China*, London: Penguin Random House, 2007; Vasilis Trigkas, 'Chimerica on Decline', *The Diplomat*, 4 May 2015, https://thediplomat.com/2015/05/chimerica-in-decline/; Sebastian Heilmann, *Red Swan: How Unorthodox Policy Making Facilitated China's Rise*, HK: The Chinese University Press, 2018. On a wider theoretical perspective, the work that has most challenged modernization theory is Samuel P. Huntington, *Political Order in Changing Societies*, New Haven: Yale University Press, 1968. Huntington argues that economic development and the political upheaval that it inspires could lead to political decay only if political institutionalization (administrative efficiency) is lagging. According to Peter Moody, it is in Huntington's work that Chinese neoconservatives have found ideas against democratization in China; Peter Moody, *Conservative Thought in Contemporary China*, Lanham, MD: Lexington Books, 2007, pp 151–2.

7 From 1949 until 1997, institutional variance in China was minimal but economic performance varied greatly.

8 Parts of this chapter draw from Vasilis Trigkas, 'On Global Power Differentials, Moral Realism, and the Rise of China: A Review Essay', *Journal of Contemporary China* 29, no. 126 (2020): 950–63.

9 In the literature of International Relations, Robert Gilpin has developed the core theory of hegemonic transition. Kenneth Waltz is the father of the 'emulation' principle which Gilpin also saw as consequential. Gilpin, however, in his study focused mostly on diminishing economic returns and imperial overextension of the hegemon (similar to Paul Kennedy) as the drivers of hegemonic transition, while Waltz expounded a systemic theory seeing emulation occurring repeatedly and leading to a balance of power. For an empirical synopsis of convergence and the mechanisms of innovation diffusion, see William J. Baumol, 'Productivity Growth, Convergence, and Welfare: What the Long-Run Data Show', *The American Economic Review* 76, no. 5 (1986): 1072–85. Baumol is not a material determinist. As he put it, there is no mathematical function able to foresee convergence. A functional approach that takes into consideration historical and social specificities across countries is more appropriate to understand the evolution of their productive capacities. Most economists explain convergence as an outcome of diminishing returns and diffusion of innovation whereas political scientists – the structural realists in particular – see convergence as an outcome of a state's pursuit of security. A state has an *existential imperative* to copy the best practices and increase its productivity as the economy forms the basis for defence. If it fails, the state will be 'cleared out' of the system (annexed) or subordinated to second-tier status, thus losing its strategic autonomy (see discussion later on levels of analysis). For a case study on how states emulate best practices, see Vasilis Trigkas, 'China Has Its DARPA but Does It Have the Right People?', *The Diplomat*, 9 August 2017, https://thediplomat.com/2017/08/china-has-its-darpa-but-does-it-have-the-right-people/; also see Otto Hintze, 'Military Organization and the Organization of the State', in *The Historical Essays of Otto Hintze*, ed. Felix Gilbert, New York: Oxford, 1975, pp 178–215.

10 In the founding work of modern power transition theory, differential economic growth, more specifically industrial growth, is the major contributor to hegemonic shift; A.F.K. Organski, *World Politics*, New York: Alfred A. Knopf, 1958.

11 Robert Gilpin, *War and Change in International Politics*, New York: Cambridge University Press, 1981, p 176.
12 Waltz and Gilpin made only arguments relating to the impact of modernization on distribution of power in the system and did not investigate the impact of modernization on domestic polity. For modernization theorists, see note 7.
13 Daron Acemoglu, Suresh Naidu, Pascual Restrepo, and James A. Robinson, 'Democracy Does Cause Growth', *Journal of Political Economy* 127, no. 1 (2019): 47–100. The empirical literature on the impact of polity on growth is divided; see the meta-analysis Hristos Doucouliagos and Mehmet Ulubaşoğlu, 'Democracy and Economic Growth: A Meta-Analysis', *American Journal of Political Science* 52 (2008): 61–83. For a theoretical synopsis, Michael Oksenberg, 'Will China Democratize', *Journal of Democracy* 9, no. 1 (1998): 27–34.
14 'Modernization theorists' in this chapter refers mostly to 'liberals' that aspire to the one-size-fits-all development model of the Washington Consensus.
15 This belief that the economic understructure drives political change is also prevalent in Marxism. As Albert Hirschman argued, in Marxism economic forces drive material growth within an established political framework. When that rigid political framework eventually clashes with the productive forces, it will eventually collapse, overwhelmed by the powerful new social groups (classes) that were born out of economic development; Albert Hirschman, *A Bias for Hope – Essays on Development and Latin America*, New Haven: Yale University Press, 1971, pp 16–17.
16 David S. Landes, *The Poverty and Wealth of Nations*, New York: W.W. Norton and Company, 1999.
17 As noted in note 16, this theoretical construction is also endorsed by Marxist theoreticians. The economic material conditions form the basis understructure for the political superstructure. However, Marxists intellectuals believe that liberal democracy due to its internal contradictions will eventually be replaced by socialism and ultimately communism as productivity precipitously rises in those systems and a vanguard communist party literate in material determinism guides the people towards the communist 'telos of history'. In a way, in Marxism, political leadership enters the equation only when the 'objective material conditions are ripe'. It is only then that leadership can be decisive.
18 Peter Gourevitch, 'The Second Image Reversed: The International Sources of Domestic Politics', *International Organization* 32, no. 4 (1978): 888.
19 A school of thought not addressed here is that of path dependency, arguing that a decision made in the past or even an accident at some point in time could place a state on a developmental trajectory which is difficult if not impossible to be revised later, even if that trajectory is suboptimal. Reform for that school would be difficult if not impossible to be achieved. The school thus abides with a type of 'historical determinism' and has limited explanatory power on diachronic change in world politics as it attributes the success of nations to accident and circumstance. See Robert D. Putnam, Robert Leonardi, and Raffaella Y. Nanetti, *Making Democracy Work: Civic Traditions in Modern Italy*, New Jersey: Princeton University Press, 1993.
20 The authors borrow this term from Michael Beckley, *Unrivaled: Why America Will Remain the World's Sole Superpower*, Ithaca: Cornell University Press, 2018, p 7.
21 For a summary of Yan's research agenda, see Yan Xuetong, *Ancient Chinese Thought, Modern Chinese Power* (New Jersey: Princeton University Press, 2011); 'Professor Yan Xuetong Chosen by Elsevier as the Most Cited Chinese Researchers for 5th Consecutive Year', *Tsinghua Institute of International Studies*, www.imir.tsinghua.edu.cn/publish/iisen/7259/2019/20190308141339629709893/20190308141339629709893_.html.
22 Yan Xuetong, *Leadership and the Rise of Great Powers*, pp 13, 54–6.
23 Perry Anderson, *The H Word: The Peripeteia of Hegemony*, London: Verso, 2017, Chapter 9.

24 Yan Xuetong, *Leadership and the Rise of Great Powers*, p 13. As Antony Saich has put it, CPC's success is based on micropolitics and local experimentation. The party was successful when it did not try to impose ideological imperatives but rather engage in local politics pragmatically and with a reformist innovative governance agenda; see Antony Saich discussion with Elizabeth Perry, www.youtube.com/watch?v=n9Q4P_ZuVTY; Yongnian Zheng, 'China's De Facto Federalism', in Baogang He, Brian Galligan, and Takashi Inoguchi (eds), *Federalism in Asia*, Cheltenham: Edward Elgar, 2007, pp 213–41.

25 Arnold Toynbee, *A Study of History Abridged and Illustrated*, Oxford: Oxford University Press, 1972.

26 Yan Xuetong, *Leadership and the Rise of Great Powers*, p 192.

27 For a comprehensive evaluation of the theory of hegemonic tradition as a progressive research paradigm, see Jonathan M. DiCicco and Jack S. Levy, 'Power Shifts and Problem Shifts: The Evolution of the Power Transition Research Program', *The Journal of Conflict Resolution* 43, no. 6 (1999): 675–704.

28 To be sure, in the IR literature, Waltz's balance of power theory is seen as antithetical to hegemonic transition theory. Here, we argue that both theories are based on shifting power. The hegemonic transition theory sees power shifting from established to rising hegemons, while neorealism sees power shifting from a hegemon (unipolarity) to other states leading to a balanced system (bipolarity or multipolarity). The question remains: why does power shift in the first place? What is the causal mechanism driving this fundamental process in international relations?

29 In fact, Organski focused so much on industrialization as the cause of power transition that he insisted that power transition theory did not apply before 1750 and it will be rendered irrelevant in the future too. This unnecessary theoretical narrowness is an outcome of Organski's failure to see the impact of *reformist leadership* on *production structures*; A.F.K. Organski, *World Politics*, p 307. Yan addresses this in his book. For a prime example of pre-industrial power transition caused by reformist leadership that unleashed commercial-naval power, see Athanasios Platias and Vasilis Trigkas, 'Themistocles: Leadership and Grand Strategy', in E.M. Economou, N.C. Kyriazis, and A. Platias (eds), *Democracy and Salamis*, Cham: Springer, 2022, pp 99–129.

30 George Modelski, 'The Long Cycle of Global Politics and the Nation-State', *Comparative Studies in Society and History* 20 (1978): 214–35; George Modelski and William R. Thompson, 'Long Cycles and Global War', in *Handbook of War Studies*, edited by Manus I. Midlarsky, Boston: Unwin Hyman, 1989, pp 23–54.

31 That may sound similar to the concept of 'political capacity' which power transition theorists like Organski and Kugler have incorporated into their model. *Political capacity* in Organski and Kugler refers to the *managerial capability* of the state or the *effectiveness of political institutions* – a proxy index other scholars use is 'fiscal capacity' (see point on Beckley in this chapter). Organski and Kluger even argue arbitrarily that *political capacity* in great powers is similar and thus drop the variable from their model; A.F.K. Organski and Jacek Kugler, *The War Ledger*, Chicago: University of Chicago Press, 1980; for a more elaborate discussion, see Jacek Kugler and Marina Arbetman (eds), *Political Capacity and Economic Behaviour*, Boulder, CO: Westv, 1997.

32 Note that Gilpin's argument about demographics and welfarism tends to be more structural than political. Unipolar hegemons, according to Gilpin, are destined to suffer from those structural social trends and their power will eventually erode; Gilpin, *War and Change*, Chapter 4.

33 As stressed earlier, while Yan does focus on the differential between rising and ruling power, his theory is analytically more focused on the perspective of the rising power.

34 Yan's agnosticism on polity type diverges significantly from almost all works in the China series of Princeton University Press, which includes books emphasizing the political

exceptionalism of monarchical or aristocratic China. Some of the titles are indicative: *A Confucian Constitutional Order: How China's Ancient Past Can Shape Its Political Future*; *Confucian Perfectionism: A Political Philosophy for Modern Times*; *The Constitution of Ancient China*; and so on.

35 Philipp Kuhn, 'Can China Be Governed from Beijing: Reflection on Reform and Regionalism', in Wang Jungwu and John Wong (eds) *China's Political Economy*, Singapore: Singapore University Press, 1998, pp 149–66; Philipp Kuhn, *Origins of the Modern Chinese State*, Stanford, CA: Stanford University Press, 2002.

36 According to James Burnham, Machiavelli introduced that argument first. In the prince, he argues that an effective leader with dictatorial powers was strategically expedient for the unification of Italy and the defence against the French. However, in his discourses on Livy, Machiavelli argues for a republican regime once the problem of Italian unification is resolved; James Burnham, *The Machiavellians: Defenders of Freedom*, New York: The John Day Company, 1943.

37 In Yan's theory, 'capacity for reform' is a dynamic variable. Past performance is not indicative of future results. Change is constant and sclerotic polities are unable to reform decay. Yan's agnosticism on the impact of polity type on propensity for reform is thus epistemologically sound. Some modern authors often point to the Roman Republic as an exemplary historical case for the impact of solid political institutions. Yet, as Harriet Flower has demonstrated, the Roman Republic, which endured for 450 years, was not a political monolith but constantly changed and reformed its institutions. When it ultimately was replaced by the Empire, Rome continued to be the sole hegemonic force into the Mediterranean interstate system for another 400 years; Harriet I. Flower, *Roman Republics*, Princeton: Princeton University Press, 2011.

38 This argument is well established in some US elite academic circles. See Matthew Kroenig, *The Return of Great Power Rivalry: Democracy Versus Autocracy from the Ancient World to the US and China*, New York: Oxford University Press, 2020.

39 'Fiscal capacity' may be a highly restrictive indicator. Trump's digressive taxation policies (trickle-down economics), for instance, may not drastically alter the fiscal capacity of the US but they may well exacerbate social inequalities. Moreover, on the quality of government accountability, some US scholars beg to disagree with Beckley. They argue that elites that clearly made disastrous foreign policy decisions were never punished but rather continued to retain positions of power and influence; Stephen Walt, *The Hell of Good Intentions: America's Foreign Policy Elite and the Decline of US Primacy*, New York: Straus and Giroux, 2018.

40 Beckley has researched extensively on the metrics of national power: Michael Beckley, 'The Power of Nations: Measuring What Matters', *International Security* 42, no. 2 (2018): 7–44; 'China's Century? Why America's Edge Will Endure', *International Security* 36, no. 3 (2011/12): 41–78. Also, see Vasilis Trigkas, 'Review of Unrivalled: Why America Will Remain the World's Sole Superpower by Michael Beckley', *International Affairs* 95, no. 3 (2019): 750–2.

41 For the impact of big money on politics and political dysfunction on economic competitiveness, see Michael E. Porter, Jan W. Rivkin, Mihir A. Desai, Katherine M. Gehl, William R. Kerr, and Manjari Raman, 'A Recovery Squandered: The State of US Competitiveness', *Harvard Business School*, www.hbs.edu/competitiveness/Documents/a-recovery-squandered.pdf.

42 For instance, structural reform would necessitate the electoral college system to be replaced by a system based solely on the popular vote. Currently, the GOP has undertaken a concerted effort not only to block such reform but to de-enfranchise citizens in crucial swing states.

43 Yan Xuetong, *Leadership and the Rise of Great Powers*, p 192.

44 Ibid., p 194.

45 In the theory of hegemonic transition, alliances play only a secondary role if at all. The primary shift occurs because of internal growth. In the balance of power theory, alliances play a more important role; Jonathan M. DiCicco and Jack S. Levy, 'Power Shifts and Problem Shifts: The Evolution of the Power Transition Research Program': 693.
46 Ibid., 40.
47 Yan refers to a similar argument made by a prototypical realist, E.H. Carr, who argued that 'just as within the state every government though it needs power as a basis of its authority, also needs the moral basis of the consent of the governed so an international order cannot be based on power alone for the simple reason that mankind will in the long run always revolt against naked power'. Yan Xuetong, *Leadership and the Rise of Great Powers*, p 6.
48 In 2014, Yan made a pressing call for China to abandon Deng's strategy of 'hide and bide' and instead 'strive for achievement'; Yan Xueyong, 'From Keeping a Low Profile to Striving for Achievement', *Chinese Journal of International Politics* 7, no. 2 (2014): 153–84. It could be argued that China and Russia have established an 'unofficial alliance' – an entente – particularly after the war in Ukraine and the US's intensifying encirclement of China. Scholars remain divided on the degree of Russo-Chinese strategic cooperation as well as on the strategic requirements and benefits of a Sino-Russian entente. See Deborah Welch Larson, 'Can China Change the International System? The Role of Moral Leadership', *The Chinese Journal of International Politics* 13, no. 2, (2020): 163–86. For an overall assessment of the domestic debate on China's non-alignment strategy, see Liu Ruonan and Liu Feng, 'To ally or not to ally? Debating China's Nonalignment Strategy in the 21st Century', in Huiyun Feng, Kai He, and Yan Xuetong (eds), *Chinese Scholars and Foreign Policy: Debating International Relations*, New York: Routledge, 2019.
49 A closer Sino-Russian entente may, however, verify the prediction of structural realism that eventually 'power balances power'. Yet, it is because of Chinese internal growth that such a Eurasian partnership has now the potential to balance US primacy. A Russo-Chinese alliance in the 1990s would not have such a pivotal strategic effect.
50 Beckley's argument on the power of US alliances can find some theoretical attestation in the work of Stephen Walt, who explains the lack of balancing in the global interstate system and the sustainability of the US alliances as a result of a lack of threat by the US to other states. The power imbalance is not a sufficient condition leading to balancing. The balance of threat matters greatly according to Walt. It is perhaps the rise of US threat against Russia that has pushed Moscow closer to Beijing and initiated a 'quasi-alliance'; Steven Walt, *The Origins of Alliances*, Ithaca: Cornell University Press, 1987. Also see Barry Posen, *Restraint*, Ithaca: Cornell University Press, 2014.
51 Vasilis Trigkas, 'By Reaching out to Japan and Reassuring India, China Can Stop the Quad before It Even Starts', *The South China Morning Post*, 23 November 2018, www.scmp.com/comment/insight-opinion/asia/article/2174610/reaching-out-japan-and-reassuring-india-china-can-stop; for a contrarian view, see Zhen Han and T.V. Paul, 'China's Rise and Balance of Power Politics', *The Chinese Journal of International Politics* 13, no. 1 (2020): 1–26.
52 Edward Luce, 'US Democracy Is Still in the Danger Zone', *Financial Times*, 27 May 2021, www.ft.com/content/bb554492-9b15-4af0-8954-ee0f2063327c.
53 Yan Xuetong, *Leadership and the Rise of Great Powers*, p 9. Also see David E. Sanger and Jane Perlez, 'Trump Hands the Chinese a Gift: The Chance for Global Leadership', *The New York Times*, 1 June 2017, www.nytimes.com/2017/06/01/us/politics/climate-accord-trump-china-global-leadership.html; Will Burn, 'The Demolition of US Diplomacy', *Foreign Affairs*, 14 October 2019, www.foreignaffairs.com/articles/2019-10-14/demolition-us-diplomacy; Paul Haenle and Sam Bresnick, 'Trump is Beijing's Best Asset', *Foreign Policy*, 15 October 2019, https://foreignpolicy.com/2019/10/15/china-trump-trump2020-deal-beijing-best-asset/?.

54 Note that Yan authored the book in 2018 before the abandonment by the Trump administration of the Kurds in Syria, his escalation in Iran, and his incitement of the attack against the capitol. For the impact of more recent events on US credibility, see Richard N. Haas, 'The High Price of American Withdrawal from Syria', *The Project Syndicate*, 17 October 2019, www.project-syndicate.org/commentary/high-price-of-american-withdrawal-from-syria-by-richard-n-haass-2019-10.

55 The case of perfidious Albion betraying Canada in the arbitration process of 1903 concerning the US–Canadian borders at Alaska; Lionel M. Gelber, *The Rise of Anglo-American Friendship: A Study in World Politics, 1898–1906*. In this regard, America's entanglement in Eastern Europe and the Middle East (strategic periphery) undermines its strategic credibility in East and Southeast Asia (strategic core).

56 'Xi Jinping: China to Further Friendly Relations with Neighboring Countries', *Xinhua*, 26 October 2013, http://en.people.cn/90883/8437410.html.

57 Some American scholars that support a grand strategy of 'offshore balancing' argue that for the US to avoid buck passing, it would be advisable to pull back from its forward posture in the Pacific and allow regional countries to take the initiative in balancing China. The US would not retrench but rather provide support from behind.

58 Stephen Walt, *Origins of Alliances*.

59 Yan Xuetong, *Leadership and the Rise of Great Powers*, p 51.

60 Shuisheng Zhao, 'A State-Led Nationalism: The Patriotic Education Campaign in Post-Tiananmen China', *Communist and Post-Communist Studies* 31, no. 3 (1998): 287–302. On the effects of Chinese nationalism on foreign policy, see Shuisheng Zhao, 'Foreign Policy Implications of Chinese Nationalism Revisited: The Strident Turn', *Journal of Contemporary China* 22, no. 82 (2013): 535–53; Jessica C. Weiss, 'How Hawkish Is the Chinese Public? Another Look at "Rising Nationalism" and Chinese Foreign Policy', *Journal of Contemporary China* 28, no. 119 (2019): 679–95.

61 On the impact of the nationalization of opinion, see Edward H. Carr, *The Twenty Years' Crisis: 1919–1939: An Introduction to the Study of International Relations*, London: Macmillan, 1940, p 172.

62 Surprisingly, though, an American expert on China sees advantages in nationalism used strategically; Thomas J. Christensen, 'The Advantages of an Assertive China', *Foreign Affairs* 90, no. 2 (2011): 59–62.

63 Guoguang Wu, 'The King's Men and Others: Emerging Political Elites under Xi Jinping', *China Leadership Monitor*, 1 June 2019, www.prcleader.org/wusummer; Ezra Vogel, 'The Leadership of Xi Jinping: A Dengist Perspective', *Journal of Contemporary China* 30, no. 131 (2021): 693–6.

64 Suisheng Zhao, 'Xi Jinping's Maoist Revival', *Journal of Democracy* 27, no. 3 (2016): 83–97.

65 Some Chinese scholars still insist, however, that the consultative model of Chinese governance has not changed drastically. See Shaoguang Wang, 'Representational and Representative Democracy', *Open Times*, (王绍光, "代表性民主与代议性民主,開放時代), 2014; Zheng Yongnian, 'The China Model: Internal Pluralism, Meritocracy, and Democracy', in Yun-han Chu and Yongnian Zheng (eds), *The Decline of the Western-Centric World and the Emerging New Global Order: Contending Views*, New York and London: Routledge, 2021, pp 74–104.

66 In Yan's words, this would perhaps mean that reform has not progressed or that it has even regressed.

67 Yan is critical of the direction that China has taken since 2012, attributing this not to its polity type per se but to an increasingly rigid leadership at the top. Yan argues that this has become evident in the growth of the Chinese economy; Yan Xuetong, *Leadership and the Rise of Great Powers*, p 83.

68. As Robert Jervis has put it, 'the organizing scheme of levels-of-analysis grew out of Kenneth Waltz's classic *Man, the State and War*. Waltz actually used the term "images," but J. David Singer's review essay on Waltz's book used the term "levels," which has proved to be more popular'. See Kenneth Waltz, *Man, the State, and War*, New York: Columbia University Press, 1954; J. David Singer, 'The Level-of-Analysis Problem in International Relations', *World Politics* 14, no. 1 (1961): 77–92.
69. For agent versus environment-based ontology, see Sterling-Folker, 'Realist Environment, Liberal Process, and Domestic Level Variables', *International Studies Quarterly* 41, no. 1 (1997), pp 4–8.
70. Robert Putnam and Andrew Moravcsik have offered a similar reasoning, seeing leaders as the 'central strategic actors' in a strategic game between systemic stimuli and domestic politics; also see Margaret G. Hermann and Joe D. Hagan, 'International Decision Making: Leadership Matters', *Foreign Policy* 110 (1998): 132–5.
71. Kenneth Waltz, 'Structural Realism after the Cold War', *International Security* 25, no. 1 (2000): 5–41. Also see Joseph S. Nye, *Do Morals Matter? Presidents and Foreign Policy from FDR to Trump*, New York: Oxford University Press, 2020, p 8.
72. Yan Xuetong, *Leadership and the Rise of Great Powers*, p 7. This perhaps echoes the concepts of external and internal balancing present in structural realism.
73. John Mearsheimer, *Great Delusion: Liberal Dreams and International Realities*, New Haven: Yale University Press, 2018; John J. Mearsheimer, 'Bound to Fail: The Rise and Fall of the Liberal International Order', *International Security* 43, no. 4 (2019): 7–50.
74. Joseph S. Nye, *Do Morals Matter?*, pp 163, 166.
75. Surprisingly, in his earlier work from 2001, Yan had made a systemic-structural argument to explain the rise of China: 'After the US air strikes against Iraq in 1998, the Chinese realized the danger of a unipolar configuration. The frequent use of military solutions by the United States caused the Chinese to consider the necessity for constraints on the Americans'; Yan Xuetong, 'The Rise of China in Chinese Eyes', *Journal of Contemporary China* 10, no. 26 (2001): 36.
76. Steve Blank, 'Reimagining Industrial Policy for a Technological Cold War', The National Interest, 10 September 2022, https://nationalinterest.org/blog/techland-when-great-power-competition-meets-digital-world/reimagining-industrial-policy.
77. 'In Washington Talk of a China Threat Cuts Across the Political Divide', *The Economist*, 16 May 2019, www.economist.com/special-report/2019/05/16/in-washington-talk-of-a-china-threat-cuts-across-the-political-divide.
78. For a discussion of this topic, see the Tsinghua debate between Yan Xuetong and John Mearsheimer, 'Managing Strategic Competition', 17 October 2019, Tsinghua University Campus, https://mp.weixin.qq.com/s/rhxWW4OHIPMx79MceCnFdw. Also, Kenneth Waltz, *Theory of International Politics*, New York: McGraw-Hill, 1979, pp 76–7, 127–8; Marc Trachtenberg, *The Craft of International History*, New Jersey: Princeton University Press, 2006, pp 39–40.
79. In his recent speech at the Detroit Ford Electric Vehicle Center, Biden said that 'China is leading the electric race. Makes no bones about it, it's a fact'. The president then submitted that the US used to invest in R&D more than any country in the world but now China has surpassed it and they think that 'they are going to win', only to conclude that China 'will not win. We can't let them. We have to move fast'.
80. Kissinger (a classical realist and not a neorealist) once marvelled that, during the Cold War, 'the overall direction of American policy was remarkably farsighted and remained remarkably consistent throughout changes in administration and an astonishingly varied array of personalities'. Though in his latest book, he strongly emphasizes the role of leadership; Henry Kissinger, *Leadership: Six Studies in World Strategy*, New York: Allen Lane, 2022.

81 Kenneth Waltz, 'Structural Realism after the End of the Cold War'.
82 See Stephen Walt, 'US Grand Strategy after the Cold War: Can Realism Explain It, Should Realism Guide It?', *International Relations Journal* 32, no. 1 (2018): 3–22.
83 The school was first defined by Gideon Rose, 'Neoclassical Realism and Theories of Foreign Policy', *World Politics* 51, no. 1 (1998): 144–72.
84 Norin M. Ripsman, Jeffrey W. Taliaferro, and Steven E. Lobell, *Neoclassical Realist Theory of International Politics*, New York: Oxford University Press, 2016.
85 It is striking that Zhang Zhidong (one of the main intellectuals of the Self-Strengthening movement in the late Qing dynasty) made an extremely incisive remark about the impact of structure on political leadership. As he put it, 'The Dynasties following had no powerful neighbours to strive against, but heaped up large treasures of literary lore at the expense of power. This accumulation produced the hollowness of forms, and this, in turn begat weakness. Not so all the countries of Europe. These were opened up at a late period in history, fresh and vigorous. Surrounded by strong neighbours, they were always in circumstances of desperate competition, stripped for a fight and ever striving to escape destruction. Continual apprehension produced determination, and determination begat strength'. Quoted in 'The "Self-Strengthening" Movement in China, 1898', *Columbia University Resources for Educators*, 3, www.columbia.edu/cu/weai/exeas/resources/pdf/opium-self-strength.pdf.
86 Norin M. Ripsman, Jeffrey W. Taliaferro, and Steven E. Lobell, *Neoclassical Realist Theory of International Politics*, p 52.
87 In fact, neoclassical realism is based on an effort to encompass classical realism in a framework of modern social science. Classical realism going back to the great work of Thucydides in the West and the Chinese strategic corpus of the Spring-Autumn and Warring States is a complex theory. It may prioritize leadership but also incorporates systemic and political variables. See Michael W. Doyle, *Ways of War and Peace: Realism, Liberalism, and Socialism*, New York: W.W. Norton, 1997, Chapter 1, 'Complex Realism: Thucydides'; Athanasios Platias and Vasilis Trigkas, 'Unravelling the Thucydides Trap: Inadvertent Escalation or War of Choice', *Chinese Journal of International Politics* 14, no. 2 (2021): 219–55.
88 Fareed Zakaria, 'Realism and Domestic Politics: A Review Essay', *International Security* 17, no. 1 (1992): 177–98.
89 For an excellent study on complexity and strategy, see Robert Jervis, *System Effects: Complexity in Political and Social Life*, Princeton: Princeton University Press, 1997.
90 Yan Xuetong, 'IR Moral Realism Epistemology', *India Quarterly: A Journal of International Affairs* 76, no. 2. Yan at some point argues that moral realism constitutes a dualist theory. Dualist in that it stresses both political leadership and a state's capability which objectively defines national interests, and then leadership shapes the very strategy to pursue those interests (in that sense, leadership seems to be an intermediary variable). There is a need for refinement and clarification; Yan Xuetong, *Leadership and the Rise of Great Powers*, pp 61–2.
91 To be sure, the choice of leadership as a pivotal variable about hegemonic transition is not unjustified; as Robert Jervis has put it, 'a state's national security behaviour may have more to do with its leaders' personality, beliefs, and images than objective systemic constraints and opportunities', Robert Jervis, *Perception and Misperception in International Politics*, Princeton: Princeton University Press, 1976, pp 28–31.
92 'State power' is a crucial concept in neoclassical realism. As Thomas J. Christensen noted, state power depends on 'the ability of state leaders to mobilize the nation's human and material resources behind security policy initiatives'; Thomas J. Christensen, *Useful Adversaries: Grand Strategy, Domestic Mobilization, and Sino–American Conflict, 1947–1958*, Princeton: Princeton University Press, 1996, p 11. For a synopsis, see Jeffrey W. Taliaferro, 'Neoclassical Realism and Resource Extraction: State Building for Future War' *Security Studies* 15, no. 3 (2006): 464–95. For a definition of 'state power' as the tool of the leader, see Yan Xuetong, *Ancient Chinese Thought*, p 77.

93   Norin M. Ripsman, Jeffrey W. Taliaferro, and Steven E. Lobell, *Neoclassical Realist Theory of International Politics*.
94   Ibid., p 158.
95   The usual caveats apply here. Social sciences can only be based on soft positivism. Thus, the question should be framed probabilistically and in ceteris paribus. Under what conditions can leadership 'most probably' affect other levels of analysis?
96   For instance, the British parliamentarian system tends to pick more predictable leaders than the US's presidential system; Kenneth Waltz, *Foreign Policy and Democratic Politics: The American and British Experience*, London: Longmans, 1968; Gautan Mukunda, *Indispensable: When Leaders Really Matter*, Boston: Harvard Business Review Press, 2012.
97   Robert Jervis, 'Do Leaders Matter and How We Would Know?', *Security Studies* 22, no. 2 (2013): 153. Also Jack S. Levy, 'Counterfactuals, Causal Influence and Historical Analysis', *Security Studies* 24, no. 3 (2015): 378–402. For an excellent application of counterfactual analysis to investigate the impact of leadership, see Victor Davis Hanson, 'A Stillborn West: Themistocles at Salamis, 480 BC', in P.E. Tetlock, R.N. Lebow, and G. Parker (eds), *Unmaking the West: 'What if?' Scenarios that Rewrite World History*, Ann Arbor: University of Michigan Press, 2006, pp 47–89.
98   Throughout his book, Yan mentions concepts from organizational psychology, f.i. groupthink, and how these affect the quality of leadership decisions. There is space for a more systematic incorporation of those concepts into the theory of moral realism. There seems to be a potentially promising path for interdisciplinary research between political scientists and behavioural psychologists. Overall, we agree with Joseph Nye that leadership can be nurtured. Leaders can 'learn behaviour that affects outcomes'; Joseph Nye, *The Powers to Lead*, New York: Oxford University Press, 2009.
99   In our work which draws from Greek classical texts, we have introduced the virtue of sophrosyne/prudence as consequential for sound leadership and efficient navigation of the ship of state; Athanassios Platias and Vasilis Trigkas, 'Unravelling the Thucydides Trap'; also see Mark A. Meraldo, *Leadership and Transformative Ambition in International Relations*, Northampton, MA: Edward Elgar, 2013.
100   Political Psychology investigates the impact of personality attributes on leaders' ability to process information and engage in strategic action. 'These models emphasize cognitive explanations such as operational codes, the fundamental attribution error, lessons from history, the role of personality, group dynamics and group think, and the beliefs and images of leaders.' Yan in his work builds upon such models (see his arguments against groupthink), yet we believe there is much space for a more methodical engagement with political psychology and a leadership-centric theory of hegemonic transition. Classic studies of political psychology include Robert Jervis, *Perception and Misperception in International Politics*; Deborah Welch Larson, *Origins of Containment: A Psychological Explanation*, Princeton: Princeton University Press, 1985; Barbara Farnham, *Roosevelt and the Munich Crisis: A Study of Political Decision-Making*, Princeton: Princeton University Press, 1997; Stanley Allen Renshon and Deborah Welch Larson, *Good Judgment in Foreign Policy: Theory and Application*, Lanham, MD: Rowman and Littlefield, 2003; Barbara Welch, 'Shortcut to Greatness: The New Thinking and the Revolution in Soviet Foreign Policy', *International Organization* 57, no. 1 (2003): 77–109; Jack S. Levy, 'Psychology and Foreign Policy Decision-Making', in Leonie Huddy, David O. Sears, and Jack S. Levy (eds), *The Oxford Handbook of Political Psychology*, 2nd edition, New York: Oxford University Press, 2013. For a synopsis, see Margaret G. Hermann and Joe D. Hagan, 'International Decision Making: Leadership Matters', *Foreign Policy* 110 (1998): 124–37.
101   For major philosophical works on leadership and character, see Robert Faulkner, *The Case for Greatness: Honorable Ambition and Its Critics*, Yale University Press, 2007; Harvey C. Mansfield, *Manliness*, Yale University Press, 2007.

102 John J. Mearsheimer and Steven M. Walt, 'Leaving Theory Behind: Why Simplistic Hypothesis Testing Is Bad for International Relations', *European Journal of International Relations* 19, no. 3 (2013): 427–57.

103 Johnathan Kirshner, *An Unwritten Future: Realism and Uncertainty in World Politics*, Princeton: Princeton University Press, 2022.

104 Joseph M. Parent and Joshua M. Baron, 'Elder Abuse: How the Moderns Mistreat Classical Realism', *International Studies Review* 13, no. 2 (2011): 193–213.

105 On the continued relevance of classical realism in modern IR, see Michael W. Doyle, *Ways of War and Peace*.

106 Yan Xuetong, 'Xunzi's and Kautilya's Thoughts on Inter-State Politics', *Strategic Analysis* 44, no. 4 (2020): 299–311. For a similar point made to advance a comparative study of Sun Tzu and Western strategic texts, see Athanassios Platias and Constantinos Koliopoulos (in Greek), *Sun Tzu: The Art of War*, Athens: Diavlos, 2015, pp 58; 77–82.

107 The authors address this question in detail in a recent essay: Athanasios Platias and Vasilis Trigkas, 'Strategic Universality in the Axial Age: The Doctrine of Prudence in Political Leadership', *Strategic Analysis* 46, no. 2 (2022): 157–70.

108 It is important to note that in the Chinese classical strategic corpus there was a wide range of schools of thought, from idealists to moralists to realists, and so on (see the exemplary work of Alastair Iain Johnston, *Cultural Realism*, Princeton: Princeton University Press, 1992). This is also a case made in Yan Xuetong's earliest work *Ancient Chinese Thought*. A similar case can be made for the Hellenic classical corpus where Plato represented the Idealist school while Thucydides founded the realist tradition. Our argument on the universality of strategy simply means that any state that would ascribe to the idealist or utopian views would simply be cleared out of the system; that is, annexed, subjugated, or even genocidally exterminated (Waltz makes this argument about astrategic or sub-strategic state conduct). It is only the realist path that maximizes the odds of survival. For that reason, a universal cannon of strategy can only include the effective and successful theories of strategy anchored in political realism.

109 Colin S. Gray, *Modern Strategy*, New York: Oxford University Press, 1999, p 1.

110 Note that in Greek classical texts of strategy, leadership is seen as teachable and nurtured. Therefore, political treatises and biographies are written as texts extracting generalizations about the conduct of leadership that can be didactic for future leaders. As we shall demonstrate later, Thucydides spends considerable time discussing the strategic conduct of Themistocles and Pericles and the virtues that drove sound strategic behaviour. As Lisa Kallet has put it, 'Thucydides' view of utility shows that his work is didactic, so in this respect the relationship between text and reader is that between teacher and student'; Lisa Kallet, 'Thucydides Workshop of History and Utility outside the Text', in Antonios Rengakos and Antonios Tsakmakis (eds), *Brills Companion to Thucydides*, Boston: Brills, 2006, p 336. Throughout history, there have been countless works written as advisory texts for leaders. The vast majority, however, addressed absolute monarchs (see the medieval literature on Mirrors for Princes). The richness of Greek classics, however, is that advice is provided for leaders across polities. Apart from Thucydides and Isocrates's works, see Polybius, *The Histories* (in 1.1 he explicitly states that his work aims to train a statesman); Xenophon, *Education of Cyrus*; Plutarch, *Parallel Lives*. This latter work is particularly extraordinary for it investigates a wide range of leaders throughout ancient Greek history: from city founders to legislators to generals to kings to emperors to democratic statemen.

111 David Boucher, *Political Theories of International Relations: From Thucydides to the Present*, Oxford: Oxford University Press, 1998.

112 Yan Xuetong, *Leadership and the Rise of Great Powers*, p xiv.

113 Athanasios Platias and Vasilis Trigkas, 'Themistocles: Leadership and Grand Strategy'.

114 Athanasios Platuas and Vasilis Trigkas, 'Themistocles must be destroyed: Sparta confronts a rising Athens', *Historical Review of Sparta* 1, no. 1 (2022): 129–56.
115 Athanasios Platias, 'The Grand Strategy of Themistocles', in *Thermopylae and Salamis: Assessing their Importance in the Modern World*, Athens: MV Publications, 2021.
116 Diodoros Siculus, 11.41.
117 Thucydides 1.97. Interestingly, the Athenian Hegemonic system, which was built having won the consent of the allies, seems strikingly similar to the alliance system led by the state of Qi in 651 BCE. We don't have space to engage in full comparison but this could be a topic worthy of future research. See Yan Xuetong, *Leadership and the Rise of Great Powers*, p 45.
118 Thucydides, 1.95.1, 1.96.1.
119 The discussion about tributes and good will is marvellously presented in the debate between Diodotos and Cleon concerning the punishment that Athens should impose on rebellious states. Diodotos makes a clear argument for leniency based on utilitarian morality whereas Cleon supports complete annihilation of the population on purely categorical grounds. Diodotos won the argument in the ecclesia and the population of the rebellious state was spared.
120 For a comprehensive study, see Richard Ned Lebow, *The Tragic Vision of Politics*, Cambridge: Cambridge University Press, 2003.
121 Athanasios Platias and Konstantinos Koliopoulos, *Thucydides on Strategy: Grand Strategies in the Peloponnesian War and their Relevance Today*, New York: Columbia University Press, 2010, pp 72–5.
122 Thucydides, 2.8, 3.13, and 3.31.
123 Thucydides 2.8 clearly argues that Sparta enjoyed the good will when the Peloponnesian war started.
124 Athanasios Platias and Konstantinos Koliopoulos, *Thucydides on Strategy*.
125 Although Thucydides is critical of Athens's democratic political system, arguing that it can easily be highjacked by demagogues, he insists that a prudent leader can still tame this catastrophic propensity of democracies. This is fully evident when he refers to Pericles as the 'first citizen' whose leadership was so influential that Athens under Pericles was a democracy only in name. Pericles did not change Athens's democratic institutions, but through political skill, he managed to contain the exuberance of masses. Earlier, Themistocles had reformed the very political institutions of Athens. Thus, in Thucydides we can see how a leader can either reform existing institution or operate effectively within established institutions. Deng Xiaoping performed similarly as well.
126 In their study about judgment, and FP Benshon and Welch capture exactly that dimension when they say that 'Good judgments can avoid wars, or win them. Poor judgments can start wars or lose them . Stanley Allen Renshon and Deborah Welch Larson, *Good Judgment in Foreign Policy*.
127 For this point and its diachronic relevance in the tradition of realism, see Jonathan Kirshner, 'Offensive Realism, Thucydides Traps, and the Tragedy of Unforced Errors: Classical Realism and US–China Relations', *China International Strategy Review* 1, no. 1 (2019): 54, 60–2.
128 Xunzi, *Basic Writings*, trans. Burton Watson, New York: Columbia University Press, 2003, section 1.
129 Xunzi, I. 10, XII. 6–8, IV. 5 and VIII. 6.
130 Please note that while sophrosyne is a virtue guiding a leader in forming grand strategy, eunoia is a mean.
131 Jacqueline de Romilly, *The Rise and Fall of States According to Greek Authors*, Ann Arbor: University of Michigan Press, 1991.

132 Isocrates, *On the Peace*, 8.134.
133 Yan Xuetong, *Ancient Chinese Thought*, p 90.
134 Vasilis Trigkas, 'Review of the Book: The Long Game: China's Strategy to Displace American Order by Rush Doshi', *Pacific Affairs* 95, no. 1 (2022): 132–4.
135 Yan uses the term hegemony not with its original Greek connotation of 'leadership' but with the modern connotation of imperial dominance. For a comprehensive study of the concept, see Michael Doyle, *Empires*, Ithaca: Cornell University Press, 1986.
136 The US hegemonic model has been described as an 'empire by invitation' or an 'irresistible empire'. See Geir Lundestad, 'Empire by Invitation', *Journal of Peace Research* 23, no. 3 (1987): 263–77; Victoria de Grazia, *Irresistible Empire: America's Advance through Twentieth-Century Europe*, Cambridge, MA: Harvard University Press, 2006.
137 When George Kennan argued for containment as an appropriate strategy against the USSR, he had foreseen that 'The Kremlin leaders are so inconsiderate, so relentless, so over-bearing and so cynical in the discipline they impose on their followers that few can stand their authority for very long', quoted in John Lewis Gaddis, *Strategies of Containment*, Oxford: Oxford University Press, 2005, p 41. On this point, also see Athanasios Platias and Konstantinos Koliopoulos, *Thucydides on Strategy: Grand Strategies in the Peloponnesian War and their Relevance Today*, Chapter 1. The US had not always treated allies respectfully. Washington had often engaged in covert operations and regime change. Yet, overall its conduct remained much more restrained than the USSR's and core US allies like the UK, Germany, and Canada never challenged the US's authority.
138 Thucydides, 1.76.3.
139 For an exceptional analysis of the Athenian ambassadors' speech and morality in realism, see Jacqueline de Romilly, *Thucydides and Athenian Imperialism*, trans. Philip Thody, Oxford: Basil Blackwell, 1963. Also, Clifford Orwin, 'Justifying Empire: The Speech of the Athenians at Sparta and the Problem of Justice in Thucydides', *The Journal of Politics* 48, no. 1 (1986): 72–85; Clifford Orwin, *The Humanity of Thucydides*, New Jersey: Princeton University Press, 1994.
140 John Lewis Gaddis, *Strategies of Containment*, Oxford: Oxford University Press, 2005, p 389.

8

Innovation of Moral Realism and Dialogue with It

Mario Telò

A bipolar scenario for the future global order?

The 'moral realism' of Professor Yan Xuetong is challenged to bring evidence and demonstration of its eminent appropriateness in light of the urgent need to frame empirical research on the current global transition. Yan's English language books and articles are innovative in focusing on a crucial twofold question. The first question is an interpretation of the consequences of the parallel processes of a rising China and a declining US. Yan's interpretation of the inevitable change in the current multipolarity focuses on the emergence of a new bipolar world, including a new kind of Cold War. Consistent with his realist approach, Professor Yan is far more optimistic about the survival of the US superpower than about the future evolution of the EU civilian power. Moreover, Europe's expected decline, as discussed in Yan's *Inertia of History*,[1] another relevant book, would occur simultaneously with the decadence of Brazil, India, Japan, and Russia. The second question concerns the unprecedented features of the new US–China bipolarity expected to emerge within the next decade, described as a different bipolarity 'in form and content' from that of the first one of the US and the USSR from 1947 to 1991.

The reader is thus challenged to resolve the puzzle: the mutual threat of the use of nuclear weapon capabilities, the growing primacy of China in economic globalization, and the struggle for technological leadership in the digital economy will interplay in a context wherein ideological confrontation matters far less than it did in the previous bipolarity, making possible the hope of coexistence without downgrading bipolar rivalry to military conflict. Yan's theses are well presented and sometimes provocative: however, his forecast of a coming bipolarity addresses four controversial issues of both an empirical and theoretical kind.

First, does this bipolar scenario risk underestimating the US? Yan is perfectly right about the US's hegemonic decline; however, in military terms, the multipolar world is still markedly asymmetrical in favour of the US, at least for several decades to come. The gap between China and America remains considerable , 6000 n.-heads: 300 according to the annual Stockholm International Peace Research Institute (SIPRI) Report statistical data on capabilities. The main problem for America, that is, the limits of US power, is not that of China's military competition, but rather that its unique military capacity is growing increasingly unfit to cope with the nature of the most relevant global and regional challenges, including traditional and new security challenges, namely, Venezuela, Iran, Libya, Syria, terrorism, immigration, cybersecurity, climate change, and so on.

Secondly, is the forecast of a fatal decline in the relative power of India, Japan, Brazil, Russia, and the EU by 2023 exaggerated, notwithstanding its many impressive supporting data? A large part of international relations (IR) research shares the opposite foresight that the world is, and will remain, multipolar as far as the power structure is concerned,[2] even though many concede that a bipolar tendency has been making progress over the last decade or more.

Thirdly, would the formation of opposed alliances be in the interest of China and of peace? In Yan's view, bipolarity means constructing balanced alliances. In English School founder Hedley Bull's Grotian understanding, alliances may provide a first degree of institutionalization beyond anarchy.[3] However, a China–Russia alliance is the forecast not only of realists, but also of US conservative right-wing circles. Robert Kagan, Steven Bannon, and other security advisors support an 'out of area' North Atlantic Treaty Organization (NATO) engagement, notably in the Middle East and even in coordination with QUAD, to contain China. Yan is correct with regard to the relevance of this tendency. However, an alliance between China and Russia would inevitably strengthen the opposing battle in favour of a 'democratic alliance against dictatorships'. Currently, however, this tendency is one apparently disliked not only by China's leadership, which is prudent, in spite of its energy needs, about being tied too closely to a declining Russia, but also by the EU. Moreover, Canada and Japan, like the EU, are also opposed both to a China–US diarchy, a 'G2' as envisioned by superficial journalists in 2014, and bipolar confrontation, as this would force them to take a stance with the US as junior partners, so prompting relevant negative economic, cultural, and political consequences. India's illiberal Modi leadership, which is nationalist, would also strongly oppose bipolarity.

Lastly, to what extent does international political economy matter? As Professor Yan also recognizes, economic interdependence between China and the West is more relevant now than ever before (finance, production chains, technological ties, and so on). International political economists argue that, in spite of trade wars, enhanced competition, recurrent tensions, international trade, and investment interconnectivity make a win-win game (as opposed to a zero-sum game) achievable in the long run. China is about to consolidate her path towards global economy primacy, but this is happening within an interdependent world economy (contrary to that of the first bipolar world), which has political implications. In this context of interdependence, the institutionalization of international life continues in spite of regional tensions; thousands of international regimes, civil society networks, and arrangements at the bilateral, regional, interregional, and global levels are growing upwards in number and scope.

These four controversial questions share a theoretical background: complex interdependence still very much matters, as well as the institutional resilience, compatible with a multipolar power structure.

Crisis of liberalism, or the US version of liberalism?

Yan indeed addresses crucial questions regarding the kind of crisis global governance is facing: discussing his theses, based on a rare knowledge of the Western scientific literature, is a highly stimulating academic exercise. However, I feel that Yan is still underestimating the internal controversies within the West, which is divided, particularly since the George W. Bush era, according to the main European philosopher Jürgen Habermas,[4] and even more so since Donald Trump's election.[5] Yan is absolutely right in underlining both the internal and international challenges that liberalism faces. Professor Yan highlights the risk of a historically retrogressive trend towards 'one-man authoritarian regimes' and non-rule-based governance. The internal challenge of right-wing populism is indeed strong enough to have influenced decisively the Brexit referendum outcome and Trump's election in the US (as well as other elections in Hungary, Poland, and Italy, so far). The 2020 US elections, in spite of Trump's defeat, confirm that the extreme right nationalist wave is not over in the US. However, in spite of many commonalities, the transatlantic rift has deep economic, political, and cultural roots and a profound historical size.

The main objection of Chinese scholars is that NATO is still emblematic of the Western alliance's unity. The Atlantic alliance was, without doubt, essential during the Cold War and, based on shared values, critical to containing the Soviet Union through until 1991. However, since the collapse of the USSR and the end of the nuclear threat, Europe is much less in need of the US's nuclear umbrella, and the US looks less interested in the European partnership. Burden sharing is impossible without a NATO reform in favour of a stronger European pillar capable of strategic autonomy.

Like it or not, after the USSR collapse, NATO is undergoing an 'identity crisis', and still more hierarchical than multilateral. NATO kept its distance from the US sanction policy in Iran in January 2019, and was considered by Emmanuel Macron in 2019 as fast becoming 'brain dead'.[6] NATO is the victim of profound historical tendencies: the deepening transatlantic rift, distinct strategic interests, diverse threat perceptions, and alternative understandings of current and future multilateral cooperation.

Is the crisis of the West – as regards its strategic and cultural unity – a crisis of liberal values (rule of law, transparency, human rights, and minority rights)?

A large academic discussion is in progress about the 'crisis of liberalism' and/or 'the US version of liberalism'.[7] Few concepts are more controversial than that of liberalism. Within such a debate, Yan's interpretation of liberalism is twofold: on the one hand, he is aware of the theoretical dimension of this concept, but on the other, he identifies it with the liberal ideology of the 1990s. In fact, Yan considers liberalism as an 'ideology' influencing 'the international value system to the extent that the post-Cold war era is known as the liberal order'. But this definition looks to me like a narrow historicization of a political theory whose roots are in the three Western revolutions (English, American, and French) and, as Professor Yan well recognizes, in John Locke, Baron de Montesquieu, and Immanuel Kant (European) political thought. This double definition affects the conceptualization of the current transition as 'the decline of liberalism', and deserves attention.

The Chinese perception of the scope and depth of the current crisis is particularly relevant. Professor Yan argues that liberalism 'in China refers politically to Western democracy and economically to a market economy'; on the other hand, it also includes 'freedom, democracy, civil rights, secular government, international cooperation and the resultant programmes in support thereof'.[8] Yan is correct to emphasise the leading role that the US took in liberalism after WWII, including its founding of the UN and Bretton Woods institutions; however, his brilliant analysis is disappointing in welcoming the transformation of liberalism into something else, by way of the acritical citing of [Francis Fukuyama's famous 'end of history' ideology. Many confuse liberalism as political theory with liberalism as US ideology – transformed into neoliberalism by US influence on the International Monetary Fund (IMF), notably the 1989 'Washington consensus', and on the global economy. Whatever the US's instrumentalization, the true essence of liberalism in IR remains: rule-based governance, transparency, and multilateral institutionalization with shared rules and proceduresframing the two main rules: general principle of conduct and reciprocity. Here, my discussion with Professor Yan's book becomes more critical, since he considers these principles as linked to US dominance, while they are, in my opinion, humankind's neutral and common achievements. These principles may be disentangled from US domination.

The second part of this controversy deals with the alternative to liberalism. Will the new global order be based on new norms and a new centre? Is a historical change similar to that from Pax Romana, to medieval Europe, to Pax Espagnola, to Pax Britannica, and onward to Pax Americana? Is a Pax Sinica the world perspective? If not, is the true issue in global politics that of the construction of a world centre, in charge of the formation of norms, or of a new multilateral governance? In the latter case, is it possible to modernize liberalism by making it more inclusive, and more pluralist? For example, by including 'justice fairness and civility'? Or will the bipolar confrontation lead to a new Chinese hegemony? And what is the meaning of the concept of hegemony?

Conceptual divergences and convergences of hegemony and leadership

What do we mean by 'hegemony'? One of the main conceptual challenges in the disciplinary field of IR theory is the precise and correct translation of the concept of 'hegemony', which is crucial to the large literature focusing on international leadership, including Yan's recent book. However, there is an urgent need for a deeper dialogue on the conceptualization of 'hegemony'. Based on the ancient authority of the Confucian philosopher Xunzi (or Xun Kuang 313–328 BCE)[9] and Prime Minister Guanzi (or Guan Zhong, 723–645 BCE), Yan Xuetong translates hegemony as a style of leadership 'opposed to wise power', while within Western political science, it means almost the opposite: hegemony is precisely a form of wise power that is opposed to mere domination, brute force, and naked power. Xunzi opposes 'sage kings' to 'hegemony', and Guanzi confirms this bipolar opposition through the Chinese character *ba*, as opposed to *wang*, on the premise that 'human authority understands morality while a hegemon knows how to win wars'.[10] Hegemony is thus opposed to a benevolent foreign policy, whereas in Western thought, it means a rather benevolent foreign policy. Let's take the opportunity of the discussions raised in Yan's book to move towards deepening this difference through a possibly shared research agenda.

If *ba* is the correct translation of hegemonic power, we must confront the challenge of dealing with opposing conceptualizations. This is no minor issue, especially for a high-level theoretical dialogue that inevitably includes controversies. Influenced by superficial journalistic identifications of hegemony with domination, there are also, within the Western public opinion and policy maker world, several actors whose use of the concept sophisticated European scholars consider to be confused or vague. Within the international Western epistemic community, three outstanding schools of thought address this conceptualization: they are the Canadian school, the institutionalist school,[11] and Robert Gilpin's revision of the neorealist approach.

The Canadian school of IR, founded by Robert Cox and Stephen Gill, has revived the famous Antonio Gramsci thought, taking stock of the *Notebooks* written in fascist prisons between 1929 and 1935. Let's start by underlining convergences. Gramsci's theory of 'hegemony' is a theory of leadership, including what Yan defines as both 'capacity' and 'authority'. Yan also focuses on the 'mechanisms' of the rise and fall of hegemonic powers. Quoting E.H. Carr, Yan agrees with Gramsci's theory that 'mankind in the long run will always revolt against naked power'.

However, the very hard core of the Gramsci research strategy is about deepening conceptual opposition between domination and hegemony at both the domestic and international levels of politics. Hegemony combines force, including military and economic might, and consensus building. Of course, hegemony needs the background of might (capacities in Yan's language) but does not exist without the complementary moral and intellectual influence of culture, the support of intellectuals, and the conquest of civil society and of the people's minds as a common sense, all of which are crucial both before taking over power and afterwards to maintain it. In the international arena, it is the comprehensive hegemony of the internationally leading power that makes possible allies' and various partners' acceptance of its leadership. The concept's origins are in Greek; the word *hegemonia* comes from the Greek verb *hegeomai*, which means to take the lead. This leadership can be political, cultural, or commercial. The main examples are taken from Greek historians (Herodotus, Xenophon, Thucydides, Plutarch), and relate to the long conflicts between two opposing leagues, the first led by Athens (Delos), and the second by Sparta (Peloponnesus).

On the one hand, the aim of this theory is to explain international and domestic hegemonic stability. On the other, Gramsci's theory focuses also on the conditions for progressive change, whereby the progressive change takes the form of construction of a 'counter-hegemony' (whether at national or international level) that is beyond Vladimir Lenin's idea of the 1917 revolution as a violent uprising to conquer the Winter Palace in St Petersburg, and beyond that of international conquest or invasion. In this context of 'inter-subjectivity', political hegemony must be acquired before taking national or international power.[12] It is a radical turning point, not only against economic Marxist determinism of the II Internationals, but also against the Soviet strategy of 'war of movement', based on revolutionary instrumental alliances. Gramsci argues that his theory applies to every social class and every state along with the dialectic of history. Coming back to similarities with Professor Yan, Gramsci describes hegemonic crises as 'authority crises'. The same opposition between force (domination) and consensus building (hegemony) applies at the international level. Whereas the Communist International, under Stalin's leadership, defended the rhetoric of the 'general crisis of capitalism', Gramsci focused on emerging economic and cultural US hegemony through the rationalization and modernization of production and consumption (Fordism), including the private lives of workers.[13] Gramsci's concept of hegemony is part of a profound revision of both traditional Marxist traditions – Kautsky's economist determinism and the Leninist/Stalinist orthodoxy.

While Yan is interested in Gramsci's revision of Marxism, Qin indirectly addresses his cultural hegemony theory, albeit associating it, much to the reader's surprise, with Wallerstein's orthodox Marxist world-system theory.[14] In my opinion, he welcomes the Canadian school, and notably S.T. Gill's interpretation, in which the 'structure of ideas which become dominant though the forced consensus of the ruled and dominated' stands in contradiction to Gramsci's conceptual opposition of hegemony to domination. Qin is correct in associating Gramsci with the constructivist emphasis on ideational structure, while his critics sees it as vague in including Gramsci among the mainstream IR theories, underlining the systemic level of power in Waltzian terms. Identifying the focus on the global system, like Waltz did, is highly controversial; I would like to draw attention to the fact that Waltz's milestone book *Theory of International Politics* was published in 1979, but Morton Kaplan's book, which was the first to apply the concept of 'system' to IR, was published in 1965. It was, moreover, influenced by the systems theory of Talcott Parsons and David Easton[15] and not at all by Waltzian systemic neorealism. Robert Keohane also uses the concept of global system without sharing Waltz's neorealism (see later). In any event, the Gramsci notions of power and international system are far from that of European and American realist theories.

The second Western theory of hegemony has been elaborated by the neo-institutionalist school of thought, most notably by its main representative, Keohane.[16] A state can establish and consolidate its international hegemonic stability provided only that it can offer the world 'international common goods'. This signifies much more than simply reducing transaction costs, which is one of the main outcomes of regime building.[17] Military might and economic interests are not sufficient for either hegemonic stability or cooperative regime building. In accordance with this relevant – post-realist – school of thought, the world entered a post-hegemonic era when the US grand hegemonic design (from Roosevelt to Kennedy) collapsed. After the Vietnam War's heavy budgetary consequences, President Nixon's decision of 1971 has been a milestone: after the end of the dollar as stable international currency, America was, and is, whoever the president, no longer able nor willing to provide the common goods that it did from 1944 (the Bretton Woods monetary system based on the US dollar as a pillar of international stability) to 1971. What is the definition of an international 'common good'?

The concept deserves a deepened dialogue due to the different sensibilities in the West and in China.

My definition of common good is the following: a good that benefits everybody and every country, including the enemies of the leading country, like the dollar did for the entire world, including the US's main rival, the Soviet Union, over three decades.[18] The title 'After Hegemony' expresses well Keohane's theory about the decline in the US's international authority and role, which does not mean at all the end of US domination and military primacy. The previous work of historian Charles Kindleberger[19] was a coherent background for the Keohane theory.

Yan's book disagrees with this concept of 'public good': he looks to distinguish alliances from those of the 'Cold War mentality', considering alliances as 'an effective moral strategy through which leading states may win international support and also establish their authority'. However, alliances are by definition exclusive in being against certain foreign threats and against other states. If we accept alliances as a public good, then the public good for one group of states is not that for the rival group. It is hence about power redistribution, and not about providing humankind with common goods. The instrumental side of realism would eventually reappear: alliances are a step towards changing 'the international norms, the normative order and even the entire international system'.[20]

The Yan analysis and his controversial definitions of public good are, however, very stimulating for analyses of the current transition, as the following two examples clearly show.

First, between 2013 and 2017, the Transatlantic Trade and Investment Treaty (TTIP), negotiated but never signed by the US and the EU, and the Trans-Pacific Partnership (TPP), signed by the US and 12 Asia-Pacific partners, in 2015 before Trump's decision to withdraw in 2017 and Japan's unexpected decision to continue as CPTPP with the others, were the Obama administration's two relevant ways of alliance rebuilding for purposes of setting international trade norms first and foremost with 'friends' (transatlantic and trans-Pacific friends, respectively). The objective of containing China may cause Yan to classify this as an attempt towards exclusive and 'conservative leadership', while others, following Ikenberry, could emphasize the dynamic and potentially inclusive dimensions of these projects. In my opinion, far from exclusive alliances, to reach a true hegemonic leadership – in the Western understanding, one that is close to Yan's concept of human leadership – these two projects should be explicitly transformed into building blocks for a new multilateralism that eventually would include China and other emergent economies as well. In this case, however, according to my approach, the new trade standards , including environment protection, social rights, public procurement, public conflict setting mechanisms, and other innovations, could be qualified as 'public goods', rather than the first alliance scenario. The hard criticism of Trump against Obama is an argument supporting my thesis, while China's decision to support RCEP may be seen as an alliance breaker strategy dividing the Trumpian Indo-Pacific QUAD. I would like to underline that – contrary to US policy – the inclusive idea of trade arrangements as stepping stones towards larger multilateral convergences is practised by the current EU strategy: avoiding 'alliances' and simultaneously conducting high-level and comprehensive trade and/or investment arrangements with Korea, Japan, Vietnam, China (Comprehensive Arrangement on Investments, in negotiation), Australia, New Zealand, and ASEAN.

The second example is that of the evolving balance between the military and civilian dimensions of international power. According to Professor Yan and the realist tradition, the indiscriminate refusal to use coercion by military force is not only 'antithetical to the behaviour of human authority leadership', but also signifies that a state or global actor 'refuses to maintain international order',[21] thus provoking chaos. However, we may agree that both the US and Russia's interventions in the Middle East (2002–2019), far from maintaining order, instead destabilized the entire region, in their own national interest. We might also note that, by contrast, the EU's pressure on Brazil to remain in the COP 21 Paris Treaty substantively changed President Bolsonaro's previous decision to withdraw, yet involved no military threat, instead offering a trade arrangement (EU-MERCOSUR in 2019). This EU market – and trade – power (linked to the Paris COP 21 treaty and other multilateral standards) could be strictly applied to all trade and investment arrangements. Perhaps the international political economy and its hierarchy of tools can explain more than classical realism can the capacity to change another's behaviour against its will. The international implications of the Belt and Road Initiative (BRI)[22] and the 'EU Green deal'[23] offer two further examples of international politics through political-economic tools.

The third elaboration of the concept of hegemony comes from a completely different school of thought. It is by Gilpin, one of Waltz's best pupils, a remarkable political economist with a neorealist background, who unfortunately recently passed away. He addressed diffuse critiques of structural realism (the eternally anarchical international order) by deepening an issue which his master had not considered at all: that of the global system's historical changes. Gilpin answers this crucial question, which looks interesting also to Professor Yan, by focusing on the changes of global hegemony within an international order. He accordingly elaborates and shares the concept of 'hegemonic cycles' over four successive periods and stages: emergence, consolidation, challenge, and decline.[24]

This thesis is shared to a large extent by another realist political economist, Immanuel Wallerstein, who combined his Marxist background with the findings of French historian F. Braudel in drawing attention to the ideals and cultural dimensions of the cycles of international hegemony: the ideas at the centre of the world capitalist system shaping the education, values, and behaviour of the majority of intellectuals and leaders which flow from the periphery.[25] The successive Spanish, Dutch, and English global hegemonies confirmed, during the five-century history of the transformation of Western capitalism into a global system, the theory of hegemonic cycles. Will the US also experience such a cyclical decline? Or is it about to build up a new hegemonic cycle? Professor Qin rightly criticizes Wallerstein's structural determinism.

In conclusion, these three Western schools of thought – neo-institutionalism, neorealism, and Italian Marxism with Canadian followers – are as diverse as their backgrounds and aims. However, for all such scholars, hegemony is not only distinct from mere domination, but also more comprehensive, inclusive, and multidimensional. It would make no sense to propose a new concept that is synonymous with another (that of domination). Yan's book, through his sophisticated conceptualization, eventually makes the opposite understandings of this crucial concept clear to every reader, which is of uncontroversial benefit for the global epistemic community.

Nonetheless, there are some misunderstandings, as I suspected was possible after my first dialogues with Chinese scholars in the 1980s and 1990s, when the legacy of Mao Zedong was still relevant. In the early 1960s, Mao accused the Soviet Union of behaving like a 'hegemonic' power towards China, which in his understanding meant dominant, in the manner of a 'social imperialist', in light of the withdrawal of Soviet experts and the Ussuri border incidents of 1969. In the understandings of the three Western schools, meanwhile, the Soviet Union was an arrogant and dominant superpower that humiliated China , as it did Hungary in 1956 and Czechoslovakia in 1968, after renouncing every ambition to be a hegemonic and progressive power in Gramsci, Cox, Keohane, or Gilpin and Wallerstein's understandings. After reading Yan's book, every scholar may now realize that this different conceptualization is based not only on Mao Zedong but also on the interpretation of ancient background cultures: on deep cultural differences based, respectively, on Greek ancient history on the one hand, and Xunzi and Guanzi on the other. Only by identifying such initial distances can a constructive dialogue be possible.

Is this issue merely nothing more than a dry academic question? We think not.

When defining the current international disorder, or transitional system, we propose, in accordance with Keohane, Gilpin, and Gramsci, the concept of a 'post-hegemonic system', because the US is no longer either willing or able to spread the cultural and ideational dimension of its international power, or to offer international common goods as it did in the period 1944–1971. Could China or the EU replace the US as the centre of a new hegemonic stability?

The EU cannot replace the US as the Western hegemonic power, in spite of the deepening transatlantic rift. Firstly, for internal reasons, European leading thinkers understand excessive emphasis on national sovereignty not only as a risk for the EU international role but also a potential threat to regional and global peace for two reasons: first, since, for the EU, multilateralism and cooperative governance beyond the nation state are a 'way of life', the regular internal practice for 70 years of sharing and pooling national sovereignties, rejecting multilateralism would be suicide. Cooperation is under threat, while it is an ancient tradition strengthening the supranational dimension of multilateralism. In European history, the first steps, in the form of national sovereignty civilizing, towards multilateralism were accomplished in the context of the Concert of Europe during the entire 19th century, after Napoleon's defeat.[26] The alternative, tragic, nationalist model provoked two world wars. The revival of nationalism in many EU countries is a vital challenge for multilateralism and peace.

Unfortunately, the EU has again been internally challenged for the last decade by new nationalist, populist, and far-right parties that radically oppose not only the EU but also immigration and peaceful cooperation, notably with China. This is a major challenge that can be met only through successful global and regional multilateralism, not least through successful cooperation with China. Chinese scholars don't always well understand how serious the challenge is of revived nationalism. Continental Europe's dilemmas are expressions of the internal conflictual coexistence of two logics. On the one hand, we have the EU's institutional paradigm of reconciliation among erstwhile enemies, designed to put an end to (realist) 'security dilemmas and foster cooperation through strong governance beyond the state'. On the other, we are witnessing a neo-nationalist trend, animated by what Qin defines as 'populist realism'. Even though they performed poorly in the 2019 European Parliament elections and have been chastened by the new EU leadership, the large array of nationalist and populist far-right parties, from radical supporters of Brexit to opportunistic fighters for a weaker EU, namely, Jaroslaw Kacynski in Poland, Viktor Orbán in Hungary, Matteo Salvini in Italy, Wilders in Holland and Le Pen in France, nevertheless remain a long-term challenge. The far left are often converging with the far right in anti-EU circles. These big troubles also affect the cultural arena.

Nationalist revival is in the West a burning issue, often underestimated by Chinese scholars. For example, the Declaration de Paris[27] in France has revived the Catholic anti-Pope Francis and reactionary nationalist associations once deemed outmoded. Consider the line-up of those advocating neo-nationalist paradigms: Alain de Benoist,[28] and, within a different cultural context, Michel Onfray on the one hand, and Alain Finkielkraut,[29] and even Regis Debray,[30] on the other. All contest the previously dominant paradigm of post-sovereignism championed by scholars like Bertrand Badie,[31]

Pierre Bourdieu,[32] and Pierre Hassner.[33] In Italy, extreme right nationalism has been culturally weak since WWII. However, the comeback of the old 'geopolitics' has been accompanied by the revival of national fascist thought, while extreme right-wing populists are inspired not only by Benito Mussolini but also by Ezra Pound and the Russian Alexander Dugin. The Europeanist perspective articulated by the three largest cultural streams, Christian, liberal, and left, was, and is, still hegemonic in the intellectual arena, thanks to the influence of Norberto Bobbio,[34] Altiero Spinelli,[35] Umberto Eco,[36] and many others. Even Germany, by far most representative of the thought of J. Habermas and his post-national ideas of a European public sphere and European constitutional patriotism, based on the reconciliation of previous enemies and the construction of supranational democratic governance, has been challenged increasingly not only by the reemerging legacy of the sovereignist far-right tradition of Carl Schmitt but also by various neo-nationalist approaches, including the 'social Welfare nationalism' of Fritz Scharpf[37] and Wolfgang Streeck.[38]

The victories of nationalism in Western countries has already destabilized international cooperation and would risk bringing new wars in Europe and abroad, as in the past. While Europeans are mainly concerned about nationalism as a tendency that goes against internal peace and external multilateral cooperation, notably with China, the Chinese are focusing on their history of developing the country, linked to the Bandung principles (1955), and freeing themselves from colonialism through the concepts of national sovereignty and non-interference. This very relevant difference explains to a large extent the different accents in European and Chinese IR theories. According to the majority of European IRT, the Westphalian paradigm (stability through balance of power, non-interference, and national sovereignty) failed in 1914 and collapsed in 1939. I understand Yan's book as an opportunity to make a step forward in reciprocal understanding of differences. Taking distance may be the background of convergence.

The nexus of hegemony and leadership

Professor Yan's recent book allows relevant progress with regard to the intercultural dialogue towards a common language. Should one adopt the Chinese conceptualization, revived by Yan: how does one define the current US global role, symbolized by Trump's global 'America first'-based policy, and his reckless, protectionism, combining a focus on national sovereignty with unilateral will to dominance? Yan suggests a relevant nuance that distinguishes the Trump leadership from the worst ideal-type leadership, that of Hitler's Nazi world-domination design ,as well as the Japanese militarist government of 1935–1945, and its immoral, illegal, and totally arbitrary practice , qualified as 'tyrannical leadership'. Secondly, Yan proposes, in the case of Trump, the new concept of 'anemocratic[39] leadership' , as untrustworthy, irresponsible, unpredictable, double-standard-oriented,[40] similar to that of King You, last ruler of the Zhou Dynasty; he quotes G. John Ikenberry and Joseph Stiglitz in support of his critiques of Trump. All in all, his innovative conceptualization concedes to the three previously mentioned Western schools the existence of two harder alternatives to hegemonic leadership: the tyrannical and 'anemocratic' leaderships can be considered not as variations of hegemonic leadership but as alternative ideal types. From the European point of view, this is a step in the right direction towards a compromise with the Western schools' opposition of the concept of 'hegemonic leadership' to the one of 'domination'.

According to Yan, hegemonic leadership is, on the contrary, trustworthy, in accordance with a clear distinction between allies and rivals: credible with friends, and adopting the law of the jungle with enemies, which makes peace possible but unstable. Maybe this definition could apply to the US during the Cold War decades. However, there is a relevant difference between us that calls for deeper discussion: Yan includes in the same definition of 'hegemonic leadership' both the US and Soviet governments during the Cold War era.[41]

In my opinion, this evaluation of the Soviet Union's international role during the Cold War is consistent with Mao's definition of the USSR as 'hegemonic', but it conflicts not only with the Western schools mentioned earlier but also with Yan's distinctions of hegemonic and 'anemocratic' leadership.

Moreover, hegemonic leadership, in following double standards (see earlier), is opposed not only to the 'anemocratic' and 'tyrannical' kind of leaderships but also to the main features of 'human authority', which is trustworthy and consistent with international norms according to Yan. What seems difficult to accept is that the single example Yan mentions is Franklin D. Roosevelt FDR,[42] with whom the US and European literature identify their notion of US hegemony.[43] Was, then, the turning point of 1947 and the beginning of the Cold War such a dramatic change in US multilateral hegemony? A part of the Western literature agrees with Yan that the Trumpian presidency continued and framed FDR's grand universalist design of 1944–1945 (see the Bretton Woods conference of 1944 and Dumberton Oaks conference of 1944, paving the way to the UN Charter of 1945)[44] within the hard security context and imperatives of the bipolar confrontation. However, the multilateral process that the Bretton Woods conference started was kept alive, not only with the Keynes-inspired institutions of the IMF and World Bank (WB), but also with the creation of the General Agreement on Tariff and Trade (GATT), father of the World Trade Organization (WTO) which has included China since 2001. Moreover, two Eastern European countries, Yugoslavia and Czechoslovakia, decided to reject the Marshall Plan (1947–1957) and to defect under the orders of Stalin: that's why they did not receive its benefits. The US continued to provide the world with international common goods , such asthe dollar as international currency, and with cultural hegemony through the modernization and rationalization of production and consumption, cinema, music, and global promotion of the 'American way of life' for almost three decades.

Many Western academic experts analysed the dark side of US hegemony during the Cold War,[45] evident in domestic McCarthyism and witch hunts, and imperialist policies in regions of the third world such as South America and South East Asia. But hegemony means precisely that two pillars matter: consensus building and domination. This historical discussion is relevant for the current multipolar and post-hegemonic order as well. Comparative research needs to be conducted on the evolution of China's leadership within multilateral (or 'counter-multilateral', according to Keohane[46]) organizations, such as the WTO, the AIIB,[47] and, even more so, the New Development Bank, and with regard to interregional policies (BRI) from a period of cooperation towards a period of quasi-Cold War with the US.

When discussing the post-Cold War era, Yan adds the new criterion of distinguishing hegemonic from human leadership, that of 'supporting secessionism in authoritarian regimes, but not in democratic countries'. One could argue that Putin's Russia is supporting European secessionism in Georgia, Ukraine, and Moldova. And that both Putin and Trump are supporting secessionism and fragmentation of the EU (Brexit) and of regional organizations elsewhere. Trump was indeed supporting secessionism in Hong Kong, Tibet, Taiwan, and Xinjiang. These policies look to many observers like violations of international law/norms and, hence, far from hegemonic according to the previously explained meanings.

Furthermore, after reading Yan's book, what might further be explored is whether and to what extent this conceptualization of historical and long-term hegemony also affects the notion of short-term leadership. In the Western understanding (with the single exception of Robert Kagan[48]), the US's authority and international strategic credibility are undergoing an inevitable decline. In the perception of the majority of observers, the US's recent oscillations , Clinton, Bush, Obama, and Trump), are limited conjunctural changes within an inevitable post-hegemonic era characterized by the relative decline of the US's capacities and authority.

In conclusion, the four sophisticated ideal types that Yan proposes[49] with regard to the notion of leadership provide outstanding progress in knowledge; however, our conclusions are to some extent both convergent and divergent regarding their application. They are divergent as regards the US's hegemonic leadership, notably before the Cold War and, in spite of the Cold War, during two more decades, at least in the West. In the Western, largely shared, perception, the international leadership of FDR was an ideal type of 'hegemonic leadership' in the four Western understandings mentioned earlier. The 'human leadership' in Yan's conceptualization did not end with FDR's death in 1945. The multilateral option as a mode of hegemonic leadership, combining domination and consensus-building policies, continued in the difficult context of the Cold War, albeit, of course, with oscillations and contradictions. However, both the UN and the Bretton Woods institutions continued to frame the West during the 30 golden years of capitalism. In my opinion, Yan's book risks underestimating the strengths of multilateral institutional rules and procedures: they enabled the European Community (EC)/EU to gradually develop and, later on, created an inclusive framework for China and emergent economies to join the WTO, IMF, WB, and other UN institutions (the World Health Organization [WHO], the Olympic committee, the United Nations Educational, Scientific and Cultural Organization [UNESCO], the United Nations International Children's Emergency Fund [UNICEF], and the UN programme for Development [UNDP]) after the end of the Cold War and the bipolar order.

According to Professor Yan, 1945–1947 is the turning point between US 'human leadership' and 'hegemonic leadership' (when considered as mutually opposed concepts, see earlier); the definition of hegemonic leadership thus applies to both the US and the USSR: respect for commitment to allies within each camp, while applying double standards to rivals. When comparing the hierarchical Warsaw Pact (the invasion of Budapest in 1956, of Prague in 1968, and the threat to Poland in 1980) and the Sino–Soviet alliance (the break with China and the conflict in the late 1960s) with the asymmetrical yet multilateral controversial history of NATO (including tensions with De Gaulle and Willy Brandt over East–West dialogue policies, and European critics of the US Pershing Euro missiles), we must still conclude that there was a substantial difference even if the Vietnam war marked a turning point as the US hegemonic political and cultural influence.

Furthermore, in the economic realm, a comparison of the authoritarian Council for Common Economic Assistance (COMECON) with the transatlantic market during the 30 golden years of 'embedded and interdependent capitalism', combining free trade and Keynesian national policies, stands as evidence of a historical difference, and explains the reasons for the victory in the Cold War as well as the collapse of the USSR system (more so than does underlining, like realists do, the role of Reagan's missile rearmament). All in all, the two conditions of hegemony – cultural influence/authority (Gramsci) and international common goods – that the hegemonic power offered were declining, or even absent in the case of the Soviet bloc, whereas we repeat that even the USSR could benefit from the long-lasting role of the US dollar in trade stability as an international currency. We see that, on the one hand, the different conceptualizations of hegemony matter when analysing the concrete operationalization of hegemonic leadership in the period 1945–1989/1991, but on the other, that Yan's sophisticated elaboration makes the dialogue possible and deeper.

Convergence must be explored when it comes to defining the distinctive nature of the US leadership in the context of a post-hegemonic order. According to Yan, the US leadership changed from that of George Bush Senior – who implemented a 'conservative' type of leadership – to Clinton's 'proactive' type, and then to George W. Bush's 'aggressive' type, and in 2009 reverted to a 'conservative' leadership under Obama. But, 'when Trump took office in the White House, he established an aggressive economic-political leadership – a hybrid of the conservative and aggressive types'.[50] How did he radically undermine for four years the US's international leadership? Well, it might be said that neglecting to give international support to its economic camp and its allies' economic and security interests is a key index when distinguishing the difference between a hegemonic and non-hegemonic power. Neither Clinton with 'emerging markets' doctrine nor Obama with TPP and TTIP were markedly 'conservative' with regard to prospective enlarged alliances, whereas Trump is for the first time provoking the collapse of reliance on allies, as well as their shift towards more political autonomy from the US. Shinzo Abe, for instance, is proceeding with the TPP in spite of the US's withdrawal towards CPTPP; Merkel pronounced the famous 'declaration of independence' of 2017;[51] and the EU is more proactive than ever in setting up trade arrangements in the Asia-Pacific and South America (in Yan's understated language, 'conservative leadership' via economic expansion). We and other Western scholars, like Ikenberry, share Yan's attempt to seek out new concepts more appropriate for defining Trump's 'sabotage of the order to whose creation the USA contributed'; the elaboration of the notion of the 'anemocratic leadership' concept is an innovative contribution to this research. After the US 2020 presidential elections, we are challenged to conceptualize the coming Biden balance between continuity and discontinuity.

Summary

Improving communication between the Western, notably European, and Chinese epistemic communities is a valuable and shared aim. Constructing a scientific language from such convergence, in particular regarding the main concepts of political science and IR, is in the interest of progress in knowledge and of the gradual construction of a pluralist theory of IR, [52]so opening windows of opportunity for Chinese, Indian, South American, African, and European approaches, among others, beyond the overwhelming and long-standing domination of US mainstream IR theory. Yan's recent book is also both clear and innovatory in providing readers with detailed information about the deep roots of current conceptualizations in ancient Chinese thought. In general, Chinese authors like Yan provide highly relevant contributions to the challenge of transposing traditional Chinese references into contemporary conceptualization, and opening dialogue with foreign languages. Translating them into foreign languages is indeed not just a linguistic exercise. According to philosopher, semiotician, and novel writer Umberto Eco, 'translating is cheating'. Why? Because languages carry the issues not only of various disciplines but also of various 'background cultures', or 'tacit knowledge', as well as of different historical experiences.

These huge progresses in common language building that the works of outstanding Chinese scholars allow should correspond to an upgraded endeavour on the European part. We discussed in this chapter crucial concepts such as hegemony, liberalism, multipolarity, bipolarity, regionalism, and multilateralism. Diversities remain relevant, but convergences through the building of a common scientific language are increasing. Promoting and deepening this scientific dialogue is the single way out of the main danger of non-communication, if not of 'civilization clash'. It is an essential contribution of the academic communities to a deeper people-to-people bilateral and interregional dialogue.

Notes

1. Yan Xuetong, *Inertia of History: China and the World by 2023*, Newcastle: Cambridge Scholars Publishing, 2019; Yan Xuetong, *Leadership and the Rise of Great Powers*, Princeton and Oxford: Princeton University Press, 2019.
2. Charles A. Kupchan, *No One's World: The West, the Rising Rest, and the Coming Global Turn*, Oxford: Oxford University Press, 2012.
3. Hedley Bull, *The Anarchical Society: A Study of Order in World Politics*, New York: Columbia University Press, 1977.
4. Jürgen Habermas, *The Divided West*, Malden: Polity Press, 2006.
5. Daniel Deudney and G. John Ikenberry, 'Liberal World: The Resilient Order', *Foreign Affairs* 94, no. 4 (2018): 1–15.
6. 'Emmanuel Macron Warns Europe: NATO Is Becoming Brain-Dead', *The Economist*, 7 November 2019, www.economist.com/europe/2019/11/07/emmanuel-macron-warns-europe-nato-is-becoming-brain-dead.
7. Amitav Acharya, *The End of American World Order*, Cambridge: Polity Press, 2018.
8. Yan Xuetong, *Leadership and the Rise of Great Powers*, p 128.
9. Information provided by Yan's extremely useful book *Leadership and the Rise of Great Powers*, and its Appendix on 'Ancient Chinese Figures'. Professor Yan also published in 2011 *Ancient Chinese Thought, Modern Chinese Power*, Princeton: Princeton University Press, 2011. For a highly critical approach to Sinicization of the current research (as a mere legitimation function), see Anne-Marie Brady, 'State Confucianism, Chineseness, and Tradition in CCP Propaganda', in Anne-Marie Brady (ed), *China's Thought Management*, Oxford: Routledge, 2012, pp 57–9. Of course, this 'instrumental' interpretation also has applications in Western societies. However, we must recognize that the comparative reference to classical Chinese thought also allows advancements of knowledge. For this open debate, see also Daniel A. Bell, *China's New Confucianism: Politics and Everyday Life in a Changing Society*, Princeton: Princeton University Press, 2008, pp 5, 8, and 9; Valerie Niquet, '"Confu-talk": The Use of Confucian Concepts in Contemporary Chinese Foreign policy', in Brady (ed), *China's Thought Management*, pp 76–7.

10. Yan Xuetong, *Leadership and the Rise of Great Powers*, pp 27, 39, 49.
11. For a deeper presentation of these differences, see Mario Telò, *International Relations: A European Perspective*, New York: Routledge, 2009.
12. His gradualist and reformist concept of 'warfare of trenches' in Antonio Gramsci, *Prison Notebooks*, edited and translated by Joseph A. Buttigieg with Antonio Callari, New York: Columbia University Press, 2011, p 15.
13. Ibid., 'Americanism and Fordism'.
14. Qin Yaqing, *A Relational Theory of World Politics* Cambridge; New York: Cambridge University Press, 2018.
15. Talcott Parsons, *The Social System*, London: Routledge, 1951; David Easton, *The Political System: An Inquiry into the State of Political Science*, New York: Knopf, 1953; Morton Kaplan, *System and Process in International Politics*, New York: John Wiley & Sons, Inc., 1957.
16. Robert O. Keohane, *After Hegemony: Cooperation and Discord in World Political Economy*, Princeton: Princeton University Press, 1984.
17. The classical definition of transaction costs has been provided by Douglas North, 'Transaction Costs, Institutions and Economic History', *Journal of Institutional and Theoretical Economics* 140 (1984): 7–17.
18. Mario Telò, *International Relations: A European Perspective*, with Foreword by Robert O. Keohane, London: Routledge, 2009, pp 87–9.
19. Charles Kindleberger, *The World in Depression: 1929–1939*, Berkeley: University of California Press, 1973; Charles Kindleberger, *World Economic Primacy: 1500–1990*, Oxford: Oxford University Press, 1996.
20. Yan Xuetong, *Leadership and the Rise of Great Powers*, p 65.
21. Ibid., p 66.
22. On the BRI, see Mario Telò and Yuan Feng (eds), *China and the EU in the Era of Regional and Interregional Cooperation: The Belt and Road Initiative in a Comparative Perspective*, Brussels and London: Peter Lang, 2020.
23. European Commission, The EU Green Deal, December 2019. It was combined with the EU Next Generation Recovery Plan approved on 2 July and in its final version, by the European Council, 11 December 2020.
24. Robert Gilpin, *War and Change in World Politics*, Cambridge: Cambridge University Press, 1981.
25. Immanuel Wallerstein, *The Modern World System*, New York: Academic Press, 1974, 1980, 1989.
26. Mario Telò, 'The Three Historical Epochs of Multilateralism', in Mario Telò (ed), *Globalization, Europe, Multilateralism: Towards a Better Global Governance?*, Burlington: Ashgate, 2014, pp 33–73.
27. Philippe Benetton, Remi Brague, and Chantal Delsol, *La Déclaration de Paris: Une Europe en laquelle nous pouvions croire* (Paris Declaration: A Europe We Can Believe, A Manifesto), Paris: Cerf, 2018.
28. Alain de Benoist, *Contre le liberalisme* (Against Liberalism), Monaco: Le Rochée, 2019.
29. Alain Finkielkraut, 'Nul n'est Prêt à Mourir pour l'Europe' (Nobody Is Ready to Die for Europe), *Le Point*, 30 June 2016, www.lepoint.fr/europe/alain-finkielkraut-nul-n-est- pret-a-mourir-pour-l-europe-30-06-2016-2050917_2626.php.
30. Regis Debray, *L'Europe Phantôme* (Europe as a Phantom), Paris: Gallimard, 2019.
31. Bertrand Badie, *Un Monde sans Souveraineté* (A World without Sovereignties), Paris: Fayard, 1999.
32. Pierre Bourdieu, 'Pour un Movement Social Europe' en' (For a European Social Movement), *Le Monde Diplomatique*, 1999, pp 1–16.
33. Pierre Hassner, 'L'Europe et le Spectre des Nationalismes' (Europe and the Specter of Nationalisms), *Esprit*, 1991, pp 5–20.

34 Norberto Bobbio, 'Etat et Démocratie Internationale' (State and International Democracy), in Mario Telò (ed), *Démocratie et Relations Internationales* (Democracy and International Relations), Bruxelles: Complexe, 1999, pp 143–58.
35 Andrew Glencross and Alexander Trechsel (eds), *EU Federalism and Constitutionalism: The Legacy of Spinelli*, London: Lexington, 2010.
36 Umberto Eco, 'It's Culture, Not War, That Cements European Identity', *The Guardian*, 26 January 2012, www.theguardian.com/world/2012/jan/26/umberto-eco-culture-war-europa.
37 Fritz W. Scharpf, 'After the Crash: A Perspective on Multilevel European Democracy', *European Law Journal* 21, no. 3 (2015): 384–405.
38 Wolfgang Streeck, *Buying Time: The Delayed Crisis of Democratic Capitalism*, London and New York: Verso, 2013.
39 The neo-logism proposed by Yan, 'anemocratic', comes from the Greek *kratos* (power), and *anemos*, translated into English as 'wind' and into French as 'tourbillon' (strong wind): anemocratic: power of the wind, or a storm, that is, a power characterized by turbulence and storms.
40 Yan Xuetong, *Leadership and the Rise of Great Powers*, pp 45–8.
41 Ibid., p 49.
42 Ibid., p 44.
43 Not only the Keohane definition mentioned previously, but also John Gerard Ruggie (ed), *Multilateralism Matters: The Theory and Praxis of An Institutional Form*, New York: Columbia University Press, 1993; G. John Ikenberry, *The Liberal Leviathan*, Princeton: Princeton University Press, 2001; Stewart M. Patrick, *The Best Laid Plans: The Origins of American Multilateralism and the Dawn of the Cold War*, New York: Rowman and Littlefield, 2009.
44 Mario Telò, 'The Three Historical Epochs of Multilateralism', pp 33–73.
45 Tony Judt, *Postwar: A History of Europe Since 1945*, London: Penguin Books, 2005); John Lewis Gaddis, *The Cold War: A New History*, London: Penguin Books, 2006; Odd Arne Westad, *The Global Cold War: Third World Interventions and the Making of Our Times*, Cambridge: Cambridge University Press, 2006.
46 Robert O. Keohane and Julia C. Morse, 'Counter-multilateralism', in Jean-Frederic Morin et al (eds), *The Politics of Transatlantic Trade Negotiations: TTIP in a Globalized World*, New York: Routledge, 2015, pp 17–26.
47 Matthew D. Stephen and David Skidmore, 'The AIIB in the Liberal International Order', *Chinese Journal of International Politics* 12, no. 1 (2019): 61–91.
48 Robert Kagan, *The Jungle Grows Back: America and Our Imperiled World*, New York: Knopf Doubleday Publishing Group, 2019.
49 Matthew D. Stephen and David Skidmore, 'The AIIB in the Liberal International Order'.
50 Ibid., 37.
51 Quoted in Ibid.: 42.
52 Qin Yaqing, *Globalizing IR Theory: Critical Engagement*, London: Routledge, 2020.

9

Moral Realism and Sino–American Relations

Deborah Welch Larson

As China increases its power and influence on the world stage, many observers wonder how its rise will affect the current US-dominated world order. Some have suggested that the existing system will eventually evolve into two rival blocs, like the US–Soviet Cold War.[1] Conversely, rather than bipolarity, it has been suggested that world order will collapse into anarchy, including several great rival powers pursuing their own interests, with no ordering principle and little cooperation among them.[2] As in previous power transitions, China could engage in military conflict against a declining US.[3] Defensive realists believe that the US and China will eventually learn to manage their rivalry so that they can cooperate in areas of shared interest.[4]

These predictions, however, are largely derived from the Western international experience, failing to allow for contemporary differences in regional and historic contexts. One version of the future that uses classic Chinese philosophy is the concept of *tianxia* (all under Heaven) whereby all nations will defer to China's preferences.[5] In contrast, moral realism combines insights from Pre-Qin Chinese philosophers with classical realism. Based on Pre-Qin philosophy, in addition to the conventional concept of hegemony, the theory distinguishes other types of global leadership – in particular, sage king or humane authority and tyrant. A humane authority provides economic benefits and security to smaller states and thereby wins their support.[6]

The theory of moral realism implies that competition between China and the US is likely to differ from past rivalries between a rising and dominant power such as the US–Soviet Cold War. The goal of the two states is to attain or preserve higher status, which is more intangible and subjective than relative military power. Because of globalization and nuclear weapons, competition for higher status will largely take place in the realm of economics and advanced technology instead of missiles and ideology.[7] Values will also be salient as a result of the election of Joe Biden, who wants to restore America's global and moral leadership after the Trump era of withdrawal and self-interested, transactional foreign policy. The Biden administration could mark an era of competition between the US and China to shape international norms. While these differences conduce to peace, the absence of the clear geographic red lines of the US–Soviet Cold War could result in inadvertent conflicts in the maritime realm.

In the following chapter, I apply the theory of moral realism to Sino–American relations, contrasting it with power transition theory and other realist theories. The first section highlights differences between the US–Soviet Cold War and the current strategic situation between the US and China, which make a recurrence of the Cold War unlikely. The second section discusses future Sino–American competition over technology, highlighting the importance of domestic reform and political leadership, a variable emphasized by moral realism. The third section considers the risks of US–Chinese maritime rivalry, which could disrupt China's economic-based strategy. The fourth section highlights China's efforts to shape global norms, consistent with the prescriptions of moral realism. The fifth section analyses Biden's emerging value-based foreign policy and the 'power of example' as an illustration of moral realism and its possible impact on US–Chinese relations. The conclusions summarize and offer prescriptions on how to mitigate the intensity of the Sino–American rivalry.

The Sino–American rivalry becoming a cold war?

The world is likely to become bipolar over the long run, as the US relative power advantage declines, while China narrows the gap. It is difficult to make unequivocal predictions, because much depends on the quality of American and Chinese leadership, their ability to implement reforms, and the foreign policy orientation of other major states such as Russia, Turkey, or India. Even so, if there is a bipolar distribution of power, this will not necessarily lead to a Cold War between the US and China, similar to that between the US and the Soviet Union.

The Cold War was more than a normal strategic competition – it was perceived as an existential rivalry in which there could be no more than temporary, limited cooperation between the superpowers. But it is questionable whether the bipolar system made the US–Soviet Cold War inevitable. Given a bipolar distribution, the US and the Soviet Union could have defined their relationship in a variety of ways, apart from the Cold War. For example, the two states could have entered into a sphere of influence agreement dividing Europe between them. The superpowers could have pursued a détente-style limited adversary relationship much earlier, cooperating on some issues while competing on others. Or there could have been a hot war. To explain why there was a Cold War, we need to move to lower levels of analysis and consider other variables.[8]

The conditions that led to Cold War between the US and the Soviet Union included nuclear weapons, ideological competition, and the absence of interactions between the superpowers. In the contemporary era, both China and the US have more than enough nuclear weapons to devastate the other. The existence of mutual assured destruction should inhibit either side from taking actions that could escalate to a war between them.[9]

While nuclear weapons help to prevent military conflict between the US and China, the other conditions for a Cold War are absent. The differences between China and the US do not revolve around ideological issues but competition for material benefits and status.[10] Neither state is promoting the spread of its ideology or domestic system to other states. Ideological competition is a zero-sum rivalry, in which neither side can tolerate the existence of the other's political system. Soviet Marxism-Leninism held that capitalist states were fundamentally illegitimate and the imperialists were bent on destruction of socialist systems.[11] With ideology removed from the equation, competition between the US and China is less intense and much narrower in scope.

The US and China interact with each other much more frequently and over a wider range of issues than the US and the Soviet Union did. Far from a strategic embargo like the Cold War, the economies of the US and China are connected not only through trade but investment and multinational production networks.[12] Today, the US and Chinese economies are so intertwined that attempts to decouple them would wreak great damage not only on their economies but those of the rest of the world.[13] Many American manufactured products rely on Chinese supply chains, and these connections cannot be easily replaced.[14]

During the Cold War, the US containment policy aimed to isolate the Soviet Union both economically and politically. The US tried to prevent its allies from trading with the Soviet Union and imposed restrictions on exports of products that might enhance the military power of the Union of Soviet Socialist Republics (USSR).[15] Because of globalization, it is unlikely that the world will return to the mutually exclusive trading blocs of the Cold War. States do not want to have to choose between trading with the US or China. Today, states that are allies or friendly towards the US such as South Korea and Japan are major trading partners with China.[16] Yan predicts that there will be shifting alignments and coalitions depending on the issue.[17]

Technological competition

Competition between the US and China will differ in significant respects from the US–Soviet Cold War. The main arena of competition is likely to be status, rather than military power. While military power is a major contributor to status, other attributes are also important, such as economic development and technological innovation. Status is more intangible and symbolic than material capabilities, based on collective beliefs and great power status does not necessarily require a rival's military defeat.[18]

According to moral realism, the strategies used by rising powers vary, depending on the technology and norms of an era. In the late 19th century, the major powers sought to attain prestige by acquiring overseas colonies. But after WWII, the norms of self-determination eventually led to the breakup of colonial empires, such as those of Britain and France. Since the end of the Cold War and the rise of globalization, states can gain access to markets and raw materials through trade and investment without having to control territory, while nuclear weapons deter major powers from going to war against another nuclear power.[19]

Moral realism also holds that the choice of strategy depends on the type of political leadership. China is relying primarily on economics and networks to influence others and achieve great power status.[20] The US and China will compete in the economic sphere, in technological innovation, and in establishing rules to govern trade, investment, exchange rates, and intellectual property, rather than in acquiring nuclear superiority or ideological alliance blocs.[21]

To attain global power status and avoid the middle income trap, China must innovate in technology.[22] For several decades, China has invested heavily in research and development, using subsidies, industrial policy, and investment in foreign companies. Xi Jinping has set the goal for China to become a global leader in advanced technology. To that end, in 2015, China announced 'Made in China 2025', a plan to attain market dominance in ten technologies of the future, including information technology, aerospace, robotics, and electric vehicles.[23]

Competition over science and technology is less likely to escalate to war than arms racing. On the other hand, some technology has military uses and a state's relative superiority can affect the security of other states. Increasingly, Sino–American technology competition has focused on dual-use technology such as artificial intelligence, robotics, drones, cloud computing, and virtual reality, which have potential military applications. The US government perceives such Chinese policies as 'Made in China 2025' and 'military–civil fusion' as threatening American security, aiming not just at import substitution and self-sufficiency but at using Chinese state power to undermine US military superiority.[24]

Beginning with the Obama administration, the US enacted increasing restrictions on exports of sensitive technologies to Chinese firms and on Chinese investment in US firms with advanced technology.[25] The Trump administration was concerned that China's telecommunications giant Huawei might use its 5G networks for espionage. The US Commerce Department placed Huawei on a special entities list, which meant that the company was unable to purchase US semi-conductor chips without a waiver that is rarely granted.[26] By 2021, 60 Chinese companies were placed on the US special entity list.[27] In addition to increasing the number of Chinese companies subject to review, the Biden administration passed a law that will allocate $200 billion to companies engaged in basic research in advanced technologies such as semi-conductors, biotechnology, artificial intelligence, and quantum computing, the CHIPS and Science Act. This major step towards industrial policy was aimed at competing with China.[28]

The 'securitization' of economic and technological competition increases mutual mistrust and misperception.[29] At a New Economy Forum in Beijing in November 2019, former National Security Adviser Henry Kissinger warned that the US and China are on the 'foothills of a Cold War' where tensions could escalate into a conflict that would be worse than WWI.[30]

A peaceful power transition?

Conventional theories of power transition suggest there will likely be a war between a rising power of China and the currently dominant US. Contrary to power transition theory, it is unlikely that either China or the US would deliberately start a war against the other. More worrisome is the prospect that military skirmishes might occur as a result of increasing US–Chinese military interaction due to competition in the 'grey zone' of East Asian waters.

According to Robert Gilpin, over time, due to uneven growth in power among states, eventually an imbalance develops between the distribution of power and the hierarchy of prestige. Eventually, the rising state will fight a hegemonic war against the leading power in order to redistribute territory and spheres of influence as well as change the international division of labour to suit its interests.[31]

A related theoretical framework is power transition theory, which holds that upon reaching parity with the dominant state, a dissatisfied challenger will go to war to attain its rightful position within the system.[32] Whereas power transition theorists stress that the rising power's satisfaction with the system affects the likelihood of war, Mearsheimer's theory of offensive realism asserts that all states are determined to acquire more power. Mearsheimer predicts that China will try to attain regional hegemony and to push the US out of East Asia, in a version of the Monroe Doctrine.[33]

Drawing on Thucydides, Graham Allison argues that conflict between a rising power and the dominant state is caused by 'structural stresses', such as the rivalry between Athens and Sparta that led to the Peloponnesian Wars. Rising and declining powers need to be wary of falling into a 'Thucydides Trap'.[34]

Like the more conventional power transition theories, moral realism posits that there is a structural contradiction between the rising power and the existing global leader, based on anarchy and the zero-sum nature of power. On the other hand, moral realism differs from other realist models in emphasizing that rising powers have a variety of strategies from which to choose.[35] Since China is pursuing an economic-technological strategy, moral realism does not predict war between China and the US, but it does not rule it out entirely, especially a proxy war.[36] While a deliberate war is unlikely, an inadvertent military clash might occur as a result of an unplanned naval encounter. As two continent-sized powers, armed with nuclear weapons, separated geographically, China and the US are most likely to clash at sea.[37] China wants to police its coastal waters and prevent a hostile power from taking control of sea lanes on which 85 per cent of its goods travel.[38] Apart from defensive aims, the Chinese leadership is using the navy to enlarge its global leadership, as indicated by the expansion of the PLA Navy's mission beyond coastal waters to the 'far seas'. At the 18th Party Congress in 2012, the leadership affirmed that China would 'build itself into a maritime power'. In 2020, the PRC possessed the world's largest navy with about 350 ships and submarines compared with the US battle fleet of around 293 ships.[39]

At the same time that China is increasing its naval power and reach, the US has augmented its naval activities in the Asia-Pacific, as part of the 'pivot to Asia' announced by President Obama, which actually began under his predecessor George W. Bush.[40] To oppose China's increased presence in the South China Sea, the US has been conducting increasing numbers of 'freedom of navigation' operations, which China opposes, often signalling its displeasure through warnings delivered by Chinese naval ships or aircraft. As a result, China's modernized naval forces are increasingly encountering US vessels, raising the risk of a collision.[41]

The risk of escalation to the nuclear level may not deter proxy wars or low-level skirmishes. Paradoxically, the stability of the nuclear balance could make low-level naval encounters more likely, especially in the 'grey zone'. With less possibility of an existential threat to survival, one state might be willing to use force to settle a dispute over maritime sovereignty or freedom of passage, in the belief that there was little chance that the conflict would escalate to a war between the US and China.[42] Overconfidence about the improbability of escalation could make war more likely.

Unplanned encounters are more likely due to the lack of 'red lines' in terms of geography or actions that clearly cross the threshold of war. During the Cold War, the firm East–West division of Europe deterred either side from undertaking any military action against the other. Sending military forces across the line dividing Germany would have signalled the outbreak of World War III. The Sino–American rivalry in East Asia is over maritime boundaries, where there are no clear lines, and there are competing claims to sovereignty over territory in the South and East China Seas. In addition to clarifying intentions, a military invasion across recognized boundaries could have resulted in the conquest of Europe, upsetting the balance of power. Thus, the stakes of any military encounter were greater in Europe than they would be in the Asia-Pacific.[43] For the US, there is often uncertainty and ambiguity both about the facts on the ground and the applicability of international norms and law.[44] Uncertainty about how to treat naval incidents involving a collision between US and Chinese vessels could result in inadvertent escalation.

The risks of unclear red lines were dramatized by the crisis around US Speaker of the House Nancy Pelosi's 2 August 2022 visit to Taiwan. The visit of a US Speaker was not entirely unprecedented, as Newt Gingrich made a trip to Taiwan in 1997, but it occurred in the context of increasing US official contacts with the island. Viewing Pelosi's visit as a violation of the US 'One China policy' and an infringement on China's sovereignty, the PRC conducted 72 hours of live-fire drills beginning the day after she left, including launching 11 missiles in the area. Five missiles landed in Japan's Exclusive Economic Zone. The drills were carried out in six areas to the north, east, and south of Taiwan and some were within 12 nautical miles and its claimed air space. Also unprecedented was the number of incursions by Chinese warplanes and warships across the median of the Taiwan Strait. Since then, China has tried to 'normalize' this heightened military activity in the Taiwan Strait by frequent daily incursions of Chinese warplanes across the median line.[45]

The likelihood of conflict between the US and China could be exacerbated by security dilemma dynamics, whereby one state's efforts to defend its interests are perceived as aggressive by the other, potentially leading to a spiral of conflict and mistrust.[46] China regards efforts by the US to upgrade and reaffirm its alliances in Asia as offensive and threatening, whereas the US Defense Department has expressed concerns about China's modernization of its military forces and operations.[47] *The 2018 US National Defense Strategy* accused China of pursuing a long-term, whole-nation strategy and predicted that China will 'continue to pursue a military modernization program that seeks Indo-Pacific regional hegemony in the near-term and displacement of the United States to achieve global preeminence in the future'. In response, the 2019 Chinese Defense White Paper, the first since 2015, declared that it was the US that has 'provoked and intensified competition among major countries, significantly increased its defense expenditures, pushed for additional capacity in nuclear, outer space, cyber and missile defense, and undermined global strategic stability'. In contrast, China's national defence policy is characterized as defensive'.[48] Both realism and moral realism emphasize the intractability of the security dilemma.

In the wake of Pelosi's visit and increased Chinese military activity in the Taiwan Strait, efforts by the US to deter a Chinese invasion of the island by reinforcing its ties to East Asian allies and offering Taiwan increased military assistance could exacerbate the security dilemma. If China feels compelled to react strongly to each visit of a US official or politician to Taiwan, the Rubicon might be crossed where the US would take counteraction that could lead to a Sino–American military conflict.[49]

The role of international norms

Moral realism differs from other realist theories in highlighting the importance of moral authority and the establishment of new norms as the key to obtaining global leadership. Based on ancient Chinese philosophy, Yan distinguishes between humane authority (*wangdao*) and hegemony (*badao*). A humane authority attracts followers by exercising benevolent leadership and providing benefits to followers, whereas a hegemon relies on deterring potential aggressors and providing security to allies. According to moral realism, a humane authority will attract more followers and client states than a hegemon will. Yan recommends that China become a humane authority, while the US is currently a hegemon.[50]

Like liberalism, moral realism stresses the importance of norms. The establishment of norms that are widely accepted enables the leading power to maintain order without having to use coercion, which is costly. But in contrast to liberalism, which proposes individual human rights and democracy as universal principles, moral realist theory posits that great powers seek to establish norms that are in their interests. A humane authority applies moral principles even-handedly, whereas a hegemon behaves differently towards allies than neutral states or adversaries, upholding strategic credibility towards its allies but behaving according to realpolitik norms towards outsiders. The use of a double standard diminishes the moral authority of a hegemon, subjecting it to charges of hypocrisy.[51]

China has often portrayed itself as a 'new type of great power', one that differs from historical empires. China wants to be a 'moral' power, drawing on its Confucian legacy.[52] The 19th Party Congress work report of October 2017 declared that China 'offers a new option for other countries and nations who want to speed up their development while preserving their independence' and 'offers Chinese wisdom and a Chinese approach to problems facing mankind'.[53] Consistent with moral realism, this statement suggests that China wants to promote new norms as an alternative to liberalism.[54]

Xi Jinping emphasized a different set of norms through the concept of the 'community of common destiny', which he outlined in speeches to the UN General Assembly in 2015 and in 2017 at the UN office in Geneva. In both instances, he described political, security, development, culture, and environmental dimensions, advocating settlement of disputes through consultation, partnerships, openness, and multilateralism.[55] In the political domain, Xi advocates 'dialogue' as a means of settling disputes and 'partnerships' rather than alliances. In the security domain, Xi has called for a 'common, comprehensive, cooperative, and sustainable' security concept to replace the 'Cold War' mentality. In the economic domain, Xi envisions an open global economy with 'synergies between market forces and government function'.[56]

The 'community of common destiny' is associated with the Belt and Road Initiative (BRI). The BRI aims to build 'policy, infrastructure, trade, financial and people-to-people connectivity', resulting in a 'new platform for international cooperation'. Through the BRI, China will build pipelines, ports, bridges, and railways connecting China with Southeast Asia and South Asia, Central Asia, the Middle East, and Europe. Also included in the project is a 'digital silk road', to help states build internet connections through cables and 5G networks.[57]

The BRI is not just a project to build physical infrastructure and to enhance connectivity. It is envisioned as a potential means for China to increase its influence over global norms while weakening liberal norms.[58] The geographic scope of the BRI extends beyond China's traditional sphere of influence on its periphery to Europe, Africa, the Middle East, and Latin America. Those states that join the BRI and accept loans and investments will be encouraged to adopt other connectivities – such as free trade agreements, Chinese industrial standards, smart-city programmes, academic exchanges, and scientific joint research centres.[59]

The establishment of new norms requires that a sufficient number of states observe them in their conduct. The leading state may inculcate new norms by setting a good example, offering rewards for norm-consistent behaviour, and punishing norm violations. Ancient Chinese thought upholds the superiority of example setting as a means of inducing others to follow rites or norms.[60] Today, China hopes that developing countries will follow its economic model of a strong state combined with markets – the China Model.[61]

Moral rivalry

President Biden has pledged to restore US moral leadership, raising the possibility of a competition with China to shape global norms. During the Trump administration, Xi had the dimension of moral authority to himself, as Trump pursued a purely transactional, self-interested foreign policy. Moreover, contrary to the principles of moral realism, Trump was motivated entirely by his personal interests, rather than state or international interests.[62] For example, although Trump conducted a trade war with China from 2018 to 2020 to coerce Beijing into making changes in such areas as industrial policy and protection of intellectual property rights, at a bilateral meeting with Xi in Osaka, Japan in June 2019, Trump pleaded with the Chinese president to buy American soybeans and wheat to ensure that he would be re-elected as president in 2020. Trump's actions made clear that he was more concerned about his own re-election than China's trade practices. Indeed, according to his former national security adviser John Bolton, Trump viewed all foreign policy issues through the lens of his re-election effort.[63]

Trump's policy towards China was extremely inconsistent, as the president alternated between praise for Xi Jinping as his friend and escalating tariffs on Chinese products.[64] Decision making by a single leader who is motivated solely by self-interest leads to inconsistent, unpredictable policies because personal interests fluctuate more than state interests.[65] After praising Xi for his management of the COVID-19 virus over a dozen times, in March 2020, Trump began to blame China when the pandemic spread to the US, using anti-Asian rhetoric.[66] China retaliated in a foreign ministry statement by accusing the US military of manufacturing the virus in a bioweapons lab.[67] In the context of mutual blaming, cooperation between the two powers in managing the virus and vaccines was non-existent. In July 2022, two scientific studies were published in *Science* magazine indicating that the virus had originated in Wuhan's Huanan wildlife market sometime in November 2019. But without more data and cooperation from the Chinese government, much may remain unknown about the origins of the virus, which could provide scientific insights into how to contain future pandemics.[68]

Trump's amoral, bullying foreign policy severely damaged the US moral standing. According to moral realism, strategic credibility is the most important norm for a hegemon, but Trump walked away from multilateral liberal regimes previously sponsored by the US, such as the Paris Climate Change Agreement, the Trans-Pacific Partnership agreement, and the Joint Comprehensive Plan of Action (Iran nuclear agreement).[69] American power remained roughly constant, but Trump's contempt for multilateral institutions and alliance commitments caused the US to lose international influence.[70]

Biden wants to re-emphasize liberal values in US policy and to restore some of America's moral authority.[71] But he recognizes that the US cannot force other states to adopt American values. In his 20 January 2021 inaugural address, President Biden stressed that the US would lead 'not merely by the example of our power but by the power of our example'.[72] The 'power of example' resembles moral realist recommendations that a humane authority set a good example by following international norms in order to encourage emulation.[73]

By 'power of example', Biden is not just referring to US conduct on the world stage but its management of domestic problems, such as the pandemic, inequality, the deterioration of infrastructure, and technological challenges. At his first press conference, the US president declared his determination to 'prove democracy works' in order to compete effectively with China.[74] In other words, the US government must make progress in addressing social ills and inequality to offer evidence that it is competent and can get things done. In his first major foreign policy address, at the US State Department, Biden said that the US would seek to reclaim 'our credibility and moral authority' and to 'repair our moral leadership'.[75] According to moral realism, political leadership is the most important determinant of a state's relative status. To gain additional status, the leadership must carry out a successful domestic reform programme.[76]

In his first two years, Biden succeeded in getting a major pandemic relief programme, $1 trillion for building infrastructure, a measure to keep dangerous people from getting guns, and a bill that will lower prescription drug costs for seniors, extend subsidies to help people pay for health programmes, and invest $370 billion in measures to curb climate change.[77]

Biden has also reiterated his commitment to US alliances such as NATO and bilateral alliances with South Korea and Japan to restore damaged US strategic credibility, a foundational value of moral realism. 'America is back' he told the 2021 Munich Security Conference, his first public meeting with European allies. In contrast to President Trump, who several times refused to affirm the US commitment under Article 5 to defend any member of the NATO alliance, Biden promised that 'we will keep the faith' because 'an attack on one is an attack on all'.[78]

But more consequential in establishing America's moral leadership was the Biden administration's success in forging a unified NATO policy to resist Russia's invasion of Ukraine by providing military assistance to the Ukrainians and imposing sanctions on Russia. Biden was able to take advantage of the Ukraine crisis to reassert America's leadership on the global stage and to cooperate with the European Union.[79] President Biden referred to the war in Ukraine as a 'profound moral issue'.[80]

Russia's invasion of a sovereign country Ukraine placed China in a difficult situation. Chinese strategic and economic interests depended on continuing cooperation with Russia. Chinese officials defended Russia, claiming that the Russian war against Ukraine was a defensive response to NATO expansion and American aggression. But China hedged in its support for Russia, purchasing Russian oil and gas while refraining from economic or military assistance that would incur American economic sanctions.[81]

Yan Xuetong predicts that in the near future China will probably not have sufficient power to alter global norms for all states, in particular, the industrialized West. According to moral realism, without changes in norms as well as the distribution of power, the character of the international system will not change.[82] The US has exceptional leverage due to its shaping of institutions after WWII and alliance networks.[83] On the other hand, China is creating its own international institutions parallel to and separate from the US-supported system, such as the Asian Infrastructure Investment Bank, the New Development Bank, the Shanghai Cooperation Organization.

According to moral realism, structural contradictions will prevent joint global leadership between the US and China. At the same time, neither power is likely to achieve a position of unquestioned dominance as global leader in the near future. The division of authority between the US and China could lead to a lack of concerted action on problems of global governance such as climate change, drugs, counterterrorism, and migration.[84]

Summary

Future competition between the United States and China will differ in significant respects from the Cold War. If there are rival blocs, they will be looser, less ideological, and less defined by geography than during the Cold War. There could be shifting alignments and coalitions among states, depending on the issue.[85] The US and China are enmeshed in each other's economy, which provides a brake on conflict escalation.

While the Cold War between the US and the Soviet Union extended to the military, economic, and ideological domains, competition between China and the US is likely to be mainly in the domain of status and advanced technology. Because status is a matter of collective beliefs by the international community, it does not have to be zero-sum. The two states can control their status rivalry by recognizing the other's pre-eminence in different areas, following a strategy of social cooperation.[86] As part of a division of labour, China could take the lead in providing economic assistance and trade in East Asia, while the US would offer security guarantees.[87] Xi Jinping has expressed willingness to cooperate in specific areas of shared interests, such as health security, climate change, and weapons proliferation.[88]

Sino–American rivalry over technology is likely to lead to limited decoupling of US economic ties and supply lines. As the US is increasingly concerned about the security implications of off-shoring so much production, China is striving to be self-sufficient in emerging technologies to reduce the US ability to exploit technology 'choke points', such as semi-conductors. To protect its position in technology, the US has imposed additional restrictions on private exports of technology and on Chinese investments in US firms. These actions aimed at reducing the security risks of interdependence will not eliminate the pacifying effects of globalization.[89]

While past power transitions ended in war, the US and China can take steps to mitigate the possibility of an inadvertent conflict resulting from a maritime skirmish or proxy war. Given the risk of inadvertent escalation due to misperception, there should be more communication and dialogue between the Chinese and US militaries, and ongoing negotiations regarding crisis management and nuclear weapons. China and the US are larger and more powerful than any countries in history, and they need to consult the lessons of history to determine how they can exercise international leadership.

Notes

[1] Østen Tunsjø, *The Return of Bipolarity in World Politics: China, the United States, and Geostructural Realism*, New York: Columbia University Press, 2018.

[2] Charles A. Kupchan, *No One's World: The West, The Rising Rest, and the Coming Global Turn*, New York: Oxford University Press, 2012; Richard Haass, 'How a World Order Ends: And What Comes in Its Wake', *Foreign Affairs* 98, no. 1 (2019): 30; Alexander Cooley and Daniel Nexon, *Exit from Hegemony: The Unraveling of the American Global Order*, New York: Oxford University Press, 2020.

[3] John J. Mearsheimer, *The Tragedy of Great Power Politics*, New York: W.W. Norton, 2001; Graham Allison, *Destined for War: Can America and China Escape Thucydides's Trap?*, New York: Houghton Mifflin Harcourt, 2017.

[4] Thomas J. Wright, *All Measures Short of War*, New Haven: Yale University Press, 2017; Timothy R. Heath and William R. Thompson, 'Avoiding US–China Competition Is Futile: Why the Best Option Is to Manage Strategic Rivalry', *Asia Policy* 13, no. 2 (2018): 91–119; Andrew Scobell, 'Perception and Misperception in US–China Relations', *Political Science Quarterly* 135, no. 4 (2020–21): 637–64.

[5] Zhao Tingyang, 'Rethinking Empire from a Chinese Concept "all-under-Heaven"', *Social Identities* 12, no. 1 (2006): 29–41; June Teufel Dryer, 'The Tianxia Trope: Will China Change the International System?', *Journal of Contemporary China* 24, no. 96 (2015): 1015–31.

[6] Yan Xuetong, *Ancient Chinese Thought, Modern Chinese Power*, Princeton: Princeton University Press, 2011, pp 65–6, 71; Yan Xuetong, *Leadership and the Rise of Great Powers*, Princeton: Princeton University Press, 2019, pp 43, 48–50.

[7] Timothy R. Heath and William R. Thompson, 'Avoiding US–China Competition Is Futile': 105–7.

[8] Deborah Welch Larson, *Origins of Containment: A Psychological Explanation*, Princeton: Princeton University Press, 1985, pp 328–31.

[9] Fiona S. Cunningham and Taylor M. Fravel, 'Assuring Assured Retaliation: China's Nuclear Posture and US–China Strategic Stability', *International Security* 40, no. 2 (2015): 7–50.

[10] Yan Xuetong, *Leadership and the Rise of Great Powers*, pp 87–8, 90–3.

[11] Nigel Gould-Davies, 'Rethinking the Role of Ideology in International Politics During the Cold War', *Journal of Cold War Studies* 1, no. 1 (1999): 90–110.

[12] Thomas J. Christensen, *The China Challenge: Shaping the Choices of a Rising Power*, New York: W.W. Norton, 2015, p 42; Østen Tunsjø, *The Return of Bipolarity in World Politics*, pp 110–11; George Magnus, 'China and the US Are too Intertwined to Keep Up the Trade War', *Financial Times*, 7 June 2019, www.ft.com.

[13] Keith Johnson and Robbie Gramer, 'The Great Decoupling', *Foreign Policy*, 14 May 2020, https://foreignpolicy.com/2020/05/14/china-us-pandemic-economy-tensions-trump-coronavirus-covid-new-cold-war-economics-the-great-decoupling/.

[14] 'Endgame', *The Economist*, 15 August 2020, p 56.

15. Michael Mastanduno, 'Strategies of Economic Containment: US Trade Relations with the Soviet Union', *World Politics* 37, no. 4 (1985): 503–31; Michael Mastanduno, *Economic Containment: CoCom and the Politics of East-West Trade*, Ithaca: Cornell University Press, 1992; Ian Jackson, *The Economic Cold War: America, Britain and East-West Trade, 1948–63*, Houndsmill, Basingstoke. Hampshire: Palgrave, 2001; Richard N. Cooper, 'Economic Aspects of the Cold War, 1962–1975', in Melvyn P. Leffler and Odd Arne Westad (eds), *Cambridge History of the Cold War*, Volume 2, *Crises and Détente*, Cambridge: Cambridge University Press, 2010, pp 52–54.
16. Yan Xuetong, 'The Age of Uneasy Peace: Chinese Power in a Divided World', *Foreign Affairs* 98, no. 1 (2019): 40–6; Edward Wong, 'US vs. China: Why This Power Struggle Is Different', *New York Times*, 27 June 2019; Thomas J. Christensen, '"There Will Not Be a New Cold War": The Limits of US–Chinese Competition', *Foreign Affairs*, 24 March 2021, www.foreignaffairs.com/articles/united-states/2021-03-24/there-will-not-be-new-cold-war.
17. Yan Xuetong, *Leadership and the Rise of Great Powers*, p 99.
18. Minghao Zhao, 'Is a New Cold War Inevitable? Chinese Perspectives on US-China Strategic Competition', *Chinese Journal of International Politics* 12, no. 3 (2019): 371–94.
19. Yan Xuetong, *Leadership and the Rise of Great Powers*, pp 63–64, 100.
20. Ibid., pp 2, 56–57, 63, 100.
21. Yan Xuetong, 'The Age of Uneasy Peace': 46.
22. Andrew B. Kennedy and Daren J. Lim, 'The Innovation Imperative: Technology and US–China Rivalry in the Twenty-First Century', *International Affairs* 94, no. 3 (2018): 554–7.
23. Evan S. Medeiros, 'The Changing Fundamentals of US–China Relations', *Washington Quarterly* 42, no. 3 (2019): 100; James McBride and Andrew Chatsky, 'Is "Made in China 2025" a Threat to Global Trade?', Council on Foreign Relations, 13 May 2019, www.cfr.org/backgrounder/made-china-2025-threat-global-trade.
24. Orville Schell and Susan L. Shirk, 'Course Correction: Towards an Effective and Sustainable China Policy', Asia Society and Center on US–China Relations, February 2019, https://asiasociety.org/center-us-china-relations/course-correction-towards-effective-and-sustainable-china-policy: 11; Evan S. Medeiros, 'The Changing Fundamentals of US–China Relations': 99.
25. Bob Davis and Lingling Wei, *Superpower Showdown: How the Battle between Trump and Xi Threatens a New Cold War*, New York: HarperCollins, 2020, p 131.
26. Ibid., pp 25–7; Richard Waters, Kathrin Hille, and Louise Lucas, 'Trump Risks a Tech Cold War', *Financial Times*, 25–26 May 2019; Kiran Stacey, 'US Tightens Restrictions on Suppliers to Huawei', *Financial Times*, 17 August 2020.
27. James Politi, Demetri Sevastopulo, and Hudson Lockett, 'Trump Blacklist Ups Ante with China', *Financial Times*, 20 December 2020.
28. Edward Wong and Ana Swanson, 'Export Banks Are at Heart of US Plan to Foil China', *New York Times*, 6 July 2022; Ana Swanson, 'Fearing China's Drive, US Funds Chip Makers', *New York Times*, 4 August 2022.
29. Orville Schell and Susan L. Shirk, 'Course Correction': 27.
30. Evelyn Cheng, 'Fallout from US–China Trade Conflict Could be "Even Worse" than WWI, Kissinger Says', *CNBC News*, 22 November 2019, https://www.cnbc.com/2019/11/22/us-china-economic-conflict-could-be-worse-than-wwi-henry-kissinger-says.html.
31. Robert Gilpin, *War and Change in World Politics*, New York: Cambridge University Press, 1981, pp 13–15, 31, 33, 198–9.
32. A.F.K. Organski, *World Politics*, New York: Alfred A. Knopf, 1958, pp 328–9; A.F.K. Organski and Jacek Kugler, *The War Ledger*, Chicago: University of Chicago Press, 1980, p 23; Jack S. Levy, 'Power Transition Theory and the Rise of China', in Robert S. Ross

and Zhu Feng (eds), *China's Ascent: Power, Security, and the Future of International Politics*, Ithaca: Cornell University Press, 2008, pp 11–33.

33 John J. Mearsheimer, *The Tragedy of Great Power Politics*; John J. Mearsheimer, 'The Gathering Storm: China's Challenge to US Power in Asia', *Chinese Journal of International Politics* 3 (2010): 381–96.

34 Graham Allison, *Destined for War*, pp 29, 39–40. For a critique of Allison's reading of Thucydides, see Jonathan Kirshner, 'Handle Him with Care: The Importance of Getting Thucydides Right', *Security Studies* 28, no. 1 (2019): 1–24.

35 Yan Xuetong, *Leadership and the Rise of Great Powers*, pp 64, 72, 200.

36 Ibid., p 100.

37 Jonathan D. Caverley and Peter Dombrowski, 'Too Important to be Left to the Admirals: The Need to Study Maritime Great-Power Competition', *Security Studies* 29, no. 4 (2020): 580.

38 'A Chained Dragon', *The Economist*, 6 July 2019, p 35.

39 'Why China Wants a Mighty Navy', *The Economist*, 27 April 2019, p 40; Cary Huang, 'China Takes Aim at the US for the First Time in Its Defense White Paper', *South China Morning Post*, 7 August 2019, scmp.com; Office of the Secretary of Defense, Military and Security Developments Involving the People's Republic of China, *Annual Report to Congress*, 2020, p vii.

40 Nina Silove, 'The Pivot before the Pivot: US Strategy to Preserve the Power Balance in Asia', *International Security* 40, no. 4 (2016): 45–88.

41 Orville Schell and Susan L. Shirk, 'Course Correction': p 26; Østen Tunsjø, *The Return of Bipolarity in World Politics*, p 138; 'Identify Yourself', *The Economist*, 20 June 2020, pp 33–34.

42 Østen Tunsjø, *The Return of Bipolarity in World Politics*, p 129.

43 Ibid., p 136.

44 Michael Green, Kathleen Hicks, Zack Cooper, John Schaus, and Jake Douglas, 'Deterrence Theory and Gray Zone Strategies', in *Countering Coercion in Maritime Asia: The Theory and Practice of Gray Zone Deterrence*, Center for Strategic & International Studies, May 2017 (Lanham, MD: Rowman & Littlefield), https://www.csis.org/analysis/countering-coercion-maritime-asia.

45 Tiffany May and Mike Ives, 'A Drumbeat of Pressure on Taiwan, Explained', *New York Times*, 9 August 2022; 'Danger Ahead', *The Economist*, 13 August 2022, pp 33–5.

46 John H. Herz, 'Idealist Internationalism and the Security Dilemma', *World Politics* 2, no. 2 (1950): 157–80; Robert Jervis, 'Cooperation under the Security Dilemma', *World Politics* 30, no. 2 (1978): 167–214.

47 Adam P. Liff and G. John Ikenberry, 'Racing towards Tragedy?: China's Rise, Military Competition in the Asia Pacific, and the Security Dilemma', *International Security* 39, no. 2 (2014): 57–8; OSD, Military and Security Developments, p ii.

48 *China's National Defense in the New Era*, Beijing: Foreign Languages Press, 2019, www.xinhuanet.com/english/2019-07/24/c_138253389.htm; Ben Lowsen, 'China's New Defense White Paper: Reading between the Lines', 30 July 2019, *The Diplomat*, https://thediplomat.com/2019/07/chinas-new-defense-white-paper-reading-between-the-lines/.

49 'Danger Ahead', *The Economist*, p 35.

50 Yan Xuetong, *Ancient Chinese Thought, Modern Chinese Power*, pp 43, 47–51, 86–8; Yan Xuetong, *Leadership and the Rise of Great Powers*, pp 43–5, 48–9.

51 Ibid., pp 44–5, 106, 118–20.

52 Feng Zhang, 'The Rise of Chinese Exceptionalism in International Relations', *European Journal of International Relations* 19, no. 2 (2011): 310–22; Rana Mitter, 'The World China Wants: How Power Will – and Won't – Reshape Chinese Ambitions', *Foreign Affairs* 100, no. 1 (2021): 165.

53 Full text of Xi Jinping's Report at 19th CPC National Congress, www.chinadaily.com.cn/m/qingdao/2017-11/04/content_34771557.htm.
54 Yan Xuetong, *Leadership and the Rise of Great Powers*, pp 131–2.
55 'Working Together to Build a New Partnership of Win-Win Cooperation and Create a Community of Shared Future for Mankind', at the General Debate of the 70th Session of the UN General Assembly, 28 September 2015, https://gadebate.un.org/sites/default/files/gastatements/70/70_ZH_en.pdf; Xi Jinping, 'Work Together to Build a Community of Shared Future for Mankind', 19 January 2019, speech at UN Office at Geneva, www.xinhuanet.com/english/2017-01/19/c_135994782.htm. For discussion and interpretation, see Denghua Zhang, 'The Concept of "Community of Common Destiny" in China's Diplomacy: Meaning, Motives and Implications', *Asia & the Pacific Policy Studies* 5, no. 2 (2018): 196–207; Liza Tobin, 'Xi's Vision for Transforming Global Governance: A Strategic Challenge for Washington and Its Allies', *Texas National Security Review* 2, no. 1 (2018): 155–56.
56 Xi Jinping, 'Working Together to Forge a New Partnership of Win-Win Cooperation', www.fmprc.gov.cn/mfa_eng/wjdt_665385/zyjh_665391/t1305051.shtm; Nadège Rolland, *China's Vision for a New World Order*, National Bureau of Asian Research, NBR Special Report #83, January 2020, pp 38–9.
57 Full text of Xi Jinping's Report at 19th CPC National Congress, www.chinadaily.com.cn/m/qingdao/2017-11/04/content_34771557.htm; Denhua Zhang, 'The Concept of "Community of Common Destiny"': 196; Daniel Tobin, 'How Xi Jinping's "New Era" Should Have Ended US Debate on Beijing's Ambitions', Center for Strategic and International Studies, May 2020, www.csis.org/analysis/how-xi-jinpings-new-era-should-have-ended-us-debate-beijings-ambitions.
58 Nadège Rolland, *China's Vision for a New World Order*, p 40.
59 Ibid., p 41; James Kynge and Nian Liu, 'Tech's New Rulemaker', *Financial Times*, 8 October 2020.
60 Yan Xuetong, *Leadership and the Rise of Great Powers*, pp 22–3, 113.
61 Xi Jinping, 'Secure a Decisive Victory in Building a Moderately Prosperous Society in All Respects and Strive for the Great Success of Socialism with Chinese Characteristics for a New Era', speech at the 19th National Congress of the Communist Party of China, 28 October 2017, www.xinhuanet.com/english/download/Xi_Jinping%27s_report_at_19th_CPC_National_Congress.pdf. See also Yan Xuetong, *Leadership and the Rise of Great Powers*, pp 131–2; Liza Tobin, 'Xi's Vision for Transforming Global Governance': 160.
62 Yan Xuetong, *Leadership and the Rise of Great Powers*, p 8.
63 John Bolton, *The Room Where It Happened: A White House Memoir*, New York: Simon & Schuster, 2020, pp 301–2, 485.
64 Deborah Welch Larson, 'Policy or Pique? Trump and the Turn to Great Power Competition', *Political Science Quarterly* 136, no. 1 (2021): 54–5, 57, 61–2.
65 Yan Xuetong, *Leadership and the Rise of Great Powers*, pp 140–2.
66 Michael D. Swaine, 'Chinese Crisis Decision Making: Managing the COVID-19 Pandemic, Part Two: The International Dimension', *Chinese Leadership Monitor* (2020), n45, www.prcleader.org/swaine-1.
67 Steven Lee Myers, 'China Spins Tale that US Army Started the Coronavirus Epidemic', *New York Times*, 13 March 2020, updated 7 July 2021, www.nytimes.com.
68 Victoria Gill, 'Covid Origins Studies Say Evidence Points to Wuhan Market', *BBC*, 26 July 2022, www.bbc.com/news/science-environment-62307383; Michael Worobey et al, 'The Huanan Seafood Wholesale Market in Wuhan was the Early Epicenter of the COVID-19 Pandemic', *Science* 377 (2022): 951–9; Jonathan E. Pekar et al, 'The Molecular Epidemiology of Multiple Zoonotic Origins of SARS-CoV-2', *Science* 377 (2022): 960–6.

69 Yan Xuetong, *Leadership and the Rise of Great Powers*, pp 137–8.
70 Ibid., pp 56–7.
71 David E. Sanger, 'Looking to End "America First" and Re-engage with the World', *New York Times*, 10 November 2020.
72 Inaugural address by President Joseph R. Biden Jr, 20 January 2021, www.whitehouse.gov/briefing-room/speeches-remarks/2021/01/20/inaugural-address-by-president-joseph-r-biden-jr/.
73 Yan Xuetong, *Leadership and the Rise of Great Powers*, p 43.
74 David E. Sanger, 'Biden Stakes Out his Challenge with China: "Prove Democracy Works"', *New York Times*, 27 March 2021.
75 'Remarks by President Biden on America's Place in the World', 4 February 2021, www.whitehouse.gov/briefing-room/speeches-remarks/2021/02/04/remarks-by-president-biden-on-americas-place-in-the-world/.
76 Yan Xuetong, *Leadership and the Rise of Great Powers*, pp 25, 39, 82–7.
77 Michael D. Shear and Zolan Kanno-Youngs, 'A Victory for Biden, and a Bet on America's Future', *New York Times*, 12 August 2022.
78 David E. Sanger, Steven Erlanger, and Roger Cohen, 'Biden Reaffirms Alliances' Value for US Policies', *New York Times*, 20 February 2021.
79 Mark Landler, Katrin Bennhold, and Matina Stevis-Gridneff, 'After Zelensky's Plea, the West Raced to Form a United Front', *New York Times*, 6 March 2022.
80 Joseph R. Biden Jr, 'President Biden: What America Will and Will not Do in Ukraine', *New York Times*, 1 June 2022.
81 'Winning the Narrative War', *The Economist*, 26 March 2022, p 41; Alexander Gabuev, 'China's New Vassal', *Foreign Affairs*, 9 August 2022, foreign affairs.com.
82 Yan Xuetong, *Leadership and the Rise of Great Powers*, pp 170–1.
83 Wu Xinbo, 'China in Search of a Liberal Partnership International Order', *International Affairs* 94, no. 5 (2018): 1017.
84 Yan Xuetong, *Leadership and the Rise of Great Powers*, pp 65, 199–200.
85 Ibid., p 199.
86 Deborah Welch Larson and Alexei Shevchenko, *Quest for Status: Chinese and Russian Foreign Policy*, New Haven: Yale University Press, 2019.
87 G. John Ikenberry, 'Between the Eagle and the Dragon: America, China, and Middle State Strategies in East Asia', *Political Science Quarterly* 131, no. 1 (2016): 9–43; Yang Yuan, 'Escape Both the "Thucydides Trap" and the "Churchill Trap": Finding a Third Type of Great Power Relations under the Bipolar System', *Chinese Journal of International Politics* 11, no. 2 (2018): 213–18, 229–33.
88 Michael Crowley, 'Biden, Covering Range of Thorny Issues, Talks with Xi for First Time as President', *New York Times*, 11 February 2021.
89 Philip Stephens, 'Supply Chain "Sovereignty" Will Undo the Gains of Globalisation', *Financial Times*, 19 March 2021.

10

Moral Realism on Interstate Leadership in Response to Critics

Yan Xuetong

Donald Trump's inauguration as 45th president of the US in January 2017 made the 'leadership matters' concept a main topic for discussion among international relations (IR) scholars. Although none could fail to acknowledge what dramatic changes the new American leadership had wrought on interstate politics, few carried out theoretical research on the unique nature of interstate leadership according to this phenomenon.[1] As an IR theory, moral realism ascribes major changes in interstate politics to the changers in leadership types of major powers. To improve moral realism theory, this project invited seven excellent chapters on the topic. The questions and criticisms raised by the articles published in this book brought home to me the extent to which indistinct differentiations between interstate and domestic leadership hinder theoretical understanding of the interstate leadership concept. In answering the questions that the seven chapters ask, this chapter will discuss the singularity of interstate leadership, sequenced under the headings of unique nature, relative morality, quality measurement, functional conditions, and further studies.

The nature of interstate leadership

Although interstate and domestic leadership share many features, a general understanding of what actually constitutes leadership might strengthen IR theorists' grasp of its unique nature. Since the anarchic international system throws into sharp relief the differences between interstate and domestic leadership, the latter of which operates as a hierarchy, analysis from an anarchical perspective is most apposite.

Interstate leadership at the individual level of analysis

Whether interstate or domestic, the voluminous IR literature on leadership popularly defines it as a process of interaction between leaders and followers in a given situation.[2] Richard Hughes, Robert Ginnett, and Cordon Curphy say, 'Leadership is more than just the kind of person the leader is or the things the leader does. Leadership is the process of influencing others toward the achievement of group goals; it is not just a person or a position'.[3] Among the three key elements of leadership – leaders, followers, and situations – it is situations that distinguish the different natures of interstate and domestic leadership. The latter is formed within a hierarchical system, the former in an anarchical one. Their differences are comparable to those between military commanders and intellectual authorities. It is according to such differences that moral realism defines interstate leadership as a process of interaction between the national policy makers of leading powers and those of the states that follow them within an anarchical system. Since both interstate leaders and their followers are national policy makers, moral realism treats interstate leadership as an independent variable at the individual level of analysis.

Professors Kai He and Fang Yuanyuan challenge this approach, holding that moral realism should define more explicitly the concept of leadership as referring either to an individual leader or to a government/state as a group.[4] Their criticisms are very important, which indicates a need for me to clarify the question of whether interstate leadership at the individual level of analysis is a single leader or a group of individual policy makers. Empirical phenomena show that a national leadership comprises a supreme leader and his key officials, while an interstate leadership may consist of a single or more than one national leadership. As for domestic leadership, the US national leadership includes a president, vice president, state secretary, security advisor, and a few other policy makers. The Chinese national leadership includes a general secretary and several members of the Standing Committee of the political bureau of the Chinese Communist Party. In the case of interstate leadership, the UN leadership consists of the national policy makers of the five permanent members of the Security Council. The current European leadership, meanwhile, often refers to the German chancellor, the French president, and heads of the European Union (EU).

At the domestic level, foreign policies are made through consultations between the supreme leader and his key cabinet members. At the interstate level, decision making is comparable to national policy making when the interstate leadership is performed by a single great power. When interstate leadership is exercised by leaders of more than one state, decision making, in effect, constitutes the conciliation between them. Interstate leadership can be either institutional, as in the P5 of the UN Security Council, or non-institutional, as in the leadership of Franklin D. Roosevelt (FDR), Joseph V. Stalin, and Winston L. Churchill at the Yalta Conference. However, it is the supreme leader that makes the final decision on foreign policy, both at home and in the interstate arena. It is thus most realistic to treat leadership, both interstate and domestic, as a variable at the individual level.

Professor Athanasios Platias and Lecturer Vasilis Trigkas hold that moral realism 'does not take into full consideration the fundamental impact of structure on incentivizing or hindering political reform in the first place'.[5] Their criticisms suggest that my theory does not concern the impact of structure on policy making. It is clear that I have not expressed myself well enough and need to elaborate a bit further on this. It is true to say that every interstate leadership is exercised within a given interstate power structure to which leaders must defer when making foreign policy. Yet moral realism, as a dualist theory, ascribes national interests or strategic goals to a state's position in a given power structure, and its approaches to achieving such interests to the satisfaction of the strategic preferences of policy makers. Power structure, the variable at the system level of analysis, has an impact on defining exactly what national interests are, but not on deciding how to achieve them. It is the leadership that decides foreign policy, namely behaviour. Since moral realism assumes that national interests are determined by a state's position in a given power structure, its focus is on explaining the leadership's strategic preferences. That is to say, it treats power structure as a constant rather than as a variable. Fang Yuanyuan said, when 'a state's position in the system determines the context of which leadership is exercised, this then makes moral realism also a structural theory as well as an agency theory.'[6]

Interstate leadership based on national capability rather than legitimacy

Individuals exercise both interstate and domestic leadership; however, the former is based on national material capability, and the latter on institutional legitimacy. In the anarchic interstate system, it is powerful states that undertake interstate leadership, because they have the capability that weak states lack to maintain order in that system. Interstate leadership, meanwhile, is geared not to individual but to national executive capability. For instance, neither Bill Clinton nor George W. Bush exercised global leadership during the post-Cold War period based on individual capability, but rather on the US's super capability. Angela Merkel was capable of holding European leadership jointly with her French counterpart Emmanuel Macron, but not global leadership – not because her leadership capability was in any way inferior to that of her American counterparts, but due to the lesser power of Germany in comparison with that of the US.

In a hierarchical system, national leaders are charged with domestic leadership based on institutional legitimacy as opposed to material capability. In most cases, domestic leadership transitions are not precipitated by the incumbent leader's possession of fewer material resources than his successors, but by the latter's possession of the political legitimacy required to assume national power. This is why there have been so many child kings and emperors in history, and so many impotent presidents in the present day. However, when it is a civil war, military coup, or similarly violent event that precipitates a domestic leadership transition, the anarchical scenario in which it is likely to occur makes the outcome dependent on rival parties' material capabilities, rather than institutional legitimacy. This is another way of showing that interstate leadership is geared to the material capability of political entities in an anarchical system.

As national capability is thus fundamental to interstate leadership, the superpower alone has the capability to gain leadership of a unipolar system. A bipolar or multipolar system is often without any system leadership because each of the major powers is capable of repelling the leadership bids of others. A joint leadership of two superpowers or several major powers may occur if they are willing to cooperate with each other. Such a situation, however, has been less frequent in history than that of a total absence of interstate leadership in a bipolar or multipolar situation. The logic in regard to an anarchic system's requirement of leadership capability can also be applied to regional leadership. That is to say, a regional leadership may be based on a single state's capability, or on the joint capability of several regional major states. Australia's regional leadership of Oceania represents the former case scenario, and Germany and France's joint EU leadership illustrates the latter.

Interstate leadership based on partnership rather than a superior–subordinate relationship

Followers of an interstate leadership are individuals representing independent states. As followers have independent power, especially in regard to military capabilities, interstate leadership can be exercised only through consultancy between leaders and followers, rather than leaders issuing orders to followers as in a hierarchical system. The legitimacy of the national leaders of such followers is conditional upon their unquestionable loyalty to their own country. No interstate leadership, therefore, has the right to demand loyalty from any of its followers. Although real interstate status is dependent on national capability, national leaders are under no obligation to carry out orders issued by other states. The relationship between interstate leaders and followers is one of cooperation according to the will of each side. In other words, they are business partners, rather than superiors and subordinates or employers and employees.

In hierarchical institutions, whether states, governments, troops, or companies, a leadership's followers comprise individuals that are subordinate to their bosses. Followers and their leaders do not have equal rights, neither according to law nor in actual practice. The superior–subordinate relationship legitimately expects followers to be loyal to leaders – defined as representatives of the holistic interests of a given institution. In a hierarchical system, leaders and followers are never partners; they are at best patrons and clients. The leader–follower relationship of interstate leadership thus differs from the domestic leadership hierarchy as the two kinds of leadership are formed, as well as exercised, in quite different ways.

Interstate leadership based on shared rather than institutional interests

As each state has its particular independent interests, their national leaders follow the leaders of stronger powers that can protect the interests of their state and oppose those that threaten to harm them. As an interstate system inevitably includes mutually antagonistic states, its leadership often protects the interests that certain countries share at the cost of those of certain other states. Such conflicting interests between opposing states hinder the existence of holistic interests in an interstate system. Recent instances include anti-COVID-19 efforts and climate control; neither qualifies as a common interest upon which to establish a global leadership that every state finds acceptable.

Although a necessary condition, shared interests between states alone are insufficient to form an interstate leadership. This also entails the will and capability of leading states and followers to protect such shared interests. No state ever accepts the leadership of one that is weaker than themselves, due to doubts about their capability to protect their shared interests. Thus, the three elements – shared interests, a stronger capability than any follower, and the will to protect followers – constitute sufficient functional conditions for an interstate leadership. On the condition that leaders of a strong power have the will to protect followers, the larger shared interests with and the stronger capability than others, the more followers they will gain. (see Table 10.1).

Different from interstate leadership, a domestic leadership is based on a state's entire interests, naturally and legally defined as those shared by the leaders and

Table 10.1: Relationships between leading powers and other states

		Interests between leading powers and other states		
		Shared	Neither	Conflicting
Capability of leading powers	Strong	Followers	Neutrals	Hesitant opponents
	Weak	Hesitant followers	Neutrals	Opponents

ordinary people of a given state. When a domestic leadership is legitimately established, the people of that state become its followers according to the constitution. No individual has the legal right to oppose that leadership for the sake of personal interests, although they may do so in the name of the interests of the people as a whole. In light of the different interest bases of interstate and domestic leaderships, the former usually enlarges the interests that leading states and their followers share, and the latter consolidate themselves by improving the importance of national interests. For instance, the greater the number of states that face a common security threat, the more followers the interstate leadership will gain; and the more dangerous a foreign invasion threatens to be, the more solid a domestic leadership becomes.

As one who believes there is correspondence between interstate and domestic leaderships, Fang says that moral realism 'does not explore the causal relations, or even the interaction between these two levels of leadership, and the typologies of state leadership and interstate leadership do not correspond with each other'.[7] Rather than making distinctions between interstate and domestic leaderships, Fang seems to think that the two leadership categories should be in consistency. In fact, the difference in political level of domestic and interstate leaderships is only superficial. The differences between the two, as discussed previously, suggest that they are of quite different natures. Since one functions in a hierarchical system and the other in an anarchical system respectively, their types and qualities should be judged according to different criteria. In general, it is far more difficult for a leader to enact qualified interstate leadership than it is to provide qualified domestic leadership, because interstate followers are not subordinates. That is to say, a qualified domestic leadership is not equal to the demands of an interstate one. Accordingly, there can hardly be any correspondence between the domestic and interstate leadership typologies.

The relativity of interstate leadership morality

Based on the distinctions between interstate and domestic leaderships as discussed earlier, we may infer that the moralities of the two kinds of leadership are not exactly the same. It is hence necessary to examine the general characteristics of leadership morality, along with the uniqueness of interstate leadership morality, from the aspects of historical evolution, relative comparison, and a non-holistic system.

Morality that evolves with history

The concrete moral standards of both interstate and domestic leaderships evolve with historical developments. For instance, millennia passed before slavery was criticized as an immoral political system. Upon establishing the US two or more centuries ago. George Washington and other founding fathers indeed allowed slavery to continue. By 1862, however, Abraham Lincoln's administration had issued *The Emancipation Proclamation* that abolished slavery in the US. More and more American people have since come to regard slavery as immoral, yet few similarly condemn the leadership headed by Washington. The same applies to the morality of interstate leadership. At the Yalta Conference in 1945, Roosevelt, Stalin, and Churchill discussed and decided arrangements regarding their post-war military occupations of certain foreign countries. Nowadays, an independent state's uninvited military occupation is generally regarded as immoral interstate behaviour. Yet no such judgment has been made of the Roosevelt–Stalin–Churchill leadership at the Yalta Conference.

Moral realism stresses that standards of interstate leadership morality are contemporary according to history. Disagreeing with this idea, Kai He voices doubts about the possibility of making an objective judgment. He asks, 'How could we differentiate some moral norms from others? In particular, are human rights moral norms or double-standard norms? Is non-proliferation a moral norm or a double-standard norm?'[8] His questions indicate a need for me to clarity that interstate morality should be judged according to national standards or universal ones. Historical experience shows that most people are capable of making an objective judgment about a given interstate leadership in their time. For instance, Trump was the only post-Cold War American president not to launch a war, yet the leadership he headed is, in comparison with those of George Bush, Bill Clinton, George W. Bush, and Barack Obama, regarded as the least moral. This is because the criteria for judging interstate leadership morality have descended from military concerns to the political standards of our age. The threat of major war, especially nuclear war, having diminished, people judge Trump's administration mainly from the perspective of globalization rather than peace.[9] The same goes for the non-proliferation treaty. In the 1960s, most states viewed it as a double-standard norm, but now deem it a moral one.

The connotations of a given type of interstate leadership also evolve with history. For instance, the Chinese expression *ba* (hegemony) had been interpreted as a positive type of interstate leadership until the time of Mencius, when both Mencius and Xunzi distinguished it from *wang* (humane authority) – the most moral interstate leadership. In accepting this distinction, moral realism regards hegemony as a type of leadership less moral than that of humane authority. Disagreeing with moral realism in this regard, Telò, Wang, Platias, and Trigkas, all argue that hegemony should not be categorized merely as the less inhumane type of leadership associated with the original Chinese and Greek connotations of the term.[10] Their views are very insightful, reminding us about the evolution of some political concepts through history. Ignoring the cognitive evolution of political concepts will lead to theoretical confusion.

That 'hegemony' was not viewed as an immoral leadership in ancient times is true, but a universal change in this regard occurred after WWII. During the Cold War, it was mainly developing countries that perceived hegemony as an interstate leadership bent on bullying weaker states. Since the end of the Cold War, however, almost every country, including the US, has viewed hegemony as an undesirable leadership. For instance, in the 1990s, American scholars defined US leadership as a 'benevolent hegemony', in an attempt to distinguish it from hegemony's popularly pejorative connotations.[11] This evokes a similar change in attitude towards the term 'terrorism', which for centuries referred to a political belief in violent revolutionary actions in protest against unjust rule. After the 9/11 event in 2001, terrorism also became a pejorative term. Based on the changed connotations of 'hegemony' since the Cold War, moral realism categorizes hegemony and humane authority as two types of interstate leadership, and distinguishes their different characters. 'Benevolent hegemony', meanwhile, differs from hegemony in degree, but not in character.

Relative morality of interstate leadership

From the discussion in the section on the nature of interstate leadership, we may infer that any given interstate system inevitably includes hostile countries whose interest conflicts with those of others. Interstate leadership, therefore, must operate according to shared interests between leaders and followers when facing a common enemy. Such a reality prevents all states in a given interstate system from regarding every interstate leadership as moral. This implies, therefore, that interstate leadership can only be relatively rather than absolutely moral. Leadership morality is an intersubjective or external matter determined by the views of followers as well as of non-followers on leaders' policies and behaviours. First, it means that leaders' self-claimed moral actions bear no relevance to any judgment of leadership morality. Second, people judge leadership morality according to given historical situations rather than stereotypical standards. That is to say, they usually judge domestic leadership morality through historical longitudinal comparisons, and interstate leadership morality according to contemporary lateral comparisons.

In most cases, the morality of an incumbent domestic leadership is judged by drawing a comparison between it and its predecessors. The morality of a given interstate leadership, however, is judged by comparing it with other leaderships existent in the same system. There has never been a perfectly moral interstate leadership, but certain leaderships in a given historical period have clearly been more moral than others. For instance, during the first century BCE, the Han Dynasty adopted a subjugation policy towards Central Asia states whereby they accepted its leadership but were not required to render material service The Hun Empire, meanwhile, undertook a policy of slavery towards those states, demanding that they produce agricultural products through forced labour.[12] Neither of the two leaderships was moral even in ancient times, but the Han Dynasty was less inhuman to Central Asian states than was the Hun Empire. Hence, drawing comparisons between different interstate leaderships' behaviour compels less powerful states to follow the most relatively moral ones. Theoretically speaking, therefore, followers' choices are a good reference when judging the morality of a given interstate leadership.

The partiality of interstate leadership morality

It is precisely because every interstate system inevitably includes hostile states, that it is not possible for an interstate leadership to protect the interests of every states. This conflict means that the morality of interstate leadership is always partial rather than integral at the system level. When an interstate leadership carries out its duty of protecting the shared interests of leaders and followers, it cannot avoid simultaneously hurting opposing states. This is why not every state in a given interstate system may view its leadership as moral.

In thinking of international leadership as being imbued with the global morality ascribed to the leaders of modern international organizations, Feng Zhang disagrees with moral realism's understanding of the morality of international leadership from the perspective of governmental morality. He holds that the concept of governmental morality is too narrow and 'seems to leave out the entire agenda of global justice'.[13] Zhang's critique is very important because governmental morality and international morality are not always consistent. That is why I categorize morality judgment at three levels: personal, governmental, and international.[14] However, we also have to recognize the fact that all interstate leaders deem their own particular governmental morality as part and parcel of interstate morality, rather than of any other entity's. This smacks of a similar mindset wherein each political party regards its members' loyalty as moral, yet never applies such a principle to rival parties.

From another perspective, Kai He disagrees with me that the practice of international norms and maintenance of alliance credibility is inextricable from governmental morality.[15] His idea represents a view held by many scholars of liberalism and constructivism who believe that protecting peace, democracy, and human rights is the main motive for adhering to international norms. Modern international leadership indeed is concerned with human interests more than traditional interstate leadership, but it is also true that those individuals wielding international leadership put human interests in second place to their own national interests. Interstate leadership, in fact, is often exercised by leaders of strong powers whose achievement of national interest is based on maintenance of strategic credibility to their allies but not enemies, which equates to performance of their governmental duty. This reveals the undesirable reality wherein governmental morality is holistic at the domestic level but partial at the interstate level.

The partiality of interstate leadership morality implies that the strategic credibility of interstate leadership entails being trusted by followers but not by enemies. Zhang holds that my understanding of strategic credibility is flawed, and that it diverges from Xunzi's. He says 'Under the relational interpretation *xin* [trustworthy] is no longer an abstract principle, but a virtue or habit that promotes credibility and trust in constructive relationships. Yan has missed this relational aspect of the morality of *xin*'.[16] Platias and Trigkas hold that 'for a general theory of leadership, the fundamental virtues that are conducive to strategic success must be clearly recognized and framed'.[17] Zhang, Platias, and Trigkas interpret strategic credibility adopted by moral realism as a kind of virtue. Actually, it is not my intention to treat strategic credibility as political virtue; thus, it is clear that I did not express myself well enough. For the sake of clarifying it, I would like to elaborate a bit further. To moral realism, strategic credibility is the lowest rung of interstate leadership morality, and thus cannot be regarded as a virtue[18] – a view that may be compared to regarding the will not to steal as a principle of social morality too fundamental to qualify as a virtue. If applying the concept of virtue to domestic leadership is apt, then perceiving the morality of interstate leadership as virtue is inappropriate, because interstate leadership concerns itself solely with the shared interests of leaders and followers, rather than those of all states in a system. Leading powers' policy makers, moreover, are legitimately required to give precedence to protecting their particular national interests.

The morality of an interstate leadership is often judged according to the public goods it provides for the interstate community. The existence of hostile states, however, makes it impossible for an interstate leadership to provide public goods for everyone. For instance, national defence is often viewed as the public good of every citizen of a nation, but the *Non-Nuclear Proliferation Treaty*, aimed at preventing humankind's elimination by nuclear war, is not viewed as a public good by India, Pakistan, or North Korea. Such states deem it as emanating from an international leadership of double-standard. Telò questions the view that alliances provide public goods.[19] Zhang argues that making an alliance 'could aggravate relations with non-allies, with adverse consequences for the alliance itself and the overall relationship between the alliance and its target countries'.[20] The critiques by Telò and Zhang are very helpful for the improvement of moral realism according to observation of the present international phenomena.

In their present strategic competition, the Chinese and American governments hold conflicting views about alliance. The former regards alliance as a product of Cold War mentality and the latter views it as a public good for protecting the liberal world order.[21] The conflicting views about an alliance of China and the US reflect the reality that alliances are collective rather than public goods when examined at the system level, but they are indeed public goods to allies. This is comparable to non-EU states viewing the public goods of EU members as collective ones. Suggesting that international public goods should be defined according to content, Telò views norms regarding trade, environmental protection, social rights, dispute settlement mechanisms, and other innovations as public goods.[22] In fact, multilateral norms, or the treaties of these domains, cannot be welcomed by every state. Even the norms of the World Trade Organization (WTO) were opposed by Trump's administration.

Measurements of interstate leadership

As interstate leadership differs from domestic leadership; its measurement requires a set of criteria appropriate to its specific nature. Interstate leadership can protect the interests of some, but not all, states in a system; therefore, its popularity should be measured according to the numbers of its followers. And as the quality of such followers differs, the quality of an interstate leadership should be measured according to its followers' strength and weight. Literally and practically, neither popularity nor quality equates to effectiveness; thus, measurement of the effectiveness of an interstate leadership should be according to results rather than process. Leadership per se is a process.

Measurement of popularity according to numbers of followers

The popularity of an interstate leadership refers to its acceptance by states within a given interstate system. The larger the number of its followers, the more popular a leadership becomes. Bearing in mind the competition between different interstate leaderships, the proportion of the total number of countries in a given interstate system that represents its followers is the most convincing measurement of a leadership's popularity; the larger the proportion, the greater the popularity, and vice versa. For instance, America's leadership was much more popular in the early 1990s than it was in the early 2000s, and the US launched wars against Saddam Hussein's regime in Iraq during both periods. Over 30 states followed the US leadership by joining the Gulf War in 1990, but only 13 states joined in the Iraq War of 2003. Meanwhile, UN membership increased from 159 in 1990 to 191 in 2003.[23] The number of followers in the early 1990s, however, accounted for a much larger proportion of UN member states than did those in the early 2000s.

In most cases, the increase or decrease in a leading power's allies is indicative of changes in an interstate security leadership's popularity.

Professor Deborah Larson questions my idea of improving interstate leadership through making alliances, on the grounds that the security interests of allies do not always match those of the leading state.[24] It is undeniable that conflicting security interests in this regard do weaken an interstate security leadership. Leading powers' popularity hence rests heavily on their capability to maintain solidarity within alliances. For instance, during the Cold War, the US security leadership was more popular than that of the Soviets, as manifested in the expansion of the US's allies and shrinking numbers of those of its Soviet counterpart. What should be clarified, however, is that numbers of followers serve only as an indicator of leadership popularity, and not of its quality.

Measurement of quality according to strength of followers

The popularity of an interstate leadership does not equate to its quality, which refers to its impact on interstate affairs within a given interstate system. In most cases, quality measurement hinges on the total strength of followers, because independent states invariably accept the interstate leadership of those stronger than themselves. A strong follower, therefore, has a greater impact on international affairs than a single or a few weak followers; hence, the greater the strength of its followers, the greater the influence that leadership wields. For instance, an international leadership whose followers consist of a group of industrialized countries, such as the UK, France, Germany, and Japan, carries far greater international clout than one whose followers comprise a few dozen small developing countries. Thus, the stronger its followers, the higher an interstate leadership's quality will be, and vice versa. Under anarchy, interstate affairs are largely decided by a few major powers rather than a majority of states. The quality of interstate leadership, therefore, roughly equates to the power of interstate decision making. In authorizing veto power to its five permanent members, the UN Security Council was designed according to this reality.

The quality of interstate leadership rests heavily on the strategic credibility of the policy makers it comprises. Therefore, a strong state can exercise qualified interstate leadership only when its national leaders command strategic credibility convincing enough for other states to trust them. For example, although India is the strongest power in South East Asia, it is ineligible for regional leadership. India has no followers in this region, mainly because Indian national leaders do not inspire the trust of any other state in the vicinity. Cognizant of the problem of international strategic credibility, in 2021 the Chinese leader called for China's creation of a trustworthy, admirable, and respectable international image.[25] As regards national strength and strategic credibility, the quality of interstate leadership can be categorized under the four classes of solid, ordinary, brittle, and shaky (see Table 10.2).

Table 10.2: The quality of interstate leadership

		Strength of leading states	
		Strong	**Weak**
Leaders' strategic credibility	High	Solid	Ordinary
	Low	Brittle	Shaky

According to the earlier criteria, the quality of American leadership under Trump was poor. Disagreeing with this judgment, Wang holds that I underestimate the power and resilience of the US.[26] He once doubted that the Trump administration's foreign policy undermined the comprehensive capability of the US and resulted in the decline of US hegemony. His argument indicates that my theory lacks deferent criteria for measuring the qualities of domestic and interstate leaderships. Improvement of national capability is a crucial standard applied to the quality of domestic leadership but may not be suitable for that of interstate leadership. For moral realism, both national strength and strategic credibility are components of interstate leadership quality. Therefore, focusing solely on the impact of national capability on the quality of interstate leadership, and failing to take strategic credibility into account, we will possibly misjudge the quality of a given interstate leadership. In fact, when historians of the future reevaluate Trump's impact on the US's material capability, they cannot but acknowledge that, in comparison with other American leaders during the post-Cold War period, the quality of US global leadership under Trump was the poorest of all, because the US lost much support from its European allies.

Measurement of effectiveness according to results

Since interstate leadership is a process of achieving group goals, its effectiveness refers to the extent to which goals are achieved. The measurement of a leadership's effectiveness, therefore, should be according to results rather than process, because the two things are not always consistent. A leadership's success or failure in regard to certain issues is random. Neither the popularity nor quality of a leadership can guarantee its achievement of group goals in regard to any specific issue. The most recent example is US allies' support for Joe Biden's administration's withdrawal of NATO troops from Afghanistan. The result, however, whereby the Afghan government put up no resistance and the Taliban peacefully assumed national power, was far beyond their expectations. As Biden admitted, 'This did unfold more quickly than we had anticipated'.[27]

Effective or ineffective interstate leadership cannot be distinguished by virtue of a single result. Effectiveness should be gauged according to a wide range of results rather than just one, as would be the case when measuring the effectiveness of a weather forecast. A single error cannot cast doubt on the overall forecasting effectiveness of the meteorological service as a whole. This is something that the rate of accuracy, rather than a single instance, decides. The same applies to the measurement of an interstate leadership's effectiveness. For example, FDR's international leadership is regarded as having been effective, not just because it established the UN, but also due to its many economic, military, and political achievements before and during WWII.

The effectiveness of interstate leadership is also comparative, because the success or failure of an interstate leadership often rests on competition between political or military blocs. Certain leaderships have an impressive track record of good results across a wide range of situations, whereas others have difficulties in getting their work done even with the help of followers. First, measurements of leadership effectiveness should take into account the capability differences of competing parties. A weak side's victory entails more effective leadership than does a strong one. Second, measurements of effectiveness should be limited to specific areas. Some interstate issues, such as international wars versus economic crises, are more difficult to handle than others. Limiting such measurements to similar interstate issues enables a more persuasive judgment of which leadership is the more effective.

Impact of interstate leadership at the system level

Moral realism regards interstate leadership as an independent variable at the individual level, but applies it to explanations of interstate phenomena at the system level. In comparison with variables at the system level – such as power structures, cultural structures, and interstate norms – interstate leadership has greater direct impact on interstate changes than other variables. Indeed, changes in leadership type usually bring about different interstate orders, norms, and configurations.

Theoretical explanations of interstate order

IR theories explain interstate order in accordance with two aspects: the existence or absence of order, and the characteristics of a given order. The anarchy of the interstate system implies that disorder is a natural phenomenon; hence, that order requires special conditions. War represents the former and peace the latter. Upon establishment, an interstate order may turn out to be a historically unique model, such as the imperialist order between the two world wars, the hegemonic order during the Cold War, and the liberal order in the post-Cold War period.

Classical realism attributes interstate order to 'balance of power', a concept that neorealism modernizes as 'power structure'. But the latter concept cannot explain why order and disorder occur under the same type of power structure, nor the existence of different models of interstate order that have undergone no change in power structure. Constructivism regards cultural structure as the key variable in explaining interstate order. Featuring as it does the same flaws as neorealism, constructivism also fails to explain alternations of order and disorder under the same cultural structure, for instance, the period of peace between the two world wars. Constructivism is also impotent in explaining different models of order under the same cultural structure, such as the hegemonic order in the Cold War, and the liberal order in the post-Cold War period. Relative to the topic of order models, a historically evolving cultural structure cannot explain reversals of order models, such as the counter-globalization trend since 2016. Neoliberalism ascribes international cooperation to international institutions that constrain states' behaviour by reducing transaction costs. However, the alternations of order and disorder under the same international organizations, plus the current globalization trend, render neoliberalism unconvincing.

Moral realism ascribes the existence or absence of interstate order, as well as diversified order models, to the type of interstate leadership. Changes in interstate order are caused directly by the policy of leading powers. Different leadership types have different strategic preferences. Changes in leadership type, therefore, impel dramatic policy adjustments. Interstate leadership is hence more convincing in explaining interstate order or disorder, as well as different order models, than power structure, cultural structure, or international institutions. If the type of a new interstate leadership differs from the previous one, the model of interstate order will change accordingly, or otherwise remain the same.

Kai He asks, 'If China indeed replaces US hegemony in the future, but does not change the liberal norms in the system, can we say that the China-led liberal order is the same as the US-led one?'[28] My answer is yes. Nevertheless, the reality is that China wants to change rather than maintain liberal norms. Influenced by Kenneth Waltz, He also doubts whether the theory of moral realism can explain decision making.[29] His query represents a popular view shared by many scholars in IR studies. Nevertheless, it is still worth the effort of constructing theories bridging changes at system level and decision making at individual level. It may be the advantage of moral realism which is able to link these changes at the two levels through major powers' leadership. The change in leadership type can not only explain the alternations between order and disorder, but also the reversals of order models. Interstate leadership has the power to establish, as well as disrupt, interstate orders by shaping a new model of order. For instance, the present populist leaderships of major powers have disrupted the liberal order through the policies of decoupling and deglobalization.

Interstate norms are established by interstate leadership

Interstate norms are not automatically formed through state interaction. As powerful figures are the authors of all laws and regulations, interstate norms are also established by interstate leadership. For the sake of maintaining a durable order favourable to their particular national interests, leaders of dominant powers are keen to advance certain norms that constrain other states' behaviour. But to ensure those norms are effective, they must also be seen to be following them. Kai He asks, 'What will the dominant power do when its interests are seriously undermined or threatened by the norms it has created?'[30] His question is directly related to the current debate on why the Trump administration undermined the liberal order established by the US. There is a misconception among IR scholars that rising powers, but never hegemons, are revisionist states. In fact, hegemons can also be revisionist states, bearing in mind that they are capable, for the sake of their new interests, of changing the interstate norms that they themselves originally created.

In most cases, because different types of interstate leadership favour different norms, the establishment of new norms ensues after the rise of a new type of interstate leadership. The post-Cold War norm change illustrates this argument. Neither the US nor the Soviet Union dominated world leadership during the Cold War. Rather, both provided hegemonic leaderships under which interstate norms were mainly characterized by double standards, especially regarding arms control. After the Cold War, the US became the sole superpower dominating global leadership. In light of its new global interests, however, the US began to advance liberal norms according to the globalization principles mainly represented by democratization and marketization.

Disagreeing with moral realism's classification of interstate norms, He holds that a holistic view of norms sacrifices norm nuances in regard to both shaping and constituting states' interests and behaviours.[31] Since norm classification relates closely to leadership categorization, Telò holds that interstate leadership should entail subcategories, arguing that the US and the Soviets should not be viewed as the same hegemony.[32] He and Telò's views about the classification encourage moral realism to refine types of interstate leadership and norms in future improvement. Methodologically speaking, each major category always has subclasses. When applying interstate norm or leadership classifications to a wide historical range, large categories are more appropriate than smaller or more detailed ones. Subdividing complex long-term history is often difficult and problematic. Although moral realism adopts large categories of interstate norms and leaderships for the sake of applying them to both ancient and modern history, it is still possible to bring the times factor into classification.

As for what new norms may be formed amid Sino–US bipolar rivalry, that hot debate hinges on whether or not the world will fall into a new Cold War. Larson fears the risk of US–China rivalry becoming a new type of Cold War.[33] Kai He also worries about the inevitability of a new Cold War should China forfeit its ideological openness by embracing anti-US value systems.[34] Larson and He's wariness about a new cold war is shared by many people but different with mine.[35] In the digital age, the focus of China–US competition is on gaining the digital superiority that determines the winner. Since technological standards are crucial to new international norms, both China and the US globally advance their particular digital standards rather than ideologies. Although ideological conflicts cannot disappear, they will no longer constitute the core of the rivalry between China and the US. Consequently, relations with followers will be influenced by whose digital standards, rather than ideologies, are more favourable to other states.

Interstate configurations shaped by interstate leadership

Interstate configuration is composed of the material capability structure of major powers and the strategic relations between them. Domestic leadership determines the growth of a state's material capability, and the interstate capability structure rests on major powers' different material capabilities. However, strategic relations among major powers are mainly determined by interstate leadership. That is to say, any dramatic improvement or deterioration in relations between leading states and their followers can also shape the interstate configuration. Interstate leadership, moreover, can engender either the degree or type of change in interstate configuration. An interstate leadership which all major powers follow shapes a unipolar configuration, while a bipolar configuration may ensue when its competitor compels all major powers to join an alliance against that leadership.

People usually discuss interstate configuration from the perspective of material capability structure. In fact, strategic relations between major powers engender more frequent degree changes in configuration than does capability structure. It usually takes several decades for national leaders of major powers to change the interstate capability structure, but they tend to change their strategic relations with other major powers over relatively short terms. For instance, it took Chinese leaders four decades to narrow the Sino–US capability disparity, yet the Chinese policy makers took less than a year to establish strategic cooperation with the US by abandoning anti-US foreign policy in the early 1970s.

I have defined the current international configuration as a bipolarity shaped by China–US competition, according to both capability structure and strategic relations between major powers. Wang holds that I overestimate China's capability and underestimate the US's, 'because the power disparity between the US and China is still very wide-ranging'.[36] Telò views the current interstate configuration as one of multipolarity rather than bipolarity.[37] Wang and Telò's views represent many people's argument that the world is multipolar rather than bipolar. However, there is no state or any international actor currently viewed as a superpower except the US and China. It is true that there is still a big capability gap between China and the US, but one much smaller than that between China and the other major powers. For example, by the end of 2020, China's GDP accounted for 70.3 per cent of the US's, while Japan's, the third largest GDP, accounted for only 34.4 per cent of China's.[38] Besides economic capability, China and the US also possess much larger military, technological, cultural, and diplomatic capabilities than other major powers. When taking into account the other major powers' relations with the two superpowers, the bipolar configuration becomes even more obvious. Japan and the UK side with the US, and Russia with China, while Germany and France adopt a hedging strategy.

The function of institutions based on leadership

Institutional determinism is such a popular paradigm as well as belief in political science that many scholars ignore the fact that no political institution can automatically function without political leadership. This is especially true for international institutions. It is indeed international leadership that determines the functions of international institutions, and not the other way around.

Interstate leadership defines the function of interstate institutions

In his autobiography, Theodore Roosevelt emphasizes the role of leaders in good governance, arguing that good legislation cannot secure the good governance that comes solely through administration.[39] That is to say, political leadership determines whether, or the extent to which, political institutions can function. Both interstate and domestic leaders have the political power to establish, maintain, or destroy institutions. Moral realism hence regards leadership as the precondition for the formation and functioning of institutions.

The US has not provided reliable global leadership since the Trump administration, from which ensued an obvious decline in the functions of multilateral institutions. For instance, the WTO maintained the principle of free trade under US leadership, but was unable to constrain protectionism when the Trump administration abandoned that leadership. As neither China nor the US alone has the capability to provide solid global leadership, political uncertainty has become the prominent feature of the existing bipolar world, and global governance has become less and less effective.

Many people mistakenly equate governance with institutions, or even political systems. In fact, both interstate and domestic governance refers to the performance of a political leadership, as distinct from political institutions or systems. Political leadership can adopt different types of governance under the same political system, or through the same political institutions. In both interstate and domestic societies, it is the political leadership, rather than political systems or institutions, which determines the function of governance. For instance, during the Cold War, two opposing governances under Mao Zedong and Deng Xiaoping successively existed under the same political system in China. As regards global governance of the arms control regime, however, it worked well under the leadership of Clinton's administration, but lamentably under George W. Bush's administration.[40]

Interstate leadership is little constrained by interstate institutions

Telò holds that moral realism, 'risks underestimating the strengths of multilateral institutional rules and procedures'.[41] Kai He holds the similar view that moral realism 'does not pay enough attention to international institutions'.[42] Their criticisms reflect the dominating influence of institutional determinism in political science, which is mainly advocated by liberalism. Nevertheless, the interstate leadership in an anarchical system is more or less free from the constraints of interstate institutions, including the UN, which do not have the independent material capability of states. The substantive leadership of these institutions, therefore, rests on the capability of their leading members. That is to say, interstate institutions have no independent capability to punish their leading members for any violations committed against interstate norms. For instance, the UN Security Council never imposed any binding punishment in regard to the US's misbehaviour. Free from worries about possible punishment, such states exercising interstate leadership show very limited respect for the rules of interstate institutions amid conflicts between their national interests and that institution's rules.

Wang holds that moral realism should not treat leadership as the sole factor determining the rise and fall of nations, and that consideration should also be given to such factors as political opposition and bureaucratic resistance to leadership, and the severe material constraints on it.[43] Wang's argument is right that political institutions in a modern democratic system impose certain constraints on national leaders' arbitrary actions. However, how much this kind of institutional constrains work depends on whether national leaders have respect for political institutions. Therefore, the same domestic institutional constraints vary with different leaderships, such as those that had a strong impact on Obama's administration but became weak on Trump's. Compared with domestic institutions, interstate institutions have even weaker constraints on interstate leadership, because they do have the same political power as the former.

The interstate system is anarchic, but not democratic. An interstate leadership makes decisions based on its capability and interests rather than legitimacy. Interstate institutions, including NATO, do not have the independent power to prevent their or the enemy's leadership from making certain decisions. Leading members of interstate institutions decide what should be done; institutions merely implement their decisions. That is to say, interstate institutions cannot function beyond the parameters upon which their leading members' policy makers have agreed. However, that interstate leaderships experience few constraints from interstate institutions does not mean they have absolute freedom of action. Every interstate leadership exercised by leaders of major powers accords with a specific historical condition. Therefore, they must make decisions based upon changes in both interstate and domestic situations.

Future studies of interstate leadership

There is no limit to theoretical studies of interstate leadership. Formation of interstate leadership could, in itself, be an interesting topic. Based on the distinction between interstate and domestic leaderships, there are many puzzles as to how a qualified interstate leadership is established, and how transitions between different interstate leaderships occur. In regard to practical international politics, the type of global leadership that may emerge amid China–US rivalry is a particularly catchy topic.

Formation of interstate leadership

Since moral realism regards interstate leadership as an independent variable, it has not yet touched upon the issue of leadership formation. To deepen our knowledge about interstate leadership, IR scholars need to treat it as a dependent variable by studying its formation, continuation, decline, and disappearance. Talking about leadership formation automatically renders type of interstate leadership an intriguing topic. Kai He suggests studying 'What factors can contribute to these different types of leadership, domestically and internationally?'[44] I do agree with him that the factors determining types of interstate and domestic leaderships could differ; it is, therefore, best to study interstate and domestic leadership separately.

Studies on the formation of a certain type of leadership will improve our knowledge about the relationship between major powers' domestic conditions and types of interstate leadership. Platias and Trigkas suggest formulation of a generalizable leadership-centric theory of hegemonic transition, by incorporating the unit-level variable (leadership) with political psychology and philosophy.⁴⁵ Trigkas also holds that ideology plays an important role in shaping leadership type, and that scholars overlooked the fact that Chinese millennials' worldview is shaped not only by modern science and Chinese traditional culture, but also by nationalist patriotic education.⁴⁶ Their suggestions are very instructive for studies of interstate leadership types and lead me to think about two critical questions: does the type of interstate leadership shape the mainstream values at the system level, or vice versa, and is the type of interstate leadership shaped by leaders' personal values, national values, or by interstate mainstream values?

The formation of interstate leadership is often related to the issue of strategic credibility. Theoretically, the topic of strategic credibility is worthy of study from many aspects. As a dependent variable, strategic credibility relates directly to the survival and influence of an interstate leadership, while strategic credibility, as an independent variable, is concerned with the establishment of interstate leadership. The withdrawal of US troops from Afghanistan in 2021 increased US allies' doubts about the US's reliability, a phenomenon that endows practical significance upon the study of strategic credibility. Since no interstate leadership can exist when it lost trust from all of its followers, the more reasonable approach to study strategic credibility should be from the aspect of followers rather than that of leaders.

Interstate leadership in the coming decade

At the time of writing, the US is still the world's strongest power. American leadership, therefore, is the topic most attractive to IR scholars. Although moral realism is an IR theory that Chinese scholars have formulated, it seems to have had more influence on Biden than on his Chinese counterpart. At his inauguration, Biden promised to offer the world a moral realist leadership under the principle of leading by example.⁴⁷ However, strategic credibility is based on actions rather than promises. IR experts are debating to what extent Biden's strategic credibility is undermined by his poor withdrawal plan in regard to ending the war in Afghanistan.⁴⁸ Since deeds rather than words decide the type of leadership, more empirical studies are needed to ascertain what type of leadership the American government will provide the world within the coming decade.

As for the type of American global leadership, Telò holds that distinguishing between American leaderships according to each individual administration is inappropriate, arguing. 'Convergence must be explored when it comes to defining the distinctive nature of the US leadership in the context of a post-hegemonic order'.⁴⁹ Fang holds a similar view, disagreeing with the categorization of Trump and Biden as different types of interstate leadership, and arguing that there are many similarities between their policies towards China.⁵⁰ I value very much Telò's and Fang's observations of the similarities between different American leaders. Their views suggest further studies of empirical leadership types in given countries. Distinctions between empirical interstate leaderships are much more complex than those between theoretical leadership types. The similar policies adopted by different American leaders are mainly reflected in strategic goals, but not approaches. For instance, Trump and Biden share the same strategic goal of slowing China's growth, but the former adopted a unilateral approach, the latter a multilateral one.

China is already one of the two top global powers, but there are far fewer studies on the international leadership that Chinese leaders may provide in the coming decade compared with those on American leadership. According to the last amended constitution, China is most likely not to change its national leader in the coming decade. Therefore, the study of that leader's personal political ideas may constitute the groundwork for understanding the characteristics of the Chinese leadership. Currently, more foreign scholars are doing academic research on the Chinese potential global leadership than Chinese academics are, even though the latter possesses more empirical knowledge about this issue than the former.

Since types of interstate leadership are usually related to interstate ideological competition, it is reasonable for IR scholars to study the coming global leadership from that aspect. Over the last hundred years, the world has witnessed changes in interstate leadership along with waves of rising ideologies, such as imperialism, fascism, communism, nationalism, liberalism, and populism. Kai He holds, 'It is possible for liberalism to evolve and for democracy to rebuild after the current crises'.[51] His argument implies the US's possible resumption of the liberal leadership. However, He may underestimate the current decline of liberalism. Although I appreciate He's idea of thinking about the possible resurgence of liberalism in the future, I still think that we should not ignore the fact that the term 'liberalism' is experiencing a connotation transformation from commendatory to derogatory and often related to LGBTQIA+.[52] Since all possibilities are worth our attention, populism should especially not be ignored because it remains prevalent in all major powers, including China and the US. A more realist topic is how rising populism may influence formation of the new interstate leadership in the coming decade.

Summary

Although studies on leadership constitute traditional research, few have made clear distinctions between interstate and domestic leadership. That is mainly because the two kinds of leadership are often exercised by the same national leaders of hegemons. In reality, the anarchy of the interstate system endows on interstate leadership a character quite different from that of domestic leadership. Interstate leadership consists in the interaction between partners based on both national capabilities and the interests that leading states and followers share. Domestic leadership consists of superior–subordinate relations based on both political legitimacy and holistic institutional interests. The unique nature of interstate leadership determines its morality as laterally comparative and partial. For the same reason, measurements of the popularity, quality, and effectiveness of interstate leadership should be respectively according to numbers of follower states, their weight, and the results of achieving group goals.

By ascribing types of interstate leadership to changes in the interstate order, norms, and configurations, moral realism bridges individual, state, and system analytical levels. Although its theoretical explanation is applicable to both ancient and modern interstate politics, there is still room for improvement in many respects. It fails, for instance, to touch on the formation of different leadership types and the related issue of establishment and disappearance of strategic credibility. The interstate leadership classification needs subcategories to meet history's complex reality. As a universal IR theory, moral realism needs empirical studies to test its arguments, especially with regard to the type of global leadership in the coming decade. The dearth of studies on Chinese leadership, moreover, increases the risk of moral realism theory being disproved by China's foreign policy rather than the US's.

In order to deepen knowledge about interstate leadership, moral realism purposefully controls the influence of other variables on interstate politics. Such theoretical rigour begs construction of a scientific theory on interstate leadership, but it cannot provide a comprehensive explanation for any specific leadership in the same way as multivariable analysis does. In any event, the construction of IR theories, including decision-making theories, cannot replace policy analysis.

Notes

[1] When discussing interaction between states, moral realism opts for the expression 'interstate' rather than 'international', because the former is applicable to matters or situations both ancient and modern, whereas correct use of the phrase 'international' is applicable only to events after the 15th century advent of nation states. Based on ancient political thought and history moral realism advocates a universal theory for explaining both modern and ancient political phenomena between states.
[2] Richard L. Hughes, Robert C. Ginnett, Cordon J. Curphy, *Leadership: Enhancing the Lessons of Experience* 5th edition, New York: The McGraw-Hill Companies Inc, 2006, p 6.
[3] Ibid., p 21.
[4] Fang Yuanyuan, Chapter 3 in this book; Kai He, Chapter 5 in this book.
[5] Athanasios Platias and Vasilis Trigkas, Chapter 7 in this book.
[6] Fang Yuanyuan, Chapter 3 in this book.
[7] Fang Yuanyuan, Chapter 3 in this book.
[8] Kai He, Chapter 5 in this book.

9 Joseph E. Stiglitz, 'Trump's Rogue America', *Project Syndicate*, 2 June 2017, https://www.project-syndicate.org/commentary/trump-rogue-america-by-joseph-e--stiglitz-2017-06.
10 Qingxin K. Wang, Chapter 4; Athanasios Platias and Vasilis Trigkas, Chapter 7; Mario Telò, Chapter 8, all in this book.
11 Robert Kagan, 'The Benevolent Empire', *Foreign Policy*, Summer 1998, https://carnegieendowment.org/1998/06/01/benevolent-empire-pub-275.
12 Yang Qianru, 'Han Xiongnu Xiyu Zhanlue Chengbai de Yuanyin' (The Causes of the Strategic Success of the Han Dynasty and Strategic Failure of the Huns in the Western Regions), *Guji Zhengzhi Kexue* (Science of International Politics) 1, no. 3 (2016): 78–80.
13 Feng Zhang, Chapter 6 in this book.
14 Yan Xuetong, *Leadership and the Rise of Great Powers*, Princeton: Princeton University Press, 2019, p 8.
15 Kai He, Chapter 5 in this book.
16 Feng Zhang, Chapter 6 in this book.
17 Platias and Trigkas, Chapter 7 in this book.
18 Yan Xuetong, *Leadership and the Rise of Great Powers*, p 19.
19 Mario Telò, Chapter 8 in this book.
20 Feng Zhang, Chapter 6 in this book.
21 'US Role in the World: Background and Issues for Congress', 19 January 2021, pp 2–4, https://sgp.fas.org/crs/row/R44891.pdf; Xinhua, 'China Urges NATO to Abandon Outdated Cold War Mentality', *China Daily*, 26 January 2022, www.chinadailyasia.com/article/257588.
22 Mario Telò, Chapter 8 in this book.
23 *Shijie Zhishi Nianjian 1991/92* (Year Book of World Affairs 1991/92), Beijing: World Affairs Press, 1992, p 799; *Shijie Zhishi Nianjian 2004/2005* (Year Book of World Affairs 2004/2005), Beijing: World Affairs Press, 2005, p 1601.
24 Deborah Welch Larson, 'Can China Change the Interstate System? The Role of Moral Leadership', *The Chinese Journal of Interstate Politics* 13, no. 2 (2020): 175.
25 'Xin Jiping zai zhonggong zhongyang zhengzhiju di sanshi ci jiti xuexi shi qiangdiao jiaqiang he gaijin gouji chuanbo gongzuo zhanxian zhenshi liti de Zhongguo (At the 30th Collective Study Meeting of CPC Central Committee Political Bureau, Xi Jinping Stressed the Improvement and Reform of International Media Work)', *Renmin Ribao* (People's Daily), 2 June 2021, http://paper.people.com.cn/rmrb/html/2021-06/02/nw.D110000renmrb_20210602_1-01.htm.
26 Qingxin K Wang, Chapter 4 in this book.
27 'Read the Full Transcript of President Biden's Remarks on Afghanistan: Mr. Biden spoke from the White House on Monday afternoon after the collapse of the Afghan government to the Taliban', *The New York Times*, 16 August 2021, www.nytimes.com/2021/08/16/us/politics/biden-taliban-afghanistan-speech.html.
28 Kai He, Chapter 5 in this book.
29 Kai He, Chapter 5 in this book.
30 Kai He, Chapter 5 in this book.
31 Kai He, Chapter 5 in this book.
32 Mario Telò, Chapter 8 in this book.
33 Deborah Welch Larson, 'Can China Change the Interstate System? The Role of Moral Leadership', *The Chinese Journal of Interstate Politics* 13, no. 2 (2020): 176, 179–82.
34 Kai He, Chapter 5 in this book.
35 Yan Xuetong, 'The Age of Uneasy Peace', *Foreign Affairs* 98, no. 1 (2019): 40–6; Yan Xuetong, 'Bipolar Rivalry in the Early Digital Age', *The Chinese Journal of International Politics* 3, no. 3 (2020): 314–16, 340–1.
36 Qingxin K Wang, Chapter 4 in this book.

37 Mario Telò, Chapter 8 in this book.
38 World Bank, 'Gross Domestic Product 2020', *World Development Indicators Database*, 1 July 2021, https://databank.worldbank.org/data/download/GDP.pdf.
39 Theodore Roosevelt, *An Autobiography*, New York: Macmillan, 1913, p 76, www.bartleby.com/55/6.html.
40 Joseph Cirincione, 'Strategic Collapse: The Failure of the Bush Nuclear Doctrine', *Arms Control Association*, November 2008, www.armscontrol.org/act/2008-11/features/strategic-collapse-failure-bush-nuclear-doctrine#authbio.
41 Mario Telò, Chapter 8 in this book.
42 Kai He, Chapter 5 in this book.
43 Qingxin K. Wang, Chapter 4 in this book.
44 Kai He, Chapter 5 in this book.
45 Platias and Trigkas, Chapter 7 in this book.
46 Vasilis Trigkas, 'On Global Power Differentials, Moral Realism, and the Rise of China: A Review Essay', *Journal of Contemporary China* 29, no. 126 (2020): 9.
47 'Inaugural Address by President Joseph R. Biden, Jr', 20 January 2021, *The White House*, www.whitehouse.gov/briefing-room/speeches-remarks/2021/01/20/inaugural-address-by-president-joseph-r-biden-jr/.c.
48 Stephen M. Walt, 'Afghanistan Hasn't Damaged US Credibility', *Foreign Policy*, 21 August, 2021, https://foreignpolicy.com/2021/08/21/afghanistan-hasnt-damaged-u-s-credibility/.
49 Mario Telò, Chapter 8 in this book.
50 Fang Yuanyuan, Chapter 3 in this book.
51 Kai He, Chapter 5 in this book.
52 David Brooks, 'When Dictators Find God', *The New York Times*, 9 September 2021, www.nytimes.com/2021/09/09/opinion/autocracy-religion-liberalism.html.

APPENDIX 1

Written Discussion between Rajesh Rajagopalan and Yan Xuetong

A book review of Yan Xuetong's *Leadership and the Rise of Great Powers* (2019)

Rajesh Rajagopalan
First published in *India Quarterly: A Journal of International Affairs* 75, no. 3 [2019]: 405–9

Realism is dying a slow death in its current motherland, the US. It has not been popular in Europe or other parts of the world for quite some time, and America seems set to follow the same trend. Poisoned by Kenneth Waltz's expectation of the inevitable recurrence of balances of power, prominent realists (including, while he was alive, Waltz himself) have spent the better part of the last three decades looking for an elusive counter to America's unipolar power. More radical proponents of the 'defensive' realism that Waltz spawned have gone so far as to suggest that the security dilemma – one of the central tenets of realism – can be overcome through reassurance. It has become increasingly difficult to distinguish realism from liberalism in American international relations (IR) scholarship. While there are honourable exceptions to this trend, it is difficult not to despair at the state of realism as a theory.

If realism is dying in America, it seems to be prospering in China, as others have also noted. Yan Xuetong's latest book, *Leadership and the Rise of Great Powers*, is a good example. Understandably, given China's rise, Yan's focus is on how a rising power can catch up and displace the established dominant power. Much of the literature on power transitions, and indeed much of realist theory, take for granted that uneven growth of wealth in different states over time leads to the rise of new powers. Because realist theory largely refuses to look inside states, preferring only to examine how states interact with others given this uneven growth, they ignore the question of why states grow at this uneven pace to begin with. Even the latest variant within realism, neoclassical realism, which explicitly focuses on domestic variables to understand how states cope with international pressures, do not examine this question. Of course, uneven growth of states is a larger question that has motivated much work in the social sciences for a considerable period of time, including foundational works from Max Weber, though we still do not have adequate answers.

Yan's answer is the quality of political leadership. It is a complicated set of propositions that he provides, but it appears to go something like this. He argues that 'when the rising state's leadership is more capable and efficient than that of the dominant state and that of other contemporary major states, international influence is redistributed in a way that allows the rising state to eclipse the dominant state'.[1] This leadership capability is based on the leadership's capacity for reform. As Yan puts it, 'The capability of a state whose national leadership has continuously carried out prompt reforms will improve more rapidly than that of a state that has implemented few or no reforms'.[2] Yan argues that international leadership itself is a function not just of the power that an established power or a rising power can muster, but of the authority that it wields, which is dependent on its strategic credibility, which in turn depends on the moral quality of its leadership: 'the success of a rising state [is attributed] to its political leadership that adopts foreign policy according to universal moral codes'.[3] But moral power alone is insufficient; material capacity is needed too: as Yan says, 'Without superior capability, no leading state would be able to maintain international order through moral actions alone'.[4]

International leadership is thus based on national capability and strategic credibility, with greater importance being given to the latter. This is different from most forms of realism, which puts greater stock in capability than any other variable. Strategic credibility gives states authority, which Yan claims is more important than power. Strategic credibility, in turn, is dependent on both legitimacy of international leadership and the political capability of that leadership.

High credibility allows a rising state to improve a state's comprehensive capability. This allows states with even weaker resource components of capability to reduce disparity in comprehensive capability with established powers. This happens by allowing states with higher strategic credibility to attract more allies and wider international support. The number of allies is used by Yan as a key index of international strategic credibility and political popularity.[5] This is an unusual index: Yan argues than Clinton enhanced US power by expanding NATO, but Trump's devaluing of alliances is reducing US power.

Of course, much of this has as its backdrop China's rise and US–China competition: strategic credibility presents an easier path for a rising power to catch up with the established power because strategic credibility is not determined by material capacity alone. Yan argues that US behaviour has reduced its strategic credibility and allows China to close the gap because of China's higher strategic credibility, even though China is not yet a match for the US in purely material terms. And as the leading state loses its strategic credibility, the norms it establishes also falter. Why does the US not engage in reforms to compete better? Yan has an interesting and innovative answer: because the US decline is relative rather than absolute, it is difficult for US leadership to muster the 'fervour' for reforms as China can. Yan expects the US–China competition to become bipolarized, but also that it will be different from the bipolar competition of the US and the Soviet Union during the Cold War. US–China competition will not be a cold war, he argues, because there is no ideological competition between the two and because of globalization and economic and social interaction between the two. But the shift in power from Europe to East Asia (clearly, he is reluctant to use the Indo-Pacific formulation!), and the competition between the US and China over the region, also makes for bipolarization of the competition. This is a reality that Indian analysts and scholars have not fully considered.

Thus, what Yan proposes is what he calls 'a dualist theory that stresses the importance of both political leadership and a state's capability in decision making'.[6] This differs from standard realist theory which largely emphasizes (relative) power as the key variable in both state behaviour and international outcomes. Realists are not unaware of the significance of leadership, obviously. But leadership is not an easy variable to employ, and Yan's work demonstrates the dangers of wading into these murky waters.

Yan suggests four types of international leadership: humane leadership, hegemony, anemocracy, and tyranny. Humane leadership is consistently moral. Hegemonic leadership uses double standards, supportive of allies but ruthless towards enemies. Anemocratic states bully weaker states but kowtow to stronger ones; they are untrustworthy. Trump America is seen as a good example of this. Tyrannical leadership is crudely realist, consistent but untrustworthy; its leadership is based on fear, not trust.

The main question that is raised by Yan's interesting work is whether it is useful to treat leadership as a variable, as relative power is in realist theory. There is little doubt that political leadership is not just important, but indeed may be the key in determining the fate of nations and even the state of the international system. This is not a new revelation. But if IR scholars have not previously employed this as a theoretical variable, the reason is not hard to find: political leadership is not easy to use as a theoretical variable. Realists characterize polarity, for example, on the basis of a given distribution of power. Is it possible to say similarly, for example, that given a particular type of state leadership, we should expect a particular type of behaviour or even a particular type of outcome? This is definitely a possibility. But this requires that, as with power, we can define leadership types accurately and without reference to the dependent variable, either state behaviour or international outcomes. This critical problem is one reason why leadership is not generally favoured as a variable, and it is a problem that Yan's brave work cannot be said to resolve.

The key problem is that while it is easy to recognize the importance of this variable post facto, it has so far been difficult to find a way to define leadership in a theoretically usable manner, especially because of the problem of tautology: we are likely to characterize leadership as positive, based on the results it achieves. This reverses cause and effect, in effect becoming a tautology. If we define a leadership as 'humane leadership' based on its behaviour, how then can we use this characterization to predict its behaviour? Yan not only does not acknowledge the problem of tautology, he actually explicitly embraces the tautology, arguing, for example, that 'the capacity of reforms is evaluated based on the results of implementation'.[7] If the capacity for reforms is based on the results of the reforms, then how do we usefully create typologies of regimes to predict their behaviour?

Yan characterizes various regimes (admittedly, in an anecdotal manner rather than as the result of a deep case study) but these characterizations – say of the Trump presidency and its consequences for US leadership – would have been impossible to do without knowing the consequences of the Trump presidency. Further, it also appears to depend on individual judgments rather than on some empirical measure. Thus, if we disagree in our judgment about Xi's or Trump's leadership, there is no serious empirical basis for that disagreement other than how we feel about the quality of these regimes or how to characterize them in the typologies that Yan proposes. Using global public opinion polls, which appear to be the only empirical basis for leadership, is less than satisfactory. But even if we do use that empirical basis, China under the Xi regime would appear to suffer much more, especially in the Indo-Pacific region, where its image has suffered such a pounding that China in 2018 changed the leadership of its propaganda department. Moreover, such approval ratings differ from region to region: European approval ratings tend to be very different from approval ratings in the Indo-Pacific region, reflecting somewhat different relative views of the US and China. Approval ratings for China in countries such as India, Vietnam, and Japan are very low, reflecting their traditional competition. This is one reason why public approval ratings mean little in overall leadership rankings.

One puzzle, for a realist, is why any of this extension and amendment is necessary in realist theory in the first place. The growth of China's material power and the closing of the material gap between the US and China, at least for a realist, should adequately explain China's growing influence and Washington's international difficulties. Though the US still leads, the gap between the US and China is today far smaller than it ever was between the US and the Soviet Union. If that was a bipolar system, despite the wider material gap, surely the US–China competition is also one, or definitely heading in that direction.

Beyond these large problems, there are a number of smaller issues too. Yan's definition of polarity is unusual and possibly a step back. He uses alliances to partly define polarity, suggesting that bipolarity changed to unipolarity not just because of Soviet collapse but also because the Warsaw Pact collapsed. There was a time when polarity was indeed measured by alliance structures but ever since Kenneth Waltz illustrated the weakness of such formulation in the early 1960s, polarity has been measured by the distribution of state power rather than of alliances. He also repeatedly argues that the rise of Trump signifies the decline of liberalism in the West. This sounds more like hope than analysis: the values of liberalism were simultaneously never as comprehensive as its proponents hoped but also never as fragile as its adversaries fantasized. Grand arguments such as the decline of liberalism require somewhat more sophisticated argument and stronger empirical support than the odd opinion survey and the views of a few journalist critics.

On the other hand, Yan also suggests that a combination of Chinese traditional values and liberalism may prove attractive in the coming decades for other countries too. This, of course, begs the question of how such diametrically opposed ideologies can find common ground. Indeed, it is difficult to see what, if any, common ground exists between liberal individualism and Chinese traditional authoritarianism (which in today's China is veering towards totalitarianism).

But there are lessons here for American realists in Yan's occasionally stark view of the pursuit of power. For instance, about military force, he says that the 'indiscriminate refusal to use military force is a policy of national suicide, as well as an immoral principle, and antithetical to the behavior of a humane authority leadership'.[8] This is something that American realists should definitely learn from, a principle that is truer to realism than ideas such as 'reassurance' that American realists have become enamoured of late. He also argues that competition between the leading power and the rising challenger is inevitable and that it will be zero-sum,[9] another lesson for American realists, who are busy using realism to find ways in which competition can be avoided.

This is in many ways illustrative of the worldviews of Chinese IR scholars. It may or may not be representative but the fact that the leading Chinese IR scholars have such an unabashed view of how international politics operates surely tells us something about China's likely international behaviour. And, maybe it is also worth pondering if there is a parallel between the rise and decline of realism and that of nations. If so, China is definitely on the ascent.

Response to Rajesh Rajagopalan: IR moral realism's epistemology

Yan Xuetong

First published in *India Quarterly: A Journal of International Affairs* 76, no. 2 [2020]: 338–42

Leadership and the Rise of Great Powers received 16 book reviews within six months of its publication. Among them, the one by Professor Rajesh Rajagopalan is the most academically and theoretically compelling. I highly appreciate his sincere theoretical criticisms, which encourage me to rethink my theory. His review inspired me to have a written conversation with him about the epistemology of the international relations (IR) theory of moral realism.

Characterization of political leadership

Professor Rajagopalan thinks that it is tautological to characterize political leadership according to actions since characterization is used to predict actions.[10] Tautology indeed becomes inevitable when an independent variable and a dependent variable are used to define each other. Nevertheless, tautology can be avoided if we distinguish the independent variable from the dependent variable according to chronology. That is to say, the traits of actions characterizing leadership should occur before characterization, while the actions we predict should occur after establishing the characterization. In moral realist IR theory, actions refer to strategic preference. Based on past actions or strategic preference, we characterize the type of leadership. Based on that categorization we can predict the leadership's future actions or strategic preference accordingly.

The discipline of International Studies is an empirical science quite similar to psychologists. Trained clinical psychologists diagnose a patient's mental illness according to his/her past behaviours based on the Diagnostic and Statistical Manual of Mental Disorders, which is a collection of standardized traits. They then predict the potential of harmful behaviours the patient may exhibit both to themselves and others. Similarly, using standardized traits, IR scholars 'diagnose' the type of leadership based on prior policies, and then use the 'diagnosis' to predict the strategic preferences of the leadership.

For instance, not long after President Donald Trump took over the Oval Office, many American IR scholars predicted that 'uncertainty' would be the primary characteristic of Trump's foreign policy based on his policies in the first half-year of 2017.[11] A further extrapolation based on the characterization of the Trump administration's uncertainty is that America's allies will be reluctant to support American initiatives post-2017. Because of the uncertainty of Trump's strategic preferences, the Indian government also reduced its support to the Indo-Pacific strategy initiated by Trump in 2017. As reflected in the Shangri-La Dialogue of 2018, Prime Minister Narendra Modi said, 'India does not see the Indo-Pacific Region as a strategy or a club of limited members'.[12] Recently, Joseph S. Nye said, 'Donald Trump's long-term impact on US foreign policy is uncertain'.[13] These phenomena confirmed the people's early judgment of Trump's uncertainty.

Professor Rajagopalan further suggests that evaluation of reform capacity based on the results of reform implementation will make it impossible to 'create typologies of regimes and predict their behaviour'.[14] In practice, moral realism theory treats leadership type and reform capability as two distinct concepts. Leadership type is defined by the method of doing things, while reform capability by the result. Moral realism theory quantifies reform capability as a measure of leadership's proficiency, which is calculated from two elements: direction and magnitude of reform.[15] Those who successfully implemented prior reform will be categorized as having a strong reform capability, thus we can predict that the leadership will have great chance to implement future reforms successfully. For instance, based on Modi's successful reform in Gujarat, Indian people categorized him as having stronger reform capability than Manmohan Singh in 2014's general election.

Professor Rajagopalan claims that global public opinion polls cannot serve as a satisfactory empirical basis for judging a given leadership because approval ratings differ from region to region.[16] People of different regions may indeed have different views about a given leadership, but that only validates global opinion polls as the empirical judgment of leadership. The characteristic of any leadership can only be evaluated by others not by itself. The global leadership's morality depends on the collective result of all countries' evaluations, not solely on its allies or enemies. The broader coverage of global opinion polls provides a more representative base for judging a global leadership's popularity than regional ones. Since the aim is to evaluate global leadership, regional differences will not reduce the reliability of global opinion polls.

Professor Rajagopalan's criticism of the empirical reliability of global polling is applicable if IR moral realism employed value-oriented morality. However, IR moral realism subscribes to instrumental morality. Therefore, the popularity of an action determines the morality of that action, irrespective of whether the popularity is due to political values or secular interest. Philosophical disagreement over the use of value-oriented or instrumental morality is beyond the scope of my theory.

The judgement of the international configuration

Professor Rajagopalan suggests that the reduced material power gap between China and the US can adequately explain China's growing international influence and America's declining leadership in the world. Therefore, he views it as unnecessary to add the variable of political leadership into realist theory.[17] The change in the balance of power is indeed used for explaining strategies of great powers by realist theorists, but it cannot adequately explain how changes in the balance of power or international configuration occur. For instance, the closing material gap between China and the US may be able to explain the increase of China's influence and the decline of America's, but it cannot tell why the strength gap was reduced rather than enlarged.

Before moral realism theory, no realist theory has been able to explain both the decline of a hegemon and the success of a rising power with a single independent variable. The most important contribution moral realism made to realism theory is that moral realism treats the leadership of leading powers as an independent variable and attributed the change in international configuration or balance of power to the different levels of reform capabilities of various leaderships. This helps us to understand why a given rising power, but not others, can achieve its goal and why a hegemon declines simultaneously.

In addition to explaining how international configuration changes, treating political leadership as an independent variable can also explain how the type of international norms changes: when the new global leadership is a different type from the previous one, the type of international norms will change. A case illustrating this argument is the change of international norms after WWII when the United Nations was established based on America's leadership. The US provided a different type of international leadership from the traditional one provided by European powers after WWI.

By treating leadership as an independent variable, moral realism also breaks through the rigid epistemological belief that any single IR theory can only adequately function at one of the three analytical levels: individual, state, or system. Leadership is composed of individual policy makers, mainly the supreme leader and his cabinet members. They represent the governments of their states. Leadership from the leading states constitutes the international leadership, because of the status of their states in the international system. As such, these people's policies will have a strong impact on shaping international configuration, norms, order, and even the whole system.

Regarding the judgment of international configuration, Professor Rajagopalan also notes that using alliances to define polarity is a step back, and this has already been criticized by Kenneth Waltz in his early writings.[18] Waltz's understanding of polarity was strongly influenced by the Cold War bipolarity between the US and the Soviets. The two superpowers possessed about 90 per cent of nuclear weapons and 80 per cent of aircraft carriers worldwide. In such a situation, it was impossible for the rest of the world to compose a peer pole by making alliances. Nevertheless, Waltz neglected the fact that alliances have the function of strengthening a pole and facilitating the formation of a new one, even though they cannot establish a pole by themselves. For instance, nowadays, many people disagree on the judgment that the post-Cold War unipolar world is transferring towards a bipolar one between China and the US. Nevertheless, it would be very possible for them to agree on that judgment, if China had made an anti-US alliance with Russia, India, and Japan while the US had withdrawn from NATO.

The declining influence of liberalism

Professor Rajagopalan disagrees that liberalism is in decline because he feels I did not provide empirical evidence.[19] The decline of liberalism means its global influence becomes less popular than itself during the post-Cold War period from 1992 to 2015, rather than being compared with any other ideologies at present. Liberalism is still the most influential ideology in the world, but it can no longer consolidate Western countries on strategic issues as effectively as before. For instance, all Western countries joined hands to contain China in 1989, but they are no longer consolidated ideologically as solid as then. For instance, most democracies including India, Germany, France, and the UK rejected America's requirement to block the 5G technologies of Huawei, a Chinese telecommunication giant. Recently, Japan became hesitant to support America's containment against Huawei, and the local government of West Australia announced its cooperation with Huawei, ignoring the Australian central government's decision.

It is evident that Professor Rajagopalan doubts the possibility of creating a new ideology by combining Chinese traditional values with liberalism. Because of this, he rejects the idea that the combined ideology has any chance of global popularity in the future.[20] I do agree with him that such a scenario cannot happen when the people of our generation are holding the power in China and the US.[21] Nevertheless, the Chinese and American millennials and generation Z grew up in the age of post-figurative culture. Their ideology is shaped by the knowledge they get from the internet rather than that from their parents or grandparents. The same knowledge from the internet makes their ideology more similar than different. Yong Chinese and Americans do not see the world as differently as their parents do. They have a larger world outlook from their parents rather than between themselves. When they take the reign of China and the US in the next two or three decades, they will shape the world with their own world outlook.

At the end of the Cold War, Francis Fukuyama argued that liberalism would dominate the world forever. However, the history of the last decade has disproved his opinion. Opposite to Fukuyama's epistemological view of ideology's influence, moral realism theory believes that no ideology can dominate the world forever because later generations will inevitably have different ideologies to that of previous generations. The progress of digital technology will strengthen the post-figurative culture; thus, the ideological generation gap will build up in a shorter time and become wider than before. Although we cannot be sure about the combination of Chinese traditional values and American liberal values in the future, it is highly possible for the future Chinese and American leaders to offer a new kind of ideology for the world by the middle of the 21st century.

Although there have been many academic communications between Chinese and Indian scholars, it is rare to see any theoretical discussion about IR theories. For the sake of enriching modern IR theories, Chinese and Indian IR scholars should make some contribution by bringing our traditional epistemology or philosophy into IR theory. I hope my pen conversation with Professor Rajagopalan can attract more Chinese and Indian scholars to join our theoretical discussion.

Response to Yan Xuetong

Rajesh Rajagopalan
First published in *India Quarterly: A Journal of International Affairs* 76, no. 2 [2020]: 343–4

I appreciate Professor Yan Xuetong's response to my review, and for engaging in this dialogue. Realism continues to remain the central theory in international politics, at least because all others need to position themselves primarily in terms of how they disagree with it. But realism's centrality is only relative to other efforts at theorizing about international politics; its own drawbacks are many and telling. Yet, I am convinced that it is the most useful of the theories we have to work with and the most fertile field on which to grow better theories. Moreover, it is time that realism is taken seriously by non-American IR scholars because realism's roots are global, and the inheritors of Sun Tzu's and Chanakya's legacies in particular have no good reason for leaving the realist field to be tilled by others. All of these are good reasons to welcome Yan's effort in modifying and expanding realism and to endorse his call for greater theoretical discussion between Indian and Chinese scholars.

There is a more fundamental academic reason why realism could do with some fresh thinking outside of parochial American concerns, which has unfortunately become realism's staple concentrate. This parochialism has skewed realism to focus largely on great powers politics, severely limiting realism's potential power in helping understand and explain the rest of international politics, where indeed much of the warp and woof of international politics takes place.

To give just a small example, because realism is so obsessed with great power politics, and because great powers are roughly comparable in power, realism has entirely missed the dynamics and consequences of politics between unequal powers. It took a historian like Paul Schroeder to demonstrate this by identifying various strategies beyond just balancing and bandwagoning which weaker players can adopt.

I am also convinced, along with Yan and other scholars, that the capacity of states for administrative innovation which helps enhance their power is a critical and often overlooked variable. Kaufman, Little, and Wohlforth[22] and their collaborators identified this as critical; Yan bores down on this variable as key, identifying the capacity of individual leaders to drive such changes. I am certainly sympathetic; if I am still doubtful, that has to do less with the generalizability of this variable than problems that we will likely encounter in operationalizing it.

Looking at past preferences and behaviour to predict future choices is an interesting idea for resolving problems of tautology, but I do still see some difficulties. While voters and even analysts may depend on such conclusions, they are also often wrong. To give just one example, US presidents since the end of the Cold War have repeatedly promised to reduce America's footprint in global affairs, or even withdraw. None have been successful; few, other than Trump, have even tried hard. Would looking at the past perspectives of an Obama or a Trump have helped? There are other problems too: are we to trust what leaders say, especially about their motives for action? How do we compensate for instrumental behaviour, or even hypocrisy?

On polarity, the question really is why complicate matters by bringing in alliances, instead of sticking with the simpler equation of the relative power of states? To flip the question that Yan asks, would we even consider the issue of bipolarity – and I agree with him that the world is more likely moving towards bipolarity than New Delhi's fantasy about multipolarity – if China's power had not grown in the spectacular manner that it has, and, more importantly, if in doing so, it had not closed the gap with the US as much as it has, and more than any other state in the last 70 years? Moreover, the question of including alliances in measuring polarity becomes particularly problematic if we have to consider alliances beyond formal ones, as Yan appears to do when he talks about an alliance between China, Russia, India, and Japan, which would unlikely have been a formal one.

The question of how much theorizing is possible remains a fundamental one. Kenneth Waltz[23] once made a distinction between analysis and theory, suggesting that while analysis was possible about foreign policy, theory may not be. He was only objecting to expanding his structural neorealist theory to explain foreign policy but the point itself is valid: is generalization possible at all about foreign policy behaviour? Waltz, to his credit, left the question open, but three decades of effort in adapting realism to make determinate predictions about foreign policy behaviour which have not really panned out, despite many interesting insights, suggest that we should be a bit cautious. Without discounting the importance of leadership, I would propose that defining and generalising this variable still remain quite challenging, despite Yan's valiant effort.

Notes
[1] Yan Xuetong, *Leadership and the Rise of Great Powers*, Princeton: Princeton University Press, 2019, p 2.
[2] Ibid., 192.

3. Ibid., 24.
4. Ibid., 75.
5. Ibid., 41.
6. Ibid., 61.
7. Ibid., 192.
8. Ibid., 66.
9. Ibid., 72.
10. Rajesh Rajagopalan, 'Book Reviews', *India Quarterly* 75, no. 3 (2019): 407.
11. Conor Finnegan and Elizabeth Mclaughlin, 'Analysis: How Trump's Foreign Policy Has Affected Global Relations since Assuming Office', *ABC News*, 20 July 2017, https://abcnews.go.com/International/analysis-trumps-foreign-policy-impacted-global-relations-assuming/story?id=48734071.
12. 'Prime Minister's Keynote Address at Shangri-La Dialogue', *Ministry of Foreign Affairs of Indian Government*, 1 June 2018, www.mea.gov.in/Speeches-Statements.htm?dtl/29943/Prime+Ministers+Keynote+Address+at+Shangri+La+Dialogue+June+01+2018.
13. Joseph S. Nye Jr, 'Trump's Effect on US Foreign Policy', *Project Syndicate*, 4 September 2019, www.project-syndicate.org/commentary/trump-long-term-effect-on-american-foreign-policy-by-joseph-s-nye-2019-09.
14. Rajesh Rajagopalan, 'Book Reviews': 407.
15. Yan Xuetong, *Leadership and the Rise of Great Powers*, Princeton: Princeton University Press, 2019, p 13.
16. Rajesh Rajagopalan, 'Book Reviews': 408.
17. Ibid.
18. Ibid.
19. Ibid.
20. Ibid.
21. Yan Xuetong, *Leadership and the Rise of Great Powers*, pp 143, 153.
22. S.J. Kaufman, R. Little, and W.C. Wohlforth, *The Balance of Power in World History*, London: Palgrave Macmillan, 2007.
23. K.N. Waltz, 'International Politics Is not Foreign Policy', *Security Studies* 6, no. 1 (1996): 56

APPENDIX 2

'Chinese School' as an Inappropriate Title

Yan Xuetong

A growing number of IR scholars, Chinese and foreigners alike, believe that a 'Chinese School' of IR theories has been formed in the last decade.[1] This view gained popularity partially due to Amitav Acharya's effort to advance the concept of 'global IR' (GIR). Although he replaced the term 'Chinese School' with the 'Chinese IRTs' (Chinese IR theories), most IR scholars usually view them as the same and ignore the fine semantic distinction between them. Acharya believed that 'Chinese IRTs significantly enriched IR theory and discipline as a whole and especially to the quest for a GIR'.[2] His view has reinforced the belief that a 'Chinese School' exists. However, the label 'Chinese School' is a misnomer, because Chinese scholars have constructed IR theories according to different, or even antithetical, ontology, epistemology, and assumptions.

A title derived from a misnomer

As I understand it, the popularity for a 'Chinese School' reflects the anxiousness at the absence of a 'Chinese School' in political science rather than the pride for forming such a school. The push for domestically developed IR theories originated in 1987 at an academic conference in Shanghai. In the 1990s, the idea was framed as 'IR theories with Chinese characteristics'.[3] The term *Zhongguo Xuepai* (Chinese School) was coined by young Chinese IR scholars around the turn of the century.[4] After more than two decades, Chinese IR scholars have yet to reach an agreement on the issue of constructing a 'Chinese School'. In 2021, Xu Jian says, 'Because of various historical reasons, we have not yet constructed a system of IR theories with Chinese characteristics'.[5]

To understand the craving for a 'Chinese School' among Chinese IR scholars, it is necessary to mention the terminological impact of the 'English School'.

The 'English School' encompassed IR theories constructed by European scholars that shared an institutionalist framework. However, instead of naming the school after the theoretical framework, the school was associated with the nation of Great Britain, sometimes also called the 'British Institutionalists'. Unfortunately, this nomenclature practice was imitated by their Chinese colleagues. As Barry Buzan, one of the founders of the English school, noted in 2007, the name 'English School' makes an erroneous linkage between the approach of this theory and Britain: that the school was established in Britain or of serving Britain's interests.[6] Moreover, it was the European scholars rather than British ones who constructed the school, and its perspective is more historical and political than those theories created by American scholars.[7] Thirteen years later, he unequivocally stated that he did not support 'the case for national schools of IR', and that 'national schools of IR raise the dangers of letting historical baggage, such as history problems and colonial grudges, muddy the water'.[8] Although Buzan is highly regarded among Chinese IR scholars, few share his antipathy towards naming IR theories after countries.

Because the pursuit of a 'Chinese School' is based on forming a linguistic counterpoint to the questionably named 'English School', there is no theoretically sound taxonomical distinction between 'Chinese School' and other IR schools. Over the past two decades, many scholarly writings on the 'Chinese School' of IR theories have been published, but they do not share any common theoretical features. The theoretical differences between IR theories developed by Chinese scholars are wider among Chinese scholars than they are from their Western counterparts. For instance, my theory – moral realism – is a subset of realist theory, which shares the same theoretical assumptions and epistemological practices as other realist schools, such as Hans Morgenthau's classical realism. In contrast, moral realism differs more from Qin Yaqing's relational theory, which uses a constructivist framework, than from Morgenthau's theory.

Qin is a very upright and serious Chinese IR scholar and his relational theory is much more influential among Chinese IR students than moral realism. Possibly cognizant of the inaptness of the title 'Chinese School', he followed Acharya's idea of replacing 'Chinese School' with 'Chinese IR theories' in his writing published in 2020.[9] However, rephrasing the name 'Chinese School' does not define the shared theoretical foundation of different IR theories created by Chinese scholars.

Diversity beyond one school

Many scholars proposed that traditional Chinese culture is a robust base for constructing a 'Chinese School'. And yet, historically, academic schools are formed on the basis of a shared theoretical design and not on common cultural backgrounds.

Historically, no political thoughts or theories were ever identified as the 'Chinese School'. Archaeological studies show that the phrase *zhongguo* (中国, China) first appeared in the inscription on a *He Zun*, a bronze ritual wine vessel, dated to the early Western Zhou Dynasty (1046–771 BCE).[10] Since then, Chinese scholars have formed many globally acknowledged philosophical schools, notably Confucianism, Taoism, Mohism, and Legalism, which have endured the test of time. Much of their philosophical framework influenced modern political theories. None, individually or collectively, is, or ever was, titled, '*zhongguo xuepai*' (Chinese School). Why? Certainly not for the lack of popularity or influence. It is because of the huge theoretical divergences between them that effectively render the name 'Chinese School' meaningless.

Chinese political thoughts, ancient and modern, are rich, diverse, and abundant in Chinese characteristics, yet never classified as a single school. In modern China, many influential political thoughts are combinations of foreign ideologies and aspects of Chinese traditional philosophies, such as nationalism, communism, capitalism, socialism, neo-authoritarianism, and liberalism, among others. These combinations are highly complex. Not only are the foreign theoretical inspirations different, the elements of Chinese philosophical framework through which the foreign ideas were synthesized are also different. Therefore, different schools of modern Chinese political thoughts all have different assumptions, reasoning, principles, and proposals for social reform. Owing to the huge differences among one another, they can never belong to the same school. For instance, Sun Yat-sen's nationalism (the Three People's Principles), Mao Zedong Thought, and Deng Xiaoping Theory are the three most influential political thoughts. Despite the founders' shared Chinese heritage, these political thoughts were never considered to be part of a unifying 'Chinese School'. Meanwhile, none of them individually is qualified to wholly represent the diversity of Chinese thoughts.

The pursuit of a 'Chinese School' that unifies all academic disciplines is even more of an idealistic dream. The *China Newsweek* reported that certain Chinese leftists believe it possible to build a 'Chinese School' in every academic discipline through a multidisciplinary paradigm of philosophy, history, economics, politics, law, sociology, and ethnology.[11] Obviously inspired by the idea of pan-discipline Marxism, this fanciful idea contradicts the taxonomy of academic nomenclature. An academic school is a subset of a discipline, as 'apple' is a subset of 'fruit'. The name of an academic school can be coopted by other disciplines only when the existing paradigm provides meaningful distinctions within that discipline. For example, realism is a school of thought that exists in both political science and fine art. However, there is no 'realist school' of physics, because the paradigm of realism does not provide any meaningful distinction to the natural sciences – any non-realist science is by definition not science. Meanwhile, a Sinological paradigm for constructing a 'Chinese School' doesn't even exist at the moment, let alone the ability to assess whether that paradigm is universal enough to apply to all disciplines.

Summary

China's rise is the most important international issue of the 21st century, and it engenders great opportunities for Chinese scholars to construct IR theories. However, opportunities do not automatically generate theories. Building theories calls for both scientific knowledge and a creative spirit. Self-proclaimed 'national theories' have no weight until they have withstood testing by and received acknowledgement from the scholars in the discipline. In addition, the term 'Chinese School' constrains the creation of universally applicable IR theories, because it limits people's thinking to explaining exclusively the Chinese experience.

Although I hold opposite views from those Chinese IR scholars who advocate for a 'Chinese School', I must say that they are serious scholars and have my academic respect. Over the last 20-plus years, their ideals have inspired some Chinese scholars to construct IR theories which gave voice to the Chinese perspective.[12] However, considering 20 years of hard work, the progress has been limited. As Acharya said, Chinese IRT needs 'to offer more convincing proof that the concepts and explanations they propose can apply to other societies and to IR more generally'.[13] I would suggest my Chinese IR colleagues shift their focus from how to construct a 'Chinese School' to developing universally applicable IR theories.

Notes

1. Amitav Acharya, 'From Heaven to Earth: "Cultural Idealism" and "Moral Realism" as Chinese Contributions to Global International Relations', *Chinese Journal of International Politics* 12, no. 4 (2019): 468–79; Peter J. Katzenstein, 'The Second Coming? Reflections on a Global Theory of International Relations', in Yaqing Qin (ed), *Globalizing IR Theory Critical Engagement*, London: Routledge, 2020, pp 27–38; Yaqing Qin, 'A Multiverse of Knowledge: Cultures and IR Theories', in Yaqing Qin (ed), *Globalizing IR Theory Critical Engagement*, London: Routledge, 2020, pp 145–51; Yih-Jye Hwang, 'Reappraising the Chinese School of International Relations: A Postcolonial Perspective', *Review of International Studies*, published online by Cambridge University Press, 12 April 2021. www.cambridge.org/core/journals/review-of-international-studies/article/reappraising-the-chinese-school-of-international-relations-a-postcolonial-perspective/8035C0A9D7A73A130CB902145A19E487.
2. Amitav Acharya, 'From Heaven to Earth: "Cultural Idealism" and "Moral Realism" as Chinese Contributions to Global International Relations': 482.
3. Guo Shuyong (ed), *Guoji Ganxi: Huhuan Zhongguo Lilun* (International Relations: Call for Chinese Theories), Tianjin: Tianjin People's Press, 2005, p 1.
4. Ren Xiao, *Zhongguo Gouji Guanxi Xue Shi* (History of Chinese IR Studies), Beijing: Commercial Press, 2022, p 372.

5   Xu Jian, 'Yi Renlei Mingyun Gontongti Linian Wei Yinling Jiaqiang Zhongguo Tese Gouji Guanxi Lilun Jianzhe' (Strengthening Construction of the IR Theories with Chinese Characteristics under the Guidance of Human Destiny Community), *Guoji Zhanwang* (International Review) 5 (2021): 3.
6   Barry Buzan, 'Yingguo Xuepai Jiqi Dangxia Fazhan' (English School and Its Current Development), *Gouji Zhengzhi Yanjiu* (International Political Studies), 2 (2007): 101.
7   Ibid.
8   Barry Buzan, 'How and How not to Develop IR Theories: Lessons from Core and Periphery', in Yaqing Qin (ed), *Globalizing IR Theory Critical Engagement*, p 60.
9   Yaqing Qin, 'A Multiverse of Knowledge Cultures and IR Theories', pp 139–55.
10 Min Jie and Huang Yang, 'Hezun: Keyu "Xinzhong" de "Zhongguo"' (Hezun: 'China' Inscribed on the 'Heart'), *Xinhua News Agency New Media*, 3 July 2021, https://baijiahao.baidu.com/s?id=1704240662605498579&wfr=spider&for=pc.
11 Cai Rupeng, 'Chuixiang Zhongguo Xuepai de Zong Haojiao' (The General Trumpet of the Chinese School), *Zhongguo Xinwen Zhoukan* (China Newsweek) 46 (2017): 18, http://www.inewsweek.cn/2/2017-12-08/3720.shtml.
12 Ren Xiao, '"Zhongguo Xuepai" Wenti de Zaisi yu Zairen"' (Rethinking and Recognizing about 'Chinese School'), *Guoji Guancha* (International Observation) 2 (2020): 27, www.cssn.cn/zx/202011/t20201116_5217242.shtml.
13 Amitav Acharya, 'From Heaven to Earth: "Cultural Idealism" and "Moral Realism" as Chinese Contributions to Global International Relations': 469.

Selected Bibliography

Aaronson, Mike, 'Interventionism in US Foreign Policy from Bush to Obama', in Michelle Bentley and Jack Holland (eds), *Obama's Foreign Policy: Ending the War on Terror*, Abingdon: Routledge, 2014.

Acemoglu, Daron, Suresh, Naidu, Pascual, Restrepo, and Robinson, James A., 'Democracy Does Cause Growth', *Journal of Political Economy* 127, no. 1 (2019): 47–100.

Acharya, Amitav, 'Global International Relations (IR) and Regional Worlds: A New Agenda for International Studies', *International Studies Quarterly* 58, no. 4 (2014): 647–59.

Acharya, Amitav, *The End of American World Order*, Cambridge: Polity Press, 2018.

Acharya, Amitav, 'From Heaven to Earth: "Cultural Idealism" and "Moral Realism" as Chinese Contributions to Global International Relations', *The Chinese Journal of International Politics* 12, no. 4 (2019): 467–94.

Allison, Graham, *Essence of Decision: Explaining the Cuban Missile Crisis*, Boston: Little, Brown, 1971.

Allison, Graham, *Destined for War: Can America and China Escape Thucydides's Trap?*, New York: Houghton Mifflin Harcourt, 2017.

Althusser, Louis and Balibar, Etienne, *Reading Capital*, London: New Left Books, 1970.

Ames, Roger T. and Rosemont, Henry Jr (trans), *The Analects of Confucius: A Philosophical Translation*, New York: Ballantine, 1998.

Ames, Roger T., *Confucian Role Ethics: A Vocabulary*, Honolulu: University of Hawai'i Press, 2011.

Annas, Julia, 'Virtue Ethics', in David Copp (ed), *The Oxford Handbook of Ethical Theory*, Oxford: Oxford University Press, 2007.

Ashley, Richard K., 'Poverty of Neorealism', *International Organization* 38, no. 2 (1984): 225–86.

Audi, Robert (ed), *The Cambridge Dictionary of Philosophy*, 3rd edition, Cambridge: Cambridge University Press, 2015.

Auslin, Michael, '"Leadership and the Rise of Great Powers" Review: No More "Sage Kings"', *The Wall Street Journal*, 11 August 2019.

Babones, Salvatore, 'Taking China Seriously: Relationality, Tianxia, and the "Chinese School" of International Relations', *Oxford Research Encyclopedias*, 26 September 2017.

Badie, Bertrand, *Un Monde sans Souveraineté* (A World without Sovereignties), Paris: Fayard, 1999.

Bahi, Riham, 'The Geopolitics of COVID-19: US–China Rivalry and the Imminent Kindleberger Trap', *Review of Economics and Political Science* 6, no. 1 (2021): 76–94.

Barber, James David, 'The Promise of Political Psychology', *Political Psychology* 11, no. 1 (1990): 183.

Baumol, William J., 'Productivity Growth, Convergence, and Welfare: What the Long-Run Data Show', *The American Economic Review* 76, no. 5 (1986): 1072–85.

Beckley, Michael, 'The Power of Nations: Measuring What Matters', *International Security* 42, no. 2 (2018): 7–44.

Beckley, Michael, *Unrivaled: Why America Will Remain the World's Sole Superpower*, Ithaca: Cornell University Press, 2018.

Bell, Daniel A., *China's New Confucianism: Politics and Everyday Life in a Changing Society*, Princeton: Princeton University Press, 2008.

Bell, Daniel A., *Introduction in Ancient Chinese Thought, Modern Chinese Power*, Princeton: Princeton University Press, 2011.

Benetton, Philippe, Brague, Remi, and Delsol, Chantal, *La Déclaration de Paris: Une Europe en laquelle nous pouvions croire* (Paris Declaration: A Europe We Can Believe, A Manifesto), Paris: Cerf, 2018.

Bhaskar, Roy, *The Possibility of Naturalism: A Philosophical Critique of the Contemporary Human Sciences*, 2nd edition, Brighton: Harvester, 1979.

Biden, Joseph R., 'We've Got a Big Agenda Ahead of Us … The Quad Is Going to Be a Vital Arena for Cooperation in the Indo-Pacific', White House: President Joseph R. Biden, Washington, DC, 12 March 2021, www.whitehouse.gov/briefing-room/speeches-remarks/2021/03/12/remarks-by-president-biden-prime-minister-modi-of-india-prime-minister-morrison-of-australia-and-prime-minister-suga-of-japan-in-virtual-meeting-of-the-quad/.

Biden, Joseph R., 'Inaugural Address by President Joseph R. Biden, Jr.', White House: President Joseph R. Biden, Washington, DC, 20 January 2021, www.whitehouse.gov/briefing-room/speeches-remarks/2021/01/20/inaugural-address-by-president-joseph-r-biden-jr/.

Bobbio, Norberto, 'Etat et Démocratie Internationale' (State and International Democracy), in Mario Telò (ed), *Démocratie et Relations Internationales*, (Democracy and International Relations), Bruxelles: Complexe, 1999.

Bolton, John, *The Room Where It Happened: A White House Memoir*, New York: Simon & Schuster, 2020.

Bourdieu, Pierre, 'Pour un Movement Social Europe en (For a European Social Movement)', *Le Monde Diplomatique*, 1999.

Brady, Anne-Marie, 'State Confucianism, Chineseness, and Tradition in CCP Propaganda', in Anne-Marie Brady (ed), *China's Thought Management*, Oxford: Routledge, 2012.

Braun, Benjamin, Schindler, Sebastian, and Wille, Tobias, 'Rethinking Agency in International Relations: Performativity, Performances and Actor-Networks', *Journal of International Relations and Development* 22 (2019): 787–807.

Brink, David O., 'Some Forms and Limits of Consequentialism', in David Copp (ed), *The Oxford Handbook of Ethical Theory*, Oxford: Oxford University Press, 2007.

Brock, Gillian, *Global Justice: A Cosmopolitan Account*, Oxford: Oxford University Press, 2009.

Brooks, David, 'When Dictators Find God', *New York Times*, 9 September 2021, www.nytimes.com/2021/09/09/opinion/autocracy-religion-liberalism.html.

Brostrom, Jannika, 'Morality and the National Interest: Towards a "Moral Realist" Reaserch Agenda', *Cambridge Review of International Affairs* 29, no. 4 (2015): 1624–39.

Bucher, Bernd, 'Moving beyond the Substantialist Foundations of the Agent–Structures Dichotomy Figuration Thinking in International Relations', *Journal of International Relations and Development* 20, no. 2 (2017): 408–33.

Bueger, Christian and Bethke, Felix S., 'Actor-Networking the "Failed State": An Enquiry into the Life of Concepts', *Journal of International Relations and Development* 17, no. 1 (2014): 30–60.

Bull, Hedley, *The Anarchical Society: A Study of Order in World Politics* New York: Columbia University Press, 1977.

Burhnam, James, *The Machiavellians: Defenders of Freedom*, New York: The John Day Company, 1943.

Burn, Will, 'The Demolition of US Diplomacy', *Foreign Affairs*, 14 October 2019, www.foreignaffairs.com/articles/2019-10-14/demolition-us-diplomacy.

Buzan, Barry, 'The Level of Analysis Problem in International Relations Reconsidered', in Ken Booth and Steve Smith (eds), *International Relations Theory Today*, Cambridge: Polity, 1995.

Buzan, Barry, *From International to World Society? English School Theory and the Social Structure of Globalisation*, Cambridge: Cambridge University Press, 2004.

Buzan, Barry, 'Yingguo Xuepai Jiqi Dangxia Fazhan (English School and Its Current Development)', *Gouji Zhengzhi Yanjiu* (International Political Studies) 2 (2007): 101.

Buzan, Barry, 'How and How not to Develop IR Theories: Lessons from Core and Periphery', in Yaqing Qin (ed), *Globalizing IR Theory Critical Engagement*, London: Routledge, 2020.

Carlsnaes, Walter, 'The Agent–Structure Problem in Foreign Policy Analysis', *International Studies Quarterly* 36, no. 3 (1992): 245–70.

Carr, Edward Hallett, *The Twenty Years' Crisis: 1919–1939: An Introduction to the Study of International Relations*, London: Macmillan, 1940.

Carr, Edward Hallett, *The Twenty Years' Crisis, 1919–1939*, New York: Harper & Row, 1964.

Caverley, Jonathan D. and Dombrowski, Peter, 'Too Important to the Left to the Admirals: The Need to Study Maritime Great-Power Competition', *Security Studies* 29, no. 4 (2020): 580.

Cederman, Lars-Erik and Daase, Christopher, 'Endogenizing Corporate Identities: The Next Step in Constructivist IR Theory', *European Journal of International Relations* 9, no. 1 (2003): 6.

Chan, Joseph. *Confucian Perfectionism: A Political Philosophy for Modern Times*, Princeton: Princeton University Press, 2013.

Chang, Jian and Yin, Haozhe, 'Guoji lingdao diwei xin gengti zhouqi yanjiu (A Study of the New Replacement Cycle of International Leadership)', *Fudan International Studies Review* 27 (2020): 21–2.

Checkel, Jeffrey T., 'The Constructivist Turn in International Relations Theory', *World Politics* 50, no. 2 (1998): 325–7.

Chen, Qiyou, *Han Fei Zi xin jiaozhu* (New Exegeses of the *Han Fei Zi*), Shanghai: Shanghai guji chubanshe, 2000.

Chen, Zhimin and Zhou, Guorong, 'Guoji lingdao yu Zhongguo xiejinxing lingdao juese de goujian (International Leadership and China as One Facilitative Leader)', *Shijie jingji yu zhengzhi* (World Economics and Politics), 3 (2017): 18–19, 21.

Cheng, Evelyn, 'Fallout from US–China Trade Conflict Could be "Even Worse" than WWI, Kissinger Says', *CNBC News*, 22 November 2019, https://www.cnbc.com/2019/11/22/us-china-economic-conflict-could-be-worse-than-wwi-henry-kissinger-says.html.

China's National Defense in the New Era, Beijing: Foreign Languages Press, 2019, www.xinhuanet.com/english/2019-07/24/c_138253389.htm.

Christensen, Thomas J., *Useful Adversaries: Grand Strategy, Domestic Mobilization, and Sino–American Conflict, 1947–1958*, Princeton: Princeton University Press, 1996.

Christensen, Thomas J., 'The Advantages of an Assertive China', *Foreign Affairs* 90, no. 2 (2011): 59–62.

Christensen, Thomas J., *The China Challenge: Shaping the Choices of a Rising Power*, New York: W.W. Norton, 2015.

Christensen, Thomas J., '"There Will Not Be a New Cold War": The Limits of US–Chinese Competition', *Foreign Affairs*, 24 March 2021, www.foreignaffairs.com/articles/united-states/2021-03-24/there-will-not-be-new-cold-war.

Cirincione, Joseph, 'Strategic Collapse: The Failure of the Bush Nuclear Doctrine', *Arms Control Association*, November 2008, www.armscontrol.org/act/2008-11/features/strategic-collapse-failure-bush-nuclear-doctrine#authbio.

Cooley, Alexander and Nexon, Daniel, *Exit from Hegemony: The Unraveling of the American Global Order*, New York: Oxford University Press, 2020.

Cooper, Richard N., 'Economic Aspects of the Cold War, 1962–1975', in Melvyn P. Leffler and Odd Arne Westad (eds), *Cambridge History of the Cold War, Crises and Détente*, Cambridge: Cambridge University Press, 2010.

Copeland, Dale C., 'The Constructivist Challenge to Structural Realism: A Review Essay', *International Security* 25, no. 2 (2000): 189–91.

Crowley, Michael, 'Biden, Covering Range of Thorny Issues, Talks with Xi for First Time as President', *New York Times*, 11 February 2021.

Cunningham, Fiona S. and Fravel, Taylor M., 'Assuring Assured Retaliation: China's Nuclear Posture and US–China Strategic Stability', *International Security* 40, no. 2 (2015): 7–50.

Davis, Bob and Wei, Lingling, *Superpower Showdown: How the Battle between Trump and Xi Threatens a New Cold War*, New York: HarperCollins, 2020.

Davis, Bob and Wei, Lingling, 'Biden Plans to Build a Grand Alliance to Counter China', *Wall Street Journal*, 6 January 2021, www.wsj.com/articles/biden-trump-xi-china-economic-trade-strategy-policy-11609945027.

De Benoist, Alain, *Contre le liberalisme* (Against Liberalism), Monaco: Le Rochée, 2019.

Debray, Regis, *L'Europe Phantôme* (Europe as a Phantom), Paris: Gallimard, 2019.

De Grazia, Victoria, *Irresistible Empire: America's Advance through Twentieth-Century Europe*, Cambridge, MA: Harvard University Press, 2006.

Dessler, David, 'What's at Stake in the Agent–Structure Debate?', *International Organization* 43, no. 3 (1989): 441–73.

Deudney, Daniel and Ikenberry, G. John, 'Liberal World: The Resilient Order', *Foreign Affairs* 94, no. 4 (2018): 1–15.

Dian, Matteo, 'The Rise of China Between Global IR and Area Studies: An Agenda for Cooperation', *Italian Political Science Review*, no. 52 (2022): 252–67.

Donagan, Alan, *The Theory of Morality*, Chicago: University of Chicago Press, 1977.

Doty, Roxanne L., 'Aporia: A Critical Exploration of the Agent–Structure Problematique in International Relations Theory', *European Journal of International Relations* 3, no. 3 (1997): 365–92.

Doucouliagos, Hristos and Ulubaşoğlu, Mehmet, 'Democracy and Economic Growth: A Meta-Analysis', *American Journal of Political Science* 52 (2008): 61–83, https://www.fmprc.gov.cn/mfa_eng/wjdt_665385/zyjh_665391/t1305051.shtm.

Dougherty, James E. and Pfaltzgraff, Robert L. Jr, *Contending Theories of International Relations*, 5th edition, New York: Longman, 2001.

Doyle, Michael, *Empires*, Ithaca: Cornell University Press, 1986.

Dryer, June Teufel, 'The 'Tianxia Trope: Will China Change the International System?', *Journal of Contemporary China* 24, no. 96 (2015): 1015–31.

Easton, David, *The Political System: An Inquiry into the State of Political Science*, New York: Knopf, 1953.

Eco, Umberto, 'It's Culture, Not War, That Cements European Identity', *The Guardian*, 26 January 2012, www.theguardian.com/world/2012/jan/26/umberto-eco-culture-war-europa.

Elster, Jon, *The Cement of Society: A Study of Social Order*, Cambridge: Cambridge University Press, 1989.

Epstein, Charlotte, 'Theorizing Agency in Hobbes's Wake: The Rational Actor, the Self, or the Speaking Subject?', *International Organization* 67 (2013): 287–316.

Ettinger, Aaron, 'Rumors of Restoration: Joe Biden's Foreign Policy and What It Means for Canada', *Canadian Foreign Policy Journal* April (2021): 1–18.

Farnham, Barbara, *Roosevelt and the Munich Crisis: A Study of Political Decision-Making*, Princeton: Princeton University Press, 1997.

Fearon, James and Wendt, Alexander, 'Rationalism v. Constructivism: A Skeptical View', in Walter Carlsnaes, Thomas Risse, and Beth Simmons, *Handbook of International Relations*, London: Sage, 2001.

Feng, Huiyun, *Chinese Strategic Culture and Foreign Policy Decision-Making: Confucianism, Leadership and War*, London: Routledge, 2007.

Feng, Huiyun and He, Kai, 'A Dynamic Strategic Culture Model and China's Behaviour in the South China Sea', *Cambridge Review of International Affairs* 34, no. 4 (2021): 510–29.

Feng, Huiyun and He, Kai (eds), *China's Challenges and International Order Transition: Beyond 'Thucydides's Trap'*, Ann Arbor: University of Michigan Press, 2020.

Feng, Huiyun, He, Kai, and Yan, Xuetong (eds), *Chinese Scholars and Foreign Policy: Debating International Relations*, London: Routledge, 2019.

Feng, Zhang, 'The Tsinghua Approach and the Inception of Chinese Theories of International Relations', *The Chinese Journal of International Politics*, 5, no. 1 (2012): 95–6.

Finkielkraut, Alain, 'Nul n'est Prêt a' Mourir pour l'Europe (Nobody Is Ready to Die for Europe), *Le Point*, 30 June 2016, www.lepoint.fr/europe/alain-finkielkraut-nul-n-est- pret-a-mourir-pour-l-europe-30-06-2016-2050917_2626.php.

Finnemore, Martha and Sikkink, Kathryn, 'International Norm Dynamics and Political Change', *International Organization* September (1998): 888, 894.

Flower, Harriet I., *Roman Republics*, Princeton: Princeton University Press, 2011.

Fouskas, Vassilis K. and Gökay, Bülent, 'The Power Shift to the Global East', in *The Fall of the US Empire: Global Fault-Lines and the Shifting Imperial Order*, London: Pluto Press, 2012.

Fraser, Chris, 'Major Rival Schools: Mohism and Legalism', in William Edelglass and Jay L. Garfield (eds), *The Oxford Handbook of World Philosophy*, Oxford: Oxford University Press, 2011.

Friedberg, Aaron L., *The Weary Titan: Britain and the Experience of Relative Decline, 1895–1905*, Princeton: Princeton University Press, 1988.

Fukuyama, Francis, *The End of History and The Last Man*, London: Penguin, 1992.

Gaddis, John Lewis, *Strategies of Containment*, Oxford: Oxford University Press, 2005.

Gaddis, John Lewis, *The Cold War: A New History*, London: Penguin Books, 2006.

Gauthier, David, 'The Social Contract as Ideology', *Philosophy and Public Affairs* 6, no. 2 (1977): 139.

Gelber, Lionel M., *The Rise of Anglo-American Friendship: A Study in World Politics, 1898–1906*, London: Oxford University Press, 1938.

Gilpin, Robert, *War and Change in World Politics*, New York: Cambridge University Press, 1981.

Gilpin, Robert and Gilpin, Jean M., *The Political Economy of International Relations*, Princeton: Princeton University Press, 1987.

Glencross, Andrew and Trechsel, Alexander (eds), *EU Federalism and Constitutionalism: The Legacy of Spinelli*, London: Lexington, 2010.

Gould-Davies, Nigel, 'Rethinking the Role of Ideology in International Politics During the Cold War', *Journal of Cold War Studies* 1, no. 1 (1999): 90–110.

Gourevitch, Peter, 'The Second Image Reversed: The International Sources of Domestic Politics', *International Organization* 32, no. 4 (1978): 888.

Grieco, Joseph, *Cooperation among Nations*, Ithaca: Cornell University Press, 1990.

Guo, Shuyong (ed), *Guoji Ganxi: Huhuan Zhongguo Lilun* (International Relations: Call for Chinese Theories), Tianjin: Tianjin People's Press, 2005.

Haass, Richard N., 'The High Price of American Withdrawal from Syria', *The Project Syndicate*, 17 October 2019, www.project-syndicate.org/commentary/high-price-of-american-withdrawal-from-syria-by-richard-n-haass-2019-10.

Haass, Richard N., 'How a World Order Ends: And What Comes in Its Wake', *Foreign Affairs* 98, no. 1 (2019): 30.

Habermas, Jürgen, *The Divided West*, Malden: Polity Press, 2006.

Haenle, Paul and Bresnick, Sam, 'Trump is Beijing's Best Asset', *Foreign Policy*, 15 October 2019, https://foreignpolicy.com/2019/10/15/china-trump-trump2020-deal-beijing-best-asset/?.

Hampton, Jean, *Hobbes and the Social Contract Tradition*, Cambridge: Cambridge University Press, 1986.

Hassner, Pierre, 'L'Europe et le Spectre des Nationalismes (Europe and the Specter of Nationalisms)', *Esprit*, 1991.

He, Kai, 'A Realist's Ideal Pursuit', *Chinese Journal of International Politics* 5, no. 2 (2012): 183–97.

He, Kai, Feng, Huiyun, Chan, Steve, and Hu, Weixing, 'Rethinking Revisionism in World Politics', *The Chinese Journal of International Politics* 14, no. 2 (2021): 159–86.

Heath, Timothy R. and Thompson, William R., 'Avoiding US–China Competition Is Futile: Why the Best Option Is to Manage Strategic Rivalry', *Asia Policy* 13, no. 2 (2018): 91–119.

Heilmann, Sebastian, *Red Swan: How Unorthodox Policy Making Facilitated China's Rise*, HK: The Chinese University Press, 2018.

Herborth, Benjamin, 'Die via media als konstitutionstheoretische Einbahnstraße: Zur Entwicklung des Akteur-Struktur-Problems bei Alexander Wendt (The via Media as a One-Way Street in Constitutional Theory: On the Development of the Agent–Structure Problem in Alexander Wendt's Work)', *Zeitschrift für Internationale Beziehungen* 11, no. 1 (2004): 61–87.

Hermann, Margaret G., 'Explaining Foreign Policy Behaviour Using the Personal Characteristics of Political Leaders', *International Studies Quarterly* 24, no. 1 (1980): 7–46.

Hermann, Margaret G. and Hagan, Joe D., 'International Decision Making: Leadership Matters', *Foreign Policy* 110 (1998): 132–5.

Hermann, Margaret G., Hermann, Charles F., and Hagan, Joe D., 'How Decision Units Shape Foreign Policy Behaviour', in Charles F. Hermann, Charles W. Kegley, and James N. Rosenau (eds), *New Directions in the Study of Foreign Policy*, Boston: Allen and Unwin, 1987.

Herz, John H., 'Idealist Internationalism and the Security Dilemma', *World Politics* 2, no. 2 (1950): 157–80.

Hintze, Otto, 'Military Organization and the Organization of the State', in Felix Gilbert (ed), *The Historical Essays of Otto Hintze*, New York: Oxford, 1975.

Hirschman, Albert, *A Bias for Hope: Essays on Development and Latin America*, New Haven: Yale University Press, 1971.

Hobbes, Thomas, *Leviathan*, edited by Michael Oakeshott, Oxford: Basil Blackwell, 1946(1651).

Hoffmann, Stanley, *Janus and Minerva: Essays in the Theory and Practice of International Politics*, Boulder, Colo.: Westview, 1987.

Holsti, Ole R., 'The Political Psychology of International Politics: More than a Luxury', *Political Psychology* 10, no. 3 (1989): 497.

Holsti, Ole R., 'Theories of International Relations and Foreign Policy: Realism and Its Challengers', in *Controversies in International Relations Theory*, London: Red Globe Press, 1995.

Huang, Cary, 'China Takes Aim at the US for the First Time in its Defense White Paper', *South China Morning Post*, 7 August 2019, https://www.scmp.com/comment/opinion/article/3021273/china-takes-aim-us-first-time-its-defence-white-paper.

Huang, Huaixin, *Lunyu huijiao jishi* (Corrections and Exegeses of the Analects of Confucius), Shanghai: Shanghai guji chubanshe, 2008.

Huang, Weihe, 'Mozi de yiliguan (Mozi's View on Justice and Benefit)', *Zhongguo Shehui Kexue* (Chinese Social Sciences), 3 (1985): 115–24.

Hughes, Richard L., Ginnett, Robert C., and Curphy, Cordon J., *Leadership: Enhancing the Lessons of Experience*, 5th edition, New York: The McGraw-Hill Companies Inc., 2006.

Huntington, Samuel P., 'The West Unique not Universal', *Foreign Affairs*, 1998.

Hutton, Eric L. (trans). *Xunzi: The Complete Text*, Princeton: Princeton University Press, 2014.

Hwang, Yih-Jye, 'Reappraising the Chinese School of International Relations: A Postcolonial Perspective', *Review of International Studies*, 12 April 2021, www.cambridge.org/core/journals/review-of-international-studies/article/reappraising-the-chinese-school-of-international-relations-a-postcolonial-perspective/8035C0A9D7A73A130CB902145A19E487.

Ikenberry, G. John, 'The Future of International Leadership', *Political Science Quarterly* 111, no. 3 (1996): 385, 388–96.

Ikenberry, G. John, *The Liberal Leviathan*, Princeton: Princeton University Press, 2001.

Ikenberry, John (ed), *America Unrivalled: The Future of the Balance of Power*, Ithaca: Cornell University Press, 2002.

Ikenberry, G. John, 'Liberal Internationalism 3.0: America and the Dilemmas of Liberal World Order', *Perspectives on Politics* 7, no. 1 (2009): 71–87, 84.

Ikenberry, G. John, 'Between the Eagle and the Dragon: America, China, and Middle State Strategies in East Asia', *Political Science Quarterly* 131, no. 1 (2016): 9–43.

Ikenberry, G. John, 'Why the Liberal World Order Will Survive', in 'Rising Powers and the International Order', special issue, *Ethics & International Affairs* 32, no. 1 (2018): 17–29.

Ikenberry, G. John and Kupchan, Charles, 'Socialization and Hegemonic Power', *International Organization* 44, no. 3 (1990): 283–315.

Isocrates, *On the Peace*, 8, 134.

Ivanhoe, Philip J., 'Virtue Ethics and the Chinese Confucian Tradition', in Daniel C. Russell (ed), *The Cambridge Companion to Virtue Ethics*, Cambridge: Cambridge University Press, 2013.

Jackson, Ian, *The Economic Cold War: America, Britain and East-West Trade, 1948–63*, Houndsmill, Basingstoke, Hampshire: Palgrave, 2001.

Jakes, Lara, Ismay, John, and Myers, Steven Lee, 'Biden's Goals Converge in Top Envoys' Trip to Asia', *New York Times*, 16 March 2021.

Jepperson, Ronald L., Wendt, Alexander, and Katzenstein, Peter J., 'Norms, Identity, and Culture in National Security', in Peter Katzenstein (ed), *The Culture of National Security*, New York: Columbia University Press, 1996.

Jervis, Robert, *Perception and Misperception in International Politics*, Princeton: Princeton University Press, 1976.

Jervis, Robert, 'Cooperation under the Security Dilemma', *World Politics* 30, no. 2 (1978): 167–214.

Jervis, Robert, 'Do Leaders Matter and How Would We Know?', *Security Studies* 22, no. 2 (2013): 153.

Johnson, Keith and Gramer, Robbie, 'The Great Decoupling', *Foreign Policy*, 14 May 2020, https://foreignpolicy.com/2020/05/14/china-us-pandemic-economy-tensions-trump-coronavirus-covid-new-cold-war-economics-the-great-decoupling/.

Johnston, Alastair Iain, *Cultural Realism*, Princeton: Princeton University Press, 1992.

Johnston, Alastair Iain, 'What (if Anything) Does East Asia Tell Us about International Relations Theory', *Annual Review of Political Science* 15 (2012): 53–78.

Johnston, Alastair Iain, *Cultural Realism: Strategic Culture and Grand Strategy in Chinese History*, Princeton: Princeton University Press, 1998.

Johnston, Ian, *The Mozi: A Complete Translation*, Hong Kong: The Chinese University Press, 2010.

Judt, Tony, *Postwar: A History of Europe Since 1945*, London: Penguin Books, 2005.

Kagan, Robert, *The Jungle Grows Back: America and Our Imperiled World*, New York: Knopf Doubleday Publishing Group, 2019.

Kallet, Lisa, 'Thucydides Workshop of History and Utility outside the Text', in Antonios Rengakos and Antonios Tsakmakis (eds), *Brills Companion to Thucydides*, Boston: Brills, 2006.

Kant, Immanuel, translated by Mary Gregor and Jens Timmermann, *Groundwork of the Metaphysics of Morals*, Cambridge: Cambridge University Press, 2012.

Kaplan, Morton, System and Process in International Politics, New York: John Wiley & Sons, Inc., 1957.

Katzenstein, Mary F., *The Culture of National Security: Norms and Identity in World Politics*, New York: Columbia University Press, 1996.

Katzenstein, Peter J., 'The Second Coming? Reflections on a Global Theory of International Relations', in Yaqing Qin (ed), *Globalizing IR Theory Critical Engagement*, London: Routledge, 2020, pp 27–38.

Kennedy, Andrew B. and Lim, Daren J., 'The Innovation Imperative: Technology and US–China Rivalry in the Twenty-First Century', *International Affairs* 94, no. 3 (2018): 554–7.

Kennedy, Paul, *The Rise and Fall of the Great Powers: Economic Change and Military Conflict from 1500 to 2000*, London: Vintage, 1989.

Keohane, Robert O., *After Hegemony: Cooperation and Discord in the World Political Economy*, Princeton: Princeton University Press, 1984.

Keohane, Robert (ed), *Neorealism and Its Critics*, New York: Columbia University Press, 1986.

Keohane, Robert O., *International Institutions and State Power: Essays in International Relations Theory*, New York: Westview Press, 1989.

Keohane, Robert O. and Nye, Joseph, *Power and Interdependence: World Politics in Transition*, Little, Brown, 1977.

Keohane, Robert O. and Morse, Julia C., 'Counter-multilateralism', in Jean-Frederic Morin et al (eds), The *Politics of Transatlantic Trade Negotiations: TTIP in a Globalized World*, New York: Routledge, 2015.

Kindleberger, Charles P., *The World in Depression: 1929–1939*, Berkeley: University of California Press, 1973.

Kindleberger, Charles P., 'Dominance and Leadership in the International Economy: Exploitation, Public Goods, and Free Rides', *International Studies Quarterly* 25, no. 2 (1981): 242–54, 57.

Kindleberger, Charles P., *World Economic Primacy: 1500–1990*, Oxford: Oxford University Press, 1996.

Kirshner, Jonathan, 'Handle Him with Care: The Importance of Getting Thucydides Right', *Security Studies* 28, no. 1 (2019): 1–24.

Kirshner, Jonathan, 'Offensive Realism, Thucydides Traps, and the Tragedy of Unforced Errors: Classical Realism and US–China Relations', *China International Strategy Review* 1, no. 1, (2019): 51–63.

Knafo, Samuel, 'Critical Approaches and the Legacy of the Agent/Structure Debate in International Relations', *Cambridge Review of International Affairs* 23, no. 3 (2010): 493–516.

Kontos, Pavlos, *Aristotle's Moral Realism Reconsidered: Phenomenological Ethics*, New York: Routledge, 2011.

Krasner, Stephen, 'Sovereignty, Regimes, and Human Rights', in Volker Rittberger (ed), *Regime Theory and International Relations*, Oxford: Clarendon Press, 1993.

Krauthammer, Charles, 'The Unipolar Moment', *Foreign Affairs* 70, no. 1 (1990): 23–33, doi:10.2307/20044692.

Kroening, Mathew, *The Return of Great Power Rivalry: Democracy Versus Autocracy from the Ancient World to the US and China*, New York: Oxford University Press, 2020.

Kubalkova, Vendulka, *Foreign Policy in a Constructed World*, New York: Routledge, 2001.

Kuhn, Philipp, 'Can China Be Governed from Beijing? Reflections on Reform and Regionalism', in Wang Gungwu and John Wong (eds) *China's Political Economy*, Singapore: Singapore University Press, 1998.

Kuhn, Philipp, *Origins of the Modern Chinese State*, Stanford, CA: Stanford University Press, 2002.

Kupchan, Charles A., 'Empire, Military Power, and Economic Decline', *International Security* 13, no. 4 (1989): 36–53.

Kupchan, Charles A., *No One's World: The West, the Rising Rest, and the Coming Global Turn*, New York: Oxford University Press, 2012.

Kynge, James and Liu, Nian, 'Tech's New Rulemaker', *Financial Times*, 8 October 2020.

Lake, David, A., 'International Economic Structures and American Economic Policy, 1887–1934', *World Politics* 35, no. 4 (1983): 519–21.

Lake, David A., 'Regional Hierarchy: Authority and Local International Order', *Review of International Studies* 35 (2009): 20–21, 35–39.

Lake, David A., 'Legitimating Power: The Domestic Politics of US International Hierarchy', *International Security* 38, no. 2 (2013): 74–111.

Landes, David S., *The Poverty and Wealth of Nations*, New York: W.W. Norton and Company, 1999.

Larson, Deborah Welch, *Origins of Containment: A Psychological Explanation*, Princeton: Princeton University Press, 1985.

Larson, Deborah Welch, 'Can China Change the International System? The Role of Moral Leadership', *The Chinese Journal of International Politics* 13, no. 2 (2020), 163–86.

Larson, Deborah Welch, 'Policy or Pique? Trump and the Turn to Great Power Competition', *Political Science Quarterly* 136, no. 1 (2021): 54–5, 57, 61–2.

Lau, D.C., *Analects*, Book XIV, Verse 16, New York: Penguin Classics, 1979.

Lebow, Richard Ned, *The Tragic Vision of Politics*, Cambridge: Cambridge University Press, 2003.

Lebow, Richard Ned, *A Cultural Theory of International Relations*, Cambridge: Cambridge University Press, 2008.

Levy, Jack S., 'Power Transition Theory and the Rise of China', in *China's Ascent: Power, Security, and the Future of International Politics*, edited by Robert S. Ross and Zhu Feng, Ithaca: Cornell University Press, 2008.

Levy, Jack S., 'Psychology and Foreign Policy Decision-Making', in Leonie Huddy, David O. Sears, and Jack S. Levy (eds), 2nd edition, *The Oxford Handbook of Political Psychology*, New York: Oxford University Press, 2013.

Levy, Jack S., 'Counterfactuals, Causal Influence and Historical Analysis', *Security Studies* 24, no. 3 (2015): 378–402.

Liff, Adam P. and Ikenberry, G. John, 'Racing towards Tragedy?: China's Rise, Military Competition in the Asia Pacific, and the Security Dilemma', *International Security* 39, no. 2 (2014): 57–8.

Lipset, Seymour Martin, 'Some Social Requisites of Democracy: Economic Development and Political Legitimacy', *American Political Science Review* 53, no. 1 (1959): 69–105.

Lipset, Seymour Martin, *Political Man and the Social Bases of Politics*, New York: Doubleday & Company, 1960.

Liu, Ruonan and Liu, Feng, 'To Ally or not to Ally? Debating China's Nonalignment Strategy in the 21st Century', in Huiyun Feng, Kai He, and Yan Xuetong (eds), *Chinese Scholars and Foreign Policy: Debating International Relations*, New York: Routledge, 2019.

Lowsen, Ben, 'China's New Defense White Paper: Reading Between the Lines', 30 July 2019, *The Diplomat*, https://thediplomat.com/2019/07/chinas-new-defense-white-paper-reading-between-the-lines/.

Lu, Peng, 'Chinese IR Sino-Centrism Tradition and Its Influence on the Chinese School Movement', *Pacific Review* 25 (2018): 150–67.

Luce, Edward, 'US Democracy Is Still in the Danger Zone', *Financial Times*, 27 May 2021, www.ft.com/content/bb554492-9b15-4af0-8954-ee0f2063327c.

Lundestad, Geir, 'Empire by Invitation', *Journal of Peace Research* 23, no. 3 (1987): 263–77.

Luo, Zhiye (trans), *Book of History*, Changsha: Hunan Publishing House, 1996.

Lynch, Timothy J. and Singh, Robert S., *After Bush: The Case for Continuity in American Foreign Policy*, Cambridge: Cambridge University Press, 2008.

Mabee, Bryan, 'Levels and Agents, States and People: Micro-Historical Sociological Analysis and International Relations', *International Politics* 44 (2007): 431–49.

Macias, Amanda, 'Biden says there will be "extreme competition" with China, but Won't Take Trump Approach', *CNBC News*, 7 February 2021, www.cnbc.com/2021/02/07/biden-will-compete-with-china-but-wont-take-trump-approach.html.

Magnus, George, 'China and the US Are too Intertwined to Keep up the Trade War', *Financial Times*, 7 June 2019, https://www.ft.com/content/6d0534f2-8870-11e9-b861-54ee436f9768.

Mann, James, *The China Fantasy: Why Capitalism Will not Bring Democracy to China*, London: Penguin Random House, 2007.

Mansfield, Harvey C., *Manliness*, New York: Yale University Press, 2007.

March, James G. and Olsen, Johan P., 'The Institutional Dynamics of International Political Orders', *International Organization* 52, no. 4 (1998): 943–69.

Mastanduno, Michael, 'Strategies of Economic Containment: US Trade Relations with the Soviet Union', *World Politics* 37, no. 4 (1985): 503–31.

Mastanduno, Michael, *Economic Containment: CoCom and the Politics of East-West Trade*, Ithaca: Cornell University Press, 1992.

Mathews, Jessica T., 'Power Shift', *Foreign Affairs* 76, no. 1 (1997): 50–66.

McBride, James and Chatsky, Andrew, 'Is "Made in China 2025" a Threat to Global Trade?', *Council on Foreign Relations*, 13 May 2019, www.cfr.org/backgrounder/made-china-2025-threat-global-trade.

Mearsheimer, John J., *The Tragedy of Great Power Politics*, New York: W.W. Norton, 2001.

Mearsheimer, John J., 'The Gathering Storm: China's Challenge to US Power in Asia', *Chinese Journal of International Politics* 3 (2010): 381–96.

Mearsheimer, John J., *Great Delusion: Liberal Dreams and International Realities*, New Haven: Yale University Press, 2018.

Mearsheimer, John J., 'Bound to Fail: The Rise and Fall of the Liberal International Order', *International Security* 43, no. 4 (2019): 7–50.

Mearsheimer, John J. and Walt, Steven M., 'Leaving Theory Behind: Why Simplistic Hypothesis Testing Is Bad for International Relations', *European Journal of International Relations* 19, no. 3 (2013): 427–57.

Medeiros, Evan S., 'The Changing Fundamentals of US–China Relations', *Washington Quarterly* 42, no. 3 (2019): 100.

Menaldo, Mark A., *Leadership and Transformative Ambition in International Relations*, Northampton, MA: Edward Elgar, 2013.

Menon, Shivshankar, 'Book Review: Yan Xuetong, Leadership and the Rise of Great Powers', *China Report* 56, no. 1 (2020): 139–59.

Min, Jie and Huang, Yang, 'Hezun: Keyu "Xinzhong" de "Zhongguo" (Hezun: "China" inscribed on the "heart")', *Xinhua News Agency New Media*, 3 July 2021, https://baijiahao.baidu.com/s?id=1704240662605498579&wfr=spider&for=pc.

Mitter, Rana, 'The World China Wants: How Power Will – and Won't – Reshape Chinese Ambitions', *Foreign Affairs* 100, no. 1: (2021)161–75.

Moody, Peter, *Conservative Thought in Contemporary China*, Lanham, MD: Lexington Books, 2007.

Morgan, Ruth P., 'Reviewed Work(s): The Presidential Character: Predicting Performance in the White House. by James David Barber', *The Journal of Politics* 37, no. 1 (1975): 305–6.

Morgenthau, Hans. J., *Politics among Nations: The Struggle for Power and Peace*, New York: Alfred Knopf, 1948.

Morgenthau, Hans J., *Politics among Nations: The Struggle for Power and Peace*, 3rd edition, New York: Knopf, 1960.

Morgenthau, Hans J., *Scientific Man vs. Power Politics*, Chicago: University of Chicago Press, 1946.

Mukunda, Gautan, *Indispensable: When Leaders Really Matter*, New York: Harvard Business Review Press, 2014.

Neal, Patrick, 'Hobbes and Rational Choice Theory', *Western Political Quarterly* 41, no. 4 (1988): 635–52.

Niquet, Valerie, '"Confu-talk": The Use of Confucian Concepts in Contemporary Chinese Foreign policy', in Anne-Marie Brady (ed), *China's Thought Management*, London and New York: Routledge, 2012.

Norden, Bryan W. Van (trans), *Mengzi: With Selections From Traditional Commentaries*, Indianapolis: Hackett, 2008.

North, Douglas, 'Transaction Costs, Institutions and Economic History', *Journal of Institutional and Theoretical Economics* 140 (1984): 7–17.

Northouse, Peter G., *Leadership: Theory and Practice*, 7th edition, Thousand Oaks: SAGE Publications, Inc, 2015.

Nuyen, A.T., 'Moral Obligation and Moral Motivation in Confucian Role-Based Ethics', *Dao* 8 (2009): 1–11.

Nye, Joseph, 'Transformational Leadership and US Grand Strategy', *Foreign Affairs* 85, no. 4 (2006): 68.

Nye Jr, Joseph S., *Do Morals Matter? Presidents and Foreign Policy from FDR to Trump*, New York: Oxford University Press, 2020.

Obama, Barack, 'Remarks of President Barack Obama – As Prepared for Delivery State of the Union Address', White House: President Barack Obama, Washington, DC, 20 January 2015, obamawhitehouse.archives.gov/the-press-office/2015/01/20/remarks-president-barack-obama-prepared-delivery-state-union-address.

Oksenberg, Michael, 'Will China Democratize', *Journal of Democracy* 9, no. 1 (1998): 27–34.

Onuf, Nicholas G., 'World of our Making: Rules and Rule', in *Social Theory and International Relations*, Columbia, SC: University of South Carolina Press, 1989.

Organski, A.F.K., *World Politics*, New York: Alfred A. Knopf, 1958.

Organski, A.F.K. and Kugler, Jacek, *The War Ledger*, Chicago: University of Chicago Press, 1980.

Orwin, Clifford, 'Justifying Empire: The Speech of the Athenians at Sparta and the Problem of Justice in Thucydides', *The Journal of Politics* 48, no. 1 (1986): 72–85.

Orwin, Clifford, *The Humanity of Thucydides*, New Jersey: Princeton University Press, 1994.

Parent, Joseph M. and Baron, Joshua M., 'Elder Abuse: How the Moderns Mistreat Classical Realism', *International Studies Review*, 13, no. 2 (2011): 193–213.

Parsons, Talcott, *The Social System*, London: Routledge, 1951.

Pass, Jonathan, 'Gramsci Meets Emergentist Materialism: Towards a Neo Neo-Gramscian Perspective on World Order', *Review of International Studies* 44, no. 4 (2018): 595–618.

Passoth, J-H. and Rowland, Nicholas J., 'Who Is Acting in International Relations?', in Daniel Jacobi and Annette Freyberg-Inan (eds), *Human Beings in International Relations*, Cambridge: Cambridge University Press, 2015.

Patrick, Stewart M., *The Best Laid Plans: The Origins of American Multilateralism and the Dawn of the Cold War*, New York: Rowman and Littlefield, 2009.

Pei, Minxin, 'Transition in China? More Likely Than You Think', *Journal of Democracy* 27, no. 4 (2016): 5–20.

Platias, Athanassios, 'The Grand Strategy of Themistocles', in *Thermopylae and Salamis: Assessing their Importance in the Modern World*, Athens: MV Publications, 2021.

Platias, Athanasios and Koliopoulos, Constantinos, *Thucydides on Strategy: Grand Strategies in the Peloponnesian War and their Relevance Today*, New York: Columbia University Press, 2010.

Platias, Athanassios and Koliopoulos, Constantinos (in Greek), *Sun Tzu: The Art of War*, Athens: Diavlos, 2015.

Platias, Athanassios and Trigkas, Vasilis, 'Unravelling the Thucydides Trap: Inadvertent Escalation or War of Choice?', *Chinese Journal of International Politics* 14, no. 2 (2021).

Platias, Athanassios and Trigkas, Vasilis, 'Strategic Universality in the Axial Age: The Doctrine of Prudence in Political Leadership', *Strategic Analysis* 46, no. 2 (2022): 157–70.

Politi, James, Sevastopulo, Demetri, and Lockett, Hudson, 'Trump Blacklist Ups Ante with China', *Financial Times*, 20 December 2020.

Polybius, *The Histories*, translated by R. Patton, Loeb Classical Library: Harvard University Press, 1979–2006.

Porpora, Douglas, 'Four Concepts of Social Structure', *Journal for the Theory of Social Behaviour* 19, no. 2 (1989): 195–212.

Porter, Michael E., Rivkin, Jan W., Desai, Mihir A., Gehl, Katherine M., Kerr, William R., and Raman, Manjari, 'A Recovery Squandered: The State of US Competitiveness', *Harvard Business School*, December 2019, www.hbs.edu/competitiveness/Documents/a-recovery-squandered.pdf.

Putnam, Robert D., Leonardi, Robert, and Nanetti, Raffaella Y., *Making Democracy Work: Civic Traditions in Modern Italy*, New Jersey: Princeton University Press, 1993.

Qian, Mu, *Zhongguo Wenhuashi Daolun* (An Introduction to the History of Chinese Culture), Beijing: Commercial Press, 1994.

Qin, Yaqing, 'A Multiverse of Knowledge: Cultures and IR Theories', in Yaqing Qin (ed), *Globalizing IR Theory Critical Engagement*, London: Routledge, 2020.

Rajagopalan, Rajesh, 'Book Reviews', India Quarterly 75, no. 3 (2019): 407.

Reinhold, Niebuhr, *Beyond Tragedy*, New York: Charles Scibner's Sons, 1938.

Renshon, Stanley Allen and Larson, Deborah Welch, *Good Judgment in Foreign Policy: Theory and Application*, Lanham, MD: Rowman and Littlefield, 2003.

Ringmar, Erik, 'How the World Stage Makes Its Subjects: An Embodied Critique of Constructivist IR Theory', *Journal of International Relations and Development* 19, no. 1 (2016): 101–25.

Ripsman, Norin M., Taliaferro, Jeffrey W., and Lobell, Steven E., *Neoclassical Realist Theory of International Politics*, New York: Oxford University Press, 2016.

Risse, Mathias, *On Global Justice*, Princeton: Princeton University Press, 2012.

Risse-Kappen, Thomas, *Cooperation among Democracies: European Influence on US Foreign Policy*, Princeton: Princeton University Press, 1995.

Rolland, Nadège, *China's Vision for a New World Order*, National Bureau of Asian Research, NBR Special Report #83, January 2020.

Roosevelt, Theodore, *An Autobiography*, New York: Macmillan, 1913, www.bartleby.com/55/6.html.

Rose, Gideon, 'Neoclassical Realism and Theories of Foreign Policy', *World Politics* 51, no. 1 (1998): 144–72.

Rosemont, Henry Jr, *Against Individualism: A Confucian Rethinking of the Foundations of Morality, Politics, Family, and Religion*, Lanham: Lexington, 2015.

Ruggie, John Gerard (ed), *Multilateralism Matters: The Theory and Praxis of An Institutional Form*, New York: Columbia University Press, 1993.

Rupeng, Cai, '*Chuixiang Zhongguo Xuepai de Zong Haojiao* (The General Trumpet of the Chinese School)', *Zhongguo Xinwen Zhoukan* (China News Week) 46 (2017): 19, www.inewsweek.cn/2/2017-12-08/3720.shtml.

Sachs, Jeffrey D., *A New Foreign Policy: Beyond American Exceptionalism*, New York: Columbia University Press, 2018.

Saint Augustine, *The City of God*, translated by Marcus Dods, 2 volumes, New York: Hafner Publishing Co, 1948.

Sanger, David E. and Perlez, Jane, 'Trump Hands the Chinese a Gift: The Chance for Global Leadership', *New York Times*, 1 June 2017, www.nytimes.com/2017/06/01/us/politics/climate-accord-trump-china-global-leadership.html.

Sanger, David E., 'Looking to End "America First" and Re-engage with the World', *New York Times*, 10 November 2020.

Sanger, David E., Erlanger, Steven., and Cohen, Roger, 'Biden Reaffirms Alliances' Value for US Policies', *New York Times*, 20 February 2021.

Sanger, David E. and Crowley, Michael, 'A Pivotal Reset on China Policy by Biden's Team', *New York Times*, 18 March 2021.

Sanger, David E., 'Biden Stakes Out his Challenge with China: "Prove Democracy Works"', *New York Times*, 27 March 2021.

Schaik, Louise van., Sarris, Stefano., and Lossow, Tobias von, *Fighting an Existential Threat: Small Island States Bringing Climate Change to the UN Security Council*, The Hague: Clingendael Institute, 2018.

Scharpf, Fritz W., 'After the Crash: A Perspective on Multilevel European Democracy', *European Law Journal* 21, no. 3 (2015): 384–405.

Schell, Orville and Shirk, Susan L., 'Course Correction: Towards an Effective and Sustainable China Policy', *Asia Society and Center on US–China Relations*, February 2019, https://asiasociety.org/center-us-china-relations/course-correction-towards-effective-and-sustainable-china-policy.

Scobell, Andrew, 'Perception and Misperception in US-China Relations', *Political Science Quarterly* 135, no. 4 (2020–21): 637–64.

Selin, Jennifer L., 'What Makes an Agency Independent?', *American Journal of Political Science* 59, no. 4 (2015): 971–87.

Shijie Zhishi Nianjian, *Year Book of World Affairs 1991/92*, Beijing: World Affairs Press, 1992.

Shijie Zhishi Nianjian, *Year Book of World Affairs 2004/2005*, Beijing: World Affairs Press, 2005.

Silove, Nina, 'The Pivot before the Pivot: US Strategy to Preserve the Power Balance in Asia', *International Security* 40, no. 4 (2016): 45–88.

Singer, J. David, 'The Level-of-Analysis Problem in International Relations', *World Politics* 14, no. 1 (1961): 77–92.

Slote, Michael, *Morals from Motives*, Oxford: Oxford University Press, 2001, Kindle version, location 2140.

Smith, Noah, 'Trump Blazed a Trail that Clears the Way for Biden', *Bloomberg Opinion*, 20 April 2021, https://www.newsday.com/opinion/commentary/donald-trump-joe-biden-economic-policy-program-international-trade-c90750.

Smith, Steven, *Reading Althusser*, Ithace: Cornell University Press, 1984.

Snyder, Quddus Z., 'Taking the System Seriously: Another Liberal Theory of International Politics', *International Studies Review* 15, no. 4 (2013): 539–61.

Stephen, Matthew D. and Skidmore, David, 'The AIIB in the Liberal International Order', *Chinese Journal of International Politics* 12, no. 1 (2019): 61–91.

Stephens, Philip, 'Supply Chain "Sovereignty" Will Undo the Gains of Globalisation', *Financial Times*, 19 March 2021.

Sterling-Folker Jennifer, 'Realist Environment, Liberal Process, and Domestic Level Variables', *International Studies Quarterly* 41, no. 1 (1997): 4–8.

Streeck, Wolfgang, *Buying Time: The Delayed Crisis of Democratic Capitalism*, London and New York: Verso, 2013.

Taliaferro, Jeffrey W., 'Neoclassical Realism and Resource Extraction: State Building for Future War', *Security Studies* 15, no. 3 (2006): 464–95.].

Telò, Mario, *International Relations: A European Perspective*, New York: Routledge, 2009.

Telò, Mario, 'The Three Historical Epochs of Multilateralism', in Mario Telò (ed), *Globalization, Europe, Multilateralism: Towards a Better Global Governance?*, Burlington: Ashgate, 2014.

Telò, Mario, 'Building a Common Language in Pluralist International Relations Theories', *The Chinese Journal of International Politics* 13, no. 3 (2020): 455–83.

Telò, Mario and Yuan, Feng (eds), *China and the EU in the Era of Regional and Interregional Cooperation: The Belt and Road Initiative in a Comparative Perspective*, Brussels and London: Peter Lang, 2020.

Tetlock, Philip E., *Expert Political Judgment*, Princeton: Princeton University Press, 2009.

The State Department, 'The United States of America and The Republic of Korea on Working Together to Promote Cooperation between the Indo-Pacific Strategy and the New Southern Policy', 2021, www.state gov/the-united-states-of-america-and-the-republic-of-korea-on-working-together-to-promote-cooperation-between-the-indo-pacific-strategy-and-the-new-southern-policy/.

Tobin, Daniel, 'How Xi Jinping's "New Era" should have Ended US Debate on Beijing's Ambitions', *Center for Strategic and International Studies*, May 2020, www.csis.org/analysis/how-xi-jinpings-new-era-should-have-ended-us-debate-beijings-ambitions.

Tobin, Liza, 'Xi's Vision for Transforming Global Governance: A Strategic Challenge for Washington and its Allies', *Texas National Security Review* 2, no. 1 (2018): 155–66.

Tooze, Adam, 'The H-Word by Perry Anderson – Follow the Leader', *The Financial Times*, 28 April 2017, www.ft.com/content/2367a896-29b5-11e7-bc4b-5528796fe35c.

Toynbee, Arnold, *A Study of History Abridged and Illustrated*, Oxford: Oxford University Press, 1972.

Trachtenberg, Marc, *The Craft of International History*, New Jersey: Princeton University Press, 2006.

Trigkas, Vasilis, 'Chimerica on Decline', *The Diplomat*, 4 May 2015, https://thediplomat.com/2015/05/chimerica-in-decline/.

Trigkas, Vasilis, 'China Has Its DARPA but Does It Have the Right People?', *The Diplomat*, 9 August 2017, https://thediplomat.com/2017/08/china-has-its-darpa-but-does-it-have-the-right-people/.

Trigkas, Vasilis, 'By Reaching out to Japan and Reassuring India, China Can Stop the Quad before It Even Starts', *The South China Morning Post*, 23 November 2018, www.scmp.com/comment/insight-opinion/asia/article/2174610/reaching-out-japan-and-reassuring-india-china-can-stop.

Trigkas, Vasilis, 'Review of Unrivalled: Why America Will Remain the World's Sole Superpower by Michael Beckley', *International Affairs* 95, no. 3 (2019): 750–2.

Trigkas, Vasilis, 'On Global Power Differentials, Moral Realism, and the Rise of China: A Review Essay', *Journal of Contemporary China*, 29 (2020): 126.

Trigkas, Vasilis, 'On Global Power Differentials, Moral Realism, and the Rise of China: A Review Essay', *Journal of Contemporary China* 29, no. 126 (2020): 950–63.

Trigkas, Vasilis, 'R[eview of the Book: The Long Game: China's Strategy to Displace American Order by Rush Doshi', *Pacific Affairs* 95, no. 1 (2022): 132–4.

Tunsjø, Østen, *The Return of Bipolarity in World Politics: China, the United States, and Geostructural Realism*, New York: Columbia University Press, 2018.

Vogel, Ezra, 'The Leadership of Xi Jinping: A Dengist Perspective', *Journal of Contemporary China* 30, no. 131 (2021): 693–6.

Wallerstein, Immanuel, *The Modern World System*, New York: Academic Press, 1974, 1980, 1989.

Walt, Stephen M., *The Origins of Alliances*, Ithaca: Cornell University Press, 1987.

Walt, Stephen M., 'US Grand Strategy after the Cold War: Can Realism Explain it, Should Realism Guide it?', *International Relations Journal* 32, no. 1 (2018): 1–20.

Walt, Stephen M., 'Afghanistan Hasn't Damaged US Credibility', *Foreign Policy*, 21 August 2021, https://foreignpolicy.com/2021/08/21/afghanistan-hasnt-damaged-u-s-credibility/.

Waltz, Kenneth W., *Man, the State, and War*, New York: Columbia University Press, 1954.

Waltz, Kenneth W., *Foreign Policy and Democratic Politics: The American and British Experience*, London: Longmans, 1968.

Waltz, Kenneth W., *Theory of International Politics*, New York: McGraw-Hill, 1979.

Waltz, Kenneth N., 'Evaluating Theories', *American Political Science Review* 91, no. 4 (1997): 913–17.

Waltz, Kenneth W., 'Structural Realism after the Cold War', *International Security* 25, no. 1 (2000): 5–41.

Wang, Shaoguang, 'Representational and Representative Democracy', *Open Times*, 2014.

Warren, Aiden and Bartley, Adam, *US Foreign Policy and China: The Bush, Obama, Trump Administrations*, Edinburgh: Edinburgh University Press, 2021.

Waters, Richard, Hille, Kathrin, and Lucas, Louise, 'Trump Risks a Tech Cold War', *Financial Times*, May 2019, pp 25–6.

Webb, Michael C. and Krasner, Stephen D., 'Hegemonic Stability Theory: An Empirical Assessment', *Review of International Studies* 15, no. 2 (1989): 184–6.

Weber, Cynthia, 'Performative States', *Millennium Journal of International Studies* 27, no. 1 (1998): 77–95.

Weiss, Jessica C., 'How Hawkish Is the Chinese Public? Another Look at "Rising Nationalism" and Chinese Foreign Policy', *Journal of Contemporary China* 28, no. 119 (2019): 679–95.

Welch, Barbara, 'Shortcut to Greatness: The New Thinking and the Revolution in Soviet Foreign Policy', *International Organization* 57, no. 1 (2003): 77–109.

Wendt, Alexander, 'The agent–structure problem in international relations theory', *International Organization* 41, no. 3 (1987): 335–70.

Wendt, Alexander, 'The Agent–Structure Problem in International Relations Theory', *International Organization* 41, no. 3 (1987): 335–70.

Wendt, Alexander, 'Anarchy Is What States Make of It: The Social Construction of Power Politics', *International Organization* 46, no. 2 (1992): 391–425.

Wendt, Alexander, 'Collective Identity Formation and the International State', *American Political Science Review* 88, no. 2 (1994): 388–92.

Wendt, Alexander, *Social Theory of International Politics*, New York: Cambridge University Press, 1999.

Westad, Arne, *The Global Cold War: Third World Interventions and the Making of Our Times*, Cambridge: Cambridge University Press, 2006.

Wight, Colin, *Agents, Structures and International Relations: Politics as Ontology*, Cambridge: Cambridge University Press, 2006.

Wolfers, Arnold, *Discord and Collaboration: Essays on International Politics*, Baltimore: The Johns Hopkins University Press, 1962.

Wong, Edward, 'US vs. China: Why This Power Struggle Is Different', *New York Times*, 27 June 2019.

World Bank, 'Gross Domestic Product 2020', *World Development Indicators Database*, 1 July 2021, https://databank.worldbank.org/data/download/GDP.pdf.

Wright, Thomas J., *All Measures Short of War*, New Haven: Yale University Press, 2017.

Wu, Guoguang, 'The King's Men and Others: Emerging Political Elites under Xi Jinping', *China Leadership Monitor*, 1 June 2019, www.prcleader.org/wusummer.

Wu, Xinbo, 'China in Search of a Liberal Partnership International Order', *International Affairs* 94, no. 5 (2018): 1017.

Xi, Jinping, 'Secure a Decisive Victory in Building a Moderately Prosperous Society in All Respects and Strive for the Great Success of Socialism with Chinese Characteristics for a New Era', speech at the 19th National Congress of the Communist Party of China, 28 October 2017, www.xinhuanet.com/english/download/Xi_Jinping%27s_report_at_19th_CPC_National_Congress.pdf.

Xi, Jinping, 'Work Together to Build a Community of Shared Future for Mankind', 19 January 2019, speech at UN Office at Geneva, www.xinhuanet.com/english/2017-01/19/c_135994782.htm.

Xi, Jinping. 'Working Together to Forge a New Partnership of Win-Win Cooperation', report at the 19th CPC National Congress, www.chinadaily.com.cn/m/qingdao/2017-11/04/content_34771557.htm.

Xinhua Cidian (Xinhua Dictionary) 3rd edition, Beijing: Shangwu Press, 2001.

Xu, Jian, 'Yi Renlei Mingyun Gontongti Linian Wei Yinling Jiaqiang Zhongguo Tese Gouji Guanxi Lilun Jianzhe (Strengthening Construction of the IR Theories with Chinese Characteristics under the Guidance of Human Destiny Community)', *Guoji Zhanwang* (International Review), 5 (2021): 3.

Xu, Jin and Sun Xuefeng, 'Tsinghua Approach and Directions of Chinese International Relations Researches', *Global Review* 6 (2014): 19–29.

Yan, Xuetong, 'The Rise of China in Chinese Eyes', *Journal of Contemporary China* 10, no. 26 (2001): 36.

Yan Xuetong, 'Guoji Guanxi Lilun Shi Pushixing de" (International Relations Theories Are Universal)', *Shijie Jingji yu Zhengzhi* (World Economics and Politics) 2 (2006): 1.

Yan, Xuetong (ed), *Wangba Tianxia Sixiang Ji Qidi* (Thoughts of World Leadership and Implications), Beijing: Shijie zhishi chubanshe, 2009.

Yan, Xuetong, *Ancient Chinese Thought, Modern Chinese Power*, Princeton: Princeton University Press, 2011.

Yan, Xuetong, 'Why Is There No Chinese School of International Relations Theory', in *Ancient Chinese Thought, Modern Chinese Power*, Princeton: Princeton University Press, 2011.

Yan, Xueyong, 'From Keeping a Low Profile to Striving for Achievement', *Chinese Journal of International Politics* 7, no. 2 (2014): 153–84.

Yan, Xuetong, *Shijie quanli de zhuanyi: Zhengzhi lingdao yu zhanlue jingzheng* (The Shift of World Power: Political Leadership and Strategic Competition), Beijing: Beijingdaxue chubanshe, 2015.

Yan, Xuetong, 'Gaige Nengli Yingxiang Guojia Shili (Reform Capability Determines National Comprehensive Capability)', in *Daoyi Xianshi Zhuyi Yu Zhongguo de Jueqi Zhanlue* (Moral Realism and China's Rising Strategy), Beijing: China Social Science Press, 2018.

Yan, Xuetong, 'The Age of Uneasy Peace: Chinese Power in a Divided World,' *Foreign Affairs* 98, no. 1 (2019): 46.

Yan, Xuetong, *Inertia of History: China and the World by 2023*, Newcastle: Cambridge Scholars Publishing, 2019.

Yan, Xuetong, *Inertia of History: China and the World by 2023*, Newcastle: Cambridge Scholars Publishing, 2019.

Yan, Xuetong, 'IR Moral Realism Epistemology', *India Quarterly: A Journal of International Affairs* 76, no. 2 (2020): 338–42.

Yan, Xuetong, 'Xunzi's and Kautilya's Thoughts on Inter-state Politics', *Strategic Analysis* 44, no. 4 (2020): 299–311.

Yan, Xuetong and Xu, Jin, *Wangba Tianxia sixiang ji qidi* [Thoughts of World Leadership and Implications], Beijing: shijie zhishi chubanshe, 2009.

Yan, Xuetong and Mearsheimer, John, 'Managing Strategic Competition', Tsinghua University Campus, 17 October 2019, https://mp.weixin.qq.com/s/rhxWW4OHIPMx79MceCnFdw.

Yan, Xuetong, Bell, Daniel A., Sun, Zhe (eds), and Edmund Ryden (trans), *Ancient Chinese Thought, Modern Chinese Power*, Princeton: Princeton University Press, 2011.

Yang, Dali L., 'China's Long March to Freedom', *Journal of Democracy* 18, no. 3 (2007): 58–64.

Yang, Oran, 'Political Leadership and Regime Formation: On the Development of Institutions in International Society', *International Organization* 45, no. 3 (1991): 285.

Yang, Qianru, 'Han Xiongnu Xiyu Zhanlue Chengbai de Yuanyin [The Causes of the Strategic Success of the Han Dynasty and Strategic Failure of the Huns in the Western Regions], *Guji Zhengzhi Kexue* [Science of International Politics], 3 (2016): 78–80.

Yang, Qianru, 'An Examination of the Research Theory of Pre-Qin Interstate Political Philosophy', in Yan, Xuetong, Bell, Daniel A. and Zhe, Sun (eds), *Ancient Chinese Thought, Modern Chinese Power*, Princeton: Princeton University Press, 2011.

Yang, Yuan, 'Escape Both the "Thucydides Trap" and the "Churchill Trap": Finding a Third Type of Great Power Relations under the Bipolar System', *Chinese Journal of International Politics* 11, no. 2 (2018): 213–18, 229–33.

Yin, Jiwu, 'Xinli yu Guoji guanxi fenxi: Geti xinli fenxi de lilun yu shijian (Psychology and International Relations: The Theory and Practice of Individual Psychoanalysis)', *Ouzhou yanjiu* (Chinese Journal of European Studies), 1 (2004): 65, 69, 78–79.

Yu, Yixuan, 'Chaoyue baquan: Guojiguanxi zhong lingdao de xingzhi ji qi guannian jichu (Beyond Hegemony: The Nature of Leadership in International Relations and Its Conceptual Basis)', *Fudan International Studies Review* 27 (2020): 42–59.

Zakaria, Fareed, 'Realism and Domestic Politics: A Review Essay', *International Security* 17, no. 1 (1992): 177–98.

Zakaria, Fareed, *From Wealth to Power: The Unusual Origins of America's World Role*, Princeton: Princeton University Press, 1998.

Zhang, Denghua, 'The Concept of "Community of Common Destiny" in China's Diplomacy: Meaning, Motives and Implications', *Asia & the Pacific Policy Studies* 5, no. 2 (2018): 196–207.

Zhang, Feng, 'The Rise of Chinese Exceptionalism in International Relations', *European Journal of International Relations* 19, no. 2 (2011): 310–22.

Zhang, Feng, 'China's New Thinking on Alliances', *Survival* 54, no. 5 (2012): 129–48.

Zhang, Feng, 'The Tsinghua Approach and the Inception of Chinese Theories of International Relations', *The Chinese Journal of International Politics* 5, no. 1 (2012): 73–102.

Zhang, Feng, 'The Xi Jinping Doctrine of China's International Relations', *Asia Policy* 14, no. 3 (2019): 7–23.

Zhang, Feng and Lebow, Richard Ned, *Taming Sino–American Rivalry*, Oxford: Oxford University Press, 2020.

Zhang, Zhidong, 'The "Self-Strengthening" Movement in China, 1898', *Columbia University Resources for Educators*, 1997, www.columbia.edu/cu/weai/exeas/resources/pdf/opium-self-strength.pdf.

Zhang, Zhidong, 'The Concept of "Community of Common Destiny', *Asia & the Pacific Policy Studies* 5, no. 2 (2018): 196–207.

Zhao, Shuisheng, 'A State-Led Nationalism: The Patriotic Education Campaign in Post-Tiananmen China', *Communist and Post-Communist Studies* 31, no. 3 (1998): 287–302, 535–53.

Zhao, Suisheng, 'Xi Jinping's Maoist Revival', *Journal of Democracy* 27, no. 3 (2016): 83–97.

Zhao, Tingyang, 'Rethinking Empire from a Chinese Concept "all-under-Heaven"', *Social Identities* 12, no. 1 (2006): 29–41.

Zhen, Han and Paul, T.V., 'China's Rise and Balance of Power Politics', *The Chinese Journal of International Politics* 13, no. 1 (2020): 1–26.

Zheng, Yongnian, 'China's de facto federalism', in He, Baogang, Galligan, Brian, and Inoguchi, Takashi (eds), *Federalism in Asia*, Cheltenham: Edward Elgar, 2007, pp 213–41.

Index

References to figures appear in *italic* type; those in **bold** type refer to tables.
References to endnotes show both the page number and the note number (231n3).

5G networks 166, 170

A

Acharya, Amitav 45–6, 58, 69
Adhanom Ghebreyesus, Tedros 1
Afghanistan 23, 24, 120, 191, 199
agent-centric 32–3, *34*, 35–6, 121
agent-structure 8, 24, 31, 32–3, *34*, 35–6, 36–8, 39–40, 41–5, 61–2 68, 76, 158
ai 106
Alaska 44
Alliance of Small Island States (AOSIS) 45
Allison, Graham 167
Althusser, Louis 38
Ames, Roger T. 98, 101
anarchy 53, 54, 60, 62, 83
Anderson, Perry 116
anemocracy 8, 43, 64, 76, 86, 107
anemocratic leadership 8, 22, 43, 64, 77, 86, 155
Aristotle 6
Article 5 (NATO) 172
Ashley, Richard 83
Asia-Pacific region 150, 158
Association of Southeast Asian Nations (ASEAN) 151
Athens 126–8, 130, 148, 167
Australia 119, 151, 182
authoritarianism 45
Authoritarian Council for Common Economic Assistance (COMECON) 157
authority *see* humane authority; international authority
Axial Age 125

B

Babones, Salvatore 17–18
badao (*ba*) 100, 147, 169, 185
Badie, Bertrand 153
Bandung principles 154
Bannon, Steve 144
Barber, James David 4, 5

Beckley, Michael 117–19
behaviourism 37
Beijing 166
Bell, Daniel 13
Belt and Road Initiative (BRI) 129, 151, 170
Benoist, Alain de 153
Berkeley 26
Bhaskar, Roy 39, 41
Biden, Joe 6–7, 21, 44, 46, 57, 80, 89, 122, 171, 172, 191, 199
bipolarization 8–9, 19–20, 46, 57–8, 64–5, 69, 79–81, 143–5, 195–6
Blinken, Antony 44
Bobbio, Norberto 154
Bolsonaro, Jair 151
Bolton, John 171
bounded rationality 68–9
Bourdieu, Pierre 153
Brandt, Willy 157
Braudel, F. 151–2
Brazil 69, 144, 151
Bretton Woods institutions 146, 149, 155, 157
Brexit 81, 145
Britain (UK) 56
Brostrom, Jannika 36
Bull, Hedley 3–4, 144
Bush, George W. 44, 145, 158, 167, 181, 185, 197
Buzan, Barry 18

C

capitalism 68, 117, 152, 157
Carlyle, Thomas 122
Carr, E.H. 76, 83, 148
Central Asia 170, 186–7
Chen, Zhimin 4
China (PRC) 5–6, 8–9, 18, 19–20, 21, 23, 57, 63, 80, 118–20, 120–1, 129, 130, 144, 146, 151, 154, 156, 152, 156, 165–6, 167–8, 169–70, 172, 173, 180, 188–9, 190, 200

245

China Model 170
Chinese Communist Party (CPC) 18, 120, 180
Chinese Defense White Paper 168–9
Chinese IR Theories (Chinese IRTS) 16–17, 18, 21–2, 26
Chinese School (CS) 16–18, 20, 21–2
CHIPS and Science Act 166
Christian 94–5
Churchill, Winston 181, 185
civilization 21, 58
classical realism 32, 39, 76, 125, 192
Clausewitz, Carl von 130
Clinton, Bill 23, 158, 181, 185, 197
Cold War 70, 81, 129, 157, 168, 186, 194
communism 18, 129, 149, 152, 180
comparative inter-civilizational study 125
Comprehensive and Progressive Agreement for Trans-Pacific Partnership (CPTPP) 150
Concert of Europe 153
Confucianism 66–7, 95, 97, 98, 105, 106
Confucius (Kongzi) 6, 33, 42–3, 66–7, 99–100, 105, 106
consequentialism 95–6, 108–9
constructivism 37, 39–40, 41, 53–4, 59–66, 77, 193
COP 21 Paris Treaty 151
Council for Common Economic Assistance (COMECON) 157
counter-globalization 193
COVID-19 pandemic 79, 81, 171
Cox, Robert 148
Croesus 113
Cruz, Ted 122
Cultural Revolution 8, 120
Curphy, Gordon 180
Cyrus 113
Czechoslovakia 129, 152, 155

D

dao 105
Debray, Regis 153
dedao duozhu, shidao guazhu 7
deglobalization 25, 193
Delian League 127
Delphic Oracle 113
Democracy 65, 81, 115, 117–18, 146, 172
Democrats 57
Deng, Xiaoping 23, 57, 120, 197
deontology 94–5, 107
Dessler, David 37
Diamond, Jared M. 3
domestic leadership 8, 84, 180–1, 184–5
dualist theory 2, 40–1, 181
Dugin, Alexander 154
Dumbarton Oaks conference 155
Duterte, Rodrigo 45

E

East Asia 166, 167–8
Eastern Europe 57, 108, 129
Eastern Mediterranean 113
Easton, David 149
Eco, Umberto 154, 159
economic globalization 143, 163, 164
Emancipation Proclamation 185
Emperor Taizong of the Tang Dynasty 42–3
English School 37, 88, 144
Enlightenment 95
entrepreneurial leadership 3, 4
Erdoğan, Recep Tayyip 45
ethics
  role ethics 98, 107
  virtue ethics 21, 96–7, 105
ethno-centric 58
ethnology 218
EU Green deal 151
EU-Mercosur agreement 151
European Community (EC) 157
European Union (EU) 25, 144, 145–6, 151, 153–4, 157, 158, 180
exceptionalism 20–1
Exclusive Economic Zone, Japan 168

F

fa 96
Fearon, James 40
financial crisis 2008 81, 120
Finkielkraut, Alain 153
Finland 57
Finnemore, Martha 61, 62
foreign policy analysis (FPA) 76
France 153–4, 181, 182
Friedberg, Aaron 56
Fukuyama, Francis 146

G

G2 144
General Agreement on Tariff and Trade (GATT) 70, 155
Generation Z 212
Geneva 170
Georgia 108, 156
Germany 154, 158, 181, 182
Ghani, Mohammad 23, 24
Gill, Stephen 148, 149
Gilpin, Robert 53, 59, 65, 68, 115, 116, 151, 166
Gingrich, Newt 168
Ginnett, Robert 180
global international relations theories (GIR) 58
globalization 143, 163, 164, 165, 173, 194
governmental morality 7–9, 23–4, 35–6, 54–5, 59–60, 67, 82, 103, 105, 187–8
Gramsci, Antonio 37, 148–9
Greece, Ancient 125–8, 130

INDEX

Guan Zhong (Guanzi) 6, 55 66–7, 113, 147
Gulf War 189

H

Habermas, Jürgen 145, 154
Han Fei (Hanfeizi) 6, 96
Han of Qi, Duke 101
Hassner, Pierre 154
He Zun 189
Hebrew-Christian conception 94–5
Hegel, George 82, 107
hegemonia (*hegeomai*) 148
hegemonic stability 3, 53, 149
hegemony 1, 8, 18, 43, 46, 64–5, 69–70, 77, 100–1, 102, 105, 147–8, 148–52, 155, 157–8, 185–6
Hellas 127, 128
Hellenic 125–8
Helü of Wu, King 101
Hermann, Margaret G. 4–5
Herodotus 113, 148
Hitler, Adolf 22, 154
Hobbes, Thomas 6, 32, 62, 86
Hobbesian culture 62, 64
holistic control 4, 86–7, 183
Holland 153
Hong Kong 156
Hoover, Herbert 44
Huan of Qi, Duke 22, 113
Huawei 166
Hughes, Richard 180
human rights 25–6, 65, 70, 86, 169, 185, 187
humane authority 8–9, 13, 21, 64, 66–7, 76, 77–8, 86, 98–9, 102, 169
Hume, David 97
Hungary 45, 145, 152, 153
Huntingdon, Samuel P. 130n5, 131n6
Hutton, Eric L. 99
Hwang, Yih-Jye 17, 22

I

ideationalism 78
identity
 identity crisis 146
 state identity 60, 62
Ikenberry, John 3, 4, 63, 89, 150, 155
India 69, 119, 144, 190
Indonesia 119
Indo-Pacific region 44, 57, 168
Indo-Pacific strategic framework 44, 50n76
institutional leadership 4
institutionalism 149–51
institutions, international 88–90, 196–8
intellectual leadership 3, 4
international ascendancy 56–7, 68–9
International Monetary Fund (IMF) 88, 146, 155, 157

international norms 7–8, 36, 53, 59, 61, 62, 63–4, 77–8, 169–70, 194–5
international order 25–6, 32, 33, 36, 53, 55, 59, 61, 62, 68–9, 79, 88–90, 122–4, 192–3, 195–6, 196–8
inter-subjectivity 148–9
Iran 144, 146
Iraq 26, 120, 189
Isocrates 128
Italian Marxism 151–2
Italy 145, 153, 154

J

Jahn, Beate 17, 18
Japan 44, 69, 119, 144, 151, 154
Jewish thought 94–5
Joint Comprehensive Plan of Action 171
junzi 97

K

Kacynski, Jaroslaw 153
Kagan, Robert 144
Kant, Immanuel 62–3, 64, 65, 86, 95, 107, 146
Kantian democratic states 65
Kaplan, Morton 149
Katzenstein, Peter J. 17, 19
Kautilya 125
Kautsky, Karl 149
Kennedy, John F.K. 24–5
Kennedy, Paul 69, 116
Keohane, Robert 37, 149, 150
Kim, Hun Joon 20
Kindleberger, Charles 3, 69, 150
Kissinger, Henry 166
Knafo, Samuel 31
Kosovo 25
Kuhn, Philip 117
Kupchan, Charles 63

L

Lake, David 4
Laozi 6
Le Pen, Marine 153
leader-centred perspective 3
leadership dilemma 1–2
leadership formation 198–9
leadership types 4–5, 8, 22, 43–4, 64, 85–6, 104, 194–5
Lebow, Richard Ned 104
legalism 96
legitimacy 3–4, 5, 103, 118, 182, 184–5
level of analysis 121
LGBTQIA+ 200
li 98, 105, 107
liberalism 39, 79, 80–1, 145–7
Libya 26, 144
Lincoln, Abraham 185
Locke, John 6, 62, 86, 146

Lockean culture 62, 63, 64
Lydian Empire 113

M

Machiavelli, Niccolò 82
Machiavellianism 82
Macron, Emmanuel 146, 181
Made in China 2025 165
Mao Zedong 23, 43, 152, 197
Marshall Plan (1947–57) 155
Marx, Karl 6
Marxism 148–9, 164
Massacre in Melos 127
materialism 77–8
McCarthyism 156
Mearsheimer, John 25, 121, 166
Mencius (Mengzi) 6, 33, 42, 95, 97, 106, 185
Merkel, Angela 158, 181
micro–macro 31
Middle East 120, 151, 170
middle income trap 165
Ming Dynasty 60
Modelski, George 116
Modi, Narendra 144
Mohism 96
Moldova 156
Monroe Doctrine 166
Montesquieu, Charles de Secondat 146
moral obligation 107
moral realism 2, 7, 8–9, 16–17, 19, 20–1, 22–4, 26–7, 32–3, 34, 35–6, 38–9, 42–3, 45–6, 58–66, 79–81, 82–3, 88–90, 98–102, 104–9, 121, 122–3, 180–1, 185
Morgenthau, Hans J. 32, 65, 67, 76, 78, 82, 83, 104
Most-Favoured Nations 70
Mozi 6, 96
multilateralism 153
multipolar 122, 144, 182, 195–6
Munich Security Conference (2021) 172
Mussolini, Benito 154

N

national interests 18, 32, 35–6, 41, 53, 54–5, 61, 69, 78, 82, 94, 103, 105, 181, 194
nationalism 153–4
natural law 95
Nazism 22, 154
neoclassical realism 122–4, 125
neo-Confucianism 59–60, 106
neo-institutionalism 149–51
neoliberalism 53, 63, 193
neoliberals 53
neo-Marxist 38
neorealism 32, 38, 52–3, 58–9, 60, 61–2, 74, 192–3
New Development Bank 156, 173
New Economy Forum 166

New Zealand 151
Niebuhr, Reinhold 32
Nielsen, R.T. 26
Nixon, Richard 149
Nixon Library 80
Noesselt, Nele 16, 18
Non-Nuclear Proliferation Treaty 185, 188
non-organizational 5
non-subordinate 5
norms of benevolence 58
North, Douglass 68
North Atlantic Treaty Organization (NATO) 24, 25–26, 57, 60, 108, 157, 172, 191, 198, 108
Nuyen, A.T. 107
Nye, Joseph 2, 3, 4, 35, 36, 46, 103–4, 121

O

Obama, Barack 44, 89, 150, 158, 167, 185
Onfray, Michel 153
ontology 36–7, 38, 39, 41
Onuf, Nicholas 37
Orbán, Viktor 45, 153
Organski, A.F.K. 116
Osaka 171

P

Pacific Ocean 119
paradigm 18, 153, 154, 196
Paris Climate Change Agreement 46, 171
Paris COP 21 151
Parsons, Talcott 149
parts–whole 31
Party Congress 129, 167, 170–1
Pausanias 127
Peloponnesian confederate 130
Peloponnesian War 127, 167
Pelosi, Nancy 122, 168
Pershing Euro missiles 157
Persian Empire 113, 127
Philippines 45
philosophy, moral 94–8
PLA Navy 167
Plato 6
Poland 57, 145, 153
policy sovereignty 4
political capability 7–8, 33, 53, 54, 59, 61, 63–4, 67–8, 69, 76–7, 83–4, 181–2
political determinism 115–16
political institutions 3, 19–20, 24, 84, 117, 196–7
political psychology 4–5
Pomeranz, Kenneth 68
Pompeo, Mike 80
Popper, Karl 40
populism 81, 145, 153
populist leadership 1, 2, 153
post-Cold War 113–14, 146–7, 156, 181, 194
post-sovereignism 153–4

INDEX

Pound, Ezra 154
power balances 4
power structure 1, 6, 12, 44, 60, 145, 181, 192–3
power transition theory 166
Pre-Qin thought 5–6, 18–19, 35, 42–3
Protestantism 68
public goods 150–1, 188–9
Putin, Vladimir 23–4, 25, 45, 77, 108, 156
Pythia 113

Q

Qin, Yaqing 16–17, 149, 153
Qin Dynasty 22
Quadrilateral Security Dialogue (QUAD) 44, 151
quasi-Cold War 156

R

Reagan, Ronald 44
realism 77, 78, 82–3
Regional Comprehensive Economic Partnership (RCEP) 151
ren 106
righteousness 58, 99
rising state 1–2, 8–9, 19–20, 55, 75–6, 77
rites of propriety 58
Romilly, Jacqueline de 128
Roosevelt, Franklin D. 22, 44, 57, 64, 155, 181, 185, 192, 196
Rosemont, Henry Jr 98
Rousseau, Jean-Jacques 6
Russia 23–4, 25, 26, 45, 108, 144, 156, 172
see also Soviet Union (USSR)

S

sage 97, 105
sage king 84, 99, 105
Salvini, Matteo 153
Scharpf, Fritz 154
Schmitt, Carl 154
Schroeder, Paul 213
secessionism 156
securitization 166
security dilemma 168–9
self-transformation 8
Shang Dynasty 33
Shanghai Cooperation Organization 173
sheng ren 97
Shirk, Susan 57
shu 106
Sikkink, Kathryn 61, 62
Simon, Herbert 68
Sinocentrism 21–2
Sino-Hellenic system 125
Sino-Hindu system 125
situational leadership 4
Slote, Michael 106–7
Smith, Noah 44

social Darwinism 68
socialism 218, 132n17
Socrates (Σωκράτης) 6
Song-Ming period 106
sophrosyne 128
South America 156, 158
South Asia 170
South China Sea 167–8
South East Asia 156, 170, 190
South Korea 44, 50n76, 151
Sovereignty 25–6, 62–3, 88
Soviet Marxism-Leninism 164
Soviet Union (USSR) 24–5, 55, 129, 130, 148–9, 152, 157, 164
Sparta 127, 148, 167
Spinelli, Altiero 154
Spring and Autumn period 6
St Petersburg 148
Stalin, Joseph 149, 155, 181, 185
Stiglitz, Joseph 155
Stockholm International Peace Research Institute (SIPRI) 144
Stoic thought 94–5
strategic prudence 127–8
Streeck, Wolfgang 154
structural determinism 32, 115
structural leadership 3, 4
structural Marxist 38
Sullivan, Jake 44
Sun, Tzu 128
Supreme Court (US) 118
Sweden 57
Syria 26, 144

T

Taiwan 156, 168, 169
Taiwan Strait 168, 169
Taliban 24, 191
Tang Dynasty 43
Tang Taizong, Emperor of China 43
temporal parochialism 125
terrorism 186
Themistocles 126–7
Thucydides 126–8, 148, 167
Tibet 156
Toynbee, Arnold 116
Transatlantic Trade and Investment Partnership (TTIP) 63, 150, 158
Trans-Pacific Partnership (TPP) 63, 89, 150, 158, 171
Treaty of Westphalia 62
Triangular Model 4
Trump, Donald 2, 44, 46, 57, 119, 122, 145, 150, 151, 155, 171, 185, 191, 196
Trumpism 122
tui 106
Turchynov, Oleksandr 24
Turkey 45
tyranny 43, 66, 86, 107

U

Ukraine 23–4, 26, 57, 79, 108, 156
UN Charter 1945 155
UN Declaration on Human Rights 70
UN Educational, Scientific and Cultural Organization (UNESCO) 157
UN General Assembly 170
UN Programme for Development (UNPD) 157
UN Security Council 181, 190, 197
Union of Soviet Socialist Republics (USSR) *see* Soviet Union (USSR)
unipolarity 55, 119, 121–2
United Nations (UN) 70, 88, 146, 157, 180, 189
United States (US) 2, 23, 24–5, 35, 44, 46, 50n76, 56, 57, 63, 64, 69–70, 80, 108, 118–20, 121, 122, 129, 130, 146, 149–50, 154, 155–6, 158, 164, 165–6, 167–8, 169, 170–1, 173, 180, 186, 189, 191, 194, 196
unit-level variable 121–4, 198–9
universalism 20–1
US Commerce Department 166
US Defense Department 168
US State Department 172
US-China rivalry 163–4, 165–6, 166, 168–72, 173, 195
US-Soviet Cold War *see* Cold War
utilitarianism 95
utility maximizers 53–4, 59

V

Venezuela 144
Vietnam 119
Vilaça, Guilherme 21

W

Wallerstein, Immanuel 38, 149, 151–2
Walt, Stephen 135n50
Waltz, Kenneth 37–9, 52–3, 59, 60, 74, 116, 121, 122, 149
Wang, Yangming 60, 185, 191, 195–6, 197
wangdao (wang) 99, 147, 169, 185
War of Muye 66
Warren, Elizabeth 122
Warring States period 6
Warsaw Pact 129, 157
Washington, George 185

Weber, Max 6, 61, 68
wei 101
Wen of Jin, Duke 101
Wendt, Alexander 39, 40, 41, 61, 62–3, 64, 65, 86–7
Western Zhou Dynasty 22
Wight, Colin 37
Wilders, Geert 153
Wolfers, Arnold 82
World Bank 70, 88, 155, 157
World Health Organization (WHO) 1, 157
World Trade Organization (WTO) 63, 70, 88, 155, 157, 196
World War I (WWI) 56
World War II (WWII) 64
World War III 168
Wuhan 171

X

Xi, Jinping 75, 119, 120, 129, 165, 170–1, 173
Xia Dynasty 33
xin 100, 101–2, 105, 188
Xinjiang 156
Xu, Jin 18, 22
Xunzi 6, 22, 33, 42, 69, 98–102, 104–5, 108, 125, 128, 129, 147, 185

Y

Yalta Conference 181, 185
Yalta system 36
Yang, Oran 3, 4
yi 98, 99, 105
Yin, Haozhe 4
Ying Zheng 22
Yu, Yixuan 4
Yugoslavia 155

Z

Zakaria, Fareed 56
Zelenskyy, Volodymyr 23, 77
zero-sum game 65–6, 76, 164
Zhang, Yongjin 17, 19, 20
zhanlüe chengxin 100
Zhou, Guorong 4
Zhou Dynasty 33, 64, 66–7, 155
Zhou rites 64
Zhuang of Chu, King 101

www.ingramcontent.com/pod-product-compliance
Lightning Source LLC
Chambersburg PA
CBHW051534020426
42333CB00016B/1928